# WHAT CHILDREN CAN TELL US

James Garbarino,
Frances M. Stott,
and Faculty of
the Erikson Institute

# WHAT CHILDREN CAN TELL US

## Eliciting, Interpreting, and Evaluating Information from Children

Jossey-Bass Publishers

San Francisco • London • 1989

WHAT CHILDREN CAN TELL US
*Eliciting, Interpreting, and Evaluating Information from Children*
   by James Garbarino, Frances M. Stott, and Faculty of
   the Erikson Institute

Copyright © 1989 by: Jossey-Bass Inc., Publishers
                     350 Sansome Street
                     San Francisco, California 94104
                              &
                     Jossey-Bass Limited
                     28 Banner Street
                     London EC1Y 8QE

**Library of Congress Cataloging-in-Publication Data**

Garbarino, James.
    What children can tell us : eliciting, interpreting, and
evaluating information from children / James Garbarino, Frances M.
Stott, and Faculty of the Erikson Institute.
        p.    cm.—(The Jossey-Bass social and behavioral science series)
    Bibliography: p.
    Includes index.
    ISBN 1-55542-163-6
    1. Interpersonal communication in children   2. Children and
adults.   I. Stott, Frances M., date.   II. Erikson Institute.
III. Title.   IV. Series.
BF723.C57G37       1989
155.4'136—dc20                                    89-8192
                                                    CIP

Manufactured in the United States of America

The paper in this book meets the guidelines for
permanence and durability of the Committee on
Production Guidelines for Book Longevity of the
Council on Library Resources.

JACKET DESIGN BY WILLI BAUM

FIRST EDITION

*Code 8937*

The Jossey-Bass
Social and Behavioral Science Series

# Contents

**Part Three: Communication in Special Settings**

# Foreword

There was a time when children had no legal rights. They were regarded merely as the property of their parents, very much like pieces of furniture or farm animals. If we doubt the existence of this attitude, we have only to remember Dickens's famous novel *David Copperfield*: it was, as we all know, largely autobiographical. History tells us of the early deaths of countless other children who were orphaned or born out of wedlock; these children usually had to work as chimney sweeps or mill hands in textile factories, and they lived on a starvation diet and with an overdose of physical punishment.

Times have changed, and those of us who have anything to do with children think the change constitutes vast improvement over previous centuries. Yet we all know that children still are ever available victims of neglect, of abuse of all kinds, and even of infanticide. Abolishing such horrors is contingent on our understanding of their causes. And one factor of that understanding is improving our ability to communicate effectively with children. Even comparatively minor (but frequent) occurrences that affect children's lives, such as family breakups and divorces, make it essential that we examine and understand children's observations and the feelings they have formed about what they have witnessed or experienced.

There is consensus among psychologists of various schools of thought that parents are the guardians of children and are responsible for their care and discipline but that these parents are never the children's unconditional owners. Furthermore, there is consensus that children's observations and statements must be taken seriously for the sake of these children's development, as well as for our own understanding.

But what does "seriously" mean in this context? Is "seriously" the same as "verbatim"? Hardly. A child's view of reality is certainly different from our own, at least most of the time. How, then, do children's views of reality differ from ours? What do their views offer us, and under what circumstances? Is there a way for us to use their statements? Can we gauge the difference between children's thinking and adult thinking?

Perhaps we can start to answer these questions by making it clear to ourselves exactly what constitutes an adult. An adult is a human being who is biologically mature, able to reproduce, and able to master the environment—that is, to provide for survival. However, adults are also responsible for their fellow beings, especially the young and the helpless. Finally, they are people who share a set of values, such as religious beliefs, law, and a definition of friends, enemies, and symbols. And that, first and foremost, means they must have a common language.

As we look at brand-new babies, whether born in Finland or Melanesia, the difference between them and the grown-ups in their group is great. Gradually, very gradually, these babies grow into adulthood—their kind of adulthood. And that growth process includes learning their respective communication systems.

Because we, the human race, are creatures with a very long childhood, and because a baby's needs are not always obvious, it is essential that our children communicate with adults. The principal means of communication (but certainly not the only one) is language, the same language a child's caregivers speak. This sounds promising to those of us who hope to hear the truth from children. But before we get our hopes up too high for a productive dialogue, let us look at some clinical vignettes that demonstrate how and why children's statements are based on premises different from our own.

Jonah's parents spent the first years of their married life in a small college town in the Midwest. It was there that Jonah was born and spent the first nine months of his life.

It was a peaceful existence. Since both parents were employed on the campus, a third adult took care of Jonah. Peter, a graduate student in psychology, was the regular babysitter. He sat with the little boy for a number of hours every day, and he and Jonah became very fond of one another.

Then, when Jonah was nine months old, the family moved to a different campus because of a better job opportunity, and Jonah's friendship with Peter was rudely interrupted. Jonah did not seem to mind. His mother had more time for him in the new location, and Jonah developed into a cheerful and active toddler.

One day, Jonah's parents received a letter from Peter in which he announced his impending visit to their new home. Peter missed Jonah, and he had decided he would like to visit his former charge. It would be their first encounter after twenty-one months.

When Peter arrived at the house, both Peter and Jonah smiled politely by way of greeting, and then Jonah did something quite extraordinary: He got down on all fours and repeated all the little games, which he had since outgrown, that he had played with Peter in the good old days—activities such as finger games and peek-a-boo. Peter complied, and the silent dialogue of reminiscing went on for a while.

But then Jonah put his hand on Peter's knee and said clearly and urgently, "backpack," referring to his once favorite mode of transportation—for which, at nine months, he had not yet had a term.

In the time that had passed since his early association with Peter, Jonah had acquired and learned to use properly the term for a pleasurable experience of long ago. Jonah demonstrated the fact that human beings feel strongly, and recall those feelings, from a very early age. However, as young children they are as yet unable to speak about them. Thus, the difference in developmental stages between child and adult constitutes a barrier to communication and makes it almost impossible to share the truth—the *same* kind of truth, that is. There is also another kind of barrier that is emotional rather than linguistic in nature. Here is an example:

Elizabeth was an intelligent and vivacious second grader who surpassed most of her friends when it came to the 3 R's. One day soon after the neighbors' dog had given birth to three pups, Elizabeth asked her mother to tell her exactly "how human people make babies." "But Liz," said her mother, "you know all that already; we talked about that when your sister was born. You know, parents make love, and the seeds grow in Daddy's body and the little egg cells in Mommy's." "Yes," interrupted Elizabeth impatiently, "I know all that. That's what you told me when I was little. But now that I'm big I want to know what really happens."

Elizabeth's story demonstrates that real facts can be forgotten because our feelings invariably influence our perception of reality. Elizabeth, like most second graders, is at a stage in which children are ill at ease with facts and topics that seem "charged." For example, many children in this stage defend themselves vigorously against "mushy" topics and are allergic to love stories. They mostly permit themselves those passions that reflect our more aggressive impulses but not the erotic ones. And even these aggressive tendencies are difficult to own. Who has not observed the child of almost any age who does something destructive and then blames it on the cat or, better yet, on the baby brother? That is the solution the young culprit sees to avoid the consequences of his or her action, and his or her perception may well be enhanced by fear of being punished.

Fear of punishment, or fear of untoward consequences of any kind, is not the only thing that hampers a child's truthfulness. Nor is a child's ability to see reality an exclusively developmental question. Children also tend to make up stories and sometimes miss the border between reality and fantasy. All this merely indicates a rich fantasy life, which, in principle, we welcome in children and sometimes even call "creative." However, it seems that in some situations (for instance, a custody trial or an abuse situation) there are two "truths"—the child's subjective feelings and the objective reality. This is the challenge we face: to avoid or circumvent all the potential limitations of children as sources of information and make the greatest possible use of their strengths and possibilities. That is what this book is about.

*June 1989*                                                    Maria W. Piers
                                   *Distinguished Service Professor Emerita*
                                                            *Erikson Institute*

# Preface

Our goal in *What Children Can Tell Us* is to help adults understand children as they seek information from and about them. We hope to help adults better appreciate how children see the world and how their capacity for understanding develops. Thus, we seek to stimulate adults to become more attuned to and better able to communicate with children.

Adults seek information *about* children from other adults (for example, through interviews with a child's parents and with other observers). But they also seek information *from* children as informants about the children's experiences, behavior, and feelings. Adults rely on children as sources of information in courtrooms, in classrooms, in clinical settings, in program evaluations, and in day-to-day family relations.

### Audience for the Book

Adults need to understand the strengths and weaknesses, the possibilities and limitations, of children as sources of information. This need has reached crisis proportions in cases of criminal prosecution of sexual abuse and in parental custody disputes wherein some assessment of the needs and wishes of children is required by a legal and ethical mandate to serve the best interest of the child. But the need for guidance goes beyond the courtroom. Physicians, nurses, psychologists, teachers, social workers, lawyers, police, researchers, and parents all need help in soliciting and evaluating information from children as patients, as clients, as students, and simply as children being cared for.

This book is also designed to help professionals and other adults become better consumers of information from and about children. It is designed to help the reader evaluate the information about children he or she receives from other professionals. Judges and lawyers need to know whether a psychologist or social worker is presenting a plausible report of information obtained from a child. Psychologists and social workers need to know whether the legal system is justified in drawing conclusions about a child's testimony. We all need to become better consumers of professional interpretation of information from children.

## Background

A few words about what the book is *not:* First, it is not a child development text, even though it relies heavily on research and theory about how children develop. Second, it is not a textbook on assessment techniques, even though it deals with assessment issues. Third, and most important, it is not an operational manual or cookbook. Indeed, one of our most important messages is that *any* inflexible technique or pat approach is likely to fall short of the truth. The only credible approach is to start with openness toward the child as a communicator and a good grounding in child development. We hope to stimulate and inform that openness.

We began this book as a result of three one-day workshops conducted in 1986 for the Illinois Department of Children and Family Services Division of Child Protection. The workshops brought the Erikson Institute faculty face to face (and sometimes toe to toe) with a group of child welfare specialists responsible for investigating allegations of child abuse and neglect. During those three days, we began to confront three important questions that provide the foundation for this book: (1) What can child development theory and research tell us about the process of adult-child communication? (2) How far can we go in specifying concrete procedures for eliciting information from children? (3) To what extent does knowledge about adult-child communication generalize across settings (for example, child care, formal evaluative testing, medical treatment, education, protective services, custody disputes)?

With these questions in mind, we set out to review the available knowledge concerning influences on adult-child communication. Our experience with child abuse investigators had taught us a powerful lesson: Child welfare workers in the field are faced with seemingly insurmountable problems. They demand concrete solutions—even formulas—for dealing with such issues as how to obtain reliable and accurate information from children. But our knowledge of child development warns against any approach that appears simple, pat, fixed, or in any way a "cookbook" approach. Learning a set of specified procedures for communicating with children in order to elicit information is not the solution. Rather, the task is to create an understanding, steeped in knowledge of child development, of the communicative process. Armed with this understanding, the practitioner will be better able to adapt to a specific child-adult relationship in a specific setting. We have sought to document and communicate this message throughout our book. Child development knowledge (especially when combined with experience) can greatly facilitate success in adult-child communication. What it cannot do is specify the exact form that communication will take. The child, the adult, the child's relationship to the adult, the child's previous experience in communicating (or not communicating) with adults, the specific meaning attributed to the setting in which the adult-child encounter takes place— all these factors influence outcomes. Therefore, each has a bearing on what technique to use, which approach to adapt.

We believe that all of these factors must be taken into account if one is to understand adult-child communication; reality is complex, and it is conditioned by the specifics of each situation and each child. In holding this belief, we reflect an ecological perspective that holds that the best answer to the question "Does A cause B?" is always "It depends." We recognize how frustrating this is for the practitioner, and we have tried to help defuse this frustration by highlighting practice guidelines throughout the text. Each practice guideline is an attempt to specify a conclusion generalizable enough to merit cautious confidence in applying it to communication with children. These guidelines will help forge links among theory, research, and practice.

"We" are the faculty and research staff of Erikson Institute for Advanced Study in Child Development. Founded in 1966 to train graduate-level professionals to work with young children and their families, Erikson Institute engages in a wide range of teaching, training, research, and program development activities. Our focus is always the whole child in recognition of the fact that each life evidences the influence of biological, psychological, sociological, cultural, and historical forces, which act through conscious and unconscious processes. Each faculty member has had experience in the real world of children as either a teacher or a clinician. *What Children Can Tell Us* reflects this blending of theory, research, and practice. We wrote the book in close collaboration, discussing the overall themes and specific chapters as we went along. Each chapter thus reflects our collective perspective as well as the work of one or more authors.

### Overview of the Contents

Chapter One, by James Garbarino and Frances M. Stott, provides an introduction to the issues. The authors present a series of vignettes to illustrate settings in which the meaning of children's behavior is complex and difficult to understand. But more than merely introducing problematic situations, they seek to establish our empathy for the child. Children have a credible perspective on the world and their experience of it. In order to help readers better understand the child's perspective, the authors present a framework that both takes a developmental view and considers the role of the adult in determining the nature and the quality of information received from children.

In Chapter Two, Frances M. Stott explores children's self-esteem and coping mechanisms. These subtle and complex psychological phenomena influence children's performance in an information-seeking situation by affecting the way children approach adult-child encounters. While they are difficult to translate into practice, an awareness of them can enable us to better interpret the information we *do* receive.

Chapter Three, by Joan B. McLane, examines how the way children think and understand the world influences what they can communicate. While children's thinking develops with age, it is always influenced by the context in which it occurs. This chapter reviews current understanding of cognitive development in childhood.

In Chapter Four, Gillian Dowley McNamee recounts what

we know about children's language—obviously an important contributor to understanding adult-child communication. McNamee reviews how language develops as well as how it changes with different people and in different situations.

In Chapter Five, Barbara T. Bowman shows how culture permeates the expectations and thus the interactive style of both adult and child: It matters *who* each is in relation to the other. This chapter deals with cultural issues that underlie adult-child communication.

Chapter Six, by James Garbarino and Kathleen Kostelny, explores influences on adults as recipients of information from children. They show how, in many such interactions, the psychology of the adult as a hypothesis formulator and tester is particularly relevant to the outcome of the interaction. They also discuss the role of adult unconscious forces in producing, for example, denial or misinterpretation.

In Chapter Seven, Cynthia Schellenbach examines procedures for observing children in light of their role as sources of information. In addition, she illustrates the tension between the need for objective reliability (uncontaminated information) and subjective appropriateness (sensitivity to the child's needs).

Chapter Eight, by Lorraine B. Wallach, explores the use of children's fantasy as a means of gaining insight into the child's inner life, the world of thoughts and feelings. This chapter discusses ways in which play and storytelling can (and cannot) illuminate a child's functioning and experience.

In Chapter Nine, David W. Beer explores the dynamics of interviewing children. Beer argues that children and adults differ not only in their linguistic and cognitive capabilities but also in the degree to which they are familiar with the rules of interview speech and the various purposes for interviews, and he examines the important implications of these differences both for interviewing methods and for the recording and interpretation of interviews.

In Chapter Ten, Jeannie Gutierrez examines formal testing, a common clinical tool used by professionals to obtain information about children's adaptive and maladaptive functioning. She provides the professional with a framework for assessing what information can be obtained and what questions can be answered using tests.

Chapter Eleven, by Linda Gilkerson and James Garbarino, asks: How do children communicate about the care they receive at home and at school? This chapter helps parents learn what they need to know about how their children are reacting to child-care arrangements (including "self-care"/"latchkey" situations) and helps providers know how to respond to the information children give them about their families.

In Chapter Twelve, Frances M. Stott describes the nature of evaluations and therapy for use by the nonclinician. She examines how professional roles and theoretical orientations influence the type of information we seek and obtain from children in clinical settings. Stott explores the serious tension that can arise when the information flow of the therapeutic relationship is compromised by other agendas—such as conforming to evidentiary requirements of the legal process about "leading questions."

In Chapter Thirteen, Patricia Marshall and Lucinda Lee Katz examine the adult-child communicative process in medical settings. They show how the child as patient presents some special challenges to the process of communication, particularly when crucial issues of life and death are involved.

Chapter Fourteen, by James Garbarino, examines the topic of children as witnesses. As more and more children encounter the legal system (for example, in custody and child abuse cases), lawyers, judges, advocates, counselors, and parents need to understand how the legal system meets or does not meet the needs of children—and this chapter offers them some guidance.

In the epilogue, James Garbarino and Frances M. Stott take stock of what has been said in the preceding chapters and draw some conclusions about seeing and making sense of information obtained from children.

## Acknowledgments

Our work was supported by grants from the William T. Grant Foundation and the Harris Foundation. A training contract with the Illinois Department of Children and Family Services stimulated some of our thinking about the need for the book.

A group of colleagues from the United States and abroad served as an informal advisory panel, reading and commenting on the initial outline and preliminary draft. We thank them (they are listed after this preface). The editorial staff at Jossey-Bass (particularly Gracia Alkema) and two anonymous reviewers offered invaluable help through their comments on the first complete draft of the manuscript. Tough but fair, they stimulated a final round of revisions that validated the maxim "The best writing is rewriting!"

We also thank Erikson Institute's support staff for their work in preparing the manuscript: Marilyn Carter, Sharon Dudley, and Norma Richman.

*Chicago, Illinois*                    James Garbarino
*June 1989*                          Frances M. Stott

# The Authors

James Garbarino is president of Erikson Institute. He received his B.A. degree (1968) from St. Lawrence University in history and government, his M.A.T. degree (1970) from Cornell University in government and social studies, and his Ph.D. degree (1973) from Cornell University in human development and family studies. He is the 1989 recipient of the American Psychological Association's Distinguished Award for Psychology in the Public Service. In 1985, Garbarino received the first C. Henry Kempe Award from the National Conference on Child Abuse and Neglect for "outstanding contribution to the field of prevention and treatment," and in 1968 he received the Vincent DeFrancis Award from the American Humane Association for "outstanding contribution of national significance to child protection."

Frances M. Stott is on the faculty of Erikson Institute and is a clinical psychologist in private practice. She received her B.A. degree (1963) from the University of Chicago in education, her M.A. degree (1974) from the University of Chicago in educational psychology, and her Ph.D. degree (1980) from Northwestern University in educational psychology/child development. Stott's research interests include the study of children who are at risk for psychological problems, with a special focus on the children of psychiatrically ill mothers and children of divorce.

David W. Beer is research associate at Erikson Institute and a doctoral candidate in anthropology at the University of Chicago. He received his B.S. degree (1976) from Brigham Young University in anthropology and philosophy and his M.A. degree (1980) from the University of Chicago in cultural anthropology. Beer's research interests include interpersonal affect in psychiatric hospitals and investigative interviewing of alleged child victims.

**Barbara T. Bowman** is director of graduate studies at, and a founder of, Erikson Institute. She received her B.S. degree (1950) from Sarah Lawrence College in liberal arts and her M.A. degree (1952) from the University of Chicago in education. Bowman served as president of the National Association for the Education of Young Children and is a member of the National Academy of Science Panel on Day Care Policy. Her professional interests include working with young children and their teachers both in the United States and abroad.

**Linda Gilkerson** is on the faculty of Erikson Institute and is director of the infant care program at Evanston Hospital. She received her B.S. degree (1969) from the University of Kansas in elementary and special education, her M.Ed. degree (1970) from the University of Missouri in special education, and her Ph.D. degree (1978) from the University of Illinois, Urbana-Champaign, in early childhood special education. Gilkerson's interests include early intervention with high-risk infants and their families.

**Jeannie Gutierrez** is on the faculty of Erikson Institute and is a clinical psychologist in private practice. She received her B.A. degree (1977) from New Mexico State University in psychology and both her M.A. degree (1982) and her Ph.D. degree (1986) from the University of Illinois, Chicago, in clinical and developmental psychology. Gutierrez is involved in research examining Hispanic parenting styles and the effects of sexual abuse on Hispanic adolescent mothers.

**Lucinda Lee Katz** is on the faculty of Erikson Institute and is principal of the University of Chicago Lower Laboratory School. She received her B.A. degree (1968) from San Francisco State University in creative arts/music, her M.A. degree (1973) from San Francisco State University in elementary education, and her Ph.D. degree (1976) from the University of Illinois, Urbana-Champaign, in early childhood education. She has conducted research on teaching mathematics to young children.

**Kathleen Kostelny** is research associate and a doctoral student at Erikson Institute. She received her B.A. degree (1974) from Bethel College in psychology and her M.A. degree (1985) from the University of Chicago in social sciences. Kostelny previously worked at the Orthogenic School for severely emotionally disturbed children. Her research interests include children at risk for child abuse and children in dangerous environments.

**Joan B. McLane** is on the faculty of Erikson Institute. She received her B.A. degree (1957) from Radcliffe College in history and literature, her M.Ed. degree (1970) from Erikson Institute, Loyola University of Chicago, in early childhood education, and her Ph.D. degree (1981) from Northwestern University in educational psychology/child development. McLane coauthored *Early Literacy* (with G. D. McNamee, forthcoming), which is part of the Developing Child Series published by Harvard University Press.

**Gillian Dowley McNamee** is on the faculty of Erikson Institute. She received her B.A. degree (1974) from Hampshire College in culture and cognition, her M.S.T. degree (1976) from the University of Chicago, and her Ph.D. degree (1980) from Northwestern University in education/reading and language. From 1986 to 1988, McNamee was a Spencer Fellow with the National Academy of Education, pursuing her research in early literacy development with inner-city children and their families.

**Patricia Marshall** is research associate at Erikson Institute and is assistant professor in the medical humanities program, Department of Medicine, Loyola University Stritch School of Medicine. She received her B.A. degree (1974) in behavioral science, her M.A. degree (1978) in anthropology, and her Ph.D. degree (1983) in medical/applied anthropology, all from the University of Kentucky.

**Maria W. Piers** was founding dean of Erikson Institute and is Distinguished Service Professor Emerita. She received her B.A. degree (1931) from Kindergartenbildungs Anstalt, Vienna, and her Ph.D. degree (1935) from the Loyola University of Vienna in anthropology and psychology. She is the author of several books on child development, including *Infanticide* (1978).

**Cynthia Schellenbach** is research associate at Erikson Institute and assistant professor of psychology at the University of Notre Dame. She received her B.S. degree (1976) from St. Mary's College in psychology and sociology and both her M.S. degree (1979) and her Ph.D. degree (1984) from Pennsylvania State University in human development.

**Lorraine B. Wallach** is on the faculty of, and administrative director of, Erikson Institute. She received her B.A. degree (1950) in liberal arts and her M.A. degree (1970) in social service administration, both from the University of Chicago. Wallach helped found the Virginia Frank Child Development Center and Erikson Institute.

# Advisory Panel

Lucy Berliner
Harbor View Medical Center
Seattle, Washington

Judith Bertacchi
Virginia Frank Child Development
  Center
Chicago, Illinois

Joanne Bregman
Evanston Hospital
Evanston, Illinois

Donald Bross
The C. Henry Kempe National
  Center for the Prevention and
  Treatment of Child Abuse and
  Neglect
Denver, Colorado

Anne Cohn
National Committee for Prevention
  of Child Abuse
Chicago, Illinois

Jon Conte
University of Chicago
Chicago, Illinois

Graham Davies
North East London Polytechnic
London, England

Paul DiLorenzo
Support Center for Child Advocates
Philadelphia, Pennsylvania

Spencer Eth
Veterans Administration
  Medical Center
Los Angeles, California

Mark D. Everson
University of North Carolina
Chapel Hill, North Carolina

Jonathan M. Golding
Memphis State University
Memphis, Tennessee

Gail S. Goodman
University of Buffalo
Buffalo, New York

Ellen Gray
Center for the Child
National Council of Jewish Women
New York, New York

Joann Grayson
James Madison University
Harrisonburg, Virginia

Louise F. Guerney
Pennsylvania State University
University Park, Pennsylvania

Joseph C. Hanlon
Garcia and Fields, P.A.,
  Attorneys-at-Law
Tampa, Florida

Carol Harding
Loyola University of Chicago
Chicago, Illinois

Stuart N. Hart
Indiana University
Indianapolis, Indiana

Sharon D. Herzberger
Trinity College
Hartford, Connecticut

# WHAT CHILDREN CAN TELL US

# CHAPTER 1

# Communicating with Children: Introduction to the Issues

A sculptor was once asked how he did his work. He stumbled a bit trying to explain and finally fell mute. Then the interviewer changed tactics and said, "Suppose I gave you a block of stone and told you to carve an elephant." "Ah," said the sculptor, "that's easy. I would take up my mallet and chisel and carve away anything that didn't look like an elephant." The sculptor had a perspective, a concept of his goal that guided each movement.

What we seek here is a perspective on children as sources of information for adults—a perspective to inform professional practice, not a cookbook to dictate it. As adults learn more about the child's perspective, they will begin to see children as intelligent, respected actors in the adult-child communication process. As they learn that children have a comprehensible point of view, even though it is immature compared to the adult perspective, adults can improve the validity and ethical soundness of their efforts to communicate with children. What they do and how they do it will become more effective and in greater harmony with the needs and rights of children.

## Basic Issues

We seek to integrate theory and practice, and thus we begin with some concrete illustrations of the range of issues involved when adults seek and children provide information about their experience in the world, be it in routine matters or in dramatic confrontations with the potential for far-reaching consequences.

These issues arise in a wide variety of situations, and these cases form the agenda for the rest of our book. We will return to them again and again, in one form or another.

*Case 1.* When asked by a clinic physician, "How are you feeling?" a four-year-old replies, "Fine," and refuses to say more. When asked the same question by a nurse at a day-care center who knows the child, the child replies: "When I was three I got sick. I had to go to the hospital 'cause my tummy was broken. I don't want to go back there again but my mom says I have to 'cause my tummy's broken again."

*Issues.* Do characteristics of the person questioning a child affect the accuracy and usefulness of that child's anwers? Do age, sex, experience with children, and familiarity with the particular child matter?

*Case 2.* A prosecutor makes the following statement to the jury in his closing argument in the trial of a twenty-two-year-old charged with murdering a fifteen-year-old in a video game parlor, a case in which children were the only eyewitnesses: "You can give justice to a heinous, hideous crime. Tell him [the defendant] you believe those five little kids. Tell him." The twenty-two-year-old is convicted.

*Issues.* Should someone be convicted of a crime solely on the basis of testimony by children? Should children be believed in court?

*Case 3.* A ten-year-old is interrogated by a police officer about events witnessed in a crime simulation and asked to describe the woman involved.

*Q:* Wearing a poncho and cap?

*A:* I think it was a cap.

*Q:* What sort of a cap was it? Was it like a beret, or was it a peaked cap, or . . . ?

*A:* No, it had sort of, it was flared with a little piece coming out. It was flared with a sort of button thing in the middle.

*Q:* What . . . Was it a peak like that, that sort of thing?

*A:* Ye-es.

*Q:* That's the sort of cap I'm thinking you're meaning, with a little peak out there.

*A:* Yes, that's the top view, yes.

*Q:* . . . Um—What color?

*A:* Oh! Oh—I think it was black or brown.

The woman was not in fact wearing anything on her head. Nor was she wearing a poncho (Dent, 1982).

*Issues.* Are children more or less suggestible than adults? Under what conditions and in what ways do children differ from adults in these matters?

*Case 4.* A kindergarten teacher is reading stories to her class. One story portrays two teddy bears asleep together in a bed. One child responds, "That's like me and Big Tom. He sleeps in my bed too. We play our teddy bear game just like those teddy bears." At this point the teacher interrupts and steers the discussion away from this story.

*Issues.* How does one seize informational opportunities that arise in day-to-day interaction? When should one suppress them?

*Case 5.* The infamous McMartin Preschool case involves allegations of sexual abuse and grotesque psychological maltreatment of scores of children aged two to eight. Much of the information emerged in therapy sessions with the children. The initial charges, involving hundreds of counts of molestation, rape, and assault, and allegations against the seven original defendants have been whittled down in pretrial hearings and motions until all charges are dropped against five of the accused. Defense attorneys and defendants claim that the children are fabricating and were influenced by the methods used in interviewing and treatment by the clinicians and parents. Parents believe that most of the allegations against all seven defendants are true. Defense attorneys declare that many of the children's stories are so fanciful that none of their testimony can be believed. The district attorney dismisses the charges, saying, "We in the district attorney's office have an ethical and a moral obligation not to file charges where the evidence is insufficient" ("Five Freed in Sex-Abuse Case . . . ," 1986, p. 1). The lead prosecutor, however, believes that hundreds of children were molested at the school. The mental health and social services professionals involved in the case agree. A nationally televised news magazine segment sides with one of the remaining defendants, and a filmmaker discloses taped interviews with a former member of the prosecution team that challenge the foundations of the case. The parents launch a national newsletter called *Believe the Children*.

*Issues.* What influences adults' willingness and ability to believe and understand children? Can interviews be both sensitive to the child's needs and reliable for legal purposes? How valid are indirect methods of interviewing and treating children, such as doll play and picture stories? How can very young children be interviewed about extreme or bizarre forms of sexual abuse? At what age can children testify reliably in court? How does the information-seeking process differ from the therapeutic process?

*Case 6.* Six children have been invited to join a play group so that they can be assessed for entrance into a private kindergarten. All of the teachers observing the children agree that four of them, all of whom are white, would do very well and should be accepted for admission. But there is some question about the remaining two children (one of whom is Latino, the other black). Three of the teachers are concerned about the immature behavior of one boy, including his thumbsucking, and wonder whether he would make a good group member. All but one of the teachers are negative about the sixth child, a boy who exhibits aggressiveness and an inability to negotiate roles or share toys. Neither of these children has attended preschool, while all four of the others have done so.

*Issues.* What makes teachers have different opinions about children's functioning? Do the methods used to gather information make a difference? Are different expectations rooted in ideas about gender, class, or culture?

*Case 7.* A survey reports that fourth through sixth graders rate "being suspected of lying" as the most commonly encountered highly stressful event. One child puts it this way: "When someone says I am lying I get real mad if it's another kid. If a grown-up says I'm lying when I'm not, I get mad and sad. I hate it."

*Issues.* Do children lie more or less often than adults? Does this change with age? How can you tell if a child is lying? What motivates a child to lie?

*Case 8.* A young kindergarten teacher is frustrated and disturbed by her inability to engage some of her inner-city children in question-answer sessions in class. She shows them flash cards of colors she is certain they know; when she asks them what color the cards are, several do not answer her questions. Later she asks a colleague in frustration, "What's wrong with these kids?" Her colleague explains that children have to learn the question-answer format so common in schools. The colleague says, "They are used to questions that seek information the adult doesn't already possess—like, Where did you put your shoes?—and are uncertain about what the teacher wants when she asks them to respond to self-evident questions."

*Issues.* How does culture affect a child's expectations about adult inquiry? How does adult culture affect interpretation of a child's behavior? Is the school an "unnatural" culture for some children?

*Case 9.* A clinical psychologist is asked for a recommendation by the judge in a divorce case in which the parents are battling for custody over their two children, aged five and nine. "Tell me what the children think," the judge instructs the psychologist. This is the five-year-old child's account of the parental separation: "My mommy and daddy don't live together anymore. My daddy moved downtown to live with Janie. My mom was very mad at him and Janie too. My daddy said he and mom can't get along. I miss him a lot when he's not here. But maybe he's coming back when I get bigger if I am good."

*Issues.* Can a clinical interview of a child reveal what is in the child's best interests? What is the role of observation? Testing? Play sessions? How does the psychologist handle the child's feeling that she caused her parents' divorce?

*Case 10.* A two-year-old boy ran into the bathroom and saw his mother sitting in the bathtub, her hair covered with soap suds. He looked at his mother, screamed, and ran out of the room. His father told the boy to be sensible and stop making a fuss, and he tried (unsuccessfully) to haul the boy, kicking and screaming, back into the bathroom. A few minutes later, his grandmother brought the boy, still crying, back to the bathroom. His mother rinsed the soap out of her hair, the boy calmed down, and the three of them talked about how different his mother looked with her hair full of soap. The boy's father remained upset that the boy was making a big deal out of nothing.

*Issues.* At what age can a child distinguish between appearance and reality? When can a child understand that a person remains the same even though she may look quite different? Can misunderstanding of a child's level of cognitive development lead to misinterpretation of the child's behavior?

*Case 11.* A working mother leaves her six-year-old daughter in the care of her eleven-year-old son after school. She is worried about how the children feel about this self-care arrangement. She says, "Every time I ask them, they say, 'Fine, Mom.' But I'm not sure they're really telling me how they feel." Results of a study of latchkey children include the following comment by an eleven-year-old on how he feels about being home alone after school: "I just lock the door and turn on the T.V. Then I can't hear any of the sounds. But if it is quiet then I get kinda scared, you know, because there's always some kind of noises from the basement. . . . It's okay, I guess."

*Issues.* Can children report accurately on how they feel? How do we know when they are telling adults just what they think the adults want to hear? When are children capable of making important decisions about their lives?

*Case 12.* A clinical psychologist is asked to evaluate a six-year-old girl whose family has recently immigrated to the United States from Mexico. Maria was referred by her first-grade teacher, who noticed that she was unable to complete her schoolwork and often seemed sad, withdrawn, and preoccupied. The psychologist tests Maria and recommends that she be placed in a special classroom for children with mild retardation. Later, he happens to see Maria in the grocery store with her parents and siblings. Now she seems animated and manages three young brothers competently.

*Issues.* Is the exclusive use of tests a valid measure of cognitive and socioemotional functioning? Are available tests standardized for bicultural, bilingual children? What are the influences of self-esteem and coping mechanisms on school and test performance?

*Case 13.* A teacher recommends mental health counseling for a nine-year-old girl in his class because he believes she has a "major self-esteem problem." He draws this conclusion because she always averts her gaze when he or any other teacher addresses her. After seeing her, the counselor informs the teacher that this is normal behavior for children from her ethnic background. In her Indian tribe, it is considered rude for a child to look an adult in the eye.

*Issues.* How do culture and ethnicity shape adult-child communication? How much of a child's communication is universal and how much is bound by the specifics of cultural norms, expectations, and values?

How do we go about clarifying and answering the many difficult questions raised by these thirteen cases? How do we deal with the many other questions that plague adult efforts to elicit and evaluate information from and about children? We do so by going back to the basics of adult-child communication in search of a cooperative relationship, addressing a series of fundamental concerns:

- The role of adult expectations and beliefs about children in shaping adult responses to children as sources of information—for example, do adults who expect lies get lies?
- The role of basic developmental processes in shaping the child's capacity to respond to adult efforts to elicit information—for example, does immature language production ability account for differences in children's credibility?
- The strengths and limitations of alternative techniques for eliciting information—for example, how do interviews, observation, and tests differ in what they elicit from children?
- The impact of situational factors, such as stress, procedural constraints, and ethical issues, on the efficacy of adult efforts to elicit information from children—for example, is interviewing likely to produce no harm, discomfort but no extensive trauma, or unacceptable or lasting harm?

In assessing the issues raised here, we must go beyond lists of procedural do's and don't's to attend to the full range of factors that influence performance and outcome. For this we need a theory of child development and a classification scheme, a model that allows us to represent systematically the intersecting issues and dimensions involved and thus to generate principles for practitioners.

*Practice Guideline 1.1: There are few fixed and specific formulas for communicating effectively with children; adaptability to the characteristics of each child, each situation, and each adult is essential.*

### A Developmental and Ecological Perspective

In presenting a framework for thinking about children as sources of information, we take a developmental point of view that recognizes children's changing capacities in the context of a series of ongoing interactions between children and their social environments. We also see the child's experiences as subsystems within systems within larger systems, "as a set of nested structures, each inside the next, like a set of Russian dolls" (Bronfenbrenner, 1979, p. 22). This ecological perspective on children as sources of information directs our attention simultaneously to two kinds of interaction. The first is the interaction of the child as a biological organism with the immediate social environment as a set of processes, events, and relationships. The second is the interplay of social systems in the child's social environment that affect the child's face-to-face experiences. These require us to look both inward, to the child's developing capacities in the context of the family, and outward, to the forces that shape the social and physical contexts in which we seek information from and about children.

In asking and answering questions about children, we can and should always be ready to look at the next level of systems to find the questions and answers (Garbarino and Associates, 1982). Rather than focusing exclusively on the child's competence or whether or not she is making herself understood, it is equally, if not more, important to attend to the role of the adult in defining the information-seeking process. That is the message of case 3, in which the interrogator created a climate of suggestibility that led the child to make a false report. We must consider the adult's professional role and biases and the ways in which the context of inquiry is arranged—the message of case 1.

We also should look to the culture that defines the process of inquiry for all concerned: what is normal, what is permissible, what is prescribed, what is proscribed. This is the message of cases 8, 12, and 13. Culture tells us what is normal and creates a presumption of normality. We are generally more ready to attribute pathology to the foreign.

In addition, we must look at how the several systems (family, social services, social networks, legal system, and so on) are involved. Case 5 illustrates this point: court and clinic may have different goals, standards, and agendas. Serving one may make it difficult to serve the other. The biggest issue is thus harmonizing these various settings.

Not only do we consider the nature of development to be interactive, but we also believe that the process of seeking information from children is necessarily interactive. This leads us to consider two broad categories of influence on children as sources of information: aspects of children's performance and the format of adult inquiry.

## Aspects of Children's Performance

As children develop, their physical, emotional, and intellectual states and abilities change. The range of what is possible not only increases but changes in nature. Rather than viewing development as a steady progression from the time of birth, when the infant knows nothing, to adulthood, when the person has accumulated the adult store of knowledge, we see children proceeding through a series of qualitatively different stages. A three-year-old is different from a nine-year-old in many ways, some of which are relevant to the child's communication with adults. These changes reflect successive reorganizations or shifts in the quality of functioning and occur in all spheres of development, physiological, cognitive, social, and emotional.

The major task of childhood is maintaining the capacity for

continued development. Any assessment of a child's development must consider whether the child is progressing in accordance with generally accepted milestones. But these milestones are only general indicators of a child's development. It is necessary to know the developmental milestones and to have an understanding of the general characteristics of each age period; it is also necessary, however, to have an idea of the requirements for further development. What we expect of children at each stage of their lives provides the basis for determining if they are growing toward adulthood in a healthy and productive fashion.

An understanding of developmental milestones is necessary in order to understand children's ability to give statements or information about events they have witnessed or experienced. Indeed, much of the insensitive treatment of children in the legal system, for example, results more from lack of knowledge about development than from callousness.

*Practice Guideline 1.2: The better one's knowledge of normal child development, the better prepared one is to identify effective ways to communicate with children.*

A child's performance as a source of information will depend on particular capacities to perceive, remember, interpret, and communicate. These capacities develop in connection with more general intellectual and emotional capacities. Misunderstanding and misinterpreting developmental markers are common, however. Because children are constantly changing, and because our cultural expectations, theories, and research data change, adults frequently under- or overestimate children's abilities and knowledge.

**Competence and Motivation.** A major source of misinterpretation of children's competence lies in a misunderstanding of their motivation. In order to understand children as sources of information, we make the assumption that a complex interplay of forces motivates the developing child's behavior. As suggested in the previous section, development is a continuous process of adaptation in which internal processes interact with environmental and sociohistorical processes. Thus motivation arises from a number of internal and external sources. Why did the four-year-old in case 1 "lie" to the physician and "tell the truth" to the nurse? Internal and external influences were at work.

*Practice Guideline 1.3: It is important to be critical of one's own conclusions about a child's motivation that attribute irrationality or meaninglessness to the child; consider how things might look and feel to the child.*

In order to understand children's behavior and words, it is important to take account of the psychological factors that motivate their behavior. The ability to provide information depends on children's feelings about being competent, their attitudes toward adults, and the ways in which they defend themselves from difficult consequences or feelings. These issues of self-esteem and coping may influence the way children communicate. For example, they are more likely to be open to communication when they are feeling good about themselves. The child in case 13 may or may not have a self-esteem problem that is interfering with communication. The point of that case is that culture affects expression and interpretation. The same behavior—aversion of gaze—in a white American child could well mean problems with self-esteem; it might even do so in an Indian child, if it were found that the behavior took place at times when it was not normal for her culture, such as with other children.

Children who are troubled may feel the need to turn away from inquiries or respond with defenses such as denial or projection of blame onto someone else. An understanding of the ways in which self-esteem and coping mechanisms motivate children's behavior is as important as knowledge of their developing cognitive capacities. Behavior is not always what it seems—what we see and hear may be a reflection of the child's efforts to cope with overwhelming stress, rather than a reflection of reality.

*Competence in Context.* A second major source of misunderstanding has been the tendency to view a child's capacities as stable characteristics that are much the same in all situations. In Piaget's stage theory of cognitive development, for example, preschool children are characterized as egocentric and incapable of logical thinking. Recent investigators of cognitive development (such as Donaldson, 1979; Kuhn, 1984), however, have called attention to the fact that particular abilities, such as memory and perspective taking, depend not only on the level of a child's cognitive skills but on his or her particular experience and motivation, as well as on situational factors.

Just as psychologists have become increasingly aware of the role of context in all aspects of development, they have become aware of the impossibility of understanding competence and performance apart from the contexts in which they are embedded. Context refers to any physical, social, or cultural feature of an activity that channels behavior (Rogoff, Gauvain, and Ellis, 1984). There are two broad categories of contexts. The first includes those contexts relevant to the immediate assessment situation, such as the physical setting, the meaning and significance of the event to the child, and the social interaction between adult and child. This was evident in case 13, where Maria appeared incompetent at school and competent with her family in the grocery store.

*Practice Guideline 1.4: Observed behavior may not account fully for underlying capacity; always seek situations that maximize the child's opportunity to demonstrate competence.*

The second category includes background contexts, such as the child's educational, familial, and cultural history and broader cultural contexts of law and custom. Case 12 reflected this, as did cases 6 and 8. The child's familial and cultural history influence his or her performance in an assessment setting. Familiarity with the social aspects of experimental, observational, and interview situations plays a critical role in the child's ability to perform (Rogoff, Gauvain, and Ellis, 1984). The child's understanding of the purpose of an experimental task or interview question may not be the same as the experimenter's or interviewer's. For example, the child may believe that the interviewer already knows the answer to the question (as in case 8) and that the child need not give it; or, in a desire to please the interviewer, the child may make up an answer (as in case 3). The child's degree of familiarity with the adult and the nature of the relationship also are relevant to the child's performance (as in case 1). The particular characteristics of the adult—such as age, sex, race, expectations, and degree of intrusiveness—will affect the child's performance to a degree that depends on certain characteristics of the child, the setting, and the format of adult inquiry (such as an interview, observation, or test).

*Practice Guideline 1.5: In general, the more confident and mature the child, the more positively familiar the setting, and the more conversational the inquiry, the more effective the process of communication and the more valid the information will be.*

Finally, we must consider more distant forces, such as laws, social attitudes, and institutions. Law and custom, for example, may assign particular roles to the child, such as being seen and not heard. Our view about these roles can lead to misunderstanding of children's competence. Until the last decade, the view prevailed that children were dependent and vulnerable. Evidence of this paternalistic view carried to an extreme can be seen in laws governing testimony by child witnesses that viewed children as inept and as "the most dangerous of all witnesses" (Goodman, 1984b, p. 22). Skolnick (1975) suggests that children are viewed by both psychology and the law as incompetent humans who notice less, remember less, confuse fantasy with reality, and are far more suggestible than adults.

Misperceptions of children's abilities also stem from society's more recent concerns with children's rights. Those who view children as more like adults may overestimate the maturity of their behavior and testimony. Further, particularly in cases of child abuse, adults' identification with victimized children and anger at abusive adults may lead to unwarranted generalizations, such as "children never lie." This view stems in part from the belief in children as innocent, and in part from a misunderstanding of how the motivation to lie and the ability to carry it off develop with age.

We believe that children are like adults in some respects and different in others. Despite differing theoretical perspectives and the limitations of research, there is an increasing body of information about child development that provides information about differences in the capabilities of children of different ages. Of course, it cannot tell us how an individual child will perform at a specific time. At any given age or stage of development there is variability among children in what they can do. Nor can it give us a precise measure of a capacity that resides in the child, because capacities do

not exist as stable quantities in human beings. Rather, this information about children's competence can provide a framework that
guides our assessment and points to factors we should attend to.
Rather than giving us a precise map, this perspective gives us some
principles of the social geography of adult-child encounters. With
these we must find our way.

### Format of Adult Inquiry

The interaction between child and adult influences a child's
performance in an assessment setting both directly and indirectly.
In addition to the adult's relationship to the child, the personal
characteristics of the adult have significance for the way he or she is
perceived by the child. For example, the adult's race, ethnicity, and
sex may influence the child, as may appearance factors, such as a
uniform or facial hair. The adult's demeanor, style of interaction,
tone of voice, and degree of empathy will also affect the child's ability
to respond. These influences were evident in cases 1, 3, 6, and 11.

The adult's conscious and unconscious motives, attitudes,
and expectations also play a critical role in shaping the child's
performance. Just as parental expectations shape children's developing capacities, adult preconceptions can powerfully influence
children by creating self-fulfilling prophecies through nonverbal
cues (Rosenthal, 1978). Thus, adults "find" evidence that confirms
their own biases. They allow their own unexamined personal
experiences to shape their judgments.

Finally, the adult's professional role will greatly influence
the nature of the information obtained from the child. The criminal
justice system and some research paradigms, for example, require a
particular kind of objective, verifiable evidence. The mental health
system and parents, on the other hand, may be more interested in
the child's subjective experience of an event. Who you are can
influence what you want and value and what you get; case 5
illustrates this.

*Practice Guideline 1.6: Some adults get better information
from children than others; children give better information to some
adults than to others.*

We can identify a range of techniques that can be used to elicit information from children. Since both child and adult bring objectifiable characteristics as well as subjective feelings and motives to the interaction, we seek to examine multiple sources of information about children and multiple formats of inquiry to use with children. That is, we consider both clinical and empirical data from a variety of settings to be necessary. Rather than viewing these methods of inquiry and contexts for assessment as adversarial, we see them as complementary; each has its uses and limitations. In Part Three we will consider observation of children's behavior, children's play and stories, interviewing children, and the use of tests and other instruments. Multiple methods generally lead to more valid results. It is also clear that consistency of information over time, among contexts, and across methods of inquiry increases confidence in conclusions about the information given by children.

*Practice Guideline 1.7: The more sources of information an adult has about a child, the more likely that adult is to receive the child's messages properly.*

## A Model for Understanding Children as Sources of Information

On the basis of the preceding discussion and the material in the chapters to come, we have developed a classification scheme to serve as a framework for understanding children as sources of information. The issues raised by the thirteen cases presented, as well as others to follow, are encompassed by this model.

The model looks at the child and the adult in terms of two basic dimensions: orientation and competence. Together they account for variations in outcomes of child-adult communication around the seeking of information.

*Child Orientation.* The child's performance depends, in part, on the child's orientation to the assessment. Possible orientations include feeling effective and competent, wanting to please a significant adult, consciously or unconsciously defending against unbearable feelings, and being paralyzed by fear. Beyond these psychological issues stand the sociocultural features of the child's orientation: the meaning and significance of the event to the child as created by the child's specific cultural membership and experiences, and the broader cultural contexts, such as law and custom, that influence the child's attitudes and behaviors.

*Child Competence.* The child's performance also depends on his or her ability to perceive, remember, reason, and communicate; these abilities develop in connection with more general intellectual and emotional capacities. This leads us to consider basic processes in cognitive and language development and how they affect the child's competence. One feature of this competence is derived from the developmental status of the child. The process of development is continuous, but it is useful and convenient to recognize three broad time periods. In infancy (from birth to two years), the child experiences his or her world in a perceptual, action-oriented, nonverbal fashion. The infant's capacities, affects, and behaviors serve as sources of information. In the preschool period (from two to six years), the advent of language and symbolic thinking brings about the ability to share meaning with other people. The child has achieved a significant capacity to understand and respond to adult inquiry, but performance is closely tied to the contexts in which it is elicited. In the school-age period (from six to twelve years), with the development of the ability to think about thinking and the ability to think more logically, the child is developing increasingly adultlike capacities to communicate and respond. The child's motivations, however, are also becoming more complex and difficult to discern.

*Adult Orientation.* The adult's motives, attitudes, expectations, and role play an important part in defining the adult's orientation. Characteristics of the adult role also influence both the child's ability to respond and how the adult interprets and uses the information given. These characteristics include race, sex, age, ethnicity, and knowledge of children, as well as the adult's relationship to the child. Also included under orientation is the adult's position on a set of ethical issues: What rights do children have to privacy? To authority? To respect?

*Adult Competence.* Adult competence is derived from skill in recognizing the status of a child, in formulating a context that will maximize the child's performance, and in minimizing violations of the child. Together, these factors may influence the choice of technique or tactics for eliciting information from children. The following techniques reflect different degrees of adult direction in the encounter with the child, differences in the degree to which the adult stimulates and controls the interaction (thus casting the child in a reactive mode).

In observations of children's behavior, the adult, without interacting, learns from the child by watching and listening to the child's spontaneous behavior (adult direction low). In children's play and stories, the adult uses play and storytelling as a method of communicating to a child through metaphor and as a source of information from the child about her inner world of thought and feelings (adult direction moderate). In interviewing children, the adult learns interactively from a child along a continuum ranging from eliciting a narrative through asking general questions to asking specific questions. The child is an informant of his own behavior and feelings or of his experience of an event (adult direction moderate to high). Finally, through tests and other measurements, the adult learns from the child by testing the child's response to stimuli and comparing her responses to predetermined norms, standards, or established criteria (adult direction high).

*Practice Guideline 1.8: While the competence issues are obviously greatest with respect to children, information-seeking is in fact a reciprocal relationship: the more competent the adult, the less competence is required of the child.*

The chapters that follow build on this model and the thirteen cases presented in this chapter through a systematic exploration of the many features of effective child-adult communication across diverse settings.

CHAPTER 2

# Self-Esteem and Coping

The ways children feel about being competent, their attitudes toward adults, and the ways in which they defend themselves from difficult consequences or feelings all affect their ability to provide information. These factors, in turn, are influenced by the child's personal history in a particular family and in a particular community. What a child has experienced, what he expects of himself and others, and what he has learned he may or may not do can affect his performance in an information-seeking situation.

Some children have experienced approval, acceptance, and the opportunity for mastery on a regular basis. Others have experienced unrelenting humiliation, rejection, and failure (Garbarino, Guttmann, and Seeley, 1986). Some children are resilient and energetic; others are vulnerable and lethargic. Out of the interaction of a child's experiences and characteristics comes a perspective on himself, or *self-esteem,* and a set of strategies and tactics for dealing with the world, or *coping mechanisms.*

These overlapping phenomena help account for children's self-judgments and for how they marshal their resources to meet the challenges and stresses of life. Self-esteem influences how children behave and communicate. For example, when they are feeling good about themselves, they are apt to be open to communication. Conversely, they are more resistant to adult probings that threaten to expose areas of diminished self-esteem. Efforts to cope with assaults on self-esteem or other stresses may also cause the child to turn away from inquiries or to respond with defenses, such as denial or projection of blame onto someone else. Thus, an awareness of the role of these psychological processes is as necessary to information seeking as is knowledge of children's cognitive and linguistic capacities.

## A Framework for Understanding Socioemotional Development

A basic assumption of this book is that the individual and the environment are mutually influential, acting on one another dynamically to produce development. In other words, development results from encounters between children and their physical, social, and cultural contexts. As the child changes and matures, the parent responds and adapts to these changes. The child's continuing development is influenced by the parent's responses. Both adaptive and maladaptive parent-child relationships are thus the consequence of the interactions of characteristics in the child and in the family, as well as in the wider environment.

The child contributes to these interactions from the start. We used to think of newborns as passive beings, unable to see or respond except through reflex actions. Today we know that the newborn is capable of many complex behaviors that are used to get to know and to influence the environment and, particularly, the people in it. For example, infants prefer the configuration of a human face to other shapes and the sound range of a female voice to other sounds. The baby's cries are naturally received by adults as the message "Help—I need you," and its gazes and smiles are irresistible signals for social exchanges. Thus, the infant comes equipped to participate in mutual social exchanges from the moment of birth.

Unfortunately, characteristics in the child may also contribute to inappropriate interaction patterns that may lead to maladaptive parent-child relationships. For example, when an infant's features deviate from the usual pattern, they tend to elicit negative adult reaction (Holmes, Reich, and Pasternak, 1984). Thus, for example, premature infants and children with certain disabilities may make parenting more difficult or unrewarding. An infant's characteristics also may not fit well with those of the caregiver (Thomas, Chess, and Birch, 1968). For example, a child may have a high activity level, react intensely to new things and routines, be distractible, and be attracted by many things. One parent may view this child as bright, curious, and "feisty"; another parent may not notice these qualities; a third parent may dislike the child for reminding him of his own difficulties in school and of a painful childhood. Thus, a good match between baby and caregiver will enhance the relationship, while a mismatch may hamper it. As the child becomes older, her behaviors (such as poor frustration tolerance) and her subjective experiences (such as negative feelings and fantasies) may contribute to poor interactions.

*Practice Guideline 2.1: The quality of parent-child relationships cannot be assessed by taking solely the perspective of either the child or the adult; good relationships flow from the adult-child match as much as from any attribute of either party.*

In the course of development, the child forms a sense or view of the world. All a child's experiences and interactions fit together to provide a picture of herself and of the community in which she lives. What does it take for a child to form a realistic and positive view of the world, a view that will lead her outward into the world with confidence and a capacity for meaningful relationships, trust, and responsibility? It takes a world that meets the basic needs of the child for nurturance, responsiveness, stability, predictability, support, and guidance. It also takes people who value the child for who she is.

It is within the context of their caregiving environments that children not only receive protection and nurturance but extract their first understanding of the self and the world, learning the most critical lessons in becoming thinking and social beings. A child becomes what she has internalized from her family as well as from a selection of what the world offers as plausible alternatives.

### Self-Esteem and Coping Mechanisms

*Self-esteem* is generally defined as a subjective value judgment that a person makes about his or her personal worth. It consists of a combination of thoughts and feelings toward the self and the overall experience of cohesiveness and well-being (Demos, 1983). As such, "the development of self-esteem is one of the central developmental tasks of childhood" (Mack, 1983, p. 12). Self-esteem is both a conscious experience accessible to introspection and description and an unconscious process reflecting thoughts and feelings beyond awareness. A person with high self-esteem more often feels positive feelings (affects) such as confidence, worthiness, pleasure, and effectiveness. A person with low self-esteem is more apt to feel pain, doubt, shame, and sadness.

While theorists and investigators have focused on different dimensions of self-esteem (see Harter, 1983, for a review of self-esteem literature), the two most commonly cited are competence and acceptance. The first dimension or source of self-esteem derives from satisfaction taken in independent, self-generated activity—that is, from self-judgments of competence versus incompetence. Success in this dimension ultimately results in competence in the world of school and work. The second derives from approval by others—that is, from self-judgments of relatedness versus isolation. Success in this dimension results in the capacity to form intimate relationships.

The preservation of one's self-esteem serves a strong motivational function. The urgent need to protect self-esteem may result from the intensity of the pain or anxiety experienced when it falls, what Kohut (1980) calls "the experiential core of the devastating emotional event we refer to as a severe drop in self-esteem" (p. 503). Thus, feelings of competence and acceptance can influence children's motivational orientation toward engaging in tasks or communication. For example, a child who feels good about having achieved something in school is more likely to be intrinsically motivated to perform academically (Harter and Connell, 1982).

*Coping* refers to children's efforts to come to terms with problems, frustrations, threats, and challenging opportunities. Coping involves more than competence or active mastery; it implies a marshaling of resources, conscious and unconscious, to meet stresses and challenges (Murphy and Moriarty, 1976; Lazarus and Launier, 1978). Coping styles vary considerably from child to child and include a wide range of strategies for managing both the environment and the inner tension aroused by the stimulus. These devices include cognitive capacities (such as curiosity), motor capacities (such as motor and visual-motor control), affect (such as range of moods in reaction to stimuli), complex integrative capacities (such as the ability to protest actively, the ability to ask for help), and self-feelings (such as pride) (Murphy and Moriarty, 1976). Coping overlaps with self-esteem in that self-esteem is required for long-term ways of keeping comfortable, or maintaining internal integration. That is, the child with a positive sense of self-esteem is less vulnerable to stress.

Mechanisms of defense are coping strategies that have particular relevance to children as sources of information. These mechanisms are the unconscious processes that serve as defenses against anxiety, such as denial, regression, repression, projection, and displacement (Freud, 1937). These subjective manipulations serve to take the sting out of reality and allow the person to move on. The use of mechanisms of defense can be both adaptive and maladaptive. Adaptive use can be seen in children's efforts at coping with very stressful situations. In the case of illness, for example, temporary denial can serve to reduce the scope of what has to be faced and make it seem more manageable. Normal, flexible use of defense mechanisms can make reality more bearable and make it easier for the child to use other coping resources to meet his goals or challenges. Defense mechanisms are maladaptive if they interfere with effective coping.

Emerging in the early years and lasting throughout life, mechanisms of defense are an integral part of the psychological well-being of people. Although they are difficult to understand and detect, they can sometimes be inferred from a child's unexpected or discordant reaction to particular events. For example, if a child reacts with excessive tenderness where anger would be expected, it can be inferred that the child is defending himself against the guilt generated by his anger by denying the anger and assuming the opposite stance.

While knowledge of defense mechanisms can be useful to the adult in understanding the child's motivation, it is important to respect a child's use of them. An understanding of their adaptive purposes can keep us from engaging in blaming or control battles, which may force the child into an even more defensive posture. Indiscriminate interpretation or breaking down of a child's defenses can interfere with the child's ability to cope. Sometimes it helps to respond to the feeling in a child's statement, not to the overt content. For example, rather than calling a child in a custody battle on the fact that you feel she is projecting her own feelings of blame onto a sibling, it might be better to say something like "I know it's scary not knowing what will happen next."

*Practice Guideline 2.2: The best intervention with defense mechanisms is awareness. It is generally not a good idea to make them explicit to the child outside the context of a therapeutic relationship.*

Self-esteem and coping follow a developmental progression that depends on the capacities and behaviors a child brings to each level of development as well as on the ways in which the caregiving environment relates to the child interpersonally. We now turn to the development of these psychological factors and their implications for the information-seeking process in three age periods.

### Infancy (Birth to Two Years)

Prior to the advent of language, infants' behaviors and levels of development serve as sources of information about their well-being. Observations can be made of both dimensions of self-esteem. The competence or mastery dimension is derived from achieving self-generated goals. From the earliest days of life the infant is an active, information-organizing individual who is engaged in the task of adapting to her environment, discovering the effects she can have on it and the effects the environment can have on her (White, 1963). This "I know what I can do" feeling is exemplified in an eight-month-old infant's gleeful excitement as she discovers that she can pull herself to a standing position, or when she discovers her rattle hidden under her blanket.

The second dimension of self-esteem involves what Stern (1985, p. 100) refers to as "self with other." The child's sense of self-worth, based on the belief that she is a worthy and lovable partner in an intimate relationship, is derived from her countless experiences with the adults who care for her. This requires parents to be empathically responsive to the infant's individual temperament, needs, feelings, and wishes. This joy in the child becomes incorporated into the child's sense of herself. Small failures in parental empathy are unavoidable and, in fact, helpful. Occasional failures help the child learn to deal with the inevitable disappointments and become increasingly reality-oriented.

Coping styles develop in infancy as the result of the interaction between genetic or predetermined events (such as temperament) and the response of the environment (Murphy and Moriarty, 1976). For example, some infants turn away from excessive stimulation, some protest; some are detached observers, others are eager participants; some become absorbed in objects, others in activity. These methods may continue to dominate a child's coping style throughout childhood; they may change through interaction with others or be blocked or thwarted. If the child's own inclinations are thwarted or deprived because of parental pressures (stemming from the parents' own needs), alternative coping methods are developed that include complex and often maladaptive defensive patterns (Murphy, 1962).

As suggested earlier, the beginnings of infants' self-esteem and coping mechanisms can only be inferred from observation of their behavior and development. Typically, the child's mastery and coping mechanisms are observed in the context of a problem-solving situation. Both the child's successful attempts and associated affects are noted. The infant's relatedness to others is observed in the context of adult-infant interactions. This means, for example, looking for reciprocal, joyful exchanges (Stern, 1977), evidence that the mother shares the infant's subjective feelings (Stern, 1985), or evidence of a secure attachment relationship during episodes of separation and reunion (Ainsworth, Blehar, Waters, and Wall, 1978). The following case study illustrates the ways in which a clinical psychologist observed an eighteen-month-old child's relationship to her parents and some of her maladaptive coping mechanisms:

> I was asked to evaluate the progress of an eighteen-month-old girl who had been in a pre-adoptive home for the prior six months. During my first home visit, she impressed me as a serious, sober, sturdy, and self-assured little girl who appeared quite mature for her age. But I was troubled by my observations that she initiated very few interactions with her pre-adoptive parents, preferred me to them, sought my comfort

when distressed, and protested my departure, expressing an interest in leaving with me. From my first observation of her, it seemed that either her current relationship with her pre-adoptive parents was going quite poorly or she had been so damaged by the unstable and neglectful care she received in the first year of life that she could not attach to other parental figures.

My observations of her a week later during a second home visit were consistent with those of the first. She again pretty much ignored her pre-adoptive parents, seeming to prefer my attention, and again cried when I departed. She did reveal another side of herself, however. Twice during the home visit she briefly "panicked" when she was startled. In other words, she lost her composure and self-assurance when faced with something she was not prepared for. Her armor therefore was cracked.

My third visit occurred a week later. This time I observed quite a different little girl. She was clearly focused on her pre-adoptive mother, initiated interactions with her, and sought her attention, and related to me as a visitor in very appropriate ways. It seemed therefore that she was attached after all. I believe her initial reaction to me was counter-phobic in nature. She was actually quite fearful that I would take her away from her parents in whom she was significantly invested, as she had been abruptly taken from previous parent figures by previous visitors. She acted as if she wanted to leave with me as a way of gaining control over her fears. When she realized that I was only a visitor and not someone who was going to wrench her away from her attachment figures, she was able to relax and display that attachment in appropriate ways.

A week or so later I saw her in an office setting to conduct a Bayley [a standardized assessment of development]. She was unable to concentrate on the testing, even though it was well within her abilities, because of the presence of a videotape operator. It seemed that it was very important for her to know how each stranger she encountered fit into her world. After his departure, she was able to focus on the task at hand and did quite well [Mark D. Everson, pers. comm., Jan. 1987].

As Everson suggests, his initial observations led him to question whether the child's ability to relate to others had been severely hampered by her earlier experiences, or whether she was unable to attach to this particular set of parents. If Everson had made only one or two visits, he might well have been left with either erroneous impression. What he discovered over time was that the way she acted was an indication of her attempts to cope as well as she could with her understandable fears that she would be taken away once again. Everson was also able to see that her inability to master the test items on the Bayley developmental assessment was not a reflection of her cognitive competence. Rather, once again, she was responding to the presence of a stranger.

*Practice Guideline 2.3: Multiple observations as well as some knowledge of the child's history are usually necessary to establish valid patterns of information about a very young child, particularly when there is suspicion of pathology.*

### Early Childhood (Two to Six Years)

As children grow and develop, they continue to seek the satisfaction of feeling competent in mastering challenges presented by life. Language and representational thinking open up new worlds of increasingly difficult problems and situations. The child is now capable of maintaining self-generated goals in relation to specific standards, including goals that have not been linked to adult approval or disapproval (Kagan, 1981). What continues to be critical for this dimension of positive self-esteem is that the child experience a real accomplishment. Adults may encourage the child's initiative, but self-esteem is enhanced only by praise for genuine accomplishments, for children cannot be fooled by empty praise and condescending encouragement (Erikson, 1959).

Equally important to children's urge to be competent is the need for approval from significant adults and the desire to be like them and participate in their activities. After age two, children have the capacity to stand at some distance from themselves and refer to themselves as objective entities (for example, "Sally wants a cookie"). They increasingly are able first to name and subsequently to describe their feelings (Demos, 1983). These changes enable children to enter a new level of relatedness, a way of "being with" others (Stern, 1985). They are now able to relate to others by sharing ideas and feelings about themselves and the world through language. The new level of self-awareness that emerges at this stage makes a more reflective self-esteem possible because the child is now capable of making evaluative judgments about the self (Cotton, 1983).

Regulation of self-esteem depends on parental acceptance and approval of the child's self-evaluations, such as the sense that he is good (Cotton, 1983). Self-esteem is also enhanced when parents create expectations for the child by setting protective, realistic, and consistent limits on the child's behavior. The parent walks a fine line between allowing the child to experiment, explore, achieve, and control and protecting the child from both internal hazards (such as aggression or anger) and external hazards (such as a car in the street). Well-defined limits enhance self-esteem by highlighting the restrictions and demands imposed by the real world, thereby enabling the child to evaluate his performance (Coopersmith, 1967).

During the early childhood years, children increasingly admire and seek to emulate adults who appear to have authority, power, and ownership of the goods. The attraction of children to the sources of power forms the basis for the process of identification—the desire to become like the important adults in their lives. As the child increasingly internalizes the characteristics and roles of those around her, she expands her self-definition of who she is. Identification, however, can be a double-edged sword. As Breger (1974) points out, when the child adds characteristics and roles to her self-definition out of good feelings, she comes to be proud of this new part of herself. On the other hand, if aspects of the adult are incorporated out of anxiety or anger (as in identification with the aggressor), there will be an inner ambivalence about the value of the self.

Coping during these years is closely linked to self-esteem. Children with high self-esteem are generally more effective in their coping. For example, they can more easily assert themselves, control their aggression, and use adults as resources (Murphy and Moriarty, 1976). One of the most common coping strategies children employ to deal with the threat to self-esteem caused by stressful experiences or by their own limitations is symbolic play. Through play, children can regain power and control (and perhaps take revenge)—by playing dentist, for example; they can also pretend to do something they do not yet have the skills for, such as cooking dinner.

With the advent of symbolic thought and language, distortions of reality are also possible. A person can, for example, say he is happy when he is sad. It is now cognitively possible for the child to use mechanisms of defense to cope with stress. As suggested above, flexible use of defense mechanisms can be a part of healthy coping in that defense mechanisms enable the child to endure reality while he uses other coping mechanisms to meet his needs.

Maladaptive use of defense mechanisms interferes with healthy coping. Early in their lives children may develop rigid patterns of defense. For example, in a longitudinal study of coping, Murphy (1962) found that parental behavior could influence the development of maladaptive defensive processes in children by the age of two or three years. Children whose parents were teasing, punitive, or aggressive developed a pattern of anticipating blame or punishment from the adult by acting in a way to avoid risk even when there was none.

*Practice Guideline 2.4: When communicating with preschool-age children, be attentive to self-deprecating or defensive strategies on the child's part that indicate that the child anticipates emotional or physical assault; remember that the child's initial responses are often geared to prior experience rather than the current interaction.*

Young children are very reliant upon adults for approval and have had relatively little experience with information-seeking situations. Many children therefore routinely comply with adults' commands, seeking approval or perhaps a relationship.

*Practice Guideline 2.5: It is very common for preschool children to provide an answer (right or wrong) to a question just because they are seeking approval.*

Some children seem to require a parent or someone they know to be present as an ally against either the stranger or the strangeness of the situation. Others may protest actively, which may, in some cases, be a constructive way of coping with anxiety (Murphy and Moriarty, 1976). Still others, however, may be negative or may easily rely upon avoidance or denial, suggesting they are oversensitive to the reaction of others.

*Practice Guideline 2.6: Initiating a communicative relationship with a preschool child is likely to be difficult unless the adult is known to the child or the interaction occurs in a setting familiar to the child and is sponsored by someone the child knows and trusts.*

Self-esteem influences the ways in which young children respond to the demands of adults in information-seeking situations. Murphy (1962) found that the children who could best meet the challenges of new situations felt more secure about their ability to communicate and get along with new people and showed a greater capacity for struggle, or greater determination and drive toward mastery. Those who coped less well were more anxious about newness, often were more dependent on their mothers, and displayed less flexible use of defense mechanisms. The following case study illustrates a four-year-old child's puzzling response to a series of nonthreatening play sessions:

Since Rachel showed such an extreme response to new situations—despite her willingness to separate from her mother—a closer examination of her behaviors is worthwhile in an effort to understand what strangeness meant to her. The following is a review of behavior obtained in three play sessions with miniature toys with me:

Everything Rachel did the three times we saw her in the Miniature Life Toys play situation must be thought about in relation to the impression of four observers, that a new situation is overwhelming to her, almost paralyzing, certainly fraught with potentially threatening unknowns. At these times she looks like a lost child, a war-orphan or a child in some similar circumstances who is haunted by a fear of some dreadful destiny, or, as WM commented, with a "fatiguing, paralyzing sense of apartness," expressed in her "faraway, vaguely drooping attitude." It should also be remembered throughout that on the way home from each situation she relaxed quickly, seemed to be a different child, able to talk with the adults with considerable freedom, responsive to her environment, radiantly expressive when a special treat appeared, and bubbling with eagerness as she rejoined her family. Details of her behavior can be seen then as expressions of an impressionable, reactive, resilient little personality with extremely wide swings from paralyzing anxiety to glowing delight. Verbal, motor, affective, cognitive responses to these situations were all deeply affected by this persistent apprehensiveness about the unknown situation, the unknown person, from which she recovered as soon as she left the strangeness behind her, and returned to safe familiarity, or even the prospect of it. . . .

Speculations about her inability to express the flood of feelings in a new situation which everyone sensed behind her silent gaze included the following: that she did not feel free to fully exist in an unfamiliar setting, or to call attention to herself in any way. Or perhaps she was full of awe of an outside, unknown, perhaps higher-class world. Perhaps she had been overly conditioned to a brand of manners epitomized by unquestioning obedience, conformity or inconspicuousness; or perhaps she had an underlying sense of weakness and helplessness which kept her from meeting a conflict situation with any overt effort.

But she also showed a remarkable flexibility and resilience which enabled her to respond freely once she was out of the awesome or frightening new experience, and a capacity for deep sensuous delight and gratification and for sensitive non-verbal interpersonal communication through smiles and eyes, along with her capacity for representation and symbolization of experiences in fantasies which seemed to contradict the view of her as a deeply inhibited child.

It seemed clear that she was able to use tender and loving care as a reinforcement to her own coping efforts and resilience, despite her resistance when first confronting a new situation, and that she was much more free in her home setting [Murphy, 1962, pp. 33-35].

Murphy's longitudinal data indicated that for a variety of reasons (including a hospitalization during her second year of life, at which time she was confined to a crib and almost completely immobilized for three months), Rachel's sense of efficacy was low. This was particularly true in unstructured situations in which she had to initiate spontaneous organization, such as when she was placed in the middle of the floor to play with unfamiliar toys. Murphy discovered that when told or shown what to do, Rachel could perform with high efficacy and confidence.

This case illustrates the dual nature of self-esteem; Rachel had a sense of herself as cared for and approved of by others, and she did want to comply. However, her low sense of competence in certain circumstances caused her to inhibit her behavior. The role of adults in helping the preschool child to regulate self-esteem and to cope is also highlighted. While Rachel had to succeed on her own, mediation of the situation in the form of more explicit direction and support for her own coping efforts undoubtedly helped her tolerate the discrepancy between her actual and her ideal self.

*Practice Guideline 2.7: Adults seeking information from preschool children often have to play an active role in structuring the situation, providing more explicit instructions, and offering reassurance.*

## Middle Childhood (Six to Twelve Years)

As the child becomes older, the sources of self-esteem become more integrated. The self becomes the major tool for the regulation of self-esteem by acting as a selective filter for development in the areas of competence and acceptance (Cotton, 1983). This more global or pervasive sense of self means that children are now less vulnerable to minor slights, and the impact of praise on self-esteem depends largely on the value to the child of what is being praised and by whom. Self-esteem has more psychological momentum. However, negative patterns or views of the self can interfere with developing competence or identification with positive models, in spite of environmental support.

During middle childhood, the acquisition of skills and accomplishments in school (a sense of "industry") is critical to feelings of well-being, pride, and self-esteem (Erikson, 1959). The desire to do well in school leads to vitally important learning in addition to feelings of personal power. Children with disabling conditions and learning disabilities have a particularly difficult time regulating self-esteem during middle childhood. This is because of the importance of academic and athletic competence as well as the potential meaning of a disability to peers and adults in and beyond the family. When children are constantly unable to master challenges, they may experience depression, anxiety, lowered self-esteem, and other pathological symptoms.

Nonparental adults (such as teachers) and peers become increasingly important to the school-age child. Emerging cognitive and perspective-taking skills enable the child to imagine what other people are thinking, particularly what they are thinking of him. Furthermore, children can develop rules for setting expectations about their idealized self and compare themselves with others. Rosenberg (1979) has documented the effects of the child's sociological context on self-esteem. He found that self-esteem may be lowered when a child compares himself unfavorably to a dissonant reference group, as in the case of a black child attending a primarily white school. He found that it is primarily contextual dissonance that damages self-esteem, not one's ethnic or religious identifications per se.

*Practice Guideline 2.8: An adult seeking information from a child should assess the degree to which that child deviates from the norms of school and community, for example, in terms of race, social class, ethnicity, physical appearance, and participation in valued activities.*

Coping during middle childhood continues to involve a wide range of strategies. In a study of school-age children's self-reports of their coping, Wertlieb, Weigel, and Feldstein (1987) found that the most prevalent strategies were those with a focus on the self, those oriented toward problem solving rather than emotion management, and those involving overt and direct action. For example, a solution for a boy who was never picked to be a member of a team might involve improving his sports skills (self-oriented, direct problem solving) rather than telling himself he did not want to play anyway or staying inside.

Defense mechanisms such as repression (exclusion from consciousness of an idea or an experience and its associated emotions), displacement (discharge of emotions, usually anger, on people other than those who originally aroused the emotions), and projection (unconscious rejection of one's emotionally unacceptable thoughts and feelings and the attribution of them to other people) come into sharper focus during the school years (Sarnoff, 1976). It has also been suggested that lying may develop as a symptom that expresses the struggle to maintain self-esteem (Chagoya and Schkolne, 1986). As we will see in Chapter Four, children may lie out of anxiety about aggressive feelings, out of frustration over real or perceived failures, to gain an advantage, to avoid disapproval, or to appear better to others than they feel themselves to be.

*Practice Guideline 2.9: When confronted by a child who has lied, look for explanations tied to coping mechanisms; always search for the function served by the child's lie.*

With increased cognitive capacities and social awareness, school-age children begin to resemble adults in the ways in which they function as sources of information. They are less likely than younger children, for example, to seek approval from adults indiscriminately or to require an ally in strange situations. They are more capable of logical thinking and of using language to provide rational explanations. But they also become more competent at lying and more capable of seeing subtle reasons for doing so.

School-age children's self-esteem is still developing, however, and is still vulnerable, particularly in stressful situations. Their allegiance to peers is now often a powerful motivating force for sharing or refusing to share information. Peer compliance peaks between the ages of eleven and thirteen.

*Practice Guideline 2.10: When seeking information from a child approaching adolescence (age ten and up), keep in mind that there may be peer-related motives for a child's refusal to commu-nicate.*

School-age children's increased capacities also enable them to protect themselves in increasingly sophisticated ways. As suggested above, they have more reasons and are better able to use both conscious and unconscious coping mechanisms to protect themselves from real and perceived threats.

The following two case studies illustrate ways in which pre-vailing negative views of the self influence the child's efforts to cope in information-gathering situations. The first takes place in a school setting in which a child has been referred for educational testing; the second is an interview of a child in a clinical research study.

Jeb is a twelve-year-old boy in sixth grade who was referred for educational testing by his teachers because he seemed to be capable of doing all grade assignments, yet he turned in little work.

Jeb's history indicates that he lives with his parents and is the third of five living children, the only boy. His birth followed the unexpected death of an infant girl. Each summer Jeb is sent to military camp by his father, whom Jeb considers to be his best friend. During the year he and his father are both involved in play with military model making and miniature armies. Although school officials reported that Jeb's father was interested in Jeb's participation in sports, Jeb said that no sports interested him as much as computer games.

When asked about his school experiences from his point of view, Jeb commented that he had had a "hard time" with one of his teachers in the primary school; the rest of the years went well until fifth grade when, according to Jeb, "trouble started." A new student entered the class and made fun of Jeb continuously. Two other boys joined in the scapegoating, and Jeb does not think that anything was done by the adults to ease the situation. Some of his discomfort has continued.

During individual achievement testing, Jeb made running comments about himself and his performance. Before beginning any task, he made self-deprecating comments or said that he did not expect to do well. He said that he did not like to get things wrong, and when he made one minor error (his performance still scoring above expectancy for his age and grade level), he banged his fist on the desk and said, "I knew I would do something wrong."

One of the tests required sorting pictures of words into superordinate and associative categories and shifting from an original strategy/category to a second. Jeb had such pronounced difficulty with this task that I had to stop administration of the subtest.

Jeb said that he was a pessimist. When asked if he would like to know the results of testing, he said, "Why? Am I smarter than I look?" The tone of his comment was one of query, not sarcasm.

Jeb's attitude toward himself and his performance interfered with accuracy and efficiency (the tests took longer to administer and complete). Lack of flexibility and difficulty with shifting strategies hinders his current production and could interfere with creative problem solving. Jeb's insistence on wanting everything right could have a mixed impact on his learning and, subsequently, his achievement [Carol Ceithaml, pers. comm., May 1988].

In this example Ceithaml has clearly identified issues of self-esteem rather than intellectual ability as influencing Jeb's poor school performance. In addition to having problems with competence and little sense of efficacy, Jeb appears to suffer from problems with self-esteem in his relationships. One can only speculate about the origins of Jeb's poor self-esteem or the meaning and value Jeb has to his parents. It is more apparent at school, where he has poor peer relationships and seems not to trust his teachers. Jeb was able, however, to communicate some of his feelings through his words and actions, thus enabling Ceithaml to better understand his performance in the testing situation.

The following case study describes a child who is far more troubled than Jeb and whose coping mechanisms are much further from her conscious awareness. This case comes from a clinical research study of the children of psychiatrically ill mothers.

An only child, eight-year-old Nora lives with her mother, Gladys. Gladys has a psychiatric history of a brief reactive psychosis superimposed on a severe character disorder. Though from a middle-class background they live in a series of transient hotels, eating mainly in restaurants (since there are no cooking facilities). It is believed that Nora's expensive clothes are obtained by her mother's shoplifting. At the time of this interview Gladys was separated from Nora's father.

Gladys has moved Nora to five different schools within the last year because of what she describes as "difficult peers." She calls and harasses school personnel and spends a great deal of time at Nora's school, ostensibly doing "volunteer work" but basically annoying staff and other parents with her non-stop talking, criticism and complaints. Nora's teacher noted that she is not liked by her classmates and is a trouble maker who sets girls against one another. Nora complains that others are out to get her; is easily jealous, and doesn't seem to feel guilty about misbehavior. She seems obsessed, according to her teacher, with her lack of friends, frequently running and complaining to her mother. She seems to lack a sense of humor, and to take no pleasure in her accomplishments. She tends to be irregular in her school attendance.

Nora was very cooperative and compliant during her interview. She was more than willing to leave her one-room unheated apartment to go to a restaurant, where she was able to eat something while the interview took place. Nora presented herself as a happy child who is bright and pretty and has lots of friends. Her only wishes had to do with material things—a new apartment closer to school, her own room, and a pet.

Nora's statements gave evidence of an idealization of her mother from which she rarely departed. She said that she was very close to her mother (as opposed to her father) and liked her mother because she put cupcakes in her lunch and bought her stickers and books. The only hints of having a difficult time at home came when Nora said that when she and her mother fought her mother always won, and that made her sad and mad. She also said that when she hurt herself, her mother also hurt herself. When asked what she did when she was angry, Nora said that she punched and kicked a pillow. When sad, she said, "I quit crying and say to myself 'I can be brave' or I talk to my dolls."

When I returned Nora to her apartment, Gladys told me that she was going on a field trip with Nora's class. Nora said, "All my friends want to be with Donna's mom—but *I* want to be in *your* group, Mom." Gladys commented (with a smile), saying, "I have to be with the special ed kids, Nora. You're resilient and I know you can handle it" [Stott, Cohler, and Musick, 1985, pp. 6–8].

School-age children are frequently the best informants regarding their own behavior and feelings, particularly as they get older. Edelbrock and his colleagues (1985) found that the reliability of children's self-reports increases with age; it is lower for children between six and nine than for those who are ten or older. In this case, however, it is clear that it is far more than Nora's age (eight) that keeps her from being able to report accurately on her behavior and feelings. The reality of her life is so harsh and destructive to her developing self-esteem that she needs to be strongly defended against painful knowledge of herself and her life.

Longitudinal data from this study provided additional information that this was a severely troubled family. Gladys's psychopathology intensified Nora's isolation and kept her tied to her mother in an exclusive and symbiotic relationship in which a distorted reality was created and maintained by the assertion of both parties—a situation reminiscent of E. J. Anthony's (1970) description of a mother-child "folie à deux." In some ways, Gladys provided Nora with a script about their lives together that presented a happy facade. Thus, Nora's distortions were created in part by her mother and in part by her need to ward off potentially devastating feelings. Nora denied any anger toward her mother; it is likely that she sometimes displaced it onto the pillow that she punched and kicked.

Nora's telling her mother that she wanted to be in her group on the field trip illustrates Winnicott's (1965) concept of the false self. In order to please her mother, Nora had to disavow or repress her own feelings and inner experience and convey a false enthusiasm. Whether Nora's true feelings remained a private but accessible part of herself or had been relegated out of consciousness is not clear. This case illustrates the finding of the larger research study that children who were at risk for psychological problems had significantly less accurate self-appraisals than a comparison group of children who were not at risk (Stott, Cohler, and Musick, 1985).

*Practice Guideline 2.11: The better children are functioning psychologically, the more accurate they are likely to be as reporters of their feelings and behaviors. Conversely, those children whose self-esteem is most fragile are the most likely to distort both social (that is, "objective") reality and their subjective experiences.*

### Conclusion

We have discussed self-esteem and coping at the start because we believe it is impossible even to begin to gather information without recognizing that a child's emotional life is fundamentally involved in any relationship with an adult. Children have concerns about their competence and their acceptance by, or relatedness to, the important people in their lives. These concerns are translated into conscious and unconscious efforts to cope with the stresses and challenges of life, including those situations in which adults seek information from and about children.

How is all this related to the issues of competence and orientation identified in Chapter One? Most of this chapter has been concerned with the child's orientation. Self-esteem and coping, while partly rooted in competence, affect the child as a source of information primarily by influencing how the child approaches the adult-child encounter. Low self-esteem threatens the integrity of the communication process. It can interfere with, sidetrack, or thwart the exchange. High self-esteem frees the encounter to proceed as an exchange of information. The same is true of adaptive coping. It allows the process of seeking information to go forward directly.

Maladaptive coping strategies can transform the encounter into a saga of indirection, resistance, and false or misleading exchanges.

Perhaps the biggest obstacle is that children (as well as adults) are often not aware of their own self-judgments. Nor are they generally aware of all of their coping strategies, particularly mechanisms of defense. Therefore, behavior is not always what it seems—either to the child or to the adult who is seeking information. The challenge is to factor these psychological forces into the communicative process when seeking information. While this awareness may not always enable us to obtain the exact information we seek, it will at the least allow us to understand something of the nature of the information we receive.

CHAPTER 3

# Cognitive Development

Thinking develops. Children's thinking is different from adults', and, generally speaking, the younger the child, the greater this difference will be. However, children's thinking rarely fits simply into neat developmental pigeonholes. Thinking is always influenced by the context in which it occurs. Knowing whether a child is three years old or seven years old is useful for understanding that child's thinking, but it is not enough. We must also know about the social, physical, and cultural context of the child, about the people, the setting, and the task. To understand a child's thinking we must know something about that child's relationships, spoken and unspoken expectations, conscious and unconscious motivations. All of these factors affect children's thinking in complex ways; further, they affect how adults interpret children's thinking. Thus, understanding a child's thinking depends on understanding the child's developing cognitive capacities, how the child interprets and makes sense of the particular context in which thinking is being done, and how that thinking is being evaluated. Separating these factors is not easy and may not always be possible.

Taken together, the work of two major developmental theorists, Jean Piaget (1952, [1930] 1972, [1929] 1979) and Lev Vygotsky (1986, 1978), provides a useful theoretical framework for understanding the development of children's thinking. Piaget emphasized that from birth, children are active learners who explore their environments, seek new experiences, and actively try to make sense of their encounters with objects and people. Thus, even very young infants are active "information processors." Piaget also maintained that thinking progresses through a series of stages from infancy to adulthood; young children think, understand, and know very differently from older children, adolescents, and adults (1952, [1937] 1954, [1930] 1972, [1929] 1979). Recent research (Borke, 1975; Donaldson, 1979; Gelman and Baillargeon, 1983; Gibson and Spelke, 1983; Shatz and Gelman, 1973) indicates that Piaget probably exaggerated the differences in children's thinking at different stages of development. However, there is ample evidence to demonstrate that there are important differences in how children think, know, and understand and that children are not simply ignorant or inexperienced adults. Rather than describing them as stages, it may be more useful to think of developmental differences as reflecting gradual but perceptible shifts in ways of participating in and understanding experience. Thus, it is important for adults to try to understand that a child's interpretation and understanding of a situation may be quite different from their own.

Piaget's work focused on how children think, know, and understand at different stages, and he paid little attention to the social environment in which thinking and knowing develop. In contrast, the Soviet psychologist Lev Vygotsky (1986, 1978) argued that it is impossible to understand development without recognizing that it arises in specific social and cultural contexts that are an integral part of an individual child's intellectual growth and development. Research conducted in a Vygotskian framework (for example, Cazden, 1982, 1983; Cole and Scribner, 1974; Cole, 1985; Kaye, 1982; McLane, 1987; Rogoff and Wertsch, 1984; Wertsch, 1978, 1985a, 1985b; Wertsch, McNamee, McLane, and Budwig, 1980) is based on the assumption that children's thinking must be studied in the contexts in which it develops. From this perspective, children's interactions with parents and other significant people in their environment play a vital role in the development of their thinking. According to Vygotsky, all "higher mental processes"— such as metacognition, directed memory, logical reasoning, and abstract thinking—originate in social interaction. This means that mediated learning experiences—learning experiences in which another person provides some kind of assistance—are a key element in intellectual development. A good teacher's students are likely to perform more competently than a less skilled teacher's students, all other things being equal. Thus, to study the development of children's thinking, it is important to observe children as they engage in culturally valued activities and as they interact with more competent members of their culture.

We will consider the development of children's thinking in three broad developmental periods: infancy (birth to two years), early childhood (two to six years), and middle childhood (six to twelve years). We will devote the most attention to early childhood because children's thinking during this period often seems to be particularly difficult for adults to understand. This is partly because children's thinking undergoes so many changes during this period, partly because their thinking is so dependent on a range of contextual variables, and partly because their language skills are less sophisticated than those of older children and adults. (See Chapter Four for a discussion of issues in children's language development.) In describing each period, we will focus on those aspects of cognition that seem most relevant for understanding children as sources of information for adults—perception, memory, and reasoning.

Perception refers to primary ways of registering experience through the sensory capacities of sight, hearing, touch, taste, and smell. Infants are born with sophisticated sensory capacities that develop during the first year of life. After this period, perceptual growth consists largely of the development of increasing abilities to select, direct, and control perceptual processes. This, in turn, results in increasing abilities to identify, adapt to, and discriminate accurately among stimuli and to coordinate different perceptual information.

Memory involves perceiving, coding, storing, and retaining information and retrieving this information at a later time, either through recognition or recall. Memory is an active process that involves both construction and reconstruction, both conscious and unconscious inferences and interpretations (Flavell, 1985, p. 214-215). It is closely tied to other cognitive processes, particularly to perception, knowledge, and overall conceptual ability (Brown, 1975, 1978; Kail, 1984; Flavell, 1985). Memory develops along with other aspects of cognition, becoming more efficient and reliable with age, as children acquire more knowledge about the world and about their own thought processes. Thus, older children and adults are better than infants and young children at many types of memory tasks, particularly those involving the deliberate recall of past events. However, young children often display remarkably accurate recognition memory—that is, when presented with something, they can accurately remember whether they have seen it before.

Reasoning refers to the ability to solve problems and to think logically about cause and effect. A mature understanding of causality involves recognizing that "causes must come before or at the same time as their effects," that "causes need to consistently create their effects," and that the causes and the "effects must occur at the same time and place or at least be connected by a direct spatial or temporal chain of events" (Lind, 1987, p. 2). Children's reasoning gradually becomes more flexible, logical, and less dependent on concrete contextual support. As they develop, children are increasingly able to think about possibilities and abstractions and to go beyond immediate perceptual information. Even very young children can sometimes reason logically about familiar events in familiar settings, but they are much less likely to do so in unfamiliar settings or if they are asked about abstract hypothetical possibilities.

## Infancy (Birth to Two Years)

Infancy is a period of rapid physical, social, emotional, and cognitive development. Infants have remarkably sophisticated perceptual mechanisms that either are present at birth or mature in the first few months of life. They can hear, and they prefer the sound of human voices—particularly feminine voices; they can smell, and they learn to distinguish familiar smells like that of their mother's milk; and they can see well at close range, preferring human faces and recognizing familiar ones by the age of five or six months.

Piaget (1952, [1937] 1954) demonstrated that infants spontaneously explore their environments, seeking out new experiences and information and testing hypotheses as they try to make sense of their encounters with objects and people. Infant intelligence is an "unreflective, practical, perceiving-and-doing sort of intelligence" (Flavell, 1985, p. 44). Between birth and eighteen months, however, behavior that is largely dependent on reflexes changes to behavior that is increasingly organized, integrated, and subject to voluntary control. By eighteen months, behavior is increasingly guided by mental symbols and images.

Recent laboratory research (Kail, 1984; Fagan, 1970, 1973; Fantz, Fagan, and Miranda, 1975) has demonstrated that even very young infants have remarkably good recognition memory. Recognition memory, which is closely tied to perception, involves the awareness that something or someone has been seen, heard, or felt previously. Infants and young children are better at those memory tasks that depend on recognition than those that depend on recall. This is because recall depends in part on the development of the symbolic function (Daehler and Greco, 1985, p. 70) and in part on the development of memory strategies that usually evolve between the ages of six and twelve. Infants demonstrate the first signs of spontaneous recall when they begin to search for hidden objects at around seven or eight months (Ashmead and Perlmutter, 1980).

Somewhere between fifteen and eighteen months infants develop what Piaget called the symbolic function. This achievement heralds a major shift in development because the symbolic function makes it possible for the child to use mental symbols. This, in turn, makes possible mental representation and the rapid acquisition of language. Thus, the child can engage in increasingly elaborate fantasy and pretend play scenarios and can begin to solve problems mentally, without resorting to overt behavioral trial and error. Piaget observed the beginnings of mental representation in his sixteen-month-old daughter, Lucienne, as she tried to open a matchbox containing a gold watch chain. Previously, Lucienne had retrieved items from this matchbox, but only when the box was open far enough for her to shake out whatever was inside or to reach in with her finger and pull it out. This time, she tries to put her finger in the opening, but she cannot reach the chain. "Then she looks at the opening with great attention; then, several times in succession, she opens and shuts her mouth, at first slightly, then wider and wider! . . . Lucienne unhesitatingly puts her finger in the slit, and . . . pulls so as to enlarge the opening. She succeeds and grasps the chain" (1952, pp. 337–338). Piaget interpreted Lucienne's mouth movements—which mimicked the opening and closing of the box—as an attempt to think about a problem before attempting a solution. The development of the symbolic function also means that children can begin to use language to represent experience and ideas, to communicate with others, and to direct their own thinking processes. From eighteen months onward, language plays an increasingly important role in cognitive development.

Piaget observed the beginnings of problem-solving behavior toward the end of the first year, when infants develop the ability to use means-to-an-end, goal-directed behavior. For example, infants can remove an obstacle in order to reach a desired toy; they also can use one object in order to have an effect on another—for example, they can use a wooden spoon to hit a cooking pot to make a noise. When their communicative behaviors (such as crying or smiling) produce consistent responses from their caregivers, infants learn that they can have an effect on the important people in their world: I cry, mother comes; I smile, mother smiles back. Thus, infants begin to develop a sense of cause and effect through experiences in which they have an impact on their physical and social environment (Lind, 1987).

*Practice Guideline 3.1: Because infants cannot use language to tell us about their thoughts or about their developmental progress, adults must rely on what observation can tell them about an infant's cognitive, physical, and social well-being.*

Relying on observation means looking for developmental milestones, such as the ability to search for hidden objects, the ability to engage in exploratory and problem-solving behavior, and the ability to engage in playful communicative exchanges with familiar adults. A standard developmental assessment such as the Bayley Scales of Infant Development can be used to determine if an infant's progress is generally on target.

## Early Childhood (Two to Six Years)

Young children undergo extensive cognitive changes during the preschool and early elementary school years. The development of the symbolic function enables children to make rapid progress in acquiring language, using mental representations of experience, and learning an enormous amount about their world. During this period, children's ability to represent events mentally becomes increasingly complex and flexible (Nelson, 1978).

Young children make strides in their ability to coordinate perceptual information, in their recognition memory, and in their reasoning abilities. Preschool children can often reason logically in familiar contexts about familiar experiences, particularly in pretend play situations of their own devising; their thinking is likely to seem much less logical when they are asked to reason about things they know little about. Young children's thinking is closely tied to specific contexts; they have difficulty with abstractions and difficulty in paying close attention to language, particularly when it appears to conflict with what they expect in a particular situation. Young children are most likely to think logically in situations that make "human sense" to them—situations that contain materials, behaviors, and motivations that are familiar and meaningful to young children (Donaldson, 1979).

*Perception.* After infancy children are increasingly able to control their perceptual processes and to discriminate accurately among stimuli. Young children, however, continue to have difficulty with coordinating and integrating conflicting perceptual information (Flavell, 1985). During this period, two areas of perceptual development seem to be particularly relevant for children as sources of information: the ability to distinguish appearance from reality, and the ability to take visual or spatial perspectives other than their own.

Flavell and his associates have investigated the development of children's understanding of the distinction between appearance and reality in a series of ingenious studies (Flavell, 1986; Flavell, Green, and Flavell, 1986). They found that children aged three and under are particularly likely to have difficulty in distinguishing between what is apparent and what is real—between a deceptive or misleading appearance and the real identity or properties of people, objects, and events. They found that most three-year-olds and many four-year-olds consistently failed appearance-reality tasks in predictable ways (Flavell, 1986). For example, when shown a plain glass of milk that is then wrapped in red plastic before their eyes, most three- and four-year-olds will say both that the milk *looks* red and that it really and truly *is* red. If shown a red car that is then placed behind a green plastic filter, they will maintain that the car both *looks* and *is* really and truly black. On the other hand, if given a sponge that has been made to look exactly like a rock, children will not only say that it really and truly *is* a sponge, they will also maintain that it *looks* like a sponge.

When children insist that the real color of a familiar object (a glass of milk) is the color that a piece of plastic has made it appear to be (when they insist that the milk is red), they seem to be focusing on the object's immediate appearance, ignoring what they know to be true (milk is white). However, when they insist that an object *looks* like what they know it really *is* rather than what it appears to be (when they insist that the sponge that has been made to look like a rock *looks* like a sponge), they seem to be focusing on what they know to be true and ignoring what they are seeing or perceiving at the moment.

Flavell argued that young children make these errors because they have great difficulty understanding that the same object or event can have "two seemingly incompatible properties or identities," one real and the other apparent (Flavell, Green, and Flavell, 1986, p. 61). This is reflected in the difficulty many young children have in understanding that one person can simultaneously fill two roles, so that the same person can be both father and doctor, or mother and lawyer (Flavell, Green, and Flavell, 1986, pp. 72–73); it can also be seen in their difficulties with masks and disguises and with unexpected changes in appearances. For example, a young child visiting the zoo saw penguins for the first time. The display permitted the child to see the animals under water as well as on the shore. She pointed at a penguin on shore and said, "Bird!" The penguin then dived into the water and began swimming under the surface. The child pointed at it and said, "Fish!"

The ability to make consistent and accurate distinctions between appearance and reality develops between the ages of three and five as children come to understand that "the selfsame stimulus can be mentally represented in two different, seemingly contradictory ways" (Flavell, 1986, p. 418). It seems likely, as Flavell suggests, that much of this development occurs when children actively manipulate these distinctions themselves. Children can do this in the context of pretend play, when they pretend that something or someone is other than what it appears to be, giving objects and people new, temporary identities. Thus, a wooden block can become a car, or a doll's bed, or a house, and children can become mothers, firemen, monsters, or superheroes.

Flavell has related children's difficulties with the appearance-reality distinction to their difficulties with putting themselves in another's shoes—that is, with taking the visual and cognitive perspectives of another person—and in recognizing that objects and events may seem quite different from someone else's perspective. To do this, children must first understand that other people have other perspectives, and they must then make reasonable inferences about what those perspectives might be. Young children, particularly three- and four-year-olds, often appear to have difficulty in inferring what another person sees, thinks, feels, and intends.

Spatial or visual perspective-taking tasks are designed to determine whether or not one understands that what one sees depends, in part, on where one sees it from and that an object, scene, or event may look quite different from different vantage points. To assess this understanding, Piaget devised the "three-mountains task" (Piaget and Inhelder, 1956), in which children are asked to look at an elaborate three-dimensional model of three mountains, complete with such details as lakes, houses, and snow. They are then seated at the display table and the experimenter places a doll at another position around the table. Children are shown photographs of the three-mountain display taken from different angles and asked to identify the picture that shows what the doll sees. Most children under six or seven cannot do this; instead, they usually choose the picture that represents what they see from where they are seated. Piaget concluded that children under the age of seven or eight have great difficulty in taking visual or spatial perspectives other than their own, and he interpreted these results as evidence of young children's perceptual and cognitive "egocentricity"—as evidence that young children are trapped in their own points of view, unable to "decenter" and take account of perspectives other than their own.

Following this, Piaget and other researchers found evidence of "egocentric distortions" in other areas of perception and cognition, including the ability to take the role of another person and to make inferences about what that person thinks, feels, and intends (Shantz, 1975). In recent years, however, the implications of this research have been called into question; researchers have argued that young children's difficulty with many perspective- and role-taking tasks reflects their difficulty in coping with complex and abstract tasks employing materials and situations that are remote from their own experience and calling for sophisticated communicative skills (Borke, 1975; Donaldson, 1979; Shatz and Gelman, 1973). Because they do not fully understand what is being asked of them, children give the best response they can come up with at the moment—which is likely to reflect their own immediate perspective. These researchers have demonstrated that when perspective-taking tasks are simplified and presented with materials, situations, and language that are more familiar, young children can give much more accurate responses and hence appear much less "egocentric." Borke (1975) and others have argued that what looks like egocentric behavior is often an indication that children are confused, and that even adults behave in an egocentric manner when they are uncertain or confused.

Donaldson (1979) described a perspective-taking task designed by Martin Hughes (1975), in which children were presented with a schematic display of four "rooms" created by two interlocking "walls." The experimenter placed a boy doll in one room and a policeman doll at different positions in the display, and then asked children whether or not the policeman could see the boy and where the boy could hide so that the policeman could not see him. To answer these questions, children had to take account of the policeman's perspective, which was different from their own. Most children between the ages of three and a half and five were able to do this. Donaldson argued that the policeman task, unlike the three-mountain task, makes "human sense" to young children because it employs materials and situations that they find familiar and meaningful. Children are familiar with hiding (if not from policemen, then from their friends) and with looking for someone who is hiding. Thus, "the *motives* and *intentions* of the characters [in the policeman task] are entirely comprehensible, even to a child of three. The task requires the child to act in ways that are in line with certain very basic human purposes and interactions (escape and pursuit)—it makes *human sense*" (Donaldson, 1979, p. 17).

These differing responses to visual perspective-taking tasks demonstrate how difficult it can be to make judgments about young children's thinking. They indicate some of the complexities involved in sorting out issues of underlying cognitive competence from contextual variables that may affect children's performance. The results of these perspective-taking tasks have parallels in other role- and perspective-taking areas, such as the ability to understand what someone else thinks, feels, likes, and intends. Children's ability to understand the perspectives and points of view of others depends a great deal on the context—on the degree to which they can understand and make human sense of the task they are given. If the tasks are not too abstract and complex, and if they are not too remote from their own experience, children demonstrate that they can take other visual perspectives at the age of three or four. The ability to make simple but reasonable inferences about what other people feel, intend, and think develops somewhat later, generally between the ages of four and five. Thus, young children's ability to understand and to coordinate perceptual data develops gradually during the preschool years as they learn to sort out conflicting information about appearances and to coordinate differing perspectives. How children perform on specific perceptual tasks will depend a great deal on the task materials and on how the task situation is structured and presented to the child.

*Practice Guideline 3.2: In eliciting perceptual information from young children, it is important to use familiar materials and to structure tasks and situations that make human sense.*

**Memory.** Children's memory improves during the preschool years, in part because of their increasing knowledge and developing conceptual abilities (Brown, 1978; Brown, Bransford, Ferrara, and Campione, 1983; Flavell, 1985). As they acquire more elaborate and flexible event schemas and scripts, children have larger and more precise frames of reference for organizing and making sense of specific memories (Mandler, 1983). Event schemas and scripts are ways of organizing and representing familiar places, scenes, events, and routines such as "eating at home," "eating at the day care center," or "eating at a restaurant" (Nelson, 1978). Increasing knowledge and more sophisticated scripts affect memory because they provide both context and meaning for what is to be remembered, thus influencing both storage and retrieval abilities. Generally speaking, the more one knows, the more one can remember. For example, it is harder to remember "bamboo shoots" if one has never heard of them and has no idea what they are, what other things they might be like, or where they might fit in a larger scheme of things. On the other hand, knowledge and expectations can also distort memory, so that what one remembers is biased by what one knows or expects to happen in a particular situation.

Memory is also affected by the development of knowledge about one's own memory (metamemory) and the development of specific strategies for remembering (mnemonic strategies), such as categorizing and rehearsing a list of things to be remembered, or engaging in systematic memory search in order to retrieve items from memory. Young children typically appear to have little knowledge or understanding about their own memories, and they rarely use mnemonic strategies in deliberate memory tasks (Brown, 1978; Flavell, Friedrichs, and Hoyt, 1970). Thus, young children are less able than older children and adults to direct their memories for the purposes of either storage or retrieval, and they are less able to monitor the accuracy of their memories. For example, preschool children often overestimate their own memory capacities, particularly in unfamiliar tasks, where they are likely to predict that they will be able to remember many more items than they actually are able. However, they are less likely to do this in more familiar situations, such as board games (Flavell, 1985). Although young children may sometimes use strategies spontaneously, children do not use strategies consistently and reliably until the age of eleven or twelve.

Preschoolers have occasionally been observed using simple mnemonic strategies such as spontaneous rehearsal, and they are more likely to do so in familiar, everyday tasks than in laboratory situations (Todd and Perlmutter, 1980). For example, four-year-olds told to remember a location did better on an object search and retrieval task than children not told to remember, indicating some understanding of what is involved in deliberately remembering (Kail, 1984, p. 44; Yussen, 1974). Haake, Somerville, and Wellman (1980) found that preschool children were generally very competent in figuring out where to look for "lost" objects such as cameras and calculators (actually hidden by the experimenter), indicating that they could "deduce a critical search area, determined logically by the last place a lost object was seen and the first place it was found missing" (p. 1299). Flavell observed that, in general, young children are better at devising efficient search strategies for finding missing objects in the external world than they are at searching the internal world of their own minds for missing pieces of information (Flavell, 1985, pp. 227–228).

Children's lack of metamemory may help to explain why, in general, young children perform well on memory tasks that depend on recognition and poorly on those that require deliberate recall. Recognition tasks provide built-in prompts; recall requires the child to do his or her own prompting. Evidence from a number of laboratory studies indicates that "preschoolers' recognition memory is remarkably effective" (Kail, 1984, p. 32; see also Cole and Loftus, 1987; Davies, Stevenson, and Flin, forthcoming; Loftus and Davies, 1984). For example, Ceci, Ross, and Toglia (1987) found that three-year-olds were as accurate as twelve-year-olds in recognizing drawings that had been presented to them three days earlier (without information that might mislead them). Nurcombe (1986) found that four- and five-year-olds perform as well as adults on recognition memory tasks when verbal recall is deemphasized (Schneider, 1987). Davies, Stevenson, and Flin (forthcoming) found that children as young as five are as good as adults in recognizing familiar stimuli, including photographs that they had been shown previously. However, it should be noted that recognition memory is also easier than recall memory for adults, and that "both children and adults remember more on recognition tasks than on free recall tasks" (Cole and Loftus, 1987, p. 183).

*Practice Guideline 3.3: In attempting to elicit information from young children, try to structure the task to utilize recognition rather than recall memory.*

Young children are less efficient at tasks that involve deliberate recall memory and recall less on demand than older children and adults. In general, when asked to remember past events, young children are more likely to make errors of omission than older children and adults. Although they remember less on demand than older children and adults, young children's recall is likely to be as accurate as that of adults (Cole and Loftus, 1987). Preschool children make "substantial improvements in deliberate memory abilities," especially between the ages of three and four (Todd and Perlmutter, 1980, pp. 82-83); however, children's deliberate recall is not as complete as that of adults until the age of eleven or twelve (Davies, Stevenson, and Flin, forthcoming; Kail, 1984; Loftus and Davies, 1984).

Spontaneous recall is usually the most accurate form of remembering for both children and adults. Young children engage in less spontaneous recall than older children and adults; however, even very young children sometimes engage in free or spontaneous recall (Cole and Loftus, 1987; King and Yuille, 1987; Loftus and Davies, 1984). For example, Nelson and Ross (1980) found that children between the ages of twenty-one and twenty-seven months demonstrated spontaneous recall abilities for people, objects, and events. They noted that most of these memories were "cued by either the location where an event had occurred or by seeing an object or person associated with the remembered event" (p. 95). These findings mesh with those of Daehler and Greco, who argued that early memory is closely tied to the context in which the memory was originally encoded (1985, p. 72). They cited White and Pillemer (1979) in arguing that "the context at retrieval must closely conform to the context at encoding if evidence of memory is to be obtained from early periods of development" (Daehler and Greco, 1985, p. 73). Furthermore, "the circumstances of remembering greatly affect whether the memory system appears to be accurate or inaccurate. In general, memory is improved when the original physical or cognitive context is reinstated. . . . Children may especially need such contextual support" (Johnson and Foley, 1984, p. 39).

As children develop more complete event schemas and scripts for familiar experiences, they demonstrate more comprehensive and ordered recall of past events. The development of more sophisticated scripts also means that children "become better at reading between the lines" and at making inferences based on "their knowledge of the world" (King and Yuille, 1987, p. 25). Thus, in giving spontaneous accounts of past events, children as young as three and four may exhibit "substantial recall," providing detailed information on specific events that occurred between one month and one year previously. They are especially likely to recall social encounters that are "particularly salient to young children" (Todd and Perlmutter, 1980, p. 83).

More complete, better-developed scripts, however, may also interfere with memory. Both children and adults are likely "to recall rather better the more predictable and regular features of what they observed" (Davies, Stevenson, and Flin, forthcoming, p. 13), and what is remembered is likely to be biased or distorted "in the direction of typical experiences" (Kail, 1984, p. 99; Saywitz, 1987). Todd and Perlmutter (1980) found that three- and four-year-old children sometimes fail to distinguish between similar past events, combining details from scripts of familiar, recurring events. For example, when asked if she had "ever flown in an airplane," a child who had been on several airplane trips "related specific information about several different flights" without indicating that "various aspects of the information had . . . occurred at different points in time" (Todd and Perlmutter, 1980, p. 75).

Memory is sometimes distorted to conform with one's biases and stereotypes. As Kail pointed out, elementary school children's recall may be biased by their knowledge of sex-role stereotypes (Kail, 1984; Kail and Levine, 1976). For example, Martin and Halverson (1983, cited in Kail, 1984) found that when five-year-olds were asked to recall "the actions of boys and girls behaving in non-stereotypic fashion," such as "a girl sawing wood," they were likely to "transform the sex of the actor to make it consistent with sex-role knowledge," remembering a boy sawing wood (Kail, 1984, p. 97). Children's lack of metamemory suggests that young children are less likely than older children and adults to realize that their memories may be biased in these ways.

Until quite recently, it was widely assumed that the memories of young children were less reliable and more open to misleading information and suggestion than those of older children and adults (Cole and Loftus, 1987; Goodman, Golding, and Haith, 1984). Several recent research studies have found that there are no simple, clear-cut answers to questions about children's suggestibility, and considerable controversy remains (Ceci, Ross, and Toglia,

1987; Cole and Loftus, 1987; Davies, Stevenson, and Flin, forthcoming; Goodman, Aman, and Hirschman, 1987; King and Yuille, 1987; Loftus and Davies, 1984; Saywitz, 1987; Zaragoza, 1987). Overall, these studies suggest that—in some situations and for some kinds of information—the memories of young children are more vulnerable to various kinds of suggestion than the memories of older children and adults. Goodman, however, argues that "when children's memory for an event is as strong as an adult's, suggestibility differences may diminish or disappear" (1984a, p. 161). Moreover, young children "are not uniquely suggestible" (Davies, Stevenson, and Flin, forthcoming, p. 23); older children and adults are also susceptible to post-event suggestion, especially if the misleading information comes from a credible source (Zaragoza, 1987).

Several factors, either singly or in concert, make it likely that young children will be more open to misleading information and hence more suggestible than older children and adults. These include young children's general lack of knowledge and experience, their difficulty with deliberate recall, their lack of metamemory, their lack of sophisticated communicative skills and their subsequent dependence on contextual cues and information, and their eagerness to do and say what they think is expected, particularly what is expected by adults. Because young children engage in less spontaneous recall than older children and adults, and because they have difficulty with deliberate recall, they are more dependent on verbal probing by others to elicit their memories. They thus provide more opportunities for intentional or unintentional suggestions to influence what is remembered. Because of their lack of metamemory, young children know less about their own memories, are less aware of what they remember and do not remember, and are less aware of the possibility of post-event suggestion influencing what they remember (Brown, 1978; Ceci, Ross and Toglia, 1987; Saywitz, 1987).

Because of their difficulty in understanding complex language, particularly when it concerns events that are remote from their own experiences and interests, young children tend to rely on nonverbal contextual cues and information to interpret and make sense of the situations in which they find themselves. When young children try to respond to questions about what they remember, they use contextual cues to determine what is expected of them so that they can respond appropriately—which may mean responding with what they think is wanted or expected by the adults in charge of the situation. For example, young children usually perform well on tasks involving recognition memory; however, the performance of children between the ages of three and eleven on "blank lineups" tends to be dismal (Cole and Loftus, 1987). (Blank lineups are selections of photographs that do not include a picture of the suspect.) Rather than acknowledging that they do not recognize any of the photographs, young children are likely to make a false identification. They do this even when they have been warned that the lineup may not contain a picture of the suspect (Cole and Loftus, 1987; King and Yuille, 1987). Raskin and Yuille (forthcoming) have suggested that "presenting the child with a photo spread creates an implicit demand to pick out someone" (p. 7).

King and Yuille (1987) have argued that children's desire to conform to what they perceive to be adult demands and expectations may explain why six-year-olds were more likely than older children to agree with misleading suggestions about details in a previously witnessed event (for example, whether or not someone was wearing a watch). The authors observed that several children later volunteered that they "had 'gone along' with a misleading suggestion," saying what they thought they were expected to say or what they thought the interviewer wanted to hear, presumably in order to please the interviewer (King and Yuille, 1987, p. 28). Support for this interpretation is provided by Ceci, Ross, and Toglia's (1987) finding that young children are less susceptible to misleading information and suggestions if they are provided by a child rather than by an adult.

Perhaps one of the most important conclusions to be drawn from the research on memory and suggestibility is that while young children are generally more vulnerable to misleading suggestions than older children and adults, they do not seem to be any more suggestible in recalling the more "salient and memorable" aspects of events (King and Yuille, 1987, p. 27). Indeed, both children and adults are more likely to accept misleading suggestions for peripheral information and less likely to accept them for more central information (Ceci, Ross and Toglia, 1987; Cole and Loftus, 1987; Davies, Stevenson, and Flin, forthcoming; King and Yuille, 1987). For example, in a study of children's memory of a real-life stressful event (receiving an inoculation), Goodman, Aman, and Hirschman (1987) found that three- to six-year-old children were less suggestible about the central actions (being held, receiving the injection) and people (the nurse who gave the injection) than they were about peripheral aspects of the situation (details about the room in which the inoculations took place).

In a similar vein, Davies, Stevenson, and Flin (forthcoming) cited studies indicating that the memories of three- and four-year-olds are likely to be affected by suggestive questioning; that by the age of five, however, most children will reject suggestions that refer to "central events and actions that lie within the child's understanding"; and that they are more open to suggestion about "peripheral details" (p. 17). The authors noted that "the more children know about the events they are observing, the better they are able to understand them, to select and attend to what is relevant and report on this at a later time" (Davies, Stevenson, and Flin, forthcoming, p. 9). In general, it seems that young children are least likely to be vulnerable to post-event suggestion when they are asked to recall events that they understand and know something about and that they find interesting or salient.

Goodman (1984a) suggested that young children need "concrete retrieval cues," such as physical props, to assist their recall memory (p. 163). Price (1983, cited by Goodman, 1984a) asked two-and-a-half-year-olds, four-year-olds, and five-year-olds to recall events that occurred in a novel play setting. In one case they had props and in the other they did not. The five-year-olds did as well with verbal prompts as they did with physical props. However, the four-year-olds remembered many more details with props (an average of 19) than they did without them (an average of 2.5). The two-and-a-half-year-olds did poorly in both cases, but they did much better if they were allowed to return to the original scene; in this setting, they were able to recall 63 percent of the number of details the four-year-olds recalled with physical props. King and Yuille also suggested using "reconstruction techniques" such as "small-scale models of people, furnishings, objects and settings";

however, they warn that such props may also serve as "a suggestive question with young children" (King and Yuille, 1987, p. 31).

*Practice Guideline 3.4: Questions and props designed to reconstruct aspects of the context of the event to be remembered may facilitate children's recall memory.*

A key question for adults as recipients of information from children is this: How can adults help preschoolers remember without influencing what is remembered? While there are no definitive answers to this question, the following points should be kept in mind. It is important to be alert to the ever-present possibility that post-event suggestion will influence recall. Adults need to be "sensitive to the potential for misunderstanding and the possibility that a child will treat a question as a demand for an answer, rather than as an inquiry for information. . . . Any question has the potential to be suggestive to a child" (Raskin and Yuille, forthcoming, p. 8). Thus, adults must pay attention to the possibility of implicit expectations and demands in the interview situation and should try to be alert to a range of possible interpretations on the part of the child—interpretations that may be quite different from their own. As King and Yuille (1987, p. 29) observed, it is important to distinguish between "intended" and "received" tasks—between the kind of information that the interviewer intends to elicit from the child and the ways in which the child receives or interprets the request for information.

*Practice Guideline 3.5: Try to ask questions that provide guidance without making explicit or implicit suggestions.*

This is not an easy task. For example, if you ask three- or four-year-old children what they did at the day-care center, they are very likely to answer "nothing" or "playing." If you ask them about specific events that might have occurred while they were there— "Did you have hot dogs or spaghetti for lunch?" "Did you play with Susie in the playground?"—they are likely to give more complete responses. However, such directed questioning may bias their responses by implying a choice between the alternatives presented.

**Reasoning.** Children's reasoning is facilitated by the development of the symbolic function and the subsequent development of language and representational abilities, as well as by their increasing fund of knowledge and experience and by better-developed and better-elaborated scripts. In many instances, young children appear to engage in rational thinking, and they can solve a range of problems that demand a logical consideration of alternatives (Donaldson, 1979; Isaacs, [1930] 1972; Siegler, 1978). However, at times, preschool children's thinking may appear quite illogical to adults and may seem to be based on a rather shaky grasp of reality (Piaget, 1952, [1930] 1972; Paley, 1981; Flavell, 1985, 1986). There appear to be at least two reasons for this. First, the symbolic function not only makes possible the development of language and more efficient mental problem-solving activity, it also makes possible the development of mental imagery, dreams, fantasy, pretend play, stories, narratives, and the construction of "possible worlds." This allows for the expression of feelings, wishes, and fears—both conscious and unconscious—and it means that magic and fantasy are readily available as possible causal explanations.

Second, children under the age of six or seven are generally lacking in metacognition. *Metacognition* is "a very basic form of self-awareness," that of realizing "what you know and what you do not know" (Brown, 1978, p. 82). A number of research studies have found that young children are largely unaware of their own thought processes and have considerable difficulty in reflecting on them; thus they are often unaware of the boundaries between what they know and what they do not know (Brown, 1975, p. 82). Markman (1977), for example, studied young children's *metacomprehension*—their awareness of and their ability to monitor their own understanding. Six-, seven-, and eight-year-old children were given verbal instructions for a game and a magic trick and were asked to let the experimenter know if the instructions were unclear or if they needed more information. The instructions were missing vital information and hence were incomprehensible; however, only the older children indicated that they needed more information. The younger children did not seem to realize that the instructions were inadequate until they actually tried to carry out the tasks. Young children's lack of awareness of their own thinking processes has broad implications for children's thinking. It suggests, among other things, that children may not always be aware when they cross the line between fact and fantasy, or between the rational and the irrational. Thus, they may draw on magic and fantasy to fill in the gaps in their knowledge without realizing that they are doing so. Lack of metacognitive awareness, as well as the desire to please adults, may help to explain why young children often seem willing to provide answers and explanations for anything and everything they are asked, including nonsensical questions such as: "Is milk bigger than water?" (Donaldson, 1979, p. 72).

Even toddlers can sometimes make simple causal judgments (for example, turning the handle on the jack-in-the-box makes the clown pop up). However, they usually do not understand that there must be specific mechanisms linking physical causes with their effects. Because of their strong sense of temporal order, young children are likely to understand temporal causality best and to reason most logically about objects and occurrences that are part of familiar events or scripts. Delays between a cause and its effect tend to erode their ability to make accurate attributions of causality. As Piaget ([1929] 1979) discovered, young children are also likely to attribute psychological causality to physical objects and events ("the marble went down the ramp because it wanted to"). Partly because they are not yet clear about the distinction between animate and inanimate, they tend to attribute life to anything that moves ("the moon and the clouds follow me when I walk," "the sun is alive") (Piaget, [1930] 1972, [1929] 1979; Lind, 1987).

Preschool children are interested in how things work and in understanding physical causal mechanisms, although they may not be very discriminating in their criteria for causal mechanisms. Children this age seem to think that everything has a causal explanation, and they are usually willing to offer one. Thus, they may attribute causality where none actually exists, especially with frequently occurring events ("the cat goes out because the door is open"), or confuse cause with effect ("it's dark at night so I can go to sleep"). Young children have difficulty with attributing causality to dissimilar objects, and they often think that a cause should resemble its effect. For example, they cannot understand how sugar can come from a nonwhite object such as a sugar beet (Paley, 1981; Lind, 1987).

Children this age may resort to psychological explanations

for physical events when they lack information about the real causes, and they may give magical—and confusing—explanations for events they do not understand. Five-year-old Lisa did this when she tried to explain how babies are made: the mother "gets bones from dead dinosaurs and blood from a dead person and water from a glass of water" (Paley, 1981, p. 74). Children are also likely to have difficulty with causal explanations about why something did not occur and with understanding that some things can prevent other things from happening. For example, Paley reported that the children in her kindergarten class had a hard time understanding why most of the beans they had planted failed to sprout; they suggested that the beans had been stolen by robbers or "disguised as worms" by a magician (Paley, 1981, pp. 57–59). Young children also tend to have difficulty in weighing the merits of multiple, competing causative factors (did the sandcastle fall down because the sand was too wet, because it wasn't built well, or because of the wind?) (Lind, 1987).

Donaldson (1979), Paley (1981), Isaacs ([1930] 1972), and others have shown that young children can reason logically in familiar contexts about familiar experiences—particularly in spontaneous pretend play situations where they are in control of events. Indeed, preschool children can often reason logically about pretend situations and imaginary possibilities (Isaacs, [1930] 1972; Paley, 1981). For example, when two four-year-old girls were building sandcastles, one of them said that they were going to "build castles as high as the sky." Later, the other girl added, "If we did the aeroplanes would knock them down," indicating that she had a sense of logical possibility (Isaacs, [1930] 1972, p. 116). Preschool children are also likely to demonstrate logical under- standings when they reason about familiar objects and situations. For example, Isaacs ([1930] 1972) reported on a five-and-a-half-year- old boy who dropped a pair of scissors from a considerable height and commented, "They didn't break—they're metal," demonstrat- ing his sense of both compatibility and necessity (p. 146). These understandings are also evident in a five-year-old girl's response to her kindergarten teacher's mistaken announcement, "Today is Thursday" (it was actually Wednesday): "My mother said there was no school Thursday, so if it was Thursday, we wouldn't be in school." These examples demonstrate that preschool children have some understanding that "if something is true, then something else must also be true," and that they can and do make logical deductive inferences (Donaldson, 1979, p. 40).

Thus, preschool children can reason logically in familiar contexts. In general, they are more likely to think about something in a rational, logical manner the closer it is to their own interests and everyday experience with family, friends, and familiar caretakers. Young children's thinking is likely to seem much less logical, and they are more likely to resort to illogical or "magical" thinking, when they do not know much about what they are being asked about, when material is highly complex or abstract, and when it is far removed from familiar experiences, events, and scripts.

This does not mean that young children cannot serve as reliable sources of information for adults. It does mean, however, that adults must bear considerable responsibility for how they elicit information from young children—and that adults must work much harder than when they are eliciting information from older children and adults.

*Practice Guideline 3.6: When seeking information from young children, it is important for adults to try to understand the situation from the child's perspective.*

This means considering what the particular situation might mean to the child. What about the situation is likely to be most salient to the child? How would the child usually interpret situations like this one? How is this situation related to the child's other experiences? What does the child think is being asked? Why does the child think this is being asked? How might the child interpret the fact that he or she is being questioned?

## Middle Childhood (Six to Twelve Years)

During this period, formal schooling plays an increasingly important role in the development of children's thinking, particularly in the development of metacognition. Flavell observed that school-age children gradually "learn more and more about what 'the game of thinking' is like and about how it is supposed to be played." For example, children learn that "tasks and problems usually have solutions," that they usually have to "engage in some sort of cognitive activity to solve them," and that some problem-solving strategies are more effective than others (1985, p. 102). By the end of this period, children's thinking is much like that of adults.

*Perception.* Children's perspective-taking ability develops with experience and maturation. Children are able to manage increasingly complex tasks that are less directly tied to their own experience. For example, by eight or nine, they can cope with the complexities of Piaget's three-mountain task (Piaget and Inhelder, 1956). In general, children are increasingly able to coordinate information from different perspectives and points of view and to go beyond immediate appearances and make logical inferences based on reasoning about what they know must be true, rather than on what they perceive at the moment. Nonetheless, their perfor-mance on specific perspective-taking tasks continues to depend, in part, on the complexity of the task, on the communicational demands, and on how much "human sense" the task and the situation make to them.

*Memory.* There are significant changes in children's memory abilities in this period, particularly in deliberate recall memory, which by the age of eleven or twelve is as complete as an adult's (Cole and Loftus, 1987). Improvements in memory reflect children's increasing fund of knowledge and experience, the development of more complex cognitive structures, the development of more complete and elaborated scripts, and the development of mnemonic strategies.

The importance for remembering of acquiring specific kinds of knowledge and expertise was demonstrated by Chi's (1978) finding that ten-year-old children who were expert chess players were better than non-chess-playing adults at remembering a variety of chess configurations. The children's specific, expert knowledge gave them a context for remembering the patterns of chess pieces, which had little meaning for the non-chess-playing adults. As Flavell (1985) observed, "What the head knows has an enormous effect on what the head learns and remembers" (p. 213).

With the development of metacognition and metamemory, school-age children become increasingly aware of their own memories. For example, children's ability to predict their recall capacity improves with age; by fourth grade, children are as precise as adults in estimating their recall abilities (Kail, 1984, p. 30). As children acquire a range of mnemonic strategies, they learn how to store and retrieve information with increasing efficiency. Mnemonic strategies are conscious, deliberate, planful, and goal-directed means for improving memory storage and retrieval. They include rehearsal, organization, categorization, mental imagery, and elaboration, as well as the use of external aids, such as asking someone to remind you about something or writing yourself a note (Brown, 1975; Flavell, 1985, 1979; Kail, 1984). Children learn, for example, that if they want to remember something it is helpful to organize the information into categories, to make a list, or to write a note. Further, they learn to use mnemonic cues to search their memories with increasing depth, exhaustiveness, and flexibility (Kail, 1984).

The ability to combine strategies—such as by putting items into categories and then rehearsing them—develops somewhat later, usually after the age of twelve. Adolescents are also better able to select the most appropriate strategy and to adapt strategies to specific memory tasks by modifying them and using them in more flexible ways. By adolescence, children can engage in "systematic, exhaustive search" of their memories, and they have strategies for learning and remembering complex material (Flavell, 1985, p. 226).

Children's memories become increasingly reliable during this period; however—in part because metamemory and mnemonic strategies develop gradually—school-age children's memories continue to share many of the liabilities of preschool children's. Thus, the younger the child, the greater his vulnerability to the various kinds of suggestion discussed earlier. For example, in a story recall task, Saywitz found that seven-year-old children had more difficulty than twelve-year-olds "in distinguishing between their own embellishments and the actual story content. The ability to make such discriminations and to monitor output for potential errors may be a metamemory skill that develops gradually" (Saywitz, 1987, p. 39, citing Brown and others, 1977). Saywitz also found that eight- and nine-year-olds did less well than twelve- and thirteen-year-olds on a free recall task (remembering a crime episode), tending "to remember less and embellish more" (Saywitz, 1987, p. 48). Cole and Loftus (1987) found that, for reasons that remain unclear, compared to children of other ages, "eight- to nine-year-old children are most likely to add extraneous and perhaps less plausible information to their accounts" (p. 183).

During this period, children continue to have difficulties with blank lineups and thus continue to make false identifications. It is not until they are between the ages of twelve and fourteen that children are likely to recognize (or admit) that they do not know whether or not the photographs they are looking at contain the suspect; only then can they "correctly reject a blank lineup" (Cole and Loftus, 1987, p. 205).

***Reasoning.*** Between the ages of six and twelve, children develop an increasing awareness of their own thought processes and an increasing ability to reflect on and direct their own cognitive behavior (Brown, 1978; Flavell, 1979; Flavell and Wellman, 1977). Thus, they gradually become more aware of what they know and what they do not know, when they understand something—a question, a direction, a situation—and when they do not.

Along with metacognitive awareness, children develop a range of metacognitive skills and strategies—such as planning, predicting, checking, monitoring, testing, reviewing, revising, rehearsing, and categorizing—that facilitate reasoning, problem solving, and remembering (Brown, 1978). These strategies enable children to direct and control their own thought processes so that they can approach problems more flexibly and systematically, considering a range of logical alternatives and possibilities. While metacognition is clearly important for school-related tasks, it may also be related to other aspects of cognition that are important when children function as sources of information, such as their awareness and understanding of the difference between fantasy and reality and between truth and lying. (See Chapter Four for a discussion of truth and lying.) As children approach adolescence, their thinking approaches that of adults; however, school-age children's thinking still shares some of the vulnerabilities of younger children's.

*Practice Guideline 3.7: When seeking information from a school-age child, it is still important to try to understand the*

*situation from the child's perspective, and to try to understand what
the child thinks is being asked of him or her, and why.*

In addition to these cognitive and contextual issues, it is also
important to consider issues of motivation. School-age children are
increasingly aware of the need to protect themselves and their
families and friends and of their ability to do this—by telling less
than the whole truth, or by inventing a more or less plausible
account.

### Conclusion

There are no simple recipes or formulas for understanding
children's thinking at any point in their development. Understanding children's thinking is always a complex business that depends
on the child's cognitive capacity and on a range of contextual and
motivational variables, all of which interact with one another.

The matrix of issues presented in Chapter One emphasized
orientation and competence. This chapter has focused on the
development of cognitive competence. Having examined cognitive
development, we recognize that language provides one of the keys to
children as sources of information. We turn next to language
development.

CHAPTER 4

# Language Development

One of the primary ways people exchange information is through listening and speaking. The ideal way for children to provide information to adults who want to know how they think and feel, or what might have happened to them or to others, is for them to tell us in words. While children are not able to put their thoughts and feelings into words during the early months and years of life, they have other means for communicating with adults. Language skills develop slowly yet dramatically during the first five to seven years, expanding and becoming refined in subsequent years. There are limits to what children under seven can convey to others using words alone. Yet what children say, in the context of other data (for example, their nonverbal behavior, their facial expressions, and the quality of their play), can inform adults about their well-being.

The language learning process has three dominant characteristics. First, the development of language skills is a highly social, inherently dialogical process that occurs in interactions between the child and caretakers. Language development is a two-way competency that emerges between the child who is learning to talk and caretakers who listen, respond, and find meaning in the child's efforts to express himself. Therefore, those who care for the child and know him well are in a strong position to understand what the child is trying to say and what he means by certain words or phrases. As in any relationship, however, errors in understanding can occur. There are times when adults, whether familiar or strange to the child, misunderstand the information the child conveys. This can happen particularly in the face of unexpected and unpleasant events that may blind adults to what a child is saying or lead adults to faulty conclusions regarding the child's meaning.

*Practice Guideline 4.1: Learning to talk and to communicate meaning happens daily in young children's lives. Adults are part of this learning process, contributing to the building and shaping of meaning in conversations and interactions with children from the moment of their birth.*

Second, young children view and use language very differently from adults. Children's development and use of language are context-dependent—words are tied to actions and are embedded in ongoing situations and relationships with those who know the children well. It is not until roughly age six or seven that children can begin to pay attention to language itself and to give verbal reports that are not necessarily dependent on external supports (people or objects) in the immediate environment.

A third characteristic of language development is the discrepancy between what a child can understand and what a child can say—that is, between receptive and productive language. Children can understand more language than they themselves are able to produce. Infants in the later part of the first year of life respond appropriately with gestures and movements to key words signaling routines such as "bath time" or favorite games such as "where's the baby?" (Stone and Church, 1979, p. 201). By the time children are approaching three, they are able to formulate their ideas in simple yet complete sentences; further, they can understand more complex and sophisticated language in situations that make sense to them, for example, when they are read fairy tales such as *The Three Billy Goats Gruff* or *Cinderella.*

*Practice Guideline 4.2: Children under the age of seven are more responsive and attuned to nonverbal language—gestures and actions—than they are to words. They interpret words by relying on their understanding of the concrete circumstances around them. Therefore, in order to gain a full understanding of the messages children are trying to communicate, adults must rely on their observation and knowledge of children in particular situations to supplement the limited language production abilities of young children.*

The language skills of young children will be explored in three age groupings: infants and toddlers, preschool children, and children seven to twelve years of age. The descriptions of linguistic competence are broad and the age markers are rough guidelines. The discussion will then turn to factors at work when adults have conversations with young children.

### Infants and Toddlers (Birth to Three Years)

It is now generally recognized that language development begins long before babies utter their first words; it has its roots in infants' earliest interactions with caretakers. Infants are born with resources that make them readily adaptive and responsive to communication with others (Lindfors, 1987). These resources include smiling, hand movements, and an acute sensitivity to the human face and voice. Infants' gestures, sounds, and gazes become tuned very early to the rhythm of those around them and lose their initial random quality (Lindfors, 1987, p. 124). Within the first few months of life, infants develop well-regulated rules for turn-taking in interactions—a fundamental feature of any dialogue or conversation. Games such as peek-a-boo between infants and caregivers exemplify this achievement.

In the early weeks and months of life, infants experiment with a diverse range of sounds, but these soon narrow down to a limited set of syllables that form a pattern, usually consonant-vowel combinations (Lindfors, 1987, p. 118). Studies of parent-infant interactions in mainstream American families show that when parents elicit and then respond to infants' cooing and babbling by echoing and extending their sounds in more complex utterances, infants shape and fine-tune their vocalizations to approximate those they are hearing. After weeks and months of participating in daily routines with family and caretakers and engaging in simple games such as "Where's Teddy? There he is!" infants learn that sounds carry meaning. All of this learning happens before infants utter their first recognizable word.

Learning how to use gestures and sounds to convey mean-

ings and messages is an achievement that relies on infants' and their
caretakers' understanding of one another. Infants signal that they
have had enough milk by discontinuing active sucking. They
communicate unhappiness or distress in their cries. Parents and
caretakers use their intuition and experience to discern the infant's
problem—whether it be hunger, a wet diaper, feeling too cold or
warm, losing sight of a favorite object, or fear of unfamiliar sounds
or places. Adults may explore several possible courses of action
before they find out what a particular cry means, and each form of
care might be accompanied by soothing comments and questions
asking the infant if this is what she needs or wants. Adults play an
important role in children's construction of an understanding of
meanings that can be communicated. Infants do not know why they
are crying; adults help them to learn why through the particular
alternative solutions that they hold out to the infant.

The infant's first words are connected with experiences and
activities that the infant can participate in or with people that are
important in her life. A baby's first words carry a full message of
meaning; for example, a call of "ma ma" might mean "Mama,
come here" or "Mama, I love you" or "Mama, is that you?" or
"Mama, I want something to eat." The infant's utterances make
sense to those who know her well and can interpret the immediate
environmental circumstances of her intended message. At this early
stage of language development, infants can express a great deal
using very little actual language. Single words are carriers of heavy
content and are used for diverse purposes—pointing to "the
human's thrust towards making and expressing meaning in a social
world" (Lindfors, 1987, p. 128). Infants work hard at conveying
information to adults: for them it is a matter of life and death.

As babies' utterances expand to two words, they maintain the
principle of using words that accomplish major work; they do not
worry about fillers such as articles and prepositions or about correct
verb forms. This stage of speech has been called telegraphic speech
because babies are working hard at expressing essential meanings.
Their utterances demonstrate a full command of the many uses of
language: they greet people, report and comment on events around
them, ask questions, make commands, and participate in games. As
the variety of sentence types increases, so does the presence of

grammatical details in their expressive language, such as prepositions, verb tenses, and forms of the verb "to be." Their utterances
reflect meaning relations—combining, for example, an action and
an object ("see horse"), an agent and an action ("mama go"), or an
agent and an object ("mommy book").

There is little doubt now among psychologists that the
learning process is driven by the infant's interests, desires, and
determination to participate and interact with those around him.
Family members fuel the learning process by engaging in interactions with the infant and eliciting, responding to, and extending his
utterances in meaningful ways. What is striking is that there is no
direct, didactic teaching and learning going on. When an infant
babbles "na na," those around him interpret the sounds as being
meaningful and, depending on the context, say, "Do you want some
banana?" or "Yes, nana. I'm your nana" or "No? You don't want
any more?" Infants and toddlers are not corrected and told how to
say things "properly." Instead, the infant's utterances slowly and
gradually approach the adult's standard linguistic forms as a result
of his drive to communicate effectively. Infants and toddlers learn
rules and conventions of discourse by being part of a community of
speakers and listeners. This process involves trial and error searches,
in which the child creates rules and tests hypotheses.

Children's errors when speaking are signals of development
in progress. For the most part, adults respond to what they think is
the intended meaning. Adults who try to correct children's forms
usually find children unresponsive. For example:

*Child:* Her don't want any.

*Mother:* You mean she doesn't want any?

*Child:* No, her don't want any.

With time and experience, children's forms give way to the standard
linguistic forms of their family and the community of which they
are a part.

Infants and toddlers focus on language itself when they play
with its sounds, rhythms, and patterns in babbling, singing songs,
saying nursery rhymes, and making up nonsense words and phrases

(Chukovsky, 1971). They do not examine and analyze words, phrases, and particular forms of wording the way adults can. For example, a toddler is not likely to be able to respond to a question such as "Did the lady go to the store or did she just say she was going to go to the store?" However, one way that an adult might find out what happened is by setting up a scene with a dollhouse and doll figures and saying, "Show me what the lady did." Words make more sense to toddlers when used in concrete settings with materials and activities that the child can participate in and act on.

*Practice Guideline 4.3: Adults who observe and interact with infants and toddlers have to rely on nonverbal cues to understand the messages the children are communicating. Parents and caretakers develop an intuitive understanding of their infants' and toddlers' gestures and mannerisms, and skilled professionals can also. In particular, toddlers can participate in dialogues where events are acted out using dolls, puppets, and other objects. Adults who are tuned in to the language of actions, visual images, and the early sound patterns of an infant or toddler can obtain information on very young children's well-being and experiences.*

### Preschool Children (Three to Seven Years)

Preschool children have mastered the basics of oral language in that they can speak in sentences, they have a wide range of uses for language, and they have a working vocabulary for managing day-to-day life events. They can use language to inform, to ask questions, to request things, to initiate play with others, to tell jokes, to apologize, and to express anger and other strong feelings. However, closer examination of children's language development during the years from roughly age three to age seven shows that there are some limitations on children's understanding and use of language that adults need to be aware of.

Language is a tool that facilitates activities with others in day-to-day life; as the preschool years progress, it becomes a tool for talking about and reflecting on experiences outside the here and now—the past and the future. "Like the objects they manipulate, language is what language *does* for young children" (Lindfors,

1987, p. 154). But preschool children are not yet to the point where they can reflect on language itself as a tool. This shortcoming is related to children's lack of metacognitive awareness. For the most part, children are not able to think about words in and of themselves, just as they are not able to step back from their own thinking and talk about it. This is not to say that preschool children do not engage in complex logical thinking about problems and situations. The following example demonstrates preschool children's attention to detail and precision in thinking, and the way words function in their understanding of a question.

Piaget presented five-year-old children with four red flowers and two white ones and asked, "Are there more red flowers or flowers?" Most five-year-olds responded that there were more red flowers. Piaget interpreted this pattern of response as evidence that preschoolers cannot think simultaneously about the whole class (flowers) and the subclasses (white and red flowers).

McGarrigle, by changing the wording of the task, demonstrated that preschool children are able to consider subclasses and their superordinate class concurrently. He took four toy cows, three black and one white, laid them down, and told children that they were sleeping. He then asked, "Are there more black cows or more cows?" This question paralleled the standard Piagetian form, and he got the same response pattern as Piaget. Preschool children responded, for the most part, that there were more black cows. Then he added one word to the question, asking a group of children, "Are there more black cows or more *sleeping* cows?" Many preschool children were able to answer this question successfully. He discovered that the word *sleeping*—a word the children had personal experience with—placed emphasis on the whole class of cows and made it comparable to and distinct from the subclasses, black and white cows (Donaldson, 1979, p. 40).

McGarrigle and Donaldson argue that instead of a limitation in preschoolers' thinking, Piaget was studying a misunderstanding in communication. McGarrigle demonstrated that preschool children can correctly solve a class-inclusion task if the task is presented in unambiguous language. When children are asked whether there are more black cows or cows, they make the comparison between the two groups they are looking at: "black cows" and (white) "cows." When the two groups are presented as "black cows" and "sleeping cows," they can compare the subclass and the whole.

This work reflects an important principle underlying children's language development and their competence in conversations. A child is an "active interpreter of linguistic input rather than a passive recipient of interview questions" (King and Yuille, 1987, p. 30). McGarrigle's version of the class-inclusion task shows that preschool children's mental efforts include listening to the words in coordination with their perception of the adult's intentions and the logic of the overall situation.

*Practice Guideline 4.4: A slight change in the wording of instructions or in the presentation of a problem might be all it takes to change children's understanding of a question, and the way they interpret it and respond in an inquiry.*

Language development in the preschool years expands and continues the development begun in infancy. Language is developing as a tool for expressing understanding of the world as children see it and act upon it. The next step, thinking about thinking and language as objects of observation and manipulation, lies just ahead as children enter the school years.

### School-Age Children (Seven to Twelve Years)

Around the age of six or seven, a new dimension of flexibility enters children's thinking and speaking. They become more able to mentally step back from and pay attention to language itself. They begin to reflect on their own thinking and the thinking of others as objects in and of themselves. Children of this age develop a fascination with jokes, foreign words and phrases, puns, ciphers, and secret codes and languages such as Pig Latin. This reflects their interest in playing with language itself, in mastering it, and in developing more complex ways of using verbal symbols.

Their communicative skills in representing messages and ideas begin to include written as well as spoken language. Because print permeates day-to-day life in some way for most communities in this country, most children begin formal schooling knowing what print looks like, able to draw letters or letter-like shapes, and having some sense that print carries a message. Children are also likely to recognize certain words on signs, such as *STOP, McDonald's,* and *Coke* (Lindfors, 1987, p. 151). Learning to read and write makes language forms and uses more visible for children, something they can observe and study, in contrast to the more transient nature of spoken languages (Cazden, 1976). Thus, written language development facilitates children's emerging skill of looking at language as a symbol system itself, apart from the work it accomplishes in day-to-day activity.

During the school-age years, children's development is increasingly influenced by the expanding world of people (peers, schoolteachers, neighborhood acquaintances), ideas, and circumstances that children must adapt to and cope with. Their language is spurred to further development by the need to develop more complex and subtle resources for managing daily life in the world outside the immediate family (Lindfors, 1987, p. 152), and to make themselves understood by those who are not already tuned in to their system of understanding. Children become adept in mastering ways of speaking, behaving, and interacting in an ever-widening variety of cultural institutions.

This brief look at the course of language development points to a major achievement at each stage of growth. During infancy and the toddler years, children and their caretakers evolve a full-blown communication system for managing the here and now. This communication system is unique and idiosyncratic to each family, with its own set of actions, gestures, sounds, objects, and routines that are the basis for understanding others. This communication system is built on the most sophisticated premises of all communication systems—the principle of joint attention to a particular topic during a conversation, the principle of turn-taking in dialogues, and the principle of agreed-on correspondences between action or sound and meaning.

During the preschool years, children master socially accepted conventions for communication so that they can understand and be understood by new caretakers and preschool teachers. They learn to communicate about the past and the future along with their current situation. During the school-age years, children master communication through oral and written language in a wide variety of settings with a wide variety of people. In addition, they are increasingly able to reflect on their process of thinking and their use of language in these varied situations to discuss the past, present, and future.

## Having Conversations with Children

When children are talking, they are not just repeating words and sentences that they have heard others say. Young children's talk can provide rich opportunities to hear their minds at work actively trying to make sense of the world around them. This can be seen in the following conversation between a five-year-old boy and his kindergarten teacher:

> "We have three 12s in this room," Wally said one day. "A round 12, a long 12, and a short 12." Everyone at his table looked at him expectantly. "The round 12 is the boss of the clock, the long 12 is on the ruler, and the short 12 is on the calendar."
> "Why is the 12 on the calendar a short 12?" I asked.
> "Me and Eddie measured it. It's really a five. It comes out five on the ruler."
> "You mean it's five inches from the edge of the calendar?"
> "Right. It's a five." Wally stared thoughtfully at the clock. "I'm like the boss of March because my birthday is March 12. The 12 is on top of the clock" [Paley, 1981, p. 102].

Children often say things that are surprising to adults. Their comments show us that their view of the world is sometimes very different from our own. Their ideas reflect the inferences and connections that they have been able to make given their knowledge and experience in life. In this sense, their comments reflect remarkable achievements. In conversations such as the one described above, most adults intuitively know not to try to tell children that their ideas are wrong or silly. As Paley's remarks illustrate, adult responses acknowledge, accept, and encourage the child to continue this lively mental activity of putting ideas into words. In time, with experience and through conversations with others, children develop new levels of understanding; their ideas include more of the world as we adults know it.

Young children on their own have a difficult time talking about one idea for any length of time. However, adults and older children help younger children learn how to do this by helping them sustain participation in conversations with questions and comments. In the following conversation, a mother and a pre-schooler discuss the child's day:

*M:* What did you do at school today?

*C:* Working—just was working. Teacher has a magnet game. Some things are magnet and some things are not. The ones that are sticky stick and the ones that are not sticky don't stick.

*M:* Did you play on the jungle gym today?

*C:* No, I'm a watcher.

*M:* What's a watcher?

*C:* I watch everybody fall off and if they do, I go and get the teacher.

*M:* Did you have a nice ride on the school bus?

*C:* Yes. Do you know what Mr. B——— [the bus driver] says?

*M:* No, what?

*C:* "Shut up, R———," [child's name] and he turns the radio up real loud [Lindfors, 1987, p. 117].

In this conversation, the mother's questions and comments help to create a kind of oral text. If we were to remove the adult's questions, we would get a description of the child's day at school. The process of developing and elaborating on ideas in a conversation about events not in the immediate here and now prepares children for more sustained thinking and for narration, an activity that comes more easily to children over the age of seven (McNamee, 1979).

*Practice Guideline 4.5: Gathering information from children under the age of seven always involves question-answer exchanges. Adults need to ask children open-ended questions that invite them*

*to expand and elaborate on their ideas and provide a fuller*
*explanation of their thinking.*

Having conversations with young children is not always
easy. It takes time to become familiar with individual children's
logic and the connnections they make in the course of a conversation. A common characteristic of young preschool children's
conversation is *chaining*—that is, free-associating to a word or an
experience that comes to mind without always making clear its
connections to the topic at hand (Wood, MacMahon, and Cranstoun, 1980). Sometimes the adult has to accept and articulate the
connections for the child.

Wood, MacMahon, and Cranstoun (1980) describe two
tendencies on the part of adults that discourage and often prevent
children from having extended conversations: asking too many
questions, and asking closed questions—that is, test-like questions
that leave room for one-word answers only. For example, an adult
might respond to a child drawing a picture thus:

*Adult:*   What's that you're drawing?

*Child:*   A house.

*Adult:*   Oh, that's nice. What color is the house?

*Child:*   Red.

*Adult:*   Red, yes, it is red. And whose house is it?

*Child:*   My mommy's.

*Adult:*   Oh, she'll like that. Is it her birthday?

*Child:*   No.

*Adult:*   Oh, just a present?

*Child:*   Yeah.

In this type of dialogue, the adult's constant questioning leads to a
disjointed, superficial exchange. The child is not encouraged to
provide more than one-word answers. There is no room in the

dialogue for the child to have ideas and to express them or to ask his own questions. The dialogue also illustrates how an adult's questions can shape and lead the meaning of a child's utterances. In the above conversation, the adult infers that the child is drawing the house of someone in particular, and that the child's mother will receive the drawing as a gift. The adult's inferences are imposed on the child as if they were ideas that the child was intending to communicate. The conversation so far has, in fact, revealed little of the child's meanings and intentions.

Wood and his colleagues show that the issue of control is at the heart of engaging children in elaborated and extended conversations. In the above conversation, the adult keeps the conversation going on her own terms and does not allow the child to participate in determining its course. In order to draw children into an extended conversation, adults need to encourage children to ask questions and say what is on their minds even if their ideas do not make much sense to the adult or differ from what the adult expected.

Imagine that the above conversation continued as follows:

*Child:*   Superman lives in this house and he's watching TV.

*Adult.*   Mmmmm.

*Child:*   Man-of-Arms is gonna come over and they gonna go rescue the spaceship from the bad guys.

*Adult:*   Oh, that reminds me of the spaceship that you and Tony were building this morning with the "Lego" [building toys].

*Child:*   Yeah, me and Tony gonna play space invaders when he comes to my house.

*Adult:*   You two are really good friends! You have a good time when you play together.

*Child:*   Yeah, 'til my sister comes and fights. I hate my sister! Why does she always have to play too?

*Adult:*   Well, she probably wants someone to play with too. Maybe your mother can give her something to do while you and Tony play space invaders.

*Child:*   Yeah, because space invaders is boy's stuff and she hasta play with dolls.

As this dialogue unfolds, the adult's and the child's behavior changes dramatically. There is more parallel participation by the adult and the child in the conversation, rather than adult domination of the discussion. Notice that after the child made the comment, "Superman lives in this house and he's watching TV," the adult did not respond with a question but instead just acknowledged the child's idea in a nonintrusive way. By simply acknowledging the child's comment, the adult permits the child to continue his line of thinking uninterrupted by questions. As the child continues, the adult begins to participate by giving honest responses that relate to the child's interests and needs. In conversations such as this, the child has the experience of developing his ideas in a logical way. For children as for adults, talking is not only reporting on events; it is simultaneously rethinking the events and making sense of thoughts and feelings.

*Practice Guideline 4.6: Children are likely to be more talkative and more easily drawn into a conversation when they are with people that they know well, when they are in a setting that is familiar to them, and when they are given opportunities to control the direction of a conversation.*

### Problems in Having Conversations with Children

Words are not always the means that children are most comfortable using to raise problems and concerns. Under stress, children tend to utilize words less than adults might. Instead, children commonly communicate distress through disruptions of their eating and sleeping habits, through fighting and other forms of aggression, or even through withdrawal and loss of interest in play. In relying on children as sources of information about their own well-being, adults face three types of problems: situational constraints that affect children's verbal output; the many opportunities for misinterpreting children and their messages, given their inexperience and lack of skill in using language to explain themselves; and knowing whether or not children are fantasizing, pretending, or lying. In examining each of these issues, we will see that the setting of the conversation, the nature of the relationship between adult and child in reference to how power and control in the dialogue are established, and the adult's familiarity with the child will determine how problematical these issues are in an adult's inquiry.

***Situational Constraints.*** Childhood is a vulnerable stage of human development, and children are sensitive to their dependency on adults who take care of them. When they are made overly aware of their dependency, they become less spontaneous and more wary of factors in a situation that may threaten their sense of security. Children are most likely to be talkative when they are playing with others—with familiar peers, siblings, or adults—or when they are involved in day-to-day routines with people who are familiar and nonthreatening. When children feel a sense of control over the course of events in their activities and sense an open-ended situation, they will talk about, as well as play out, ideas that are on their minds.

Children are sensitive to and affected by the questions adults ask them. Preschool children and even school-age children are often reluctant to answer questions that do not appear legitimate or interesting to them—questions that children know the adult can answer for herself (Wood, MacMahon, and Cranstoun, 1980, p. 121). Wood and his colleagues demonstrated this principle in a study carried out with preschool children and their mothers. They invited three different groups of mothers and their four-year-old children to come to a playroom for a play session. One group of mothers stayed in the room and played with their children. The second group of mothers watched their children playing in the playroom under another adult's supervision over closed-circuit TV. The third group of mothers were brought to a separate room for coffee and conversation while their children played. These mothers genuinely did not know what their children did in the playroom.

After the play session, children went with their mothers to

another room for a snack. The mothers had been asked to engage their children in conversation about their activities during the play period. The conversational efforts of mothers in the first and third groups did not go well. The children whose mothers had been with them resisted and avoided answering questions about what happened. The mothers who knew nothing at all were also not very successful in getting their children to talk about what had happened. The children seemed to find the task of reconstructing an account of their activities difficult, and the mothers' questions were not specific enough to elicit clear accounts of their children's activities.

The mothers who had watched their children over closed-circuit television engaged their children in the most elaborate and sustained conversations about what they had been doing. The children perceived their mothers' questions as genuine; further, the mothers could frame intelligent questions to draw out information on salient parts of their children's experience. These findings are unsettling because adults usually do not have the knowledge that mothers in this group had. However, we learn from this that asking questions that children know we know the answer to may deter their participation in a conversation. Also, knowing something about the child's experience in a situation will help an adult ask informed questions to which children can respond with more detailed information.

*Practice Guideline 4.7: The more adults know about what a child has experienced, and the more awareness professionals have of the typical activities of children and their patterns of thinking, the more effective they will be in engaging children in conversations that elicit information about their well-being.*

The setting for such question asking and conversation is also an important determinant of children's responsiveness. Children are far less likely to talk and reveal information when formal demands are placed on them, such as in a testing situation, a formal interview, or a structured adult-led conversation (Cole, Dore, Hall, and Dowley, 1978). The sociolinguistic William Labov demonstrated this principle in his classic study of black children in Harlem in the early 1970s. These children performed very poorly on standardized interview tasks with school psychologists and were characterized as "verbally deprived." Labov demonstrated that when school-age children were engaged in conversations in more relaxed, open-ended, and informal situations, they became highly verbal. He concluded that "the social situation is the most powerful determinant of verbal behavior and that an adult must enter into the right social relation with a child if he wants to find out what a child can do" (Labov, 1972a, p. 236). This is difficult for many adults, particularly when they approach the child through their professional identity as lawyer, police officer, doctor, judge, or nurse.

*Practice Guideline 4.8: Adults are more likely to understand and communicate effectively with children when they adopt an informal conversational style, dispensing with the accoutrements of adult professional roles.*

To acknowledge the difficulties in getting information from children in structured and formal settings is not to say that children cannot be helpful sources of information for adults in such situations. It means that adults need to be extremely careful in how they arrange these interviews. Children will feel less vulnerable and fearful when they have a parent or caretaker with them while talking with a professional adult, familiar or unfamiliar. However, if the relationship with the familiar caretaker is dominated by feelings such as anger or fear, this person can have the opposite effect on the child, serving to compromise what the child will tell others.

*Practice Guideline 4.9: Preschool and school-age children usually need the support and encouragement of a trusted and familiar caretaker to mediate their interactions with authority figures or with people whom the child perceives could hurt him, such as a police officer or a doctor.*

**Being Misunderstood.** Because verbal explanations are not children's forte, they are in a prime position to be misunderstood by adults. As Korbin, an anthropologist, points out, children sometimes think that they have told something to adults, but the message does not always comes through in a way that adults can understand. She points out that in the McMartin case of alleged sexual abuse of preschool children in California, parents asked their children why they did not tell them what was going on in school. "In addition to the enormous fear that the children felt that has been extensively written about and discussed, the children also responded that they HAD told their parents, for example, telling them that they did not want to go to school. The parents didn't ask further questions about why, and so the children assumed (some of them) that their omnipotent parents knew what was going on. This is not to blame the parents who were responding to what they often thought were normal school avoidance and separation problems" (Jill Korbin, pers. comm., Jan. 1987). This unfortunate case points out the need for adults to consider carefully the meaning of what children say and of their nonverbal behaviors.

Another example of misunderstanding young children is provided in the Australian film *Careful, He Might Hear You*. This film contains an interview between a judge and a school-age boy for the purpose of a custody decision. The boy's two aunts were vying for guardianship. The boy had a preference for one aunt and told her so. This aunt told the boy that if this was what he wanted, he would have to tell the other aunt himself. When the case came to court, the judge called the boy into his chambers to discuss the matter privately. In a brief interview he asked the boy why he had told his aunt that he did not want to live with her. The boy responded that the other aunt had told him that he had to tell her himself. The judge assumed that this aunt was prompting the boy; he asked no further questions and awarded custody to the aunt whom the boy did not want to live with (Jill Korbin, pers. comm., Jan. 1987).

Adults must be cautious in the inferences and conclusions they draw from what children say. In *Careful, He Might Hear You*, the judge is kindly but far too hasty in his interview to gain a full understanding of the child's point of view, and the child is not given an explanation of why he is being asked these questions. The child is misunderstood and left without opportunity to explain himself.

*Practice Guideline 4.10: Part of creating adequate conditions for children to provide adults with information is ensuring that children understand the purpose of an inquiry, and that they have enough time to explain themselves in nonthreatening conversations.*

**Lying.** *Webster's* dictionary defines lying as making a false statement that one knows is false, especially with the intent to deceive or give a false impression. Researchers have recently pointed out that the ability to lie begins in the toddler years and can be viewed as a developmental achievement because it marks the infant's discovery that her mind and thinking are separate from her mother's. This same understanding is marked by toddlers' discovery of the word *no,* which helps them delineate the boundaries between their own desires, thoughts, and feelings and those of others (Chagoya and Schkolne, 1986). Children do not always provide us with accurate accounts of what has happened to them; young children's accounts of experiences can and do include intentional and unintentional or unconscious distortions and changes of the facts. The question for children of all ages is not whether or not they are lying, but what factors are operating that influence what they say to adults at any one time.

Children change their facts in recounting an event for many of the same reasons as adults: to protect themselves and those they love, to avoid punishment, and to get something that they want for themselves. Lying is not always self-serving; feelings of loyalty to one's parents, the desire to keep the family together, and the desire to protect parents from hearing about bad and painful experiences will affect the way events are reported. Likewise, responses of disbelief or anger by adults may change what children say. In addition, the stress of the interview situation itself—with potentially frightening authority figures—may inhibit or distort the recounting of events. Under any of these circumstances, children may say what they think adults want to hear.

The following conversations between Mrs. Paley, a kindergarten teacher, and her pupils provide a picture of some of these pressures operating in young children's lives.

*Eddie:* I told my dad the truth. I was fighting with my brother and my dad came in and said, "Who did this?" because we made such a mess. We threw everything on each other and dumped the whole box on the floor. I said it happened by accident.

*Teacher:*    Was it an accident?

*Eddie:*    Yes.

*Teacher:*    But you said you did it on purpose.

*Eddie:*    Yeah, but I didn't want to get yelled at.

*Teacher:*    Did your father believe you?

*Eddie:*    He really did. See, I told you it was the truth.

*Teacher:*    Has anyone ever told a lie?

*Everyone:*    No! No!

*Teacher:*    Let's act out a scene in which someone tells the truth just as George Washington did when he cut down the cherry tree. I'll put these pictures on the table and, Wally, you take one picture and hide it. Then I'll ask who did it and you tell me. (I close my eyes and Wally takes a picture of Lincoln and puts it in his cubby.)

*Teacher:*    Oh, my favorite Lincoln picture is missing. Who took it?

*Wally:*    I did.

*Teacher:*    Good for you, Wally. You told the truth.

*Wally:*    I found it on the sand table. I didn't know who it belonged to.

*Teacher:*    Wally, is that supposed to be the truth?

*Wally:*    I didn't want you to say that I stoled it.

    Even in a role-playing game, Wally had to protect himself. Any response that shielded him from adult disapproval or punishment was a good and an honest response.
    The same day, the subject of honesty came up again, but this time it was not simulated. The sand table was

saturated with water, and the water was dripping on the floor. I had warned the children not to do this and I was angry.

*Teacher:*   Who poured in all the water?

*Everyone:*   Not me. I didn't.

*Eddie:*   Maybe someone came in and did it while we were out.

*Tanya:*   Maybe the sink leaked into it. That could happen.

*Teacher:*   I would like to know who did it, please, so I can ask that person not to do it again!

*Tanya:*   Maybe it was Eddie.

*Eddie:*   It was not! Maybe it was Tanya!

*Teacher:*   Okay, look. I don't care who did it. How can we make sure that it doesn't happen again?

*Wally:*   You put the water in from now on.

Anger from an adult and perhaps fear of punishment make a child weak. Wally always liked to wet his own sand, but my irritation made him unsure of his ability to do it properly. I was certain that Eddie was the culprit because I had seen him overwater the sand table before. Yet Wally reacted as if he were guilty and expected to be punished [Paley, 1981, pp. 138–139].

These conversations are striking for several reasons. Here a skilled and experienced master teacher is leading a discussion with normally developing five-year-old children facing life's everyday problems. This conversation is taking place in January of the school year; the teacher knows the children well, and the children respect and trust her. The situation appears optimal for an adult to elicit the truth from young children. The discussion shows that in a seemingly nonthreatening role-play situation and later in a real classroom situation, the truth needs a disguise in order to protect the children's emotional integrity. In far more emotionally charged situations, and with adults that are less familiar, we can only assume that the need to protect themselves is operating strongly in young children.

These conversations illustrate another factor at work in preschool children's language development. Sometimes just saying the words makes an idea become real; denying an action can make a child feel that he or she did not actually do it, regardless of the actual events. As Paley describes it, "the appearance of honesty is as good as the honest act itself. . . . 'If you have not had a turn, raise your hand,' says the teacher. A hand shoots up; it is someone who has already had a turn. To the adult this is a blatant lie. But the child may feel he has not had a proper turn or that others have had more turns. He may simply wish he has not had a turn so he can have another. None of this matters anyway, for if the teacher believes him he feels he has told the truth" (1981, p. 137). Adults may view young children as perpetual liars in such day-to-day situations, but this view seems shortsighted. As Paley found, there are always strong feelings and reasons motivating children's behavior and responses. Rather than discounting their behaviors and comments as lies or potential lies, it is more useful for children's and adults' inquiries in the long run to study and eventually discern the probable meaning and message the child is trying to communicate.

The research findings of Yamamoto (1979) on children's reactions to being considered a liar support the idea that adults should worry less about whether or not children are lying, and focus more on understanding why children make a particular statement at a certain point in time. Yamamoto surveyed 367 children in fourth through sixth grades in order to understand which life events they considered most stressful. The children rated twenty events on a scale from one to seven, seven representing the most upsetting. The seven events with the highest average ratings were "losing parent" (6.90), "going blind" (6.86), "academic retainment" (6.82), "wetting in class" (6.74), "parental fights" (6.71), "being caught in theft" (6.63), and "being suspected of lying" (6.52).

Children were also asked if they had experienced each event. Being suspected of lying was reported by 82.3 percent of the children (a rate higher than any other event except "not making 100," which was rated less stressful at 3.75 on the scale). For events rated 6.0 or higher, the only events approaching "being suspected of lying" in prevalence were "parental fights" (64.0 percent) and "a poor report card" (46 percent). Yamamoto's survey demonstrates school-age children's awareness of adult expectations for veracity and their frequent, stressful experiences of being suspected of lying.

Adults sometimes become suspicious of young children's reports because some of the facts are changed in different interviews about the same events. In one case (Gutierrez, 1987), a five-year-old girl living in the custody of her father told her mother that her uncle, the father's brother and a priest, had "touched" her in a "funny way" that made her feel bad. He had lifted up her dress, pulled down her tights, and touched her "down there." Her mother called the state protective services agency, and an investigation was made by both police and state investigators. When the child was interviewed by police, she changed her story—she said that it was a man at the grocery store who had done this to her, not her uncle. The case was eventually closed for lack of evidence.

A closer examination of the sequence of events that took place suggests several reasons for the change in the child's story. In her initial report to her mother, she said that the uncle had told her not to tell anybody because everyone would "get in trouble." The child refrained from talking about it until it became too much for her to manage—she was having nightmares and needed comfort and therefore told her mother. The mother's initial response to her daughter was one of disbelief. Young children are highly sensitive to such adult reactions; children are not likely to repeatedly claim something that makes a parent doubt them or even become angry. As Yamamoto (1979) found, the experience of being considered a liar is enormously stressful for young children.

The child's interview with the police was ill-fated from the start; the child was alone with two police officers for this questioning. Given her age, the sensitive nature of the problem, and the unfamiliar authority figures in intimidating uniforms, the child needed someone she knew and trusted to be present to help mediate and remind her of the purpose of the conversation. It is important to note that the child held to her story about what happened to her and changed only the part about who did it—the part of the report that was most upsetting to her parents, and the part that would threaten a family member's safety. Because this child's parents were already separated and she had, in a sense, lost her mother (in that her father had custody), it is hard to imagine her implicating anyone in the family network of wrongdoing and thus taking the risk of losing more than she already had.

*Practice Guideline 4.11: Children's sense of loyalty to family members, no matter how abusive and hurtful, is very strong and is likely to preclude children from saying things that would betray them.*

This case study demonstrates the range of psychological factors that can operate on young children in stressful situations. It further illustrates the importance of allowing children to participate in establishing the conditions under which they feel safe to talk. Once the child is comfortable talking, adults need to anticipate the range of psychological factors that may be operating to shape the child's report. The child's effort is an attempt to make sense of what has happened to her in the past as well as what is happening to her in the present.

### Conclusion

What adults learn from talking with young children has as much to do with the adult's competency, sensitivity, and knowledge about the child and his way of thinking and speaking as it does with the child's linguistic competencies. "Communicative skill is an attribute of speaker-listener pairs, not just the speaker" (Melton and Thompson, 1987, p. 14). Therefore, adults who want to question young children must understand what kinds of questions and comments open the floor for conversations with young children and what closes off dialogue. As Melton and Thompson conclude, "As a matter of policy, we should be concerned not with children's competency per se, but instead their competency *in interaction with* that of the factfinder" (1987, p. 14).

This chapter has focused on the competence features of the matrix presented in Chapter One, particularly the child's linguistic competence. A child's verbal reports are influenced by the child's age, by the setting in which the conversation takes place, by the person engaging the child in conversation, and by the child's understanding of the immediate situation that he finds himself in. Children can provide us with verbal accounts of events in their lives when adults can arrange for an appropriate social situation, and when they take the time to understand the complexity of the ways in which children communicate messages. Understanding verbal messages usually requires additional information from observations and interactions with a child in more than one context.

# CHAPTER 5

# Culturally Sensitive Inquiry

In a multicultural society such as our own, one of the most perplexing problems in eliciting information from young children is how to make inquiries sensitive to the child's culture. Inquiry is inextricably bound to interpretation. Culture affects how the informant and the questioner view the event or situation being discussed. For example, a teacher who notices reddened marks on a child's body will want to find out if the child has been abused. The teacher and the child understand what it means to be hit, but they may not understand it in the same way. The child may see being hit with a switch as an appropriate punishment for misbehavior. Communities define appropriate discipline differently, and each community has standards of care that are understood by participants in that community (Garbarino, Guttmann, and Seeley, 1986).

For a family member to hit a child within the context of community-accepted discipline has different psychological meaning to a child than when the event is unexpected and unwarranted from the child's and the group's point of view. Children who think of a switching as "okay" within the family or community definition of fair punishment for a disobedient or delinquent act may not feel angry and helpless, and they may easily tell the teacher what happened. On the other hand, children who live in families and communities in which such a spanking is considered demeaning may feel shamed and reluctant to discuss it.

Teachers also have culturally defined ideas and attitudes about hitting children. For some adults, all physical discipline is unacceptable. Others give broad latitude to parents before judging physical punishment abusive. A teacher may even question the sense of responsibility of a parent who fails to whip a disobedient or delinquent child. These differing attitudes toward spanking children give the teacher's question shades of meaning that children are quick to understand and that may increase or decrease the child's willingness to respond.

In addition to possible differences in how the adult and child interpret the event under discussion, the specific interview situation (its location, the motives of the participants) may lead each party in the interchange to hear the questions and answers differently. In the school environment, the child may perceive the teacher as a potential enemy, as a threat to the family. Seeing the teacher this way, the child may refuse to respond to questions. In another setting (at a neighborhood hamburger shop with a trusted adult), the child may feel far freer to explain the facts as he knows them. The adult is also affected by the context of such an investigation. In school, the teacher may quickly notify the authorities of suspected abuse by people she does not know, but she may be reluctant to report a close friend or family member for the same or similar behavior.

Finally, the style of communicating itself is culturally related. Oral language and nonverbal communication (eye movements, posture, facial expression) convey meanings that are interpreted within the cultural framework of child and teacher. A child may be silent when questioned by an adult because of her group's suspicion of strangers, or their idea of good manners in the face of prying, or a taboo on the subject being raised. The interviewer brings ideas about the meaning of silence as well, and may consider it a form of rudeness, or an expression of fear, or sign of low intelligence. The original intent of the inquiry can become lost as the interaction itself evokes culturally mediated feelings in each participant about the other.

Adults must understand cultural meanings from the child's point of view as well as from their own. While adults cannot exclude all of their biases, recognition and understanding of their own values and ways of thinking help avoid ethnocentric interpretations. Reflection on one's own group's practices and beliefs is an important aspect of cross-cultural communication.

*Practice Guideline 5.1: Sensitive inquiry places the burden of understanding the cultural meaning of behavior on the adult.*

All peoples address similar human problems. A Christian man in England shows respect for his religion by taking off his hat but keeping on his shoes, while a Muslim in an Arab country will show similar respect by keeping on his hat and removing his shoes (Evans-Pritchard, 1962). It is a mistake, however, to assume that the differences in how groups think, feel, and act consist in nothing more than simply using different words or actions for the same phenomena. "The worlds in which different societies live are distinct, not merely the same world with different labels attached" (Chilcott, 1987, p. 206).

For instance, truth and falsehood may be defined quite differently depending on whether lying is viewed as sinful, clever, or adaptive. The meaning of an untruth told by an inner-city child who is "covering" for a powerful gang member is not the same as one told by a suburban child in a safe community who does not want to snitch on a friend. Both children may lie, but for one it may be the reasoned response to a threat to the survival of the entire family, while for the other it is an impulsive gesture to avoid a minor embarrassment to a friend.

*Practice Guideline 5.2: The culturally sensitive professional looks for the parallels in the behaviors of children of various groups, while still appreciating the differences between the groups' perceptions of the world.*

People belong to a variety of overlapping groups that may coincide or conflict with each other (Patterson, 1975). But within communities, groups are not organized haphazardly. Rather, they are bound into complementary and reciprocal relationships with one another. The culture forms an overarching framework that ties together the various groups in which individuals claim membership. It makes day-to-day life comprehensible, coherent, and predictable (Evans-Pritchard, 1962, p. 19).

Patterns of interactions are established early, but they are not straitjackets that bind the cultural participant in all situations to a narrow range of responses. Because a child usually responds in a particular way in a given situation does not mean that he is incapable of another response, only that the response given is the preferred or "normal" one in the context as the child understands it (Bruner, 1970). Questioning black children in their own homes and in their own language, for instance, has led to higher performance on standardized tests than is achieved in school settings. Labov described an eight-year-old black boy who was monosyllabic when interviewed by a community member in a standard interview situation. The same child was an articulate and enthusiastic speaker when the interviewer went to the boy's apartment with a friend, lay on the floor, provided potato chips, and talked about a taboo subject in dialect (Cole and Bruner, 1972). This highlights the importance of social context in assessing competence.

Cultural patterns change over time as new environmental challenges present themselves and give considerable range to individuals in their interactions with others of their own community as well as those from different communities. Particular features of a culture, however, may linger in an individual's behavior after their function has passed, thus becoming an impediment to successful adaptation. This is particularly characteristic of first-generation immigrant groups who need the security that traditional beliefs and practices bring, but whose children often suffer from the misfit between the ideas of their family and community, on the one hand, and those of their new society, on the other. This makes the behavior of first- and second-generation immigrants difficult to predict; sometimes they respond according to the old culture, sometimes they adopt the behavior of the new.

### Cultural Identity

Who one is shapes what one does. What one does shapes who one is. The reciprocal relationship between the child and his social group's cultural practices results in the establishment of identity. The culture of family and community directly affects how children experience the world—what goals and objectives are presented to them, what relationships are available to them, what behavior and practices are recommended to them—and it is from these experiences that their definition of themselves, their identity, arises.

Erikson (1950) points out that it would be a mistake to

assume "that a sense of identity is achieved primarily through the individual's complete surrender to given social roles and through his indefinite adaptation to the demands of social change" (p. 368). In fact, identity builds. Sometimes it is more responsive to group norms and expectations, sometimes less so, as the individual strives to integrate the cultural roles ordained by family and community with her own needs, abilities, and wishes. Some of the most important identity groups are determined by age, sex, ethnicity, and social class.

*Age.* Children occupy a unique place in every group and expectations for them are enormously varied. For instance, groups vary in terms of the age at which children are expected to tell the truth, to be responsible and reliable (Korbin, 1981). If children are not considered to be competent, to "have sense," and to be able to tell the truth until seven or eight years of age, adults and children may not take a child's perceptions or pronouncements seriously. Inappropriate expectations of very small children and infants, often implicated in child abuse and neglect in Western nations, may be related to cultural definitions of the nature of children and childhood. Some religious groups, for example, may condone practices considered abusive by the larger society in the effort to save children from what they consider a greater danger. Adults' expectations of these children and the children's beliefs about themselves are different from those of children from more mainstream religious communities.

*Practice Guideline 5.3: Culturally sensitive inquiry requires an appreciation of the place of children in their families and communities and of the constraints and prerogatives this place may give them in their interaction with adults and with other children.*

*Sex Roles.* One of the most significant group memberships for all human beings is determined by their gender. While biological factors dictate some similarity in sex roles as they have evolved across culture groups, there is also considerable variation. In the United States, each cultural community has defined gender roles in a somewhat different way. For instance, a number of investigators have pointed to the strong maternal role played by women in black communities as compared to mainstream white communities (McAdoo, 1981) and to the macho image of males in Hispanic families (Tores-Matrullo, 1980).

It would be a mistake, however, not to acknowledge an American influence on how all groups define sex roles. One of the facts of the second half of the twentieth century is the trend toward androgyny, the result of the women's movement and various economic forces. Today, children's gender-specific models are often confused, ambivalent, and conflict-laden. As a consequence, their behavior may differ sharply from that of their parents and older members of their community. Such generational differences often make it difficult for all adults to obtain information from young people regarding their behavior, particularly gender-related behavior, and most especially sexual behavior.

Sex-related cultural expectations are important variables affecting how children respond to adults of both the same and the opposite sex. Sensitivities regarding males' interactions with female children are found among many ethnic and social-class groups, and sexual behavior and thoughts are often a taboo subject for discussion between males and females. Many groups restrict communication about sexual matters between children and people outside the family, even with adults of the same sex.

*Practice Guideline 5.4: Adults attempting to obtain sexual information from young children must be particularly alert to sex roles and sexuality and their implications for communication.*

*Ethnicity.* In the United States, one of the most meaningful units of cultural identity is ethnicity. Although there is a national identity that is powerfully felt, for many Americans national identity is filtered through the ethnic community. Cultural values and norms of behavior brought from other countries are transformed in ethnic enclaves in the United States (McGoldrick, 1982, p. 4).

Racial identity is a special instance of ethnicity because it differentiates people not only by their actions and common ancestry but also by their current visual appearance or past racial identifier. (Race in the United States is not a biological marker but rather a social definition relating to the African, Indian, Latino, or Asian, as opposed to Caucasian, origin of at least one ancestor.) Although there may be physical similarities among people of the same race, there are enormous cultural variations within races and great similarities among people categorized as belonging to different races.

Children as young as three are well on their way to developing attitudes about their own group and other groups (Katz, 1982). The significance of racial and ethnic identity to children depends on specific experiential factors, such as the homogeneity of their environment, their group's sense of social and economic importance, and the extent of prejudice perceived or discrimination experienced.

*Practice Guideline 5.5: The professional cannot assume a child's subjective feelings of ethnic or racial identity on the basis of physical characteristics or an ethnic label.*

**Social Class.** Another group identity that has considerable impact on behavior is social class. Social class, while primarily defining economic status, carries with it behavioral expectations that range from educational achievement to table manners. Although social class is more fluid and less clearly marked in a democracy like the United States than it may be in other political systems, its influence, nevertheless, is strongly felt. The economic status of families has wide-ranging effects on children's development. Income determines a broad array of factors, from the amount of time parents can spend with their children to the safety of the environment, the number and kinds of objects available for children's play, and the opportunities to participate in various social groups.

Identity groups set standards of conduct and styles of interaction that may support or conflict with the other groups in which the individual may have membership. For example, Rogler, Malgady, Costantino, and Blumenthal (1987) warn of the importance of distinguishing between "acculturated Hispanics who can be treated as if they are Anglos and those who require some sort of special treatment modality reflecting their adherence to Hispanic culture" (p. 568).

*Practice Guideline 5.6: In assessing a child's response to adult questioning, it is essential to know which of the many social groups to which a child belongs he or she sees as holding sway in a particular context.*

## Barriers to Cross-Cultural Communication

*Racism.* In the United States, all ethnic groups are minorities, but not all minority groups share a similar national environment. People of color (blacks, Latinos, Asians, and Native Americans) are often the victims of prejudice that results in discrimination and devaluation by the European ethnics. Ogbu (1978) attributes the difference in the treatment of what he calls "caste-like minority groups" (p. 23) to majority-group prejudice rather than to genetic, individual, or social-class differences. Further, he asserts that the behavior of blacks (and members of other caste-like groups) can be understood only against the backdrop of racism. He explains the poor school performance of many blacks as a reaction to the diminished opportunities available to them.

Another explanation for the unequal treatment of blacks and other caste-like minorities is that their culture is deficient in essential ways; their children, therefore, do not develop the skills necessary to function effectively in the mainstream (see Tulkin, 1972, for a discussion of cultural deficits as cultural differences relevant to child development). Their poor performance in educational and work environments is believed to be caused by their culture, which limits and constrains their development. This perspective, often called the culture of poverty (Lewis, 1966), posits that poor communities have cultures that are self-perpetuating and essentially pathological. According to this view, the culture of poverty encourages behaviors and attitudes that are maladaptive to mainstream achievement and effectively disqualify members from participating in the more complex and education-dependent majority culture. Bernstein (1961), for instance, contends that lower-class children learn a restricted language code that ill fits them to participate in activities that require an elaborated code such as is expected in school.

More recently, the high achievement of some Asian children in relation to white children has led to a belief in the superiority of Asian culture as a vehicle for socializing children for academic success. While this new appreciation of the cultural configurations of a previously caste-like minority is a welcome development, it is not yet clear that such appreciation will exempt Asians from further discrimination in mainstream institutions.

Adults' beliefs about either exceptionally good or especially poor achievement based on racial identity inevitably affect their expectations and, therefore, their interactions with children of color. Inappropriately high or low expectations of children inevitably result in a misfit in communication. The educational literature is replete with examples of how teachers change their interactions with children they perceive as being more or less capable (Rosenthal, 1968).

*Practice Guideline 5.7: Adults who question children must be particularly aware of their own beliefs regarding the status of minority racial groups; racism can affect their understanding of the information gathered.*

Of all classes and regional groups, black Americans tend to adhere to racial-group beliefs and behavior most tenaciously (McAdoo, 1981). They tend to be more socially isolated and show greater similarity in thought and action across social class and other social divisions than members of other ethnic groups. Cross-racial inquiry can, therefore, be particularly difficult, since racism or the expectation of racism confounds relationships between minorities of color and whites. Blacks are more likely to turn to family, friends, ministers, and church members during periods of stress than to outsiders (Hines and Boyd-Franklin, 1982). McAdoo (1977) found resistance in blacks to airing the family's "dirty laundry" outside the family.

*Practice Guideline 5.8: Whether discrimination is intended or not, many racial minorities expect prejudice from the majority group and are reluctant to discuss sensitive topics with them.*

Defensive behavior, which may include withdrawal, aggression, passivity, and rage, is not an uncommon response to cross-racial communication, even from children who have not personally experienced prejudice and discrimination. Similarly, children who come from more privileged groups may learn to feel and act in an overbearing and superior manner with other groups. Feelings of superiority may transcend other status variables, such as age or social position. Status transformations based on race, ethnicity, or religion may complicate communication between high- and low-status adults and children.

*Practice Guideline 5.9: Adults who interact cross-culturally must recognize and learn to deal with the status expectations and coping mechanisms used by both victimized and privileged groups.*

Adults from low-status groups may also have difficulty obtaining information from children of their own group. Some adults accept the stereotypes of their group that are projected by the majority and are disrespectful of members of their own community, particularly those who are poor and powerless. Furthermore, some adults need to create social distance between themselves and less successful group members and, therefore, are unable to use their firsthand knowledge of their culture. For instance, paraprofessionals who go to work in social service programs may come to identify with the institutional goals and workers and reject the behavior of their former peers, refusing to "hear" with an ear tuned to the community (Musick and Stott, forthcoming).

*Practice Guideline 5.10: Adults must be aware of their own status needs and attitudes when interacting with children of their own and different groups.*

*Stereotyping.* Cultural descriptions of groups are useful guides for interaction, but they must be used with caution. Even relatively homogeneous groups reflect differences in social class, religious affiliation, educational background, regional residence, and esthetic interest. Further, groups that are perceived by others to be homogeneous, such as Native Americans and Hispanics, consist of a variety of different groups. Native Americans are divided by tribal affiliation, and Spanish-speaking groups have cultural roots in Mexico, Central and South America, and the Caribbean as well as Spain. In addition, the degree of Americanization differs, particularly among new immigrant groups.

Garbarino and Ebata (1983) stress the complexity of trying to categorize the behavior of groups sharing ethnic and racial identity.

In analyzing ethnic differences in child abuse, they note that "when class and ethnicity are confounded, we always run the risk of confusing legitimate ethnic differences in style with the deleterious effects of socio-economic deprivation" (p. 774).

*Practice Guideline 5.11: Generalizations from group norms regarding an individual's behavior must be regarded as tentative and potentially misleading unless verified.*

***Biculturalism.*** Children from ethnic groups that are most different or most excluded from the mainstream culture often learn to live in two separate worlds, in their own ethnic enclaves and in the larger community. Such children become bicultural, able to switch culturally encoded behavior depending on the context in which they find themselves. This permits them to retain their family or primary identity and at the same time to function in the larger society. Biculturalism, however, sometimes carries the seeds of bitter conflict when the social groups involved have beliefs and practices that cannot be reconciled. "No matter how well educated an Indian may become, he or she always suspects that Western culture is not an adequate representation of reality. Life, therefore, becomes a schizophrenic balancing act wherein one holds that the creation, migration, and ceremonial stories of the tribe are true and that the Western European view of the world is also true. Obviously, this situation is impossible although just how it becomes impossible remains a mystery to most Indians. The trick is somehow to relate what one feels to what one is taught to think" (Wise and Miller, 1983, p. 353). While biculturalism may be an asset in facilitating communication between members of different groups, it can also be misleading when the child switches "identity" because of the topic discussed or the context in which the inquiry takes place.

*Practice Guideline 5.12: Adults must be aware of the potential for conflict and ambivalence in children's understanding of and response to inquiries.*

### Cultural Style

Cultural identity, determined by group membership (race, gender, ethnicity, social class), defines, on one level, who one is and what one's status is. Cultural style refers to the underlying chords that orchestrate how one organizes the world and expresses oneself. It is in worldview that the influence of culture is apt to be most pervasive and most subtle. All human communities have a perspective on life, a philosophy for living that underlies behavior. For example, Afro-Americans' worldview leads them to approach people with caution, wariness, and a sense of distrust (Shade, 1982, p. 220).

In recent years, considerable research has focused on the cognitive and perceptual styles of various cultural communities (Cole and Bruner, 1972; Shade, 1982; McGoldrick, 1982; Gray and Cosgrove, 1985; and Hilliard, 1982). This research suggests that cultural groups vary along a number of different continua, such as their definitions of proper caregiving and discipline, health and illness, courtesy and rudeness, and personal-institutional relationships.

*Caregiving and Discipline.* Although all communities have definitions of child abuse and neglect, there are differences in their definitions and ratings of abusive and neglectful behaviors. A study of six ethnic groups—Filipino, Japanese, Samoan, Vietnamese, Mexican-American, and Blackfeet Indian—revealed that all of the informants believe that some aspects of their child-rearing practices are misunderstood as abusive by the larger community (Gray and Cosgrove, 1985). "According to this study, the protectiveness of Japanese and Filipino mothers who are not intent on raising 'rugged individualists' can be misperceived by Westerners as stifling to the child's emotional health. So, too, the severe physical discipline mentioned by the Samoan respondents may be perceived as physically harmful" (Gray and Cosgrove, 1985, pp. 395–396).

*Health and Illness.* Ethnic groups vary in the way they respond to and communicate about pain, the frequency of various symptomologies, their beliefs about the causes of illness, their attitudes toward helpers (such as physicians), and their preferred modes of treatment (McGoldrick, 1982, p. 6). This leads, for instance, to different assessments of psychological complaints in German and Iranian communities; Germans are willing participants in talk therapy, while Iranians prefer medicine to relieve their psychological discomfort (Winawer-Steiner and Wetzel, 1982; Jalali, 1982).

*Courtesy and Rudeness.* A classic case is found in the plight, cited earlier, of an Ottawa Indian girl whose teacher believed she had low self-esteem and referred her for psychological testing and counseling. The teacher's belief was based on the fact that the child seldom made eye contact when the teacher spoke to her. The teacher did not know that for Ottawa Indians (and other Native American tribes), it is a "sign of disrespect" to look an older person in the eye (Wise and Miller, 1983, p. 350).

*Personal-Institutional Relationships.* For Puerto Ricans, family is the overriding consideration in assessing obligations. Maintaining close personal relationships with family and friends is one of their highest priorities, frequently overruling the demands of institutions and systems. "For a Puerto Rican, life is a network of personal relationships. He trust persons; he relies on persons; he knows that at every moment he can fall back on a brother, a cousin, a compadre. He does not have the same trust for a system or an organization" (Fitzpatrick and Travieso, 1980, pp. 109). Differences in style and goals of personal and personal-institutional relationships are transmitted through child-rearing techniques and other conditions of life for the child. For instance, Japanese mothers spend more time soothing their infants than American mothers, who are more apt to stimulate their infants. "American mothers, partly to fulfill their own expectations of appropriate effective behavior, encourage open, expressive, assertive, self-directed behavior while the Japanese mothers seek quiet contented babies" (Super and Harkness, 1982, p. 10). Differences in mother-child interaction set the stage for later differences in social organization.

While differences in cultural style significantly affect how people interpret the world and respond to it, there is no reason to believe that there are substantive differences in the capabilities of people (Cole and Bruner, 1972).

*Practice Guideline 5.13: The task in cross-cultural communication is to grasp how different groups express meaning through their behavior.*

## Language

All social groups have a wide range of language uses available to them, and they differ in the tasks and situations in which these uses are brought to bear. Florio-Ruane (1987) reports two studies in which the home language of children differed from or overlapped the language expected in school situations. A study of Italian-American children and their Italian-American teacher showed congruence between the teacher's permission for children to "chime in" on the answers to math problems and their "chiming in" during dinner-table conversation.

Children must learn to respond to the subtleties of language as it is used in various group settings by different people. The question "Where did you come from?" illustrates the dilemma. Is the right answer a geographical place (Chicago), an anatomical place (mommy's tummy), or a biological process (the confluence of egg and sperm)? Children learn to use and interpret language within their community, but they often make mistakes as they try to match their behavior to their group's expectations.

Language also has emotional connotations. Even when people know more than one language, they may not respond equally well in all the languages. Emotional expression is often freer and more spontaneous in one's native tongue, whereas the use of a second language may foster intellectual defenses and control (Rogler, Malgady, Costantino, and Blumenthal, 1987).

People often have negative beliefs and attitudes about nonstandard dialects spoken by low-status groups. Thus, the child who answers the question "Are you hungry?" by responding, "Ah bees," may be considered unable to answer the question because of the deficiency in his language. A more realistic interpretation, however, is that the child is competent to translate the question into his own language and respond correctly and that he is a participant in a social system in which groups do not share a communication code. The listener's interpretation may range from disgust with the child's poor language expression to appreciation of his bidialectic ability or concern about the dual linguistic system with which Americans live.

*Practice Guideline 5.14: Culturally sensitive inquiry must recognize that children use words to convey emotional as well as linguistic meaning through language and must consider which language a child is most apt to use to express feelings as well as information.*

## Conclusions

This chapter has focused on the orientation features of the matrix presented in Chapter One, particularly the interplay of the child's and the adult's orientation. The goal of a culturally sensitive interview is to help the child give as clear an account as possible of her understanding of an event. In order to understand the meaning of this event, it is useful to have a working knowledge of how members of the child's community interpret such happenings and to determine whether or not the child has already been brought into this understanding. Since the questioning adult may not already have such knowledge, it may be necessary to ask an adult from the child's own community for help in making this judgment.

The adult is responsible for setting a stage for interaction that the child is likely to understand in terms of both place and participants. Here, adult orientation is inseparable from adult competence. Who may or should ask questions of whom, about what, when, and where are critical variables in obtaining a meaningful account of a child's experience. Culturally familiar persons, places, and languages are apt to elicit the most meaningful communications from children.

It should be apparent that passing an inquiry through a cultural filter is extremely complex. Florio-Ruane (1987, p. 186) suggests that the following questions may assist adults:

1.  What is happening, specifically, in the social action that takes place in this particular setting?
2.  What do these actions mean to the actors involved in them, at the moment the actions take place?
3.  How are the happenings organized in patterns of social organization and learned cultural principles for the conduct of everyday life—how, in other words, are people

in the immediate setting present to each other as environments for one another's meaningful actions?

4. How is what is happening in this setting as a whole related to happenings at other system levels outside and inside the setting?

5. How do the ways everyday life is organized in this setting compare with other ways of organizing social life in a wide range of settings and at other times?

No discussion of culturally sensitive inquiry can be concluded without considering the ethical implications of cross-cultural questioning. The unequal power relationship between adult and child automatically presents ethical issues in such interrogations. But when the unequal relationship extends to the social groups to which adult and child belong, the ethical issues become even more problematical. When the goal of the adult is to ferret out behaviors, beliefs, and attitudes of children's families and communities that are at odds with those of the institutions the adult represents, inquiry can quickly become an unfair imposition. To what extent an adult, through his or her questions, is free to judge, interfere with, or impose on the socialization of a child whose culture is different is a question with which the culturally sensitive inquirer must struggle, and one to which we will return.

CHAPTER 6

# Adult Biases
# and Expectations
# About Communication

Social psychologists have long known that expectations and social forces can affect adult perception and judgment. Decades ago, Asch (1951) demonstrated that adults perceive movement of a stationary point of light projected on the wall of a darkened room (the "autokinetic effect"), and that adult reports of the distance the light moved could be influenced by expectations established by the reports of other adults. Even when there is nothing to see, social pressure can produce reports of movement.

*Practice Guideline 6.1: Social pressure can result in distorted perception; adults should be especially self-critical when seeking information in the context of strong social pressure.*

Asch's findings are derived in part from the fact that perception and cognition are neither passive nor strictly objective processes. Rather, the individual (or group) brings meaning to each stimulus or experience. These preexisting categories provide the starting point for each new act of knowing. When the new experience or stimulus fits in with these expectations, it may be incorporated, or *assimilated,* to use Piaget's term. If it does not fit, it may be disregarded as irrelevant or invalid. When the new experience or stimulus is beyond the absorption capacity of the existing expectations but is not disregarded, those expectations, or *schemas,* are changed to fit the new information, and what Piaget called *accommodation* takes place (Piaget, 1976, pp. 69–82).

Hundreds of studies conducted by social psychologists testify to the existence of a powerful need for cognitive consistency. This need translates into an impulse to resolve cognitive dissonance by dissociating painful or inconsistent connections or by rearranging one's interpretations of experience.

For example, consider the situation of a parent who asks a child how it feels to be home alone after school. If this "latchkey" arrangement is the parent's only apparent option, the parent needs the child to answer, "It feels fine." The parent may be reluctant even to ask if she or he fears that the child will answer in a way that will expose parent and child to distress. In such a situation, the adult's need to hear something may result in a host of nonverbal and subtle verbal cues to the child—and perhaps even an unconscious unwillingness to see and hear.

In a more powerful example, a parent may be confronted by a child alleging sexual abuse at the hands of a trusted adult. If the parent believes the child, the parent must accept a challenge to his or her concept of "trusted adult." An alternative is to discredit the child's report—perhaps charitably to conclude that the child misinterpreted the trusted adult's behavior. Another is to redefine the trusted adult as a criminal. Violated expectations require action of one sort or another; the motive to deny discrepancies between experience and expectation is strong.

*Practice Guideline 6.2: Assimilation is generally preferable to accommodation from an emotional standpoint, at least in matters of personal or cultural significance. This puts pressure on the process of adult-child communication when that communication touches on threatening topics or violates taboos. It may require that the adult modify his or her self-concept as a "good" parent (or a "good" social worker, lawyer, psychologist, nurse, physician). We can see that clearly in the case of efforts to define child abuse.*

Adults have expectations about the meaning of childhood experiences. These expectations reflect conclusions drawn from experience as well as prejudice. An area in which the role of these expectations has been documented is that of adult perceptions and evaluations of child abuse.

A recent national survey (National Committee for Prevention

of Child Abuse, 1987, pp. 2–5) revealed that 73 percent of adults believe that "repeated yelling and swearing at a child . . . often or very often . . . leads to long-term emotional problems for the child." In contrast, only 41 percent of adults believe that "physical punishment of a child often or very often . . . leads to injury to the child." The former suggests that most adults have drawn the conclusion that verbal abuse is a threat to development, but that "ordinary" corporal punishment is not.

This is interesting because the definition of what is and is not abuse hinges on a community judgment that particular ways of treating a child are inappropriate and damaging (Garbarino and Gilliam, 1980; Garbarino, Guttmann, and Seeley, 1986). The origins of such a community judgment lie in a mix of professional expertise and scientific knowledge, on the one hand, and culture and local standards, on the other.

The process of community definition of what is and is not abusive is thus both an important influence on and a consequence of how adults interpret the experience of children. Clinicians recognize that "You can't diagnose what you don't believe exists." Adult concepts of abuse thus are important in the ability of adults to be recipients of information about abuse from children.

### Sources of Adult Bias

What are the sources of differences in adult hypotheses about communication in adult-child relationships? Two major categories are personal experience and prejudicial attitudes or bias. Sharon Herzberger's research sheds some useful light on this issue (Herzberger, 1985). Herzberger interviewed 139 young adults and asked them to respond to a series of hypothetical disciplinary interactions between parent and child (Herzberger and Tennen, 1985). Each posed a child misbehavior and a parental disciplinary response. The misbehaviors had previously been rated according to adult perceptions of "deserving of punishment"; the eight disciplinary responses—four emotional punishments and four physical punishments—all had previously been rated from moderate to severe according to adult assessments.

Respondents were grouped according to whether or not they

reported having had a similar experience as a child. The 139 respondents then rated the parent-child interactions according to whether or not they were abusive. In general, if respondents had experienced a particular form of punishment, they were much less likely to define it as abusive, much less likely to predict it would have emotional consequences for the child, and more likely to define the situation in which punishment was inflicted as the child's fault.

However, another preliminary study conducted by Herzberger and her colleagues (Howe, Herzberger, and Tennen, 1988) revealed that clinicians who reported having been abused (most often emotionally) as children "view abuse of others as more serious than those without such a history" (p. 112). This is presumably due at least in part to their self-selection as helpers, as well as their having processed their own experiences through training and practice. Of course, one might also argue that this reflects unprocessed anger at their parents, anger that is translated into criticism of others. Can we resolve this issue? A close look at Herzberger's study indicates that the behaviors in question meet the current objective criteria for abuse established by the public process of community decision making, a process that provides the official basis for all child protective service.

No doubt the findings with respect to nonclinicians reflect a complex mix of influences. Some of these include the motive to rationalize one's own experiences ("this happened to me and I'm okay"), the role of family experience in defining basic social relations ("abuse is what someone else does; this is just the way discipline was handled in my family"), and childhood egocentrism ("if this happened to me it must have been my fault").

All these concerns are present in decisions adults make about reporting experiences by children that constitute child abuse within the legal definitions that manifest community standards. Here we see the processes of cognitive consistency–seeking at work in force as adults seek to maintain their view of the world and reconcile that view with children's horrible experiences. Of course, another influence at work here is concern that reporting abuse will lead to official inaction or a poorly conceived intervention that will make the child's situation worse.

*Practice Guideline 6.3: Unless they have carefully examined and fully processed their own experience, people are less likely to recognize as abuse treatment that is similar to treatment they themselves experienced as children (or that they themselves, or people like them, practice).*

Adults' unexamined personal experience can shape behavior and judgments inappropriately in interaction with children. An example of how a mother's fantasies influenced her overt behavior toward her baby comes from Stern's (1977) study of interactions between a mother and her twin sons.

At three and a half months there were repeated exchanges in which the mother and one twin, Fred, would gaze at each other. Fred would avert his face as a signal to avoid further contact and to leave him alone. The mother would not respect this communication but would instead try to make eye contact again. Fred would respond with a more exaggerated aversion of his face. As soon as the mother looked away, however, Fred would look back at her, and the cycle would begin again until Fred was in tears.

With her other twin, Mark, the mother respected the signal to avoid further eye contact and virtually never tried to force it. Mark was able to begin and end eye contact with his mother when he wanted. When the boys were seen at one year of age, Fred seemed notably more fearful and dependent than Mark; he often used aversion of his face to break off contact with other people. Mark, on the other hand, greeted people openly and looked them straight in the eye.

Stern's behavioral data provided a picture of how parent and infant interacted and was useful in diagnosing a problem of maternal intrusiveness. He went beyond this observation, however, to interview the mother in order to understand her subjective beliefs and fantasies about her boys. As she spoke, she revealed that she felt Mark was more like herself, while Fred reminded her of certain characteristics of her husband that she did not like. This belief system appears to have contributed to and sustained her different interactive styles with the two children and her inability (unwillingness, in a sense) to be an effective communicative partner with Fred.

Adults must always be careful that they do not let their own unexamined personal experiences inappropriately shape their judgments. Research on the transmission of child abuse across generations concludes that one of the most important mediators of intergenerational transmission is the degree to which childhood experiences of maltreatment are unprocessed and unexamined and become part of the unconscious (Kaufman and Zigler, 1987). Alice Miller has explored these issues in *For Your Own Good* (1983) and *Thou Shalt Not Be Aware* (1984). As a result of differences in processing experiences of child maltreatment, the intergenerational transmission rate can vary from 5 percent to more than 75 percent (Kaufman and Zigler, 1987).

*Practice Guideline 6.4: A major concern in understanding adults as recipients of information from children is the adults' own unresolved childhood experiences.*

Unprocessed memories of victimization may be a particular problem in the matter of adults receiving information about sexual abuse. Survey evidence suggests that from 20 to 25 percent of all women and 10 percent of all men have been sexually abused (Finkelhor, 1984). Thus, the odds are high that children giving information about sexual victimization will encounter adults who have themselves been victimized and (in light of our historical failure to treat victims) have unprocessed memories that can impede accurate evaluation and response. Denial of such experiences and their relegation to the unconscious are common.

When fully processed, however, the experience of victimization might well serve as a powerful motivator to help. Adults who have no direct experience of sexual victimization might stand somewhere between "processed" and "unprocessed" former victims. They might be less likely to be biased one way or the other because of their lack of exposure to sexual victimization. But they might also be less likely to understand indirect communication by a child ("you can't diagnose something if you don't know it exists"). It is an issue meriting further study, one on which we do not have a great deal of information at present.

*Practice Guideline 6.5: To prepare themselves for dealing with information from children who may have been sexually*

*abused (that is, all children), adults should explore and confront
their own childhood experiences with sexual victimization.*

## Bias and Expectations in Adult Decision Making

Over twenty years ago Silver and his colleagues (Silver,
Barton, and Dublin, 1967) reported that more than 20 percent of the
physicians they surveyed said they would not report cases of
suspected physical abuse that came to their attention. More recently,
James and his colleagues (James, Womack, and Strauss, 1978) found
that 62 percent of a sample of pediatricians and family physicians
said they would decline to report a case of sexual abuse brought to
their attention unless the family supported making such a report.

In a study of eighteen psychiatrists and eighty-three psychologists, pediatricians, and family counselors, Attias and Goodwin
(1984) found that more than half the psychiatrists but less than a
third of the other clinicians said they would not report a family to
child protective services in the case of an eleven-year-old girl who
describes graphically to her school counselor fellatio and cunnilin-
gus with her natural father, ongoing for more than two years, if the
child later retracted the allegation. The authors link this in part to
widespread misunderstanding of the likelihood that such retractions, rather than the original allegations, are false. They base this
on the finding that false allegations by children are rare, but
retractions are usually the result of coercion or fear of family
disruption.

It seems safe to say that reporting has improved since the
1960s and 1970s. Nonetheless, a recent study of professionals'
reporting of sexual abuse cases tells us that the issue is still alive.
Using a self-selected sample of professionals with special interest in
or responsibility for sexual abuse cases in New England, Finkelhor
(1984) found that 64 percent said they reported such cases to
protective services when faced with them, in compliance with their
legal mandate. The breakdown across professional groups ranged
from 48 percent for mental health professionals to 76 percent for
school personnel.

Who you are (at least professionally) seems to affect what you
do about reporting. Mental health professionals may believe,

perhaps correctly, that they have the skills necessary to handle these cases themselves and that reporting will only muddy the waters and undermine the family's prognosis. Teachers, on the other hand, may feel that handling child sexual abuse is beyond the scope of their mission and perhaps their competence.

These decisions may be consciously made and based on knowledge of self and the relevant social realities. Or they may stem from powerful unconscious forces associated with the potential reporter's own unexamined childhood experiences or adult feelings. This is the wild card in considering child abuse reporting and the role of adults in the process of soliciting and receiving information from children.

It is clear that bias or predisposition is an active element in the day-to-day life of children and the adults they encounter. Parents have expectations that affect what they do to stimulate and respond to their offspring. Teachers have expectations that affect their response to children in the classroom. Adults have expectations for children in courtrooms and clinics, expressed through the often subtle tone set by authority figures such as judges and physicians. For example, research reveals that a judge's attitude, even though not openly expressed, is evident in the tone set when the judge instructs the jury in criminal cases and it appears to be capable of *doubling* the likelihood of a jury returning a guilty verdict, at least in cases where the judge's knowledge of a defendant's prior record of felonies is concerned (Blanck, 1985).

Where children are involved, most of the evidence concerns the power of preconceptions to influence outcome via their impact on motivation and responsiveness. Rosenthal (1978) has reviewed 345 studies consistent with such a model of these effects (the "Pygmalion" effect), a model that emphasizes the role of nonverbal cues as the link between expectations and altered outcomes.

Interestingly, women are, on average, more adept at interpreting nonverbal cues (Hall, 1985). This finding has implications for understanding why and how children are better information sources for some adults than for others. It suggests a hypothesis to explain the often-made observation that women are generally, although not invariably, more successful than men at building rapport with children in clinical interview situations.

Sensitivity to nonverbal cues may have far-reaching implications for improving the child-adult communicative process, even in
settings well beyond abuse. For example, Rowland (1987) reports
that dentists often misinterpret the emotional response of their
young patients, attributing fear when children are actually
experiencing pain. The problem seems to be that the facial cues of
pain (eyebrows lowered and drawn together, eyes wide) are
mistakenly attributed to fear. Dentists are predominantly male and
presumably less attuned to nonverbal cues. This suggests the need
to sensitize all clinicians—perhaps men in particular—to the
nonverbal cues of children as part of professional training. Such
training could help ground adult expectations better in the realities
of child-adult communication.

Practice Guideline 6.6: Sensitivity to nonverbal cues from
children is an important feature of adults who are effective recipients of information from children; this should be a focus of all
professional training.

How relevant are adults' expectations in understanding
adults' responses to children as sources of information in child
abuse allegations? Research by Everson and Boat (1986) testifies to
the possibly dramatic importance of such expectations. They
surveyed child protective service workers in all 100 counties in
North Carolina. The survey focused on rates of substantiation in
sexual abuse allegations and on expectations concerning the
incidence of false statements—both fictitious accounts and false
retractions—about sexual abuse by children and adolescents.

Everson and Boat reported that of 124 cases involving
children under the age of three, 48 percent of the reports were
substantiated, 1.6 percent were determined to be false reports, and
none was retracted. Among 301 reports involving three- to six-year-
olds, 60 percent were substantiated, 1.7 percent were determined to
be false, and 2.7 percent were falsely retracted. Among 414 reports
involving six- to twelve-year-olds, 55 percent were substantiated, 4.3
percent were false, and 5.8 percent were falsely retracted. Among the
410 adolescent cases, 57 percent of the reports were substantiated, 8.0
percent were false, and 5.0 percent were falsely retracted.

Of course, the determination that a child's account was a

false report reflects the results of the protective service investigation. Substantiation means there was sufficient evidence to proceed officially. Unsubstantiated cases may involve actual abuse, but they are not provable. (However, some analyses document a 50 percent incident of substantiation of physical, sexual, or emotional maltreatment in such cases within two years; Rick Green, pers. comm., 1987). Cases that are clearly intentional false reports are classified as such and are differentiated from unsubstantiated cases.

These age-related differences in the incidence of false reports are particularly interesting in light of two findings about developmental trends in honesty. The first is that "the data for specific tests of overt moral conduct . . . provide little evidence of a continuing development of honesty with age" (Burton, 1976, p. 178). The second is that researchers have observed a trend toward growing consistency with age: older children become more consistently honest or dishonest, whereas younger children are more inconsistent (Burton, 1976). To what do we attribute the higher rate of false reports among adolescents?

Among the eighty-eight protective service workers reporting in Everson and Boat's study, some reported a rate of fictitious accounts of 15 percent or more. This led to a separate study of twenty-four randomly selected workers from the original thirty-four workers who had described at least one fictitious report of sexual abuse in their experience. These twenty-four were randomly matched with twenty-four of the fifty-four respondents in the original survey who did not detect a false report.

Everson and Boat asked these workers to report on their expectations about the frequency of lying by children and adolescents in allegations about sexual abuse. They asked: "Suppose you saw 100 children . . . who said they had been sexually abused. On average, how many of those children do you think would be lying or not telling the truth about the abuse?" (Everson and Boat, 1986, p. 4). The question was asked for groups of children under three, three to six, six to twelve, and twelve to eighteen years old.

Among the group of forty-eight workers, the average expectation of lying for all ages was 8.7 percent. Lying was expected from 4.3 percent of children under three, 2.7 percent of three- to six-year-olds, 6.6 percent of six- to twelve-year-olds, and 15.8 percent of twelve- to eighteen-year-olds; the most significant comparison was between adolescents and all other ages. This gives a baseline for professional expectations about children as sources of information in the important matter of child sexual abuse allegations.

This is not the whole story, however. The workers who had actually classified cases as false reports expected higher rates of lying by children than those who did not report having received a false account. This difference was particularly evident for expectations about adolescents. Workers who had received false reports expected 12.2 percent of all children and 19.6 percent of adolescents alleging sexual abuse to be lying; those who had not received false accounts expected 5.2 percent of all children and 11.9 percent of adolescents to be lying.

The most interesting finding in Everson and Boat's analysis is that those who reported having investigated a false report had had an overall substantiation rate of 47.8 percent in the previous year; those who did not report having investigated a false report had had a substantiation rate of 69.4 percent. The differences between the two groups of workers did not seem to be derived from the number of years they had served as protective service workers, the number of cases of sexual abuse they had ever dealt with, or their perceived comfort in dealing with such cases. Were the false reports really false? Did they increase the workers' level of competence in detecting future false reports, while at the same time giving them more accurate expectations about the likelihood of children and adolescents lying about sexual abuse? Or did these workers approach their task with an inappropriately high level of suspicion? We cannot know for sure because we do not have an independent assessment of these cases.

Everson and Boat offer the following conclusion: "We believe that these findings suggest that many [child protective service] workers may have difficulty believing that children tell the truth when they report sexual abuse. Rather than beginning an investigation with the attitude that the child is to be believed unless there is convincing evidence to the contrary, these workers seem to view the child, and especially the adolescent, with a great deal of suspicion. A retraction is then accepted, not as a predictable phase of the disclosure process, but as evidence that the child is lying, confirming the worker's worst suspicions" (1986, p. 6).

Some adults begin with the working hypothesis that children often lie about sexual abuse. In Everson and Boat's study it is not possible to be sure about the direction of effects. Did one group expect more lies because they had encountered more liars? Or did they believe they had encountered more liars because they expected more lies?

*Practice Guideline 6.7: When investigating allegations made by children of sexual abuse, the most effective approach is to start with a willingness to believe and a recognition that most child-initiated allegations are grounded in real experiences (even if those experiences themselves do not constitute sexual abuse).*

Everson and Boat's report from the field leads us to consider the result of laboratory studies conducted by Mahoney and his colleagues that deal with the processes adults use in confirming and discarding hypotheses. Mahoney's research has dealt with factors that influence the strength of convictions about hypotheses. Its relevance to our concerns should become apparent in light of Everson and Boat's study, in which it appears that adult hypotheses about whether children and adolescents are prone to lying about sexual abuse may influence their behavior as professionals.

DeMonbreun and Mahoney (1976) tested the impact of alternative patterns of encountering data on self-reported confidence in a hypothesis. Adult participants rated their confidence about a hypothesis concerning a mathematical rule used to predict the outcome of an experiment. They were given outcomes for twenty trials and asked to rate their confidence after each trial. They were told that there was some random error in the experimental procedure; thus, their hypotheses might be correct and yet might not be verified in every single test. What they were not told was that the data they received were prearranged and hence independent of their hypotheses. All participants finished with 50 percent successful predictions.

Forty percent of the subjects remained 98 percent confident in the validity of their hypothesis at the end of the twenty trials, even though not more than 50 percent of their predictions had been successful. If we assume that these results can be generalized beyond the laboratory to the world in which practitioners and other adults form hypotheses about children and their behavior, the results direct us to consider what those hypotheses are. Everson and Boat's results make this far more than simply an interesting matter of the psychology of science; it is a matter of direct and concrete importance for children, particularly children caught up in adult interrogations.

Mahoney (1986) notes that this matter of affirming and discarding hypotheses is clearly a powerful issue no matter what the domain of interest. He cites Mitroff's (1974) study of forty-two geoscientists at the National Aeronautics and Space Administration. These scientists were confronted with the results of the Apollo 11 through Apollo 16 missions to the moon. Mitroff found that as new data became available about the validity of previously held hypotheses concerning the geoscience of the moon, the scientists "displayed intensely emotional responses to the data returns and were generally very tenacious in holding to their original hypotheses" (Mahoney, 1986, p. 5). In fact, one-third of the scientists reacted to disconfirming evidence by rejecting the evidence as poorly acquired. Mahoney replicated this finding experimentally in his work.

That confirmatory bias operates in the interrogation of children by adults seems clear. How does it operate? DePaulo and Pfeifer (1986) report on the selective success of professional interrogators in discerning lies. DePaulo and Pfeifer had college students and police investigators listen to audiotapes of sixteen people's statements, each of which contained two lies and two truths. The two groups were equally able—or rather, unable—to discriminate between truths and lies in this situation, but the police were more confident of their judgment as the test progressed.

These results parallel Starr's (1982) findings in studying the inability of professionals (and students) to reliably identify abusive parents on the basis of a brief observation—in this case, a videotaped segment of parent-child interactions. Some abusive parents were easy to identify; others were much more difficult. Interestingly, Starr reported that in some cases clinicians achieved a success rate lower than chance, and lower than that attained by college students and nurses. Perhaps the confidence of the police and other professionals stems from similar origins, such as peer support in the absence of empirical validation, and thrives when selective perception of results is possible. We must bear in mind that confirmatory bias can imply both that some adults will invariably reject accounts given by children and that others will invariably accept accounts given by children.

*Practice Guideline 6.8: It is extremely difficult to make valid assessments on the basis of tiny samples of behavior or behavior observed in only one mode (as in the case of the audiotapes).*

*Practice Guideline 6.9: Professionals may be likely to overestimate their ability, to be inappropriately confident of their ability, and to overvalue their own hypotheses about what they see and hear.*

These hypotheses may do a disservice to children and to the pursuit of truth. This is certainly consistent with recent evidence disputing the validity of the customary interview of the child by a trial judge (the voir dire) to determine the child's competence to testify in court. The voir dire appears to be of very limited validity (Melton, 1986).

### Lying in Adult-Child Communication

To understand fully how adults function as recipients of information from children, we must better understand where normal lying fits into adult-child relationships. Research and clinical commentary on lying have primarily focused on lying as it is related to psychopathological development. Only recently has attention been directed to how lying plays a positive role in normal development. Current research suggests that lying is as essential to normal development as telling the truth (Goleman, 1988). Some psychiatrists view the inability to lie—the George Washington syndrome—as a neurotic manifestation (Goldberg, 1973). Furthermore, according to Ekman, lying is an indication of psychological growth in a child. Essential human skills, such as independence, perspective taking, and emotional control, are the same skills that enable children to lie (Ekman, 1989).

Before a child is able to lie, he must know what the truth is. Developmentally, the child's cognitive processes must be mature enough to recognize the difference between fantasy and reality (Freud, 1965). Once this maturation has occurred, the ability to either conceal or reveal the truth emerges, and the concept of lying develops.

Recent research has found that most children learn to lie effectively between the ages of two and four. In one study, three-year-olds were instructed not to look at an appealing toy when the researcher left the room. Later, they were asked if they had done so. Ninety percent of the children had looked at the toy; of these, one-third told the truth and admitted they had peeked, one-third lied and said they had not looked, and one-third would not say what they had done. The children who refused to reveal what they had done represented a transitional phase in the development of lying: these children wanted to lie but did not yet have the necessary skills. Behaviorally, they exhibited the most nervousness of the three groups. In contrast, the children who lied appeared calm and relaxed, suggesting their satisfaction with being able to lie effectively (Lewis, Stanger, and Sullivan, 1989).

While the motivations for some lies are obvious—for example, personal gain or avoidance of punishment—the motivation for other lies is not so readily discernible. Here we must look for developmental clues. One such issue occurs around separation-individuation, where lying is seen as a major determinant of autonomy for the child during the course of normal development.

According to some researchers, the child's first successful lie is extremely important in the formation of the ego and a necessary condition for the child's ability to separate psychically from the parents (Goleman, 1986; Ford, King, and Hollender, 1988). Lying is a vehicle through which the child can test her limits in determining a separate identity from her parents. When a child's lie is believed by her parents, the child realizes that her parents cannot know or control her thoughts. Thus, being able to lie successfully can be a developmental transition enabling the child to have a more realistic view of her parents and others.

*Practice Guideline 6.10: Lying plays a positive role in the differentiation of the self, enabling the child to become an autonomous person with a will of his or her own.*

Adolescence is a time when issues concerning autonomy reemerge (Goldberg, 1973). In an effort to maintain independence from their parents, adolescents often engage in testing limits with them; this frequently involves lying and deceitful behavior. Additionally, in order to enhance admiration from peers, adolescents frequently fabricate or exaggerate accomplishments. Adolescents also conceal information or communicate indirectly by means of strategic interactions in efforts to enhance their self-esteem. Goffman (1969) explains strategic interactions as those experiences with others that have the goal of acquiring, concealing, or revealing information. Strategic interactions evolve during early adolescence, when a higher level of mental ability is acquired (what Piaget, 1976, pp. 59-60, called *formal operations*) and the ability to make calculations about another person's thinking and behavior develops. Skill in strategic interactions develops as adolescents become more adept at distinguishing between their own thoughts and those of the persons they are interacting with (Elkind, 1980).

*Practice Guideline 6.11: As young adolescents become more adept at conceptualizing other people's thoughts and behaviors, their strategic interactions become more effective in acquiring, concealing, or revealing information.*

Although lying has been defined as a conscious intent to deceive, it is essential to recognize that the motivation as well as the content of a lie can be determined by unconscious mechanisms, such as denial and repression. For instance, a lie that is told over and over can gradually come to be believed by the teller as well as the person to whom it is told. If a child's lies are believed by adults, the lies seem real to the child, while the truth seems false. In this way, painful memories of traumatic events may be viewed as not true or as only fantasies (Fenichel, 1954).

Some researchers have suggested that pathological lying can have its roots in factors such as child abuse and emotional trauma (Ford, King, and Hollender, 1988). Just as multiple personality disorders are linked to devastating traumatic experiences in childhood, some observers believe that lying can serve as another means of hiding from the self and others that which is too painful to expose. In this sense, pathological lying may be an indicator of the existence of abusive and traumatic experiences in childhood. For example, a nine-year-old girl who was removed from her home after it was discovered that she had been sexually abused by her half-brothers and physically abused by her mother not only lied about her childhood experiences (she claimed to have an ideal family) but also continually lied about many other aspects of her life (winning awards in school, being a champion swimmer, appearing on TV). Thus, through her need to conceal from others her horrible childhood experiences, she generalized this pattern of deception to other aspects of her life, transforming herself into a more acceptable person both to herself and others. Although dynamically related to normal lying, this extreme pattern of fabrication is evidence of extremely negative life experience coming to dominate a child's life rather than being assimilated.

*Practice Guideline 6.12: When a child's lying becomes persistent and compulsive, it is destructive to normal development and is labeled pathological lying—that is, habitual and indiscriminate lying, well beyond what social conventions allow.*

While lying by children and adolescents is often viewed as wrong or immature by adults, lying nevertheless plays a significant role in adult-adult and adult-child interactions. A recent study found that adults admit to lying an average of thirteen times a week; the actual number of lies may be even higher (Goleman, 1988). Certain types of social lies—white lies (those told to avoid hurting others' feelings), altruistic lies (those that protect the innocent), joking lies (those intended to entertain), and self-preservation lies (those that present one in a better light)—form a major component of adult social interactions. These types of lies are not only unquestionably accepted but tacitly expected as well (Goleman, 1986). Not participating in social lies is considered at best impolite and at worst pathological.

Adults regularly tell social lies to children. According to Henry, many parents do not "know how and when to tell their children the truth. It is so much a tradition in our culture to conceal the 'ugly side' of life from children, that it takes intelligence, sensitivity and even training to communicate realities to them" (Henry, 1973, p. 160). For example, to avoid the unpleasant topic of death in a hospital with many terminally ill children, it is an accepted practice among the professional staff that when a child dies, the rest of the children are told that the child was taken to the seventh floor (the hospital has six floors). Many adults even consider some lies to children to be developmentally beneficial—for example, telling a child his scribbles on a piece of paper is the best drawing of a horse they have ever seen. Traditional myths such as Santa Claus, the Easter Bunny, and the Tooth Fairy are routinely presented to children as fact. While these fictions may not be developmentally harmful and are mostly developmentally enhancing, they illustrate the extent to which adults initiate and encourage socially acceptable lying in children.

Adults frequently suppress truth telling in children by encouraging politeness at the expense of honesty. Only in very young children is total candor excused, and even this makes adults uncomfortable. For example, a white preschooler attending an integrated school who remarks during snack time that her classmate's skin is the same color as the chocolate pudding makes her teacher squirm. It is obvious that such spontaneous and natural observations are taboo. Although this type of remark by very young children is usually tolerated by adults, older children learn to suppress comments that they perceive adults do not want to hear. This applies to significant matters (such as disclosures of sexual abuse) as well as relatively unimportant ones (such as pointing out the shortcomings of adults). Thus, decisions about disclosing or withholding the truth are based on how the child perceives the information will be received by the adult. If children believe they will be punished or humiliated for telling the truth, they may alter the truth or conceal it entirely. It is in this sense that the lying or truth telling of children is a function of the way adults behave as recipients of information from children.

The ways in which adults react to children's lies are also important. Adult responses of physical punishment, rejection, ignoring, amusement, or manipulation can encourage or suppress lying behavior in children (Smith, 1968). The specific patterns of verbal behavior that emerge during childhood may then continue throughout the rest of the child's life (Ford, King, and Hollender, 1988).

Goldberg (1973) cites a compelling example of a lying interaction between mother and son: A three-year-old boy announced at dinner that the family doctor had telephoned that morning with instructions for him not to eat any vegetables. His mother said she would call the doctor to see if this meant the very special vegetables she had particularly prepared for him. The boy then said that he had spoken to the doctor again just before dinner and that the doctor insisted that he was not to eat any vegetables, special or not, under any circumstances. When the mother replied that the doctor must not have understood how very special these vegetables were, and that she would call the doctor to clear up the misunderstanding, the boy, in a panic, blurted out that the doctor had just died. While amusing, the crucial point of this incident is that both the child and mother were lying to each other—only the mother was more skilled at it and used her power to dominate her child. While it would be unreasonable to assume that any parents are totally truthful, a family dominated by parents who habitually lie in order to get their own way is likely to produce related pathological lying in their children.

*Practice Guideline 6.13: Adults control and define the terms for normal lying; when adults abuse this power they may undermine future interactions with the child and encourage pathological lying.*

Children learn from adults that to get along in the adult world, not only must they learn to be skilled liars, but they must also ignore certain lies in others (Goleman, 1986). This is especially true for social lies, in which, in order to be successful, the deception must be overlooked. For instance, when an unwanted dinner invitation is turned down because of "previous plans," the inviter is allowed to save face, while at the same time it is implicitly understood that he is not to notice the untruth. Additionally, clues to other people's verbal and nonverbal behavior that may differ from what they are actually saying must be ignored—for example, one is not to point out that the person who is saying how much he likes his neighbor is clenching his fists while he talks. The consequence of this is often a type of collective self-deception illustrated in the classic fairy tale "The Emperor's New Clothes." Unfortunately, those who detect and state the truth are often ostracized. Rosenthal and his colleagues found that people who were skilled at correctly interpreting a person's slips and nonverbal cues were considered to be rude and even to be eavesdropping, while people who did not detect discrepancies in others' verbal and nonverbal behavior were readily accepted (DePaulo, Zuckerman, and Rosenthal, 1980).

Thus, lying plays a significant role in the development of children. Lying is also an essential part of adult-child interactions, at least as much as it is of adult-adult interactions. Children are sensitized from an early age to see only what adults want them to see, and not necessarily to see the truth. Children also learn from adults that certain lies are essential for smooth social interactions. This recognition provides some of the context for understanding adults as recipients of information through their participation in dialogues with children.

*Practice Guideline 6.14: Adults must acknowledge lying as a normal part of a child's repertoire of coping strategies, not simply dismiss it as immoral or immature behavior.*

### Adult Bias in Policy and Practice

Adult hypotheses about children as sources of information are embedded in institutional policy, in community ideology, and in individual belief systems. For example, until recently, children (unlike adults) were presumed incompetent to testify in court unless proven otherwise. The guiding hypothesis was that children are unreliable witnesses in general, and that the good child witness is a rare exception. As several historical reviews make clear (Melton, 1986; Bross and Michaels, 1986), there has been a strong confirmatory bias at work. In Michigan, for example, police routinely ordered polygraph (lie detector) tests for child witnesses. Over 147 were administered with only one child failing the test before the practice was abandoned (Groth, 1980). How well would adults have fared under such a policy?

Fueled by an overextension of Sigmund Freud's psychoanalytical model of childhood seduction fantasies (or even misled by Freud's own work—see, for example, Masson, 1984), many professionals have assumed that the preponderance of sexual abuse allegations made by children (particularly girls) are fictitious and result from seduction fantasies. The tenacity with which this hypothesis is held is all the more interesting (and perhaps revealing) in light of studies demonstrating the empirical rarity of fictitious allegations initiated by children. The most commonly cited recent study is Jones and McGraw's (1987) analysis of 309 allegations, only forty-five of which were found to be fictitious when evaluated by staff predisposed toward, not biased against, them. The fictitious allegations were of two types: thirty-six were initiated by adults (typically during custody disputes, and frequently by adults who had themselves been sexually abused) and nine were made by adolescents who had been sexually assaulted on an earlier occasion.

False allegations that are initiated by children without prompting from adults are rarely taken seriously enough to show up as official reports. This finding should be an operating principle for those who seek to communicate with children about sexual abuse allegations.

*Practice Guideline 6.15: Children rarely invent allegations of sexual abuse on their own initiative; adults are a more likely source of false allegations.*

Because of the problem of substantiation, some child protective service units now shy away from cases in which sexual abuse is alleged by adults in the context of child custody disputes. One result of this retreat from a commitment to investigate all allegations, of course, is to leave some children at heightened risk for victimization. The complexity of adult motives in sexual abuse allegations (particularly in the context of custody disputes) heightens the importance of children as sources of information in these situations.

Are children likely to lie and fantasize about sexual abuse on their own? One view says no: "The fantasy of young children is so inextricably interwoven with actual experience, so reflective of wishful thinking and pleasure principle material, so likely to have mastery as a theme, and so easily differentiated from reality, that sexual abuse is not likely to be a theme of the fantasy in the first place, and therefore, will not be the stuff of lies" (deYoung, 1986, p. 557). The classical Freudian view, however, asserts that seduction fantasy is a plausible, common source of false allegations about sexual abuse.

How do we reconcile these positions? Perhaps the bridge between these two contradictory viewpoints is the finding that real traumatic stress can produce negative fantasies—the post-traumatic stress syndrome—and that these fantasies can generate false allegations some time after the actual assault. This explains how some of the adolescent victims of assault came to make false assertions of new victimization in Jones and McGraw's (1987) study.

Severe trauma can and does produce negative fantasy, even in young children (Terr, 1983). This view is actually consistent with one interpretation of Freud's view that his female patients had in fact been sexually assaulted at one time, and that their "seduction fantasies" were the result of these real traumatic experiences, not the autonomous creations of the children in the absence of actual experiences. Children who are suffering delusions also invent stories that they believe to be true, such as in the case of a girl who "borrowed" a story of being abused from her best friend, with whom she closely identified, and who in fact had been abused.

*Practice Guideline 6.16: Fantasy is rarely the source of false allegations by children; more likely possibilities are that the child has been persuaded to lie (for example, that he or she has been coerced, threatened, or told that the falsehood serves a higher purpose such as family unity) or that the child is delusional (for example, that he or she is clinically depressed and creates stories that he or she believes to be true).*

This is not to say that children never lie about sexual abuse. However, false allegations by nonabused children appear to be uncommon. The "news" about false allegations made by children is their rarity, not their frequency. It seems that much of the lying about sexual abuse is attributable to adults: parents who prompt or even coerce lying by children (perhaps more frequently to deny rather than allege), perpetrators whose assault on a child produces traumatic stress and ultimately a false accusation against someone else, and perpetrators who falsely deny having victimized a child. Some is attributable to psychopathology.

This heightens the role of adults as recipients of information, of course; further, it directs our attention to the particular psychic convenience of the belief in the proposition that children often lie about sexual abuse. Why the strong confirmatory bias attached to the hypothesis that allegations are false? Where does such a bias come from, and how does it operate?

An important source of such adult confirmatory bias is unconscious cognitive processing, as evidenced by denial and repression. Denial and repression play important roles in adult psychology, particularly in sexual matters. Recent developments in neuroscience have begun to document not only the existence of unconscious filtering of information but the processes involved as well (Goleman, 1987). Although they have questioned the exact sequence of mechanisms proposed by Freud for this censoring process, contemporary students of cognitive science have validated the existence of unconscious and preconscious sensory processes. Although for most of us the existence of unconscious forces in human behavior may seem self-evident, the fact that some deny their existence or relevance makes it worthwhile to take the time to outline their importance.

Zajonc (1984) and his colleagues have demonstrated that even when a person is not aware of having perceived something (such as a geometric shape flashed on a screen), the unconscious reception and storage of that information can influence later behavior (such as the choice of a shape from among a group containing the original "unseen" one). This perceptual filtering of neutral information is not the whole story, of course.

In a process that takes only tenths of a second, the unconscious processors can screen upsetting or troubling information from conscious awareness—a process referred to as "selective inattention." In the words of one review: "Our capacity to deceive ourselves seems to depend upon our ability to deflect attention away from whatever might be too troubling to face" (Goleman, 1987, p. 28). That child sexual abuse is a prime candidate for selective inattention should come as no surprise, for there are few things more threatening.

Roland Summit, a veteran of dealing with child sexual abuse, puts it this way:

What makes the issues so difficult is not their power but their paradox. Most of us are survivors of childhood. We are intimidated and embarrassed by the shadows of our past. It was good to become enlightened, imperative to become strong and sure, vital to replace fearful feelings with comforting beliefs. It is normal to be an adult. It is healthy to take charge. It is necessary to know. Who can dare slip back to experience the feelings and vulnerabilities of a dependent child?

Besides all those basic growth and power issues, each of us is challenged in our personal beliefs and loyalties. If we are loyal and respectful to the memorial image of our own parents, and if we are protective of appropriate hierarchies of enlightenment and power, can those securities stand the test of believing that a pediatrician has molested a patient or that a father has sodomized his own three-year-old? If mothers are vital to our experience of caring and being cared for, can we contemplate that a woman could enjoy forcing feces into the mouth of her infant? And could such a woman be at the same time the trusted organizer of a parent cooperative preschool? Most of us insist that she would be found, if at all, only in Bedlam. . . . Even beyond the challenge to positive anchors of security, sexual abuse of young children assaults our psychological defenses. Anyone betrayed and molested by loving caretakers in childhood will try to establish a protective mythology: "They were right and good; I was bad and provoked my own suffering (and if I could only learn to be good they would love me)." By learning to be hyperalert and intuitively sensitive to clues of displeasure, abused children can learn to protect adults and to scapegoat themselves, making reasonable order out of intolerable chaos. An adult survivor of such a childhood may be very good at helping others in distress even while despising the child who elicits that distress. Many practitioners in the helping professions are

themselves victims, hidden even from themselves. Some will
be incapable of empathy with abused children. Others, further
along in their partial recovery from abuse, can feel only for the
children and against the offenders. Child sexual abuse gives
new meaning to the old adage "Physician, heal thyself"
[Summit, 1986, pp. xii–xiii].

The use of denial in dealing with information from children is not
homogeneous or universal; while every consciousness is shielded by
a censoring unconsciousness to some degree, some are more
shielded than others.

Luborsky, Blinder, and Schimek (1965), for example, have
documented a link between assessments of an individual's reliance
on psychological defense mechanisms and his perceptual response
to ambiguous photographs—for example, one that presents a naked
woman and a clothed man reading a newspaper. "Repressors" were
found to look at the reading man but not the naked woman. In
other research, repressors were shown to respond to sexual
statements without conscious arousal, while psychological assessment indicated a high level of arousal (Goleman, 1987). Ever-
increasing sophistication in measuring the neurological and other
psychological evidence of unconscious processing has provided
important support for the necessity of incorporating psychodynamic influences into our model of adult-child communication
around topics such as sexual abuse. However, the reality of
unconscious processing does not mean that all adult responses to
children as sources of information are rooted in denial, repression,
and other defense mechanisms.

*Practice Guideline 6.17: While some adult-child communica-
tion problems result from adult defense mechanisms, others do not;
some result from simple cognitive errors, and sometimes adults
simply mis-hear children or misunderstand a child's meaning,
without there being any particular psychic significance to the
mistake.*

Simple misunderstanding occurs frequently when children
are learning to speak or encountering new words. For example, a
nonparental adult may have trouble understanding a two-year-old's

speech because it contains idiosyncratic conventions with which only a parent is familiar. A child hearing a phrase for the first time may substitute similar-sounding familiar words in place of the unfamiliar words (such as "garden angels" for "guardian angels"). A four-year-old who comes home from nursery school announcing that they are celebrating "King Arthur's birthday" may in fact be about to celebrate Martin Luther King's birthday.

The dichotomy between psychically significant and insignificant communication problems parallels the results obtained by research on "slips of the tongue." Some verbal misstatements conform to the notion of a "Freudian slip," in the sense that they reflect a breakthrough from the unconscious, an "unintentional" suspension of the censoring process. For example, men asked to respond to a sentence completion task in the presence of a sexually stimulating situation provided more sexually significant responses than men not so stimulated (Motley, 1987). For example, they used "climax" rather than "finale" or "conclusion" to complete the sentence, "Tension mounted at the end, when the symphony reached its ———." Similarly, in a tongue-twisting word-pairing task, sexually stimulated men were more likely to say "fat passion" instead of "past fashion," and "nude breasts" instead of "broad nests." Men led to fear electric shock slipped up on "damn shock" for "shame dock," and "cursed wattage" instead of "worst cottage."

Other such "mistakes" appear to arise from simple "technical" errors in information processing. These mistakes are properly attributed to the stimulation of multiple, similar words by the initiation of the process of speaking one of them. Thus, for example, in a task where the phrases "let double" and "left decimal" are paired, an attempt to say "dead level" can lead instead to "led devils." Similarly, attempting to say "computer printout" may result in saying "comprinter puteout."

These are not emotionally or socially significant. This distinction rests on the belief that not all behavior has emotional or social significance for the unconscious and its censoring mechanisms. Freud recognized this, of course ("Sometimes a cigar is just a cigar"). But the truth of this statement complicates our task in assessing adult behavior in the context of communication with children.

*Practice Guideline 6.18: Some adult errors are benign, but others are consequential; some are simply technical problems, while others derive from adult defense mechanisms.*

These errors are different, at least in degree, from the conscious refusal to believe that occurs in some (perhaps many) intrafamilial sexual abuse cases. The mother who refuses to believe her child's allegation of sexual abuse against a father, stepfather, or mother's boyfriend is engaged in a dramatic form of denial. Such a mother is faced with a major threat to her world, and the self-protective feature of denial may be enhanced still further if the allegation seems to document the mother's failure as a parent and perhaps revive memories of the mother's own sexual victimization. In neither case does this absolve the parent from her protective responsibility toward the child, although it may temper an outsider's evaluation of the mother.

*Practice Guideline 6.19: If treatment is to go forward, the well-being of children eventually must take precedence over the self-protective psychological needs of the parent; the same is true of any professional who approaches children with strong confirmatory biases at work on behalf of inappropriate hypotheses.*

### Conclusions

The appropriate response to the problem of confirmatory bias is to ensure that adults have no axes to grind in their communication with children as sources of information about important matters. How do we accomplish this? While we may never accomplish it fully, we can work at getting adults to become aware of and to confront their unconscious biases. Further, we can work at improving the social technology of adult-child communication to minimize benign errors. Doing this requires careful attention to processes and procedures in all assessments involving children.

In Chapter Fourteen we will introduce an emerging technique for objectively assessing the validity of a child's narrative account. This procedure, known as statement validity analysis, imposes measures of internal consistency and the developmental appropriateness of language and concepts used in reporting events to determine the probable validity of an account. This approach can do much to counteract adult confirmatory bias.

*Practice Guideline 6.20: In the absence of any simple recipe for getting at the truth, the most important thing we can do is to prepare ourselves as adults to be open to effective communication with children, to be sensitive and unbiased recipients of information.*

How do we do this? It is not easy, of course, but an effective strategy includes the following things. First, recall that human behavior is best understood in human terms. Look first for an explanation of puzzling behavior that affirms the basic humanity of the actor. Why would you act the way a child is acting? Why would your child act that way? Empathy requires this basic affirmation that people are people. Second, recognize that everyone has a culture, even you yourself. Culture influences what we see and hear from a child as well as how we interpret what we see and hear. When dealing with a child who seems different, look at how that child's background and culture give meaning to his behavior in his own terms. Then think again about your own culture. Third, enter into a dialogue with your peers about adult-child communication and about your own experiences and assumptions about children (and their relationships with adults).

Most of us carry around psychological baggage that can affect our capacity to empathize with children as well as adults. Rigorously seek to understand why you are drawn to one child and repelled by another, why one child seems truthful and another deceitful. Do these children awaken memories or associations that influence the objectivity (in a sense, the fairness) of your dealings with this child here and now? There is no cookbook for self-analysis, but that does not absolve each of us of the responsibility to make the effort, and to get as much help as we need to accomplish the goal.

CHAPTER 7

# Observing
# Children's Behavior

Observation is a valuable key to understanding children's behavior. Children continually provide us with information through their fantasy behavior. Consider the following situation: A three-year-old boy is playing at home with a doll and a pipe. He dresses the doll and says, "Now have some fun. Take your cocaine and put it in the pipe and smoke it." What is the child telling his parents through this unusual example of play behavior? In this situation, the vocabulary is unusual for a child three years of age. The behavior reconstructed by the child is out of context. The child in this situation apparently had knowledge of techniques for using cocaine. The professional may use this information as a clue to initiate additional observations of spontaneous behavior in which the child demonstrates knowledge of drug use.

*Practice Guideline 7.1: Young children communicate through their behavior even more powerfully than through their words; by observing systematically the behaviors and behavior patterns of young children, we may tap into an additional source of information from children beyond efforts to elicit verbal reports.*

### Purpose of Observation

"If we could say that understanding a child is like a mystery, then taking records is the gathering of clues. Like experienced detectives, we must recognize the significant clues, we must develop special skills" (Cohen and Stern, 1958, p. 1). Some of these clues reflect where a child is developmentally. Others reflect the presence of troubling emotions. For example, anxious children may display symptoms such as eye twitching, rocking or swaying, or an inability to sleep or eat.

*Practice Guideline 7.2: Because symptoms are often manifest in spontaneous behaviors, observation is a tool that is particularly well suited to seeking information about emotional problems children are confronting.*

Observation is a natural method that parents learn to use to collect information about children. For example, in a study designed to discover how parents identify the symptoms of normal childhood illness and when parents seek medical intervention, parents reported that they observed a child's behavior changes during illness (Schellenbach and Susman, 1981). In fact, parents suggested that children's behavior changed dramatically during illness. For example, during an episode of illness children appeared lethargic, showed a decrease in appetite, and an increase in behavioral signs of insecurity or vulnerability, such as clinging and whimpering. Interestingly, parental behaviors during childhood illness also changed; parents tended to be more lenient and more indulgent with their ill children.

Some professionals rely heavily on observational methods as an aid to understanding child behavior. Consider, for example, the observational information obtained by a child psychologist regarding a two-year-old's attempts to cope with fear by creating an imaginary playmate.

One afternoon as I entered the door of her grandparents' house, I found my niece just about to leave with her grand uncle. Jan did not greet me, if anything, she looked a little annoyed at my entrance. Still ignoring me, Jan pulled on white cotton gloves and clasped her patent purse in her hand in a fine imitation of a lady leaving for an afternoon engagement. Suddenly, she turned and frowned at something behind her. "No!" she said firmly. "No, Laughing Tiger. You *cannot* come with us for an ice cream cone. You stay right here. But Jannie can come with us. Come along Jannie." And she stepped out the door with her uncle, swinging her purse grandly. Later, the child was asked why the tiger was called a "laughing" tiger. She replied, "He doesn't roar. He never scares children. He doesn't bite. He just laughs." Why could he not go for an ice cream cone? "He has to learn to mind. He can't have everything his own way" [Fraiberg, 1959, p. 16–17].

Selma Fraiberg (1959) reports these observational data in her classic work, *The Magic Years.* Fraiberg suggests that the tiger appeared as a strategy to enable a powerless little girl to deal with her fears of large animals.

There are two steps involved in collecting information from children: observation and interpretation. Observation involves the recording of objective facts about child behavior in various contexts. Interpretation involves choosing explanations (usually derived from theories of child development) of why children behave in specific ways.

*Practice Guideline 7.3: Professionals should avoid relying on hunches or unsubstantiated judgments in citing reasons for children's behavior patterns; a way to gather more accurate information is to observe child behavior directly.*

Classic works on emotional development by Goodenough (1932) and on play behavior by Parten (1942) utilized observation to shed light on social development. In an early study by Goodenough (1932), the researcher instructed the observers to record details regarding a very clear manifestation of anger by a child. The details included immediate cause or provocation for anger and behavior expressed (undirected energy, such as jumping; resistance, such as pouting; and retaliation, such as attack), as well as an assessment of the individual in control and the outcome of the act. A typical observation follows: "A child is drawing his toy wagon when the wheel catches in the rocker of a chair. Any or all of the following forms of behavior may appear. He may stand and scream (undirected energy), he may pull and tug at the wagon or chair (resistance), or he may kick it again and call it names (retaliation). Similarly, the child may respond to a suggestion that it is time to go to bed by throwing himself on the floor and kicking (resistance accompanied by a display of undirected energy, both headings to be numbered 1) or he may run away or scream 'no, no!' (simple resistance), or he may strike or kick at the person making the suggestion (retaliation, likely to be accompanied by some resistant behavior in this instance, but not necessarily so)" (Goodenough, 1932, p. 10).

*Practice Guideline 7.4: Observation of a child in a naturalistic setting can yield insights into that child's characteristic behaviors. As is evident from accounts by parents, professionals, and researchers, behavioral observations provide a rich resource of information to adults.*

Bell's (1968) work clarified the necessity to observe the child as an active agent rather than as simply the "effect" of adult and environmental "causes." Subsequent research has documented the relationship between child characteristics and adult behavior, particularly such attributes as physical attractiveness, temperament, and level of aggression. For example, on average, bright and attractive children are likely to be more popular with peers and with adults. Children may show a lack of predictability in eating and sleeping schedules and may have extreme difficulty making transitions from one environment or activity to another; the "moods" or temperamental qualities of these children may present a challenge to the most patient parent. Thus, the personality characteristics of the child have an observable effect on the parents' behavior.

### Observable Behaviors

Just what exactly do we observe in a child's behavior? As in the examples provided, we can observe the child's actions, words, style, and feelings and interactions.

Observations are richer if we record how a child feels about her actions, details on how she does something as well as the setting, and the frequency and substance of interactions with adults, peers, and objects. Of course, the further we go beyond concrete behavior, the more at risk our observations are of being biased by our own assumptions and expectations (whether of cultural or individual origin). A diverse array of questions may be answered by collecting observational data. The following is an illustrative list of questions that may be explored with observational techniques:

- Does the child show behaviors that indicate fear of specific persons?
- Does the child show secure, positive atttachment to a caregiver?
- Does the child display a familiarity with illegal drugs that is unusual for young children?
- In what ways is the child showing a positive adjustment to a foster home placement (positive mood, stable eating and sleeping patterns)?
- Is the child showing progress in adjustment to school?
- Is the child displaying behaviors indicative of abuse?

All of these questions may be appropriately addressed by gathering data from observational methods. However, there are some types of questions that cannot be answered by naturalistic observation. For example, a child's level of reading comprehension is best assessed by presenting the child with a paragraph followed by a series of questions that test the child's knowledge of the themes and facts within the text. In contrast, the level of a child's social development is best assessed by a series of observations of the child interacting with peers. Alternatively, if the goal is to assess the presence of depression or fear, the best assessment tool may be a checklist of symptoms.

*Physical Development.* One way to measure physical development is to assess the child's level of competence in motor abilities. The first criterion for selecting a sample of behavior is to select a sample of time that will allow a representative number of opportunities for demonstration of motor abilities to occur. Consequently, one must observe the child in a context that promotes motor activity, such as a playground or a backyard. Following is an example of a rating form that can be used during a thirty-minute observation of motor activity in a school setting:

A. List all large muscle activities you observe during a thirty-minute period (such as running, skipping, hopping, climbing, riding a tricycle):

B. Rate the child's competence in each type of activity on a scale from very competent to incompetent:

| 5 | 4 | 3 | 2 | 1 |
|---|---|---|---|---|
| very competent | highly competent | competent | low competence | incompetent |

C. Rate the child's general level of muscle coordination from excellent to poor:

| 5 | 4 | 3 | 2 | 1 |
|---|---|---|---|---|
| excellent | very good | average | poor | very poor |

D. Assess the child's level of overall activity on a scale from very active to inactive:

| 5 | 4 | 3 | 2 | 1 |
|---|---|---|---|---|
| very active | active | medium | low | inactive |

The observer may also plan to observe small motor abilities by following a similar set of procedures. The observer should plan a set of definitions for each point on the scale.

*Cognitive Development.* In contrast to physical development, it is far more difficult to observe cognitive development. Other techniques—such as interacting with the child, seeking information from other adults, and using screening and standardized instruments—are far more productive. However, a common approach to observing cognitive behavior is to use a theoretical framework such as Piaget's as a way of looking for evidence of developmental progression. For example, as discussed in Chapter Eight, the changing forms of a child's play, which became more complex and differentiated as the child develops, reflect newly acquired cognitive abilities. A two-year-old child, for example, who is spontaneously grouping objects according to category (such as shape or function) or performing sequential acts (such as stirring in the pot and then in a cup) is displaying more cognitive sophistication than the child who manipulates one object at a time. An eight-year-old may demonstrate cognitive competence in his or her understanding of the rules of football or chess.

The best way to assess children's cognitive behavior through naturalistic observation is to watch them while they are engaged in different kinds of problem-solving activities, such as putting together a puzzle, building a block structure, or making a drawing. It is equally important, however, to observe the child when she is interacting with a more capable peer or with an adult and receiving assistance or instruction in a problem-solving activity. Is the child able to make use of the assistance to solve the problem? What kind of metacognitive awareness does the child demonstrate? For example, is she aware of what she understands and when she needs more information? Does she "catch on" to the strategies needed to solve the problem? (In such a situation it is, of course, important to pay attention to the nature and quality of the assistance being provided, and to try to assess whether or not it seems appropriate in helping the child accomplish the task at hand.)

*Emotional Behavior.* In the study of emotional behavior, observers have focused on three components: the physiological substrate of emotion, such as blood pressure or adrenalin levels; the subjective experience or cognitive label associated with the experience; and overt expressive behaviors, such as facial expressions, motor behaviors, vocalizations, and gaze behaviors associated with specific emotional experiences (Izard, 1977). Facial expressions appear to be linked to specific sets of conditions in the environment. For example, one would expect to observe sadness and crying when a young child experiences pain or loss. Similarly, research suggests that a mother vocalizing to her infant is a reliable condition for eliciting pleasure. Emotional expression is also characterized by cyclical variation. For example, an episode of crying will usually begin with whimpering, escalating to crying and full-blown wailing if the child is unattended. Each of these emotions is linked to specific functions that are adaptive for the individual.

*Social Behavior.* The observer of social behavior may focus on the interaction of a child with adults or peers in a variety of settings. These may include routines or responses to materials in fantasy play situations. Routines are viewed most typically as behaviors that accomplish goals for the child. These behaviors must be completed on a regular basis to maintain an orderly schedule for the child. Routines involve bathing, eating regular meals, and alternating periods of rest and activity, separation and reunion. In observing a routine, we may want to record the initiator for the behavior, the setting in which the behavior occurs, the behaviors, and the effect that characterizes the interaction. For example, at bedtime one might structure an observation with the following set of questions:

- Who or what was the initiator of the bedtime? Did an adult initiate the routine? Did the child look sleepy? Was it impulsively initiated by the child?
- What is the setting? Is the child in a residential setting or a group home? Is the bedtime an opportunity for leisurely storytelling, or a hurried task? Is the child alone or with other children?
- What are the behaviors of the persons involved in the interaction? If the activity was initiated by an adult, specify the reactions of the child—is the child anxious or relaxed in anticipation of bedtime? Does the child resist in any way? Does the child seem familiar with the routine and proceed easily, or does he appear hesitant? Does the child appear engaged in the process or does he appear distant or removed? Does the child initiate play or appear fearful?

*Practice Guideline 7.5: In seeking information from a child through naturalistic observation, the professional should seek out settings that are familiar to the child and that are likely to elicit the behaviors of interest.*

The following is an example of a narrative record about a child residing in a group home: "As the time for preparation for bedtime was announced, Phillip appeared hesitant and fearful. He continued to play intently at his block rather than beginning to clean up in order to prepare for bed. The child-care worker told him twice before he initiated any activity to put away the block. Then she suggested a bath, and Phillip protested by saying, 'no bath.' When he refused to move into the bathroom, his body became very rigid as she attempted to pick him up. He was crying for about five minutes before the child-care worker was able to soothe Phillip. He stepped hesitantly into the tub, appeared wary of the water toys she had placed there for him. Eventually, he was able to engage himself with the toys in the bath."

*Practice Guideline 7.6: When observing routines, it is important to note that routines are interpreted differently by children and adults. For adults, routines are simply a means to an end. For children, however, routines can be occasions for play and fun, unless the child is anxious or fearful. For example, most parents are familiar with the child's need to use a bathtime for playing with toys, blowing bubbles, spraying water, or almost any activity other than washing.*

Dropping off a child at school is a routine that presents a special opportunity for observing the nature of the child's attachment to the parent or caregiver. If the child shows distress when the parent leaves but is able to be comforted by another adult caregiver, the child is probably positively attached to the parent. If the child is not visibly distressed by the exit of the parent and does not seek the comfort of another caretaker, the child is likely to be insecurely attached. A disorganized pattern of behavior is often associated with abused children. In this pattern the child appears to be disoriented and distracted, unable to focus attention. The child who exhibits this type of behavior is likely to remain upset without deriving comfort from the caretaker (Ainsworth, Blehar, Waters, and Wall, 1978).

***Use of Materials.*** Professionals can also learn about children by observing children's use of materials. One way to organize observations of children's use of materials is to focus on a series of questions (Cohen and Stern, 1958). How does the child handle the clay physically (squeezing, pulling, rolling, slapping, stroking)? What does he do with the clay (make figures, balls, cookies)? How does he use the space available to him? In observing the child's use of blocks we may use the following questions as guides: Which materials are appealing to the child (blocks of assorted sizes, small apparatus such as wheels, windows, ladders, vehicles)? What forms does the child construct? Does the child confine herself to a small space or spread into a larger area? Does the child play alone or in group settings? How is the structure used? In dramatic play? In building?

Most important for the professional seeking to use the child's behavior as a source of information is the style with which the child performs these activities. These include the affect that characterizes the behavior (gleeful, sad, drowsy), body movements (active, quiet), posture (stiff, relaxed, nervous), degree of effort (very little, laborious, moderate, weak), and style (intense, free, happy-go-lucky, distractible). The professional should summarize information collected over several occasions in this way. This information permits us to see patterns of change in the child's behavior over a period of time and to detect themes that may shed light on the origin of a problem behavior.

The following is an example of a summary of a child's overall use of materials. The various items from the records, when brought together in a summary, are easily written up as a sketch of a youngster's use of materials.

> Iris, age 3:
> Materials most used by Iris are sand, mud, crayons, easel paints, finger paints, and water. Just recently she has begun to use the clay to make cakes with cookie cutters or make imprints with any article handy. At first her attitude toward materials was one of indifference, but now she is interested in what she is making and comes to show it to the teachers or children. Paste on her hands at first annoyed her so that she did not want to use it. Today she was pasting and I was delighted to see a paste smear in her hair, and Iris concentrating intently on her creation.
>
> When a new material was introduced she looked at it but did not attempt to play with it. Recently we received train and track, musical bells, new dishes, and started a new project of covering our rug chest. She wanted to be part of each group, except dishes, and went from one thing to another as fast as she could. This was so unusual that we almost gasped in surprise. The part that gave us the biggest thrill was this morning when two children were taken upstairs to cover the chest. Iris went to the toilet and on the way back noticed what

was going on. Going up to a big five-year-old she said, "Give me hammer" in a demanding voice. Teacher said she could have a turn next. Stamping foot, trying to pull the hammer from Lucy's hand, she replied, "Now, I want it right now." Not receiving it instantly, she came down to tell the other teacher her trouble. She did get a turn and then went to the musical bells. While there are still materials she has not touched, such as blocks, setting table with dishes, cars, she is adding to her play more materials each day. Outside equipment is now, and has been from the beginning, used without fear of falling. Every piece of equipment has been used by her, and with good control of muscles, expressions and movement of body indicating extreme satisfaction. The swing is the one place where she always hums and sings [Cohen and Stern, 1958, p. 39].

Running records are excellent sources of information on any type of behavior that involves interaction with others, that is, social behavior. The advantages of such records are enhanced validity and richness; the disadvantage is a decrease in reliability related to the unstructured nature of the observations.

   *Practice Guideline 7.7: Professionals must recognize that reliability and flexibility are inversely related: the more informal, flexible, and naturalistic the strategy for observing, the greater are the problems of reliability.*

## Increasing the Reliability of Observation

How do we increase reliability? There are at least three methods: time sampling, event sampling, and checklists. A behavior record is a narrative description of ongoing behavior sequences that describe the setting, the people who are present, and a stream of ongoing behaviors. The observer records the actions, words, and interactions of children in as much detail as possible. The basic goals are to record what behaviors occur and how they occur.

   *Time Sampling.* Time sampling is a coding scheme in which the observer notes whether a specified behavior occurs within a time interval. For example, a professional may be interested in observing the number of occasions in which a child responded positively to overtures by an adult caregiver. As in a study by George and Main (1979), the professional may observe the child's behavior during a twenty-minute sample in a variety of settings (home, day care, treatment) in order to detect patterns of avoidance or responsivity.

The advantages of a time sampling procedure are three. First, anyone can record behavior in intervals because the technique simply requires paper and pencil. Second, the training demands on the observer are minimal. Finally, reliability is generally high if the behaviors under study are defined clearly. This technique also has limitations. For example, because the time sampling procedure records the occurrence of a behavior only once during the interval, the sampling technique does not permit the study of duration of behavior. A second disadvantage is that the sampling technique does not permit the study of behavior sequences.

*Event Sampling.* In contrast to time sampling, event sampling defines the sample not by the time interval but by the frequency or duration of the event. For example, one may choose to study all observable occasions of aggression that occur within a one-week period. Parents and teachers may collect data on the circumstances under which bouts of aggression tend to occur, such as the time of day, the target of aggression, the goal of aggressive behavior, and the outcome. Over a period of time, the professional should be able to detect patterns in the behavior that may serve as an information base for intervention.

*Checklist.* Another type of observation that is useful to professionals is the checklist. A checklist is a simple device used to record the presence or absence of a symptom. Checklists have been used widely by professionals as a technique to summarize an array of symptoms displayed by a child.

Achenbach's Youth Self-Report, for example, is a checklist designed to measure social adjustment. This test is a 118-item inventory designed to assess reports from children and teenagers about both behavioral problems and competencies. The Youth Self-Report is based on the Achenbach Child Behavior Checklist, developed by Achenbach and Edelbrock (Achenbach, 1978; Achenbach and Edelbrock, 1979) at the National Institute of Mental Health. The checklist is an indicator of both behavioral problems (such as anxiety, low self-esteem, depression) and competencies in the school and social arenas.

Behavior problems are assessed on two dimensions, externalizing and internalizing. Examples of externalizing behaviors for girls from twelve to sixteen are "getting into fights," "talking back," and "hanging around with kids who get in trouble." Examples of items describing internalizing behaviors are "unhappy," "sad or depressed," "withdrawn," and "nauseous." Behavior competencies are also measured in school, social, and school performance categories. Norms for behaviors of 1,300 nonreferred youths and 1,300 referred clinical samples are available for comparison (Achenbach, 1978; Achenbach and Edelbrock, 1979).

Clinicians may choose to develop a unique checklist to catalogue symptoms. The Referral Problems Checklist shown in Exhibit 1 has been used to represent aggressive problems of children participating in a study by Patterson, Reid, Jones, and Conger (1975, p. 28).

*Practice Guideline 7.8: Checklists can be useful to professionals in their attempts to organize a summary of behavior, to detect changes in behaviors following intervention, or to make an assessment of a behavioral adjustment in relation to a set of norms from children of similar ages.*

## Adults' Assumptions About Children's Behavior

Why is it important to uncover personal assumptions about behavior? Observing is a human process involving both the observer and the observed. Therefore, the assumptions and beliefs of the observer influence the quality and quantity of the information gathered. There are distinct advantages and disadvantages associated with the process of observation. The advantages of the observation process are that humans are usually sensitive and perceptive, thereby adding a unique dimension of depth to the quality of information obtained. Professionals engaged in observation are capable of gathering descriptive information on streams of behavior; they can also describe how the behavior was performed or

## Exhibit 1. Referral Problems Checklist.

Over the past six months, have any of the following been problems?
(Interviewer: Check items as needed.)

| | Home | School | Community | Other |
|---|---|---|---|---|
| 1. Aggressiveness | | | | |
| 2. Arguing | | | | |
| 3. Bed-wetting | | | | |
| 4. Competitiveness | | | | |
| 5. Complaining | | | | |
| 6. Crying | | | | |
| 7. Defiance | | | | |
| 8. Destructiveness | | | | |
| 9. Fearfulness (unreasonable) | | | | |
| 10. Fighting with sibs | | | | |
| 11. Fire-setting | | | | |
| 12. Hitting others | | | | |
| 13. Hyperactiveness | | | | |
| 14. Irritableness | | | | |
| 15. Lying | | | | |
| 16. Negativism | | | | |
| 17. Noisiness | | | | |
| 18. Noncomplying | | | | |
| 19. Not eating (at mealtime) | | | | |
| 20. Pants-wetting | | | | |

*Source:* Reprinted with permission from Patterson, Reid, Jones, and
Conger, 1975.

the style that characterized the interaction with other children or
with objects in the environment. The disadvantages of human
observation are that human beings, as opposed to standardized tests,
tend to be inconsistent, nonstandard, and unreliable in their observations. In other words, personal assumptions may bias observations. Naturalistic observation provides an opportunity for insight
while it opens the door to bias. Systematic observation provides

precision, but its results, while technically accurate, may miss the point of a child's behavior.

There are many reasons that observational data show a lack of reliability. Observing is rarely a neutral process. The observer's expectations may easily influence the observation process, either consciously or unconsciously. There are at least two ways in which expectations may influence observational records. First, individual differences among children may result in a systematic pattern of expectations from observers. Second, the behavior being studied may be particularly salient to an observer.

Systematic individual differences among children may result in a biased sample of behaviors. The most common type of error in observing involves systematic omission of certain types of behaviors (failing to record behaviors when they actually occur). The difference between the accounts of two observers is illustrated in this excerpt from the research of Yarrow and Waxler (1979, p. 41):

> *Observer A:* "Come on, Johnny." Johnny slows his pedaling of the trike he is riding. More insistently, "Come John, let's chase Bobby." Johnny frowns. "Aw, come on." With this command, Johnny jumps off the trike and chases after Bobby with Bart.

> *Observer B:* Bart calls urgently to Johnny, "Come on, come on, let's chase Bobby." After some hesitation, Johnny gets off his trike and runs to join Bart, follows after him, after Bobby.

In this example, it is clear that both observers recorded similar behaviors in a given incident of toddler play. However, the level of detail in the observers' recordings of the incident differs. This is a common occurrence among observers. As a consequence, it is difficult to assume a pattern exists, since behaviors may have been missed. On the other hand, when a strong pattern is apparent from the data, one may have greater confidence about this pattern. It is interesting to note that when one asks about the extent of agreement between observers on the sheer number of occurrences contained in the excerpts above, the reliability increases. Therefore, the records that were less reliable regarding a sequential order of episodes of behavior now showed greater reliability for number of occurrences. This is an example of the limits on the statements one can make on the basis of the data.

There are other sources of systematic error in observation as well. Studies suggest that observers may have specific behaviors prominent in their minds. For example, observers are likely to have gender-based expectations for appropriate behavior that affect what they see and record. The reliability of observer records on boys regarding number of aggressive contacts is higher than the reliability for girls. In contrast, observers appear to be consistently more reliable when recording incidents of expression of warmth among girls. A similar pattern is evident for observer expectations for child-care professionals who interact differently with boys and girls. In a study of the number of cold receptions of children by nursery school teachers, observers tended to be more reliable for boys than for girls (Yarrow and Waxler, 1979).

This error may be related, in part, to the expectations that observers hold for individual children. It may be that when an observer labels a particular child "aggressive" or "warm," an expectation is set up for future behavior from the child. This trend may be especially true for observers who focus on gender differences in levels of aggression and prosocial behavior among boys and girls. Cultural differences can have a similar effect. For example, in the individualistic culture of the United States, few studies observe cooperative behavior; in the collective societies of Eastern Europe, cooperative behavior is the major focus of study.

### Influence of Context on Behavior Sampling

Behavior is shaped by the context in which it is embedded. Under some circumstances, the context is critical in producing the behavior under study. For example, the playground is essential in providing the conditions necessary to observe motor activity. Similarly, the expression of fear appears to be less likely when a toy or game is used as a mediator in the interaction (Emde, Gaensbauer, and Harmon, 1976).

Further empirical data in support of the differing effects of context were cited in a study by Yarrow and Waxler (1979). These researchers compared the observations of children and teachers in a variety of settings, including indoor play, outdoor play, and lunch. The data suggest that the correlations among social behaviors across settings were very low. Such findings underscore the fragility of observational data and point to the need for additional research on the effects of special settings (such as the courtroom) on child behavior.

*Practice Guideline 7.9: Behavior is very much context-specific; we must not be too eager to expect generalization of behavior across settings.*

## Qualities of a Good Observer

Most people have the potential to become good observers, particularly professionals who have valuable years of experience with children. Observers are most effective when they are able to remain unbiased, inconspicuous, and unobtrusive, interested and motivated but not intrusive.

Researchers have identified and summarized five characteristics of a good observer (Yarrow and Waxler, 1979). First, the observer must be able to sustain attention without tuning out. Because the task of observation requires close attention to similar behaviors, perhaps over an extended period of time, observers must be skilled at maintaining attention without losing the ability to distinguish nuances in behaviors. Second, the observer must be capable of discerning specific kinds of behavior in an array of stimuli presented to them. Frequently, observers are professionals who work directly with children in group settings, such as a preschool, a hospital ward, or a therapy group. In these settings, the professional may be confronted with the challenge of observing behaviors amid much environmental stimulation. Third, a person who is concerned about details and order is likely to be a good observer. Even when presented with a high level of stimulation, the person who is alert to detail can take down details and impose order at a later time. Fourth, a person who is aware of her own personal biases and assumptions about behavior will recognize these biases and work toward objectivity in observing facts about children's behavior. Finally, a person who tends to approach life with an analytical and introspective style is likely to be a good observer. Such a person is skilled at observing behavior as a way of life.

## Conclusions

The primary purpose of observation is to seek information from children's spontaneous behavior. It is particularly well suited to gathering information about young children who have difficulty verbalizing. While adult bias may affect the interpretation of what is observed, experience and self-awareness can minimize its influence. According to the matrix of competence and orientation presented in Chapter One, here we have been concerned most immediately with adult competence (with issues and orientation lurking in the background as always). We turn next to a more detailed look at a special category of observation, that of the child at play. As we have underscored at several points in this chapter, play offers a special window into the child's life.

CHAPTER 8

# Communicating Through Play and Storytelling

Information gained from and about children through their play is used increasingly by professionals concerned with children and families, such as child welfare workers in their investigations of abuse and violence, judges and officers of the court in their decisions about child custody and other matters regulating parent-child relationships, and teachers in preschool settings (Haynes-Seman and Hart, 1987; Herzog, 1986; Bresee, Stearns, Bess, and Packer, 1986).

Adults use play and stories to learn about children in three ways. The first is to assess the developmental level and competence of the child. Play observations can complement the information gained from other techniques used to study children. Although play and stories provide information about children of all ages, the play of infants and preschoolers is a particularly powerful tool for assessing their cognitive, social, and physical development. For this reason our focus is on children under six years of age. Stories and play also provide information about the inner life of the child. How children feel about the people and events in their lives and how they perceive the world about them are often interpreted by adults on the basis of play observations and written or dictated stories.

Finally, adults use play and stories to communicate with children about stressful experiences in their lives. Children who have been physically or sexually abused, particularly by parents or relatives, may have difficulty talking about it. Children who have witnessed violence in their homes or neighborhoods may be too frightened to discuss it coherently. Children who have been abducted by an estranged parent may feel too conflicted about their loyalties to both parents to testify against the abductor. In less dramatic situations, play and stories can also reveal how a child feels about a camp experience, a new school, or the birth of a sibling, serving either as an aid to verbal communication or as a substitute for it.

Over the years, theorists and researchers have defined play in many different ways (Millar, 1969; Singer, 1973). In the 1800s, Spencer explained play as the method children use to rid themselves of energy not expended in seeking food or maintaining life (Millar, 1969). This viewpoint has come to be known as the "surplus energy" theory, and its remnants can still be seen in the use of recess in elementary schools to allow children to blow off steam after sitting still during their lessons. At the turn of the century, Hall defined play from an evolutionary viewpoint, describing children's games as recapitulations of the life of primitive man (Millar, 1969). Play with water reflected the time when people lived near the sea and depended on it for a living. In the late nineteenth century, Karl Groos proposed that in play the young of all species (or at least all mammals) practiced the skills needed for survival as adults (Millar, 1969). Kittens chasing balls of yarn developed skills needed to catch mice for food.

Among contemporary students of play, differences still prevail concerning its definition, but Garvey's five criteria define play in a way that is comprehensive and practical (Garvey, 1977). Play is pleasurable or has a positive value for the player. It is intrinsically motivated with no external purpose or required outcome. It is spontaneous and not compulsory. It requires active participation by the player. And it has a definite relationship to what is "not play," that is, to the real world.

## Play and Development

In the study of play, the work of Jean Piaget (1952, 1962) stands out. Through observation of his own three children, he demonstrated how changes in their play reflected the growth of their intelligence from the sensorimotor period through the use of symbols to operational thought.

Play reflects a growing child's increasing competence. When we observe infants at play, we see changing forms that become more complex and differentiated as children grow and acquire new abilities. In play, children practice over and over again what they have learned.

Several studies have established a developmental sequence of infant play behavior (for example, Inhelder, 1971; Sinclair, 1970; Fenson, Kagan, Kearsley, and Zelazo, 1976; Rosenblatt, 1977). At six months, the child manipulates one object at a time. As the child develops, his play gradually includes the use of two or more objects, culturally appropriate associations between objects (placing the cup on the saucer), the grouping of objects according to category (such as shape or function), and the performance of sequential acts (stirring in the pot and then in the bowl).

Symbolic or pretend play emerges in the toddler stage, somewhere between sixteen and twenty-four months. It begins with the child imitating her own behavior and then the behavior of others. As imitative behavior becomes separated from the original perceived behavior it represents the child's first manifestation of the use of symbols.

Although it is seen in the toddler, pretend play is the hallmark of the preschool years. Increasing complexity and improved organization are observed in the play of children over three years of age. Both children's play and stories become more coherent and recognizable themes appear. Some observers believe that symbolic play may help children develop the ability to understand the difference between appearance and reality.

*Practice Guideline 8.1: Through their pretend play, preschool children gain an increasing ability to manipulate fantasy and reality. They know the difference bewteen pretense and reality, particularly if it concerns their own activity, and if they are in a benign environment and not under stress.*

Children dealing with strong feelings may regress in their ability to make this distinction. An example of this kind of temporary regression is referred to by Gould (1972, pp. 77–84) as "fluctuating certainty": a school-age child knows that her friend who is playing at being a witch is really a little girl, but she nonetheless cannot protect herself from being frightened. Her certainty about reality is shaken by the strength of the feelings aroused during the game. This kind of regression can be observed when playing monsters gets out of hand and children become genuinely scared. It can happen as the result of deliberate efforts by adults to terrorize children or "accidentally" in the course of teasing children (Garbarino, Guttmann, and Seeley, 1986). In less traumatic situations a child can regress, as in the case of the preschool child who usually engages in complex, sociodramatic play but for a time after the birth of a sibling consistently takes the role of "baby" in solitary play.

*Practice Guideline 8.2: When we use play observations to assess physical, cognitive, or emotional status, we must be aware of the stresses or traumas a child may be encountering at that particular time.*

Just as adults talk about a trauma over and over again in an effort to come to grips with it, so children play out their traumatic experiences (Erikson, 1950). However, this does not mean that all of children's play or stories are a direct reflection of reality. Young children have a very rich fantasy life that is often expressed in their play and stories. They use symbols to express both their fantasies and the realities of their lives.

*Practice Guideline 8.3: Children often play out or tell stories that reflect a need to master an overwhelming or traumatic experience.*

The games of school-age children reflect their growing intellect and their ability to deal with many factors at the same time. It is at this time that children turn to more structured games that allow them to practice living within the confines of more explicit rules—a task shared by adults in all cultures. Although games epitomize the play of school-age children, pretend play and fantasy remain an important part of their lives. We can still see fantasy in the stories they weave about their drawings or the models they build.

## Communicating Through Play

Play has enhanced our understanding of how children develop emotionally and how they perceive and interpret the people and events in their lives. Because play can reflect a child's inner world, it is often used in both diagnostic and therapeutic work with children as a substitute for spoken language. It is accepted that verbal communication is not always the best way to gain information from or about a young child. The language of children, particularly young children, is often not adequate to express what they really know and feel. For example, hospitalized children are often unable to ask questions about their condition or about the medical procedures to which they are subjected. Yet in the hospital playroom, in the presence of supportive and accepting adults, they are able to play out some of their fears and concerns and to discuss what is happening to them.

*Practice Guideline 8.4: When children are in a state of anxiety because of illness or traumatic experiences or because they have been subjected to ongoing deleterious situations, communication becomes even more difficult and unreliable; play can complement language as adult and child seek to communicate with each other.*

The mutual misunderstandings that can result from a conversation between a child and an uninstructed adult are endless. Recall the cartoon depicting a child imagining his father sitting at his office desk, tied to the chair, while his mother explains that Daddy is not home for dinner because he is "tied up at the office." A child's limited vocabulary, a setting in which the child is not comfortable, a new relationship between child and adult, an adult's lack of understanding about how a child of a particular age thinks are only some of the aspects of verbal exchange that can cause confusion in an adult-child conversation. Play can help.

Another important reason for employing play as a medium for communicating with children and gaining information about them is that play allows children to deal with anxiety-producing or sensitive material as if it were someone else's problem (Bateson, 1976). Through play, children can express their wishes and needs, their thoughts and feelings, as if those feelings and wishes did not really belong to them. Sometimes they attribute their unacceptable feelings to dolls or stuffed animals; sometimes they assign them to playmates.

*Practice Guideline 8.5: When children can express feelings and thoughts as if they belonged to someone else, they can reduce their fear of the consequences associated with them.*

Preschool children are particularly sensitive to negative feelings about people close to them. Because young children often confuse thought with action, they are vulnerable to anxiety about their bad feelings or wishes. The little boy who is angry with his father and wishes he would go away can be confused about whether his wish will really come true. That is why, for example, young children who have lost a parent through death or divorce may feel responsible for the loss even though in reality it has nothing to do with them (Wallerstein and Kelly, 1980).

Denying ownership of threatening or distasteful ideas is accomplished in play through the use of symbols. Symbolic play can take several forms. It can substitute one object for another or use an object to represent a person. The player can take on a different role or transfer feelings or emotional states from one player to another, either real or pretend. The little girl who plays that the bad mommy sends the baby away does not have to acknowledge that it is really she who wants to get rid of her sibling. The little boy who pretends that he destroys the monster may not realize that he is angry with his father for being drunk and abusive to his mother.

*Practice Guideline 8.6: In play situations, children can recall unpleasant events more easily because they can pretend the occurrences happened to other characters, such as stuffed animals or dolls.*

Play also affords children the opportunity to reverse the roles they play in reality. Instead of being passive and helpless, they can take on active roles. They can imagine themselves as the perpetrators rather than the victims. In play, children can pretend to do to others that which has been done to them. The child can pretend to be the doctor giving the shot, instead of the frightened patient receiving it. The opportunity to reverse roles in play entices children to approach both real and imagined themes that might be too frightening or distressing to talk about directly with an adult.

Through symbolic play, children can express ideas and feelings that would ordinarily be taboo (Peller, 1978). In their play children use metaphors and pretense to help distance themselves from the content and from the characters being enacted. Distancing oneself from the moment affords a feeling of safety and allows children to play out problematical material more easily.

Distancing in play is most evident when children express their feelings about people who are important to them. The relationships between children and their parents, siblings, relatives, friends, teachers, and neighbors are central to their emotional status. If we are to explore this aspect of their existence, children must be able to express their feelings about the important people in their lives, people they depend on for sustenance, for security, for love, and for emotional support. When their feelings are negative, children may be reluctant to talk about them. They may even block them out, so that they remain unconscious and unavailable. This response occurs most often when the feelings concern parents and other caregivers who are responsible for the children. A mother in a shelter for homeless families showed the child-care worker a story that her five-year-old daughter had dictated about a little girl who bought her mother a present. The worker was surprised because the same child had told the worker a story about a bunny who hated her mother for making her daddy go away. The worker decided that the child was able to use stories to express her negative feelings to the worker but had to reassure her mother about her love.

Adults are powerful figures in the lives of children and are often perceived by children as omnipotent and omnipresent. Putting deep-rooted feelings about such important people into words is difficult enough, but children have an added burden when trying to tell about conflicting or ambivalent feelings. Even adults find it hard to accept their feelings of both love and hate directed toward meaningful people in their lives. So it is easy to understand that children can be confused and inarticulate when they experience such conflicting emotions (Mahler, Pine, and Bergman, 1975).

Ted may hate his mother for always scolding and embarrassing him in front of his friends, but he also loves her, a love based on their early relationship when she took care of him. When asked about his feelings, Ted finds it impossible to express such complex and conflicting emotions, but play allows him to communicate with adults about his feelings.

Anna Freud (1950), Melanie Klein (1949), and other early psychoanalysts were the first to substitute play for verbal communication in diagnosing and treating their young patients. Although they differed in their approach to child analysis, both Freud and Klein based their work with children on early psychoanalytic theory. Since that time, psychoanalysts and other practitioners, such as Virginia M. Axline (1939) and Clark E. Moustakis (1953), have continued to use play with children as a therapeutic tool, as a means of studying children, and as an avenue for communication. It has become the standard in working with children.

### Communicating Through Storytelling

Storytelling is another means of learning about children's experiences and their emotional states. Storytelling has been tried with preschoolers (Paley, 1981, 1986), but it is more likely to be successful with older, more verbal children. Eliciting stories from children is often combined with other activities, particularly with drawing. Winnicott (1971) invented the squiggle-drawing method, in which he engaged a patient in making up stories about the doodles each of them produced. Claman (1980) combined Winnicott's technique with the mutual storytelling method of Gardner (1971) to devise the squiggle-drawing game. Gardner participated with his patients in storytelling. After the child told a story, Gardner told the same story but with a different, healthier ending. In this way, he helped the child see alternative solutions to his problems without the child's having to own up to his difficulties or feelings.

In his squiggle-drawing game, Claman (1980) alternates with his child patient in making a drawing out of a squiggle, telling a story about the drawing, and answering questions the other party may ask about the story. In this way, Claman is able to give direction to the stories being told. Other therapists have elicited stories about children's drawings or paintings, while some have simply asked children to produce a made-up story. Like play, the exact use of storytelling differs from one therapist or inquirer to another. Some therapists or diagnosticians frame the story to elicit information about a particular subject. Others prefer not to influence the child's efforts, so that the production represents only the child's thoughts and feelings, and the subject matter is freely chosen.

Storytelling has also been used as a group activity. Alice Eberhart (1979) reports on group storytelling as a part of a therapeutic program for preschool youngsters and in family therapy sessions at the Child Development Center of Topeka State Hospital. In that setting the purpose of storytelling is therapeutic, but storytelling might very well be tried in situations where it is necessary to elicit information from a group of children about a shared experience.

As a technique for communicating with children, storytelling shares with play the advantage of encouraging children to deal with information or feelings that may cause guilt, shame, anxiety, or fear. Some of the mechanisms that support communication are the same in storytelling as in play. Storytelling allows children to distance themselves from frightening or unacceptable emotions by attributing them to characters in their stories. When either external prohibitions or internal inhibitions forbid children to acknowledge or express their feelings or discuss the events in their lives, the characters, be they people or animals, can do, say, think, or feel much that a child would not be allowed.

Through the fantasy woven into their stories, children can make good things happen. They can get even with people who have wronged them, identify with the daredevil hero or heroine, and give a fair share to those who deserve it. However, like fairy tales, the stories children tell also include unpleasant things. Fairy tales do not avoid the difficult. Rather, they give children the message that meeting challenges head-on is the way to overcome hardship and to be victorious. According to Bettelheim (1976), fairy tales help children understand themselves and others and thereby give meaning to their lives. Fairy tales do, however, have happy endings, something lacking in many of the stories told by children who are in stressful situations. The little boy who tells his worker a story about his uncle getting shot and blood pouring down his shirt is not making up a fairy tale with a happy ending. Rather, he is telling about something he has seen, and is perhaps soliciting help in dealing with it.

*Practice Guideline 8.7: Sharing in the telling of stories can provide adults with an opportunity to talk to children about their feelings or the frightening events in their lives. The adults can communicate through the characters in the story rather than directly to the child. Questions can be asked about what happened to "the little girl" in the story instead of what happened to the child being questioned.*

## The Role of the Adult

In using both play and storytelling to gain information from and about children, it is the adult seeking the information who sets the stage and frames the interactions that take place between adult and child. The way in which practitioners encourage children to play or tell stories may vary from very open situations to highly structured play interviews.

In some situations children are allowed to explore freely, to select toys from a large and varied assortment, and to make up their own games. This kind of experience is often provided when a therapist is trying to determine the cause or the severity of a child's emotional problems. In such a diagnostic situation, it is important to allow the child to "tell" the therapist through play how he or she perceives the problem. In other words, the emphasis is on the child's ideas, and efforts are made by the therapist to avoid projecting his or her own biases or predilections onto the scene.

In his book *Childhood and Society*, Erik Erikson (1950) describes two play sessions with Mary, a three-year-old, who has been brought to his office by her mother for an evaluation of her recent disturbing behavior. Without words, the patient and therapist communicate with each other on many levels. The child is able to express the underlying fears that are the cause of her nightmares and odd behavior, and the therapist is able to use that information, along with facts given by the mother, to help the parents supply the support necessary for the child to cope with her fears. These play sequences illustrate well the unstructured approach to evaluation and diagnosis.

At the other end of the range of possible play settings is one in which the adult is trying to communicate with a child through play about a very specific event or set of circumstances. If a social worker is trying to determine if a child has been sexually molested and is not able to see the child more than once or twice, it may be necessary to direct the child's attention to the question at hand. In such circumstances it is more effective to provide a limited number of toys, including a set of dolls, and to structure a game that mirrors the situation to be evaluated. It is in situations such as these that sexually detailed dolls can be of benefit in sorting out the facts of a situation and in determining the child's perception of what happened. Sexually detailed dolls are most often used as an aid when an adult is interviewing a child, rather than in a play session. However, their use in interviews with children—particularly when the results of those interviews are the basis of court evidence—is still being debated ("Debate Forum," 1988). This issue is discussed in more detail in Chapter Nine.

The adult can provide a variety of play situations, ranging from the most unstructured to the most structured. Some practitioners include sand, water, clay, soft toys, and pillows as props. These items encourage the expression of feelings more than ideas. Anna Freud (1950) uses the example of a child who comes to the therapist's office after an appointment with the dentist and proceeds to cut up and tear paper. The child's anger at the dentist expresses itself in a generalized display of aggression, rather than in a game that mirrors the event in the child's life that caused the anger— namely, the visit to the dentist.

*Practice Guideline 8.8: When it is important to understand a child's feelings about a situation, unstructured materials allow children to express affect without having to concern themselves with ideas.*

But there is more to consider than the setting and the toys when engaging children in diagnostic or information-getting situations. The character of adult-child interactions is of paramount importance in these circumstances. Obviously, it is advantageous for adult and child to have a relationship built on trust.

But building trust takes time. Often children need to test the adult. They have to find out if the adult will still like them even if they show their worst behavior. Children also test to see if the adult is able to protect them from themselves and from others. This does not mean that play sessions cannot be meaningful and fruitful outside an established relationship.

The example cited above concerning Erikson's young patient Mary illustrates well the potency of an initial interchange between a small child and a sensitive, knowledgeable adult. Winnicott invented his squiggle game to be used specifically within a limited number of interviews (Winnicott, 1971).

*Practice Guideline 8.9: When children are able to trust adults and to feel protected by them, they are more willing to open up and express their innermost thoughts through play or storytelling.*

Unfortunately, many people attempting to communicate with children through play and storytelling are not as sensitive or as knowledgeable as they need to be. This is why we emphasize the importance of knowledge of normal child development and experience with children, rather than training in a fixed set of techniques, as the foundation for the successful gathering of information from children.

When unskilled adults deal with children in trouble, they often make mistakes. One of the most common is not understanding children's communications. The dangers of interpreting and misinterpreting children's play and stories fall into two general areas. The first is that the adult misreads the message in the child's play or stories and is left with false information. A typical example is the little girl in a preschool group who is spanking her doll and calling it bad. Teachers might interpret this play as evidence that the child is physically and psychologically punished at home. Although this play may reflect the child's home life, it may also reflect the child's inner concerns about being bad. The play may be more indicative of the child's developing conscience, and her message may be one calling for more control from the adults so that she does not have to be so harsh with herself. Trying to determine whether a child's play or story reflects real-life experiences or inner turmoil can be a most difficult task.

*Practice Guideline 8.10: When children present disturbing images in play or in stories, adults should seek to learn more about the child's life circumstances and experiences through further contact with the child and with adults who know the child well; treat disclosures in play and storytelling as hypotheses for further study and testing, rather than as concrete conclusions or explicit narrative accounts of experience.*

The second common error adults make in information-gathering sessions with children is to interpret indiscriminately the unconscious meaning of their play or stories. Without knowing the details of a child's life, including the inner psychic structure and the external circumstances, it can be harmful to interpret the meaning of either play or stories. If the ideas or feelings expressed are unconscious and the child is unaware of them, making them explicit without preparation and in a nonsupportive context can interfere with a child's attempts to cope with a difficult situation.

The dangers of premature and inappropriate interpretations are often seen when adults are dealing with children in crisis. In an effort to encourage expression of emotion or to help the child open up to the adult, the practitioner rushes ahead and unwittingly breaks down the child's defenses. An important tenet of crisis counseling is to help the person in crisis maintain the defenses that are still functioning. Van Ornum and Mordock (1983) caution against insisting that a child discuss something before he is ready. For example, a child may keep changing the subject when questioned by an adult about his parents' divorce. Instead of saying to the child, "Every time I mention your parents' divorce, you change the subject," the adult can support the child's attempts to handle his feelings by saying, "I know you try to think about pleasant things whenever you start worrying about your Mom and Dad. That's a good way to make yourself feel better." When we seek information from children we face ethical issues, particularly when there is the danger of making children aware of unconscious thoughts or feelings.

*Practice Guideline 8.11: It is only in the context of a safe, supportive, ongoing relationship with a knowledgeable and skilled practitioner that a child should have unconscious material interpreted and made conscious.*

Although we look to play to learn about children, many of the most severely traumatized and disturbed children are unable to play at all, or at least in a fashion that communicates to adults (Gould, 1972; Schaefer, 1976). Stressful situations can cause children to be so inhibited that they are unable to express themselves in any medium, including play or storytelling. Further, growing up in chronically disorganized families can produce children who are themselves disorganized, unable to focus on play or storytelling or to produce a coherent scenario.

*Practice Guideline 8.12: Trying to use play and storytelling with children who are severely disturbed or disorganized is likely to be ineffective, particularly if there is insufficient time to build a relationship with the child and teach the child how to play or tell a coherent story.*

## Guides to the Use of Play and Stories

Even when children are capable of productive, organized play or storytelling, there is no simple guide to separating their fantasies from reality. But there are some rules of thumb that give direction to the efforts of those whose job it is to gain information from and about children.

Older children can be interviewed to supplement the use of play or storytelling. Interviews allow the adult to discover the child's perception of his own play or story, or at least the child's "public interpretation," and help the adult understand what motivated a particular fantasy. Combining interviews with play observations or storytelling is like asking an adult patient to talk about a dream. The associations make clear the specific meaning the dream has to that patient.

Older children can also relate facts about their current situation and provide some history. But with younger or nonverbal children, it is essential to gain information from outside sources. In the example of Erikson's young patient Mary, specific information about the child's infancy and the current family situation was necessary in order to make a diagnosis; that information came from the child's mother.

Practice Guideline 8.13: *The most important principle is that neither play nor stories can be used alone to determine the facts of a child's life nor to assess development; other information is essential to making an assessment or establishing the truth about a situation.*

In observing children's play or working with their stories, it is important to look for recurring themes. Recurrent themes alert the adult to possible areas of concern for the child. They can represent anxiety about real-life events or struggles about unresolved intrapsychic conflicts. Because the themes may take different forms, using different characters or different situations, it is important to identify the underlying message. For example, a child may repeatedly use the theme of a large creature hurting a smaller one to represent his fears of his father. The characters may change from animals to birds to people, and the sequence of events and the settings may change, but the theme remains the same.

Practice Guideline 8.14: *It is important to note the repetition of a theme, for it indicates that the theme has special meaning for the child.*

Adults should also be alert to sudden disruption in a child's play. Erikson discusses this phenomenon in *Childhood and Society* (1950) and attributes it to the child's being overwhelmed by the impulses being expressed. Play disruption signals the breaking down of defenses and therefore of the ability to organize and express, even nonverbally, the ideas or feelings aroused by the situation. Play disruption does not, however, make clear whether the disintegration of defenses is related to memories of real experiences or to the impact of inner emotion.

## Conclusions

Because children express themselves best through their play and stories, adults can learn much about a child by using these avenues for observation and communication. They provide information that tells us a great deal about a particular child and how that child sees the world. That information has to be interpreted by the adults using it, and the accuracy and exact meaning of the interpretation depend on the skill of those adults. This does not negate the value play and stories have in providing information about the child. Play and stories are an important part of the evidence an adult needs to accurately assess a child's competence or state of mind, or to ascertain the truth about particular events in the child's life. However, that evidence must be used judiciously and with caution.

The information children give us through their play and stories has to be interpreted in light of their developmental status, their current life situation, and their history. In other words, children must be viewed within the context of their total life experience. The onus is on the adults to make intelligent and sensitive use of what children tell them through their play and stories. And the adults must depend on their knowledge and skill to use that information wisely.

CHAPTER 9

# Guidelines
# for Interviewing Children

Interviewing is an important way for adults for obtain information from children. In legal proceedings, verbal testimony is essential to tie physical evidence of child abuse to a perpetrator. In research, asking children to solve problems allows us a glimpse of their cognitive processes. In therapy, interviewing is combined with observation and other kinds of interaction to piece together a picture of the child's inner world.

With the help of skilled professionals, even young children can provide rich verbal accounts of their own experiences and of their understanding of the world around them. It must be remembered, however, that interviewing is an adult form of inquiry. Traditional methods of interviewing assume that the interview participants share an adultlike level of linguistic and interactive competence. Since children vary in their linguistic and interactive competence, and since the language ability of young children is essentially different from that of adults, it cannot be assumed that interviewing methods suitable for adults will work with children. The adult interviewer must be conscious of the competence of the child and respond accordingly. It is also important to know how to interpret interview results. They are not necessarily self-evident—an interview record may not straightforwardly reflect what happened, how a child feels, or what a child knows. It is, therefore, also important to know how to compile and evaluate the interview record. This chapter addresses these issues in turn.

## The Interviewing Process

Most of what we know about interviewing we know from interviewing adults, from our experience being interviewed as adults, and from research done on adult interviewing. The assessment of psychopathology in children, for instance, traditionally depended on interviews with parents or other adults. Treating the child as an informant about her own feelings, behaviors, abilities, and social relationships is a relatively recent phenomenon (Edelbrock and Costello, 1984).

Young, O'Brien, Gutterman, and Cohen (1987) have identified twenty-six common sources of interview misinformation. They include the structure of the interview instrument itself (for example, the sequence of questions, ambiguous or vague terms), the respondent (memory lapses, the experience of questioning as stressful), and the interviewer (variable emotional intensity, recording errors). More than half of the factors listed by Young as problems in clinical interviews of adults are also commonly mentioned in connection with interviewing children; Table 1 presents these common factors.

Implicit in the problems presented in Table 1 are common underlying assumptions about the simplicity of the communicative process in the interview (see Mishler, 1986; Brenner, 1981; Cicourel, 1981, 1982, 1986; Dexter, 1970; Mehan, 1979). This is seen, for instance, in the location of difficulties in three categories when the relationship between the interviewer and the respondent is probably the most important determinant of the interview's outcome (Parker, 1984). The core assumption is that the interview is a series of psychologically independent and discrete stimulus-response pairs, where the stimulus is the question and the response the answer.

The stimulus-response model of interviewing is inadequate on two counts. First, careful studies based on actual recordings of "standardized" interviews indicate that it is extremely difficult to standardize interviews—to ask the questions exactly as they are written, to completely control other interviewer effects, to eliminate all contextual references, all irrelevant "stimuli" (Mishler, 1986). In fact, even proponents of this approach to interviewing admit that

Table 1. Common Sources of Interview Misinformation.

| Structure of the Interview | Respondent | Interviewer |
|---|---|---|
| Lack of specificity in the question | Need to give socially desirable answers | Interviewer characteristics[a] |
| Concepts of question are complex and multidimensional[a] | Lack of understanding of the questions[a] | Preferences and biases[a] |
| Sequence of questions | Memory lapses[a] | Variable emotional intensity[a] |
| Number of questions[a] | Experience of questioning as stressful[a] | Variable verbal facility |
| Question structure[a] | No true opinion[a] | Variable understanding of the questions |
| Unwarranted assumptions in the question | Differing emotional intensity among respondents | Recording errors |
| More than one question embedded in a single question | Variable perceptions of the situation and purpose[a] | |
| Sensitive or threatening element in the questions[a] | Timing of interview | |
| Wording of the question: Inexact terms Ambiguous or vague terms Complex terms and sentences[a] Biased words | | |

[a]Commonly cited in interviews with children.
*Source:* Young, O'Brien, Gutterman, and Cohen, 1987, p. 614.

from 25 to 40 percent of the questions asked contain or are accompanied by clarifying remarks and other interviewer effects (Bradburn, Sudman, and Associates, 1979; Cannell, Lawson, and Hausser, 1975; Brenner, 1982; Dijkstra, van der Veen, and van der Zouwen, 1985).

Second, even if it were possible to specify the stimulus by controlling the delivery of the interview question, the nature of the response would not necessarily be clear. Interview responses have meaning and as such are subject to the same constraints as all meaningful conversation.

*Practice Guideline 9.1: Responses are influenced not only by the question that immediately precedes them but by several pre-*

*ceding questions and answers. Responses are influenced by what the respondent thinks the questions mean, what he feels the interviewer will accept as an answer, and what he thinks will be the consequences of providing the information.*

Recent studies suggest that it is more valid to think of interviews as a special kind of speech event (Erickson and Schultz, 1982; Mishler, 1986; Briggs, 1986). Speech events are "activities, or aspects of activities, that are directly governed by rules for the use of speech" (Hymes, 1967, p. 19). They imply "a set of social relationships enacted about a set of schemata in relation to some communicative goal" (Gumperz, 1982, p. 166). One advantage of the speech event model is that it describes the nature of communication in the interview situation. Interview communication requires the coordination of numerous factors, ranging from the meanings of words to the social roles of the participants in the wider society. The ability to perform well in an interview is a form of communicative competence.

Communicative competence is "knowing which expressions can be used under what circumstances to convey which meanings" (Hymes, 1971a, 1971b; Briggs, 1986, p. 43). Communicative competence requires not only linguistic competence but also an understanding of the social and cultural rules for using language. For example, it would generally not be appropriate to interrupt a priest saying mass, even if one's English were flawless. Similarly, in some cultures it would be equally rude for a child to contradict an adult (a fact that could prove critical in a courtroom cross-examination).

In many interview situations much of the discussion has to do with clarifying the range and type of response the interviewer wants and negotiating the difference between the interviewer's desire for information and the willingness of the respondent to provide it (Briggs, 1986). Communicating in this way requires a form of competence peculiar to interviews and employs a range of linguistic and nonlinguistic devices.

For example, in medical histories the length of responses is regulated by the rapid pacing of questions (Mishler, 1984). In counseling interviews the clinician may gently restate the question, sending the message that although he will listen to whatever the client wishes to say, the last thing the client said was not quite what he was looking for, and the client should try again to respond to the question (Mishler, 1986). In oral examinations questioners often use the next question to cut off the student as soon as it is clear that she knows the answer.

*Practice Guideline 9.2: Clarification and negotiation of the interview's goals and rules is carried out not only in words, but also in gesture, posture, facial expression, tone of voice, and rate of speech.*

Whether conducted with adults or children, interviews are highly complex social interactions. A successful interview requires the coordination of a large number of social and linguistic elements. Any of these elements can, if neglected, either prevent the interview from proceeding or render the results of the interview misleading or useless.

*Practice Guideline 9.3: The interviewer, who frames the situation and largely controls the interaction, cannot assume that the respondent's communicative competence does or can match his. Interviewers are responsible for adjusting their interviewing methods to the communicative competencies of the respondent.*

## Children's Communicative Competencies and Limitations

If the interviewer is to keep in mind the communicative competence of children, she must know which aspects of their communicative competence are relevant to interviews. We can point to four: the child's psychological competence to be interviewed, his state of cognitive development, his language development, and his level of socialization.

*Psychological Competence.* As we saw in Chapter Two, an understanding of the ways in which self-esteem and coping mechanisms motivate children's behavior is as necessary to information seeking as is an understanding of their other capacities. A child's ability to give statements or information will depend on the strength of his need to be competent and please the adult inter-

viewer as well as his need to defend himself from difficult consequences or feelings.

Until a child reaches school age, maintenance of self-esteem
is highly dependent on approval from significant adults. Therefore,
when being interviewed, children may rely on avoidance or denial
to protect themselves against the judgments of others. It may be
helpful to a young child to have a significant adult present to
provide reassurance and periodic reminders of the purpose of the
interview. Of course, this would not be appropriate were the adult-
child relationship defined by fear or hostility, or were the adult the
object of the interview. Always, but especially in the absence of a
parent or other significant adult, the empathic attention of the
interviewer is critical to the successful completion of the interview.

In addition to demonstrating genuine acceptance of and
interest in the child's responses, the interviewer should let the child
exercise some control in the interview. When children become too
conscious of their dependency on adults they become less spontaneous and more wary of factors in the situation that may threaten their
security. Feeling some sense of control in the situation allows them
to attend to the purpose of the interview.

Children from whom we seek information must cope with
two different kinds of stress. One kind has to do with the unfamil-
iarity of the interview situation—trying to understand the adult
interviewer and the reasons for having the interview, trying to
respond to the questions and to please the interviewer. This is
common to interviews of both children and adults (Young, O'Brien,
Gutterman, and Cohen, 1987). It is of particular importance to
avoid putting a child from whom information is to be obtained
under unnecessary stress. Such stress can decrease competence in
remembering information (Peters, 1988). For instance, the stress of
avoidable repeated interviewing in child sexual abuse cases may
cause the child to alter her story if she interprets the repetition of the
interviews as evidence that she has somehow failed in her attempts
to describe what happened. More research is needed on the effects of
interview stress on children's interview performance (Goodman,
Aman, and Hirschman, 1987).

The other form of stress that is important to adults seeking
information from children is the stress of victimization or the

trauma of witnessing a violent event. The pain and terror associated with certain experiences may be so difficult for a child that he exhibits symptoms of a post-traumatic stress disorder, which may include denial (Pynoos and Eth, 1984). When a child appears not to remember, the interviewer should consider the possibility that the child is using denial to protect himself from the stress of the situation.

In a study of children's memories of having blood drawn, Goodman, Aman, and Hirschman found that the intermediate levels of stress experienced by the child patients did not inhibit, but in fact enhanced, their memory of the event: children's memory of the act of drawing blood was much more complete and accurate than their memory of the technician or the room in which blood was being drawn (Goodman, Aman, and Hirschman, 1987). However, Peters found that 58 percent of children confronted with their assailants in a lineup opted not to tell the truth because they were afraid (Peters, 1988). It should be kept in mind that language is not always the easiest means of expression for young children, especially when it is used outside the context of established relationships.

*Practice Guideline 9.4: When interview situations create stress in the child, he will often use other channels of communication, such as crying, aggression, withdrawal, or general lethargy. While such outbursts may require firm control, they should be viewed as the child's attempts to express discomfort rather than personal attacks on the interviewer or her motives.*

**Cognitive Competence.** In Chapter Three we learned that younger children remember less than adults, are more likely to be deceived by appearances, are more susceptible to post-event suggestion, are less able to coordinate complex perceptual information, are less likely to engage in deliberate recall, are more likely to engage in magical thinking, are less likely to know what they do and do not know, and are more likely to be affected by the interview context. However, children can often perform well, and what young children do remember is as likely to be accurate as what adults remember. They are not significantly more suggestible than adults in recalling what they understand to be the salient and memorable aspects of events. And, like adults, they are more likely to accept misleading suggestions about matters peripheral to the central event.

How is it possible to help children to remember without influencing what is remembered? Adults must be aware of the limitations on young children's cognition and avoid asking children questions that would require them to exceed their capabilities. Adults must also be aware of the possibility of other implicit expectations and demands in the interview situation.

A rule of thumb is to try to understand the interview situation and the specific question being asked from the perspective of the child. This is difficult to do, since, to a certain extent, adults are always aliens to the world of children. This varies, however, as a function of an adult's experience, training, empathy, and relationship with the specific child being approached.

As children reach school age, perception, memory, and reasoning begin a gradual transformation. School-age children become better able to focus attention and integrate an increasing amount of information into their memories. They begin to use mnemonic devices and become aware of the difference between what they remember and what they do not remember, what they know and do not know. This process is assisted considerably by the development of literacy, as is the development of causal reasoning. This is a gradual process, however; the memories of school-age children continue to share many of the characteristics of preschool children's.

Young schoolchildren are still very sensitive to contextual cues and to what they perceive as the adult's demands or expectations, and they are likely to respond to these whether they have real information or not. They are more likely than older schoolchildren to need questioning to elicit recall; thus, they are more vulnerable to post-event suggestion. They are less sure of what they know and do not know. They are most likely to offer information that is reliable when talking about events that are part of or related to their own interests and experience.

*Practice Guideline 9.5: Children are most likely to offer information that is reliable when talking about events that are part of or related to their own interests or part of their everyday experience.*

The burden of assessing and monitoring the state of the respondent's cognitive development rests on the adult interviewer. Until ten or eleven years old, the child may not be capable of telling the interviewer when he does not remember, does not know, or does not fully understand. Often it is not that the child wants to obstruct the adult—the child is not capable of doing what the interviewer is asking of him, and thinks that by fabricating a response he is responding to the wishes of the interviewer.

*Language Competence.* If a child has some ability to use language, a skilled and sensitive interviewer can assist the child to express herself and to describe objects and events external to the interview situation (Jones and Krugman, 1986). To accomplish this, the interviewer must take account of the child's linguistic development.

In Chapter Four we learned that early language development occurs through the interactions between an infant and her primary caretakers. Even after the onset of language, toddlers still use language much as they use gestures and crying or smiling, and understanding their words requires attention to nonlinguistic cues. They do not communicate in words alone. Parents and caretakers understand toddler communications intuitively, partly because they have taught their children to communicate and partly because of what they have learned from their experience with the children (Goody, 1978a). Skilled professionals can also interpret the communications of this age group, especially when children are encouraged to supplement their communications by using dolls, puppets, and other objects.

*Practice Guideline 9.6: Preschoolers are much more proficient using language in familiar settings with familiar adults than they are in new places or new activities with people whom they consider strangers.*

*Practice Guideline 9.7: Preschoolers are much more proficient using language to describe persons, objects, or events than to clarify, evaluate the truth of, or reflect on statements.*

One must be careful, however, not to equate a child's level of language usage in a particular setting with his cognitive ability. Developmental researchers have been able to make significant differences in children's performance on experimental tasks by taking pains to be sure the children fully understood what was being asked of them (Donaldson, 1978). The basic approach is to take nothing for granted, to rely on modes of communication familiar to the child, and to constantly be alert to the possibility of misunderstanding in both directions.

It is not likely that the preschool child will be familiar with specialized nouns unless they relate to some aspect of her experience. For instance, Sivan found that 28 percent of the names assigned to body parts by nonabused three- to four-year-olds were incorrect; for four- to five- and six- to seven-year-olds the percentage of errors decreased to 10 percent and 8 percent respectively (Sivan, Schor, Koeppl, and Noble, 1988). The definitions of nouns or noun phrases may vary—a child's conception of "private parts" (including, for instance, her fingers) may differ considerably from her parents'. Pronouns and prepositions are not used reliably by children until ages five to seven (Steward, 1987).

Although children can imitate a variety of actions very early in life, they have trouble describing new actions, and they often must be creative in the application of limited language to the acts and motives of others (for example, in a sexual abuse case a child described an adult male's ejaculation with the sentence "the man wet my pants"). This may lead to difficulties in describing new or unfamiliar actions of adults. While children can generally understand more complex sentences than they can produce (de Villiers and de Villiers, 1979), those they produce can act as a guide for the length and complexity of adult questions. It is helpful for the adult to use the child's terms for key objects or events when asking for clarification or further elaboration. Usually children can be expected to overcome these difficulties by age seven (Steward, 1987).

*Practice Guideline 9.8: Interviewers should assess the vocabulary and grammatical complexity of statements made by child respondents and adjust their questions and comments accordingly.*

*Competence in Sociocultural Communication Conventions.*
Communicative competence requires not only linguistic competence but also an understanding of the social and cultural conventions for using language in a given setting. In the interview setting,
as in any conversation, the convention of turn-taking plays an
important role. Participants have to know what a turn is, how to get
one, what to do when they have one, and how to relinquish it
(Sacks, Schegloff, and Jefferson, 1974). Another convention that is
closely related to turn-taking is the *adjacency pair,* a type of
conversational exchange that has two parts, one of which follows
the other, such as greeting-greeting and question-answer (Lindfors,
1987). These conventions for language use are learned, as is
language, through interactions with people who use them.
Participation in an interview requires understanding turn-taking,
adjacency pairs, and several other conventions.

Satisfactorily interpreting and responding to questions in
interviews is a complex process. The respondent must interpret the
language of the question. She must monitor the interviewer's
gestures, tone of voice, inflection, expression, and rate of speech to
see whether they alter the sense of the question. She must understand what type of question is being asked and what type of
response that type of question elicits. She must understand the
relevance of the interview context to her response—how much of an
answer is required, what kind of information is pertinent, whether
she is supposed to respond with knowledge or speculation. When
the respondent gets off the track in adult interviews, a brief
discussion can get things back on the track. Such discussions,
however, require metalinguistic reflection ("What did you mean
when you said *x*?") and, therefore, are not always possible with
younger children. This places the responsibility for making the
relevant response conventions explicit squarely on the shoulders of
the adult interviewer. She should do everything possible to make
requests for information explicit. Take nothing for granted!

At an early age children learn the social conventions
governing two particular kinds of questions—caretaker questions
and teacher questions. But the conventions associated with teacher
and caretaker questions differ considerably from those of the
interview situation. Dillon defines the conventions of the interview

question thus: "Both the questioner (Q) and the respondent (R) presume that Q does not know the answer and that R does know it, that Q desires and needs to know the answer and believes that R will supply it, and that Q . . . expects R to give a true answer" (Dillon, 1982, p. 151).

Caretakers carry on the majority of their discourse with children in questions that are not used to elicit information. Rather, caretakers' questions express an immediate concern of the questioner and direct the attention of the child who is present to the concern. Keenan, Schiefflin, and Platt (1978) point out that requesting information is the least common immediate concern of caretakers asking questions of children; most questions are rhetorical. Caretakers usually expect agreement or behavior compliance from the child, not information.

*Practice Guideline 9.9: Young children whose primary experience is with caretakers' questions may not understand that an interviewer's question is a request for information; for them questions are as likely to imply direction as inquiry.*

Once children reach school, they come into regular contact with questions seeking information. For example, elementary school science teachers are likely to ask as many as two or three information questions per minute (Wilson, 1969). However, teachers' questions entail assumptions that reverse those of the interview situation. Whereas in the interview the questioner is assumed not to know the answer to the question, in the classroom the teacher does know the answer. The interview respondent would normally be thought to be capable of providing the answer, but teachers do not necessarily believe this (Dillon, 1982). In fact, teachers often use questions to assess what is already known so that they can add to it. Their questions thus seek to identify the limits of knowledge in a child. Pupils generally answer such questions with brief comments and come to think that it is proper to answer all adult questions in this way, whereas they give long and complex answers to questions from peers (Boggs, 1972; Mishler, 1978).

*Practice Guideline 9.10: School-age children may feel that adult interviewers already know the answers to the questions they are asking and thus may either severely curtail their responses or not respond at all.*

The amount of power or authority exercised in the question is called *valence*. Children are very sensitive to this feature of adult-child communication. Pure information questions, in theory, have neutral valence. They simply seek information and have no effect on the relative status of the questioner and respondent. Control questions, on the other hand, have positive valence, meaning that they establish the relative dominance of the questioner over the respondent. A common control question that parents ask their children is, "What are you doing?" This question does not request information about the activities of the child to whom it is addressed, but means "Stop that!" As Tammivaara and Enright point out, it is extremely difficult for adults to ask questions that do not appear to children to have positive valence, because children are used to such questions and are subordinate in most of their relationships to adults (Tammivaara and Enright, 1986).

*Practice Guideline 9.11: Special care must be exercised in interviewing children, especially young children, to avoid convey-ing the impression that a request for information is a demand; even when questions are asked in a neutral tone, the child may assume they have valence.*

Questioning conventions vary across cultures and classes, meaning that normally developing children in two social groups may learn quite different conventions. Ester Goody describes an important variation in rules governing the use of information questions (Goody, 1978b). In middle-class England (and other industrial nations), children begin to bombard their caretakers with informational questions at about age four. This sometimes irritat-ing practice is looked on as a developmental milestone in children. It is, however, as much cultural as it is developmental. In some cultures informational questions are thought to have positive valence. Consequently, in such cultures children almost never ask questions of their elders (only of their peers or those younger than they).

While some children may have had substantial experience with intergenerational information questions by the age of four, others will have learned that intergenerational information questions are inappropriate. In an interview with an adult, such a child would assume that the purpose of the questions was not really to request information, and that the correct response was not information, but deference.

## Interviewer Competence

Interviewing children places great responsibility on the adult interviewer. She must not only arrange the interview setting, but must assess and continuously monitor the child's competence and make appropriate adjustments as the interview progresses. In addition, the interviewer must monitor herself. In Chapter Six, we discussed the origins of adult biases and their influence on the elicitation of information from children and its evaluation and use by adults. The relative weight of adult evaluations and children's statements in the production of adult knowledge and policy virtually ensures that adult biases will overwhelm children's information when there is a contradiction. This is why it is so important for adults to be reflective about their biases and make special efforts to understand children's information and distortions from an empathic point of view. Professional and personal characteristics of the interviewer may significantly influence both the information a child provides in interviews and how that information is interpreted.

*Interview Purposes.* In addition to matching the interview to the child's communicative competence and carefully monitoring her own influence on the interview, the adult interviewer must remain cognizant of the purposes of the interview. She has to strike a careful balance between adapting the interview to the needs of the child and accomplishing the adult purposes of the interaction. It is important to understand the purposes of the interview for two reasons. First, the purposes of the interview include the intended uses of the information obtained; thus, they determine the type of information that the adult seeks from the child and the standards that must be met in order for that information to be acceptable. Second, the adult will have to make special efforts, because of the competence of the child, to communicate those purposes clearly.

Interviews with children have three general purposes: to do research about children, to learn about a child who requires clinical assessment or screening, and to get information for the purposes of an investigation about something a child saw or experienced. Each has its own standards for acceptable information, but for our purposes it is the latter two that hold the greatest interest. Researchers, for instance, attempt to design and administer questions so that they yield very specific kinds of information, whereas clinicians are interested in a wide range of associations. Investigators are generally concerned with the child's cognitive, linguistic, and psychological competence to make a statement, in addition to what the child has to say about an event.

One interview can have multiple purposes. For example, when a clinician is asked to interview a child prior to an appearance in court, he may have a dual purpose: (1) to assess the child's psychological state and detect symptoms of trauma or long-standing emotional disturbance and (2) to obtain an account of what happened to the child. In such cases, it is important to keep each purpose of the interview in mind, because questioning methods and information that are acceptable for one purpose may violate the standards of another.

Reversing the order of questions or confusing one type of information with another may render the information useless. This is particularly important in multipurpose interviews that include an investigative component. Since nearly all research indicates the superiority of information obtained from a child during free recall (supplemented, in the case of younger children, with nonsuggestive probes), some authorities propose delaying evaluative and clinical questions until the child's spontaneous recall of an event and all follow-up questions related to it have been completed (Raskin and Yuille, forthcoming).

*Practice Guideline 9.12: It is important to keep the purpose of each question in mind, because questioning methods and information that are acceptable for one purpose may violate the standards of another.*

When interview purposes are to be combined in the same interview, one should consider the effect on the child. Certain roles may be fundamentally incompatible. For instance, while therapists take a supportive, accepting stance toward the responses and statements of the child, investigators must take a more critical and questioning stance. This will be especially confusing for young children, who find it difficult to comprehend adults playing different roles.

If a child is to undergo successive interviews by authorities and professionals with different purposes, the order of the separate interviews should be considered. This is especially true when investigative interviews are involved, since certain interview methods may "contaminate" the child's information, causing it to be dismissed as evidence. Research findings indicate, however, that even among three-year-olds, post-event suggestion is unlikely to recur during free report in subsequent interviews (Goodman, Aman, and Hirschman, 1987). Thus, even young children can survive the rigors of multiple interviews if those interviews are done sensitively and in good faith, without efforts to break the child or the child's story.

*Interview Types.* The variety of techniques used in interviewing children makes it difficult to set forth a unified typology of interviews. We can note certain dimensions, however. Interviews may be arrayed along a continuum from unstructured to structured. In unstructured interviews, the interviewer asks a limited number of questions and encourages the child to narrate or describe or reflect in his own words. The basic strategy in the narrative interview, a form of the unstructured interview, is to elicit a description of events in the child's words: "Tell me what happened." The child being interviewed (the narrator) is given maximum control over the order and manner in which events are described. Because of this freedom, narrative interviews yield information whose meaning to the child can be ascertained with relative ease. Such unstructured interviews may yield insight into misapprehended or previously unknown facets of the child's experience.

Structured interviews, by contrast, use codified questions and generally employ specific response options, giving the interviewer maximum control over the response of the child. This facilitates the application of statistical techniques by ensuring comparability and consequently favors the development of generalizations, replica-tions, and predictions in research studies. Structured interviews are also more comprehensive and reliable for clinical use in that they outline the targeted behaviors, symptoms, and events to be covered, thus reducing the information variance (Edelbrock and others, 1985). They provide little opportunity, however, for the interviewer to assess the meaning of questions and responses to the child respondent and, thus, reveal little about the child's perceptions of the interview. This makes it difficult to specify the degree to which the child perceives certain questions as demands for a response.

It is useful, when thinking of structured interviews, to distinguish between semistructured and highly structured interviews. While both types ensure comprehensiveness by defining the range and types of information to be gathered, semistructured interviews allow more flexibility in the interview itself, making it possible to tailor the interview schedule to the competence of the individual child. Highly structured interviews, which allow less flexibility, also require less judgment on the part of the interviewer, thus reducing the possibility of interviewer-induced error. As yet there is no definitive research finding on the relative value of highly structured and semistructured interview schedules for psychiatric assessment and screening purposes (Edelbrock and others, 1985; Hodges, McKnew, Burbach, and Roebuck, 1987). Debate also continues concerning the relative value of structured and unstructured interviews. When eliciting information about an event, however, research favors beginning with an unstructured, free report–style format (Dent and Stephenson, 1979; King and Yuille, 1987; Goodman, 1984a; Goodman, Aman, and Hirschman, 1987).

It is worth noting that all the structured and semistructured psychiatric interviews reviewed in the September 1987 issue of the *Journal of the American Academy of Child and Adolescent Psychiatry* (American Academy of Child and Adolescent Psychiatry, 1987) are for use with children aged six and older. Because of the state of their language and metacognitive development, younger children will generally have more difficulty responding freely to structured interviews.

*Practice Guideline 9.13: Barring substantial and unforeseen advances in structured interviewing of young children, it will remain necessary to use less structured interviews with preschool children and young schoolchildren.*

*Interviewing Techniques.* Knowing something about the child's experience will help the interviewer ask more informed, intelligent questions to which the child will be more likely to respond in detail. In interviewing alleged child victims (of sexual abuse, for example), there is some debate about whether knowing the allegations and other background information is prejudicial to the outcome of the interview (White, Strom, and Santilli, 1986; Boat and Everson, 1986). Objectivity, however, depends on what the interviewer presents to the child, not what the interviewer knows. Information obtained prior to the interview should be used only as a general guide to the areas the investigation will touch on and as a source of background material from which to construct questions ("Your uncle says you visited your friend Ronnie's house last night") (Boat and Everson, 1986).

The adult must be careful in selecting the setting and context for the interview. Context, as noted above, is a very important influence on children's memory. Interviews should be held in a neutral, relaxed setting relatively free from distractions. There should be cushions or mats to enable the interviewer to sit on the same level as the child. A selection of tools and props to assist the child and interviewer may be included, depending on the age of the child. The interviewer's knowledge of the child's age, sex, and background will help him select appropriate items.

An interviewer kit containing familiar items selected because they facilitate communication and help build rapport is helpful when seeking information, especially from younger children. Interviewers often find it useful to include one or more of the following in their kit: felt-tipped markers or crayons and paper, a dollhouse and dolls, puppets, modeling clay, and toy telephones. If sexually detailed dolls are to be used, they should be present with other props and tools (issues concerning the use of anatomical dolls will be discussed in a separate section below). The interview should not be held at nap time, mealtime, or in the late afternoon.

Young children may have a familiar person—one with whom they have a positive relationship—present to periodically reassure and remind them of the purpose of the interview, unless, in the judgment of the interviewer, the situation dictates otherwise. Observers should observe through a one-way window. If such a window is not available, observers should be directed to sit behind the child and not to respond to anything the interviewer or child says or does. Neither the interviewer nor the observers should wear uniforms or other such clothing, which could intimidate the child. Videotaping or audiotaping of the interview may eliminate the need for observers, but in investigative interviews it should be done only after legal consultation.

*Regulating the Interviewing Relationship.* The sociolinguist William Labov pointed out that the social situation is the most powerful determinant of a child's verbal behavior. Consequently, if an interviewer wants to find out what a child knows, she must enter into the right social relationship with the child (Labov, 1972a; see also Parker, 1984). Questioning establishes a relationship between the questioning adult and the responding child. For instance, questions that highly restrict the possible responses of the child place the adult in control of the interaction. Children sense this and may either refuse to respond at all or respond in terse, often one-word, answers. They respond better to open, indirect questions, which leave a substantial (but not infinite) range for response, and to questioning sequences that let the child exercise some control by initiating and terminating the discussion of new topics at least as much as the adult. Having said (with adult encouragement) what they would like to say about a given topic, children will respond to narrow and directed probes. But the timing of such probes, their position in the flow of the interview, is of the utmost importance in maintaining an appropriately balanced relationship and in facilitating the adult's receipt of information (Tammivaara and Enright, 1986).

Balance in the interviewer-child relationship is also important because of suggestion. An imbalanced relationship may be interpreted by the child as a demand for an answer when there is none. This appears to be the problem when children are asked to select a photograph of an assailant from a set of photos that does not actually contain one of the assailant (King and Yuille, 1987). Children perform poorly on such blank lineups. While a balanced relationship between adult interviewer and child is ideal for obtaining information, it requires special effort to maintain.

*Practice Guideline 9.14: Where possible, the adult interviewer should avoid controlling the behavior of the child, should allow diversions from the subject at hand, and should embed questions in routines and activities already familiar to the child, or in words, drawings, and actions that the child introduces in the interview situation.*

Certain kinds of interviews may take more than one occasion to complete. When the child shows boredom and restlessness, it may be because he has reached the limit of his attention and participation.

Another important aspect of interviewing children is empathy, a genuine appreciation of the feelings and perceptions of the child and an interest in understanding the world or some part of it in the way the child does. A child's emotional, verbal, and behavioral expressions are the result of monumental intellectual and emotional effort and should be understood as such. To activate such interest in the child's perceptions, memories, and feelings requires overcoming what Garfinkel (1967, p. 73) called the "et cetera" principle. According to this principle, communication between adults is facilitated by their ability to "fill in" the unstated understandings necessary to make their conversations complete.

*Practice Guideline 9.15: An adult talking to a child cannot assume that there is a shared understanding of either language or feeling, but must work continuously to ensure that he and the child are operating on the same wavelength.*

***Questioning Techniques.*** The content and manner of questioning are important determinants of interview outcomes. Wood and his associates (Wood, MacMahon, and Cranstoun, 1980; Wood and Wood, 1983) found that the number and type of questions teachers asked significantly affected the number and length of preschool children's statements in a conversational situation. Further, they discovered that by altering her style, a teacher could affect dramatically the number and length of children's statements. They concluded that open questions and encouraging responses ("Oh really!" "I see") are keys to encouraging children to talk. This is consistent with the finding among researchers that witnesses of all ages provide more accurate information when they are freely narrating than when they are responding to direct questions (King and Yuille, 1987; Dent and Stephenson, 1979; Goodman and Reed, 1986; Jones and McQuiston, 1985).

To be effective, questions must be appropriate for the developmental level of the child being interviewed. There are qualitative differences in language, comprehension, reasoning, and memory between adults and preschoolers. The following suggestions are intended to ameliorate some of the difficulties in interviewing these children:

- Use sentences with only three to five more words than the number of words in the child's average sentence.
- Use names rather than pronouns.
- Use the child's terms; if necessary, elicit them. If elicitation is impossible, use various terms in your question to be sure the child understands, and monitor his response to be sure.
- In order to determine if you have been understood, ask the child to repeat what you have said rather than asking, "Do you understand?"
- Rephrase questions the child does not understand. Repeating a question may be taken as an indication that the child has given an incorrect answer and the child may change his answer.
- Avoid asking questions involving a time sequence.
- Be careful in interpreting responses to very specific questions. Children are apt to be very literal.
- Do not respond to every answer with another question. Merely acknowledge the child's comment. This will encourage the child to expand on his previous statements (Boat and Everson, 1986).

A method for assisting a young child to recall what he remembers, particularly when the subject of the interview is a recurrent event, is to help him refer to routines with which he is familiar, such as the pattern of activity surrounding bedtime (script memory). Sometimes a child can recall more of a particular event if he thinks of it as connected to a particular script with which he is familiar. For example, in the case of suspected recurrent abuse, rather than asking a direct question such as "What did Daddy do last Tuesday?" one might ask the child to recount a script: "What happens when Daddy puts you in bed?" (King and Yuille, 1987).

*Other Methods of Obtaining Information.* Interviewers often resort to supplemental methods to obtain information from children who are unable to give it verbally for developmental or emotional reasons. A common method is the use of props to stimulate memory, to supplement language ability, or to facilitate communication in the interview setting. Props can be used to recreate the setting of an event, permitting the child to enact the event itself. A dollhouse and dolls, for instance, can be used to help describe a domestic event that is either too complex or too traumatic to describe in words. Pretending to talk on the telephone may act as a vehicle for talking with the interviewer (and may also help the child feel a sense of control over the interview, since he can stop the conversation at any time by hanging up). Human figure drawings can be useful in both projective and abuse investigation interviews (Miller, Veltkamp, and Janson, 1987).

Closely related to the use of props in interviewing is observing imaginative play. We learned in Chapter Eight that observing imaginative play has been used as a method of obtaining information from children in therapeutic contexts for years. Play provides trained observers with information about a child's fantasies, his fears and anxieties, and his relationships with important others. Healthy play involves the expression and resolution of anxieties and problems; it also includes exploration and investigation. If the child has enough language ability, an adult can often carry on a low-key conversation about the subject of the play. Because of its interpretive nature, this method of obtaining information is primarily useful in therapeutic and clinical research contexts, and it should be verified where possible through triangulation with other kinds of information.

Another method of asking children questions is the photo lineup, used in sexual abuse investigations to avoid having the child feel confronted by his assailant. A photo of the accused is included with photos of other persons and the child is asked to identify the assailant. Children of all ages can correctly identify the assailant from among the photos. When the assailant's picture is removed and the remaining pictures are again shown to the child, however, young children often make false identifications. There appears to be a demand implicit in the request to select a photo that young children cannot resist, even when the person whose photo is sought is not in the set of photos being examined. King and Yuille (1987) suggest that interviewers who wish to use the photo lineup could make it less suggestive to the child by demonstrating failure to find a photo that looks like the assailant, and explaining that this result is acceptable.

*Using Sexually Detailed Dolls.* One method of interviewing alleged victims of sexual abuse involves sexually detailed dolls, also known as sexually anatomically correct (SAC) dolls. SAC dolls are distinguished from normal dolls by their adult- and child-sized male and female genitals and bodily orifices and sometimes by body hair. These sexually detailed dolls are used in interviewing alleged victims of sexual abuse who either do not have the vocabulary to describe being abused or are so traumatized that they cannot discuss what has happened. Because of the dolls' design, it is possible for children to use them to demonstrate abuse they have experienced. Because of young children's limited understanding of sexual differences and sexual activity, proponents argue that a child's demonstration of sexual activity with the dolls suggests that he has been sexually abused.

SAC dolls are in widespread use by physicians, child protective service workers, law enforcement agencies, and mental health practitioners, and it is likely that their use will continue to grow (Boat and Everson, 1988). Although there are at least three published protocols for the use of SAC dolls in interviews with alleged victims of sexual abuse (White, Strom, and Santilli, 1986; Everson and Boat, 1986; Friedman and Morgan, 1985), there is as yet no agreement concerning how dolls can best be presented, what kind of specific interview training is necessary, what level of training in child development is necessary, or how the results of the interview should be interpreted and recorded (Boat and Everson, 1988).

The dolls are the subject of substantial debate. At issue are two questions: (1) Are the dolls suggestive—do they encourage nonabused children to demonstrate sexual abuse? (2) Since we do not yet have a conclusive answer to the first question, and since there are a host of other unanswered questions concerning the dolls, should the dolls be used at all?

Some research has been done concerning the suggestiveness of sexually detailed dolls. White and her colleagues (White, Strom, and Santilli, 1986), in a study intended to compare the results of a structured interview using SAC dolls with parental reports of suspected abuse, interviewed twenty-five children referred because of suspected sexual abuse and twenty-five nonreferred children. While the SAC doll interviews with referred children elicited behaviors indicative of sexual abuse, the interviews with nonreferred children did not. Sivan, Schor, Koeppl, and Noble (1988) investigated the way 144 three- to eight-year-old nonreferred children interacted with SAC dolls under a variety of conditions designed to help children play comfortably in an unfamiliar laboratory playroom. Sexually detailed dolls were less interesting to the children than other toys in the room. Although the sexual body parts of these dolls were explored by children, role playing of explicit sexual behavior was not observed. Less than one percent of over 5,000 observed interactions with the dolls were aggressive, none while the dolls were undressed. Sivan concluded that the dolls were not very different from other toys and that unusual behavior with such dolls should be taken seriously.

Boat and Everson (1988) studied the interactions of 206 nonreferred two- to five-year-old children with sexually detailed dolls. The children were shown four dolls, asked to choose one, and an interview about body parts and functions was administered (White, Strom, and Santilli, 1986) as the dolls were undressed. After the interview the children had the opportunity to explore the unclothed dolls. There was substantial manual exploration of the genitals, anus, and female breasts of the dolls, but the incidence of manual exploration decreased steadily as age increased. Four children demonstrated clear genital intercourse with the dolls while the interviewer was in the room. Another five children demonstrated clear genital intercourse when the interviewer was not present. Everson and Boat conclude that since nine children not under any suspicion of being abused demonstrated clear genital intercourse, a demonstration of intercourse during a doll interview cannot be considered a definitive marker of abuse.

Goodman and Aman (1987) studied the effect of sexually detailed dolls when used in interviews of three- and five-year-old children concerning a staged event. Included in the interviews were objective questions about the event, misleading questions about the event ("Show me where he touched you"), and misleading abuse questions ("He kissed you, didn't he?"). They found that the dolls did not contribute to incorrect answers to questions, either objective or leading, that might lead to reports of sexual abuse.

While the results of three of these studies seem to indicate that sexually detailed dolls are not suggestive, Boat and Everson's study raises doubts about the reliability of the doll interview as an investigative tool. Even if their cases are eventually explained away, much research remains to be done. The studies mentioned above did not include social group membership or socioeconomic status. There is no research as yet assessing the impact on reactions to the dolls of the child's previous sexual exposure and sexual knowledge, different methods of using the dolls, the child's prior medical or physical experience (such as genital exams or the use of suppositories), or the familiarity of the child with the interviewer and interview setting. And we know nothing about the stability of young children's behaviors with the dolls over time (Boat and Everson, 1988). These variables will also have to be examined as factors affecting the response of referred children to sexually detailed dolls.

Given the inconclusiveness of evidence compiled to date and the enormous number of remaining research questions, should sexually detailed dolls be used at all? Recent issues of the *Journal of the American Academy of Child and Adolescent Psychiatry* have included a debate on the merits of doll interviews as the basis of expert testimony (Yates and Terr, 1988). Yates suggests that evaluators should continue to use the dolls but should not base conclusions on doll play alone. Terr likens the dolls to hypnosis, once suggested as an investigative shortcut but later shown to have far too many shortcomings, and suggests that SAC dolls are far too suggestive for judicial use.

There is little question that, in the hands of competent professionals, sexually detailed dolls can be a useful reconstructive technique. Competent professionals, however, have at their disposal a variety of reconstructive tools, some of which, such as human figure drawings, are less vivid and perhaps less potentially suggestive than the dolls. Until further research on the suggestiveness of the dolls is complete, caution should be used with dolls in judicial proceedings. Consideration should be given to other forms of interviewing prior to using dolls. Sexually detailed doll interviews, if done, should be done as soon after the alleged abuse as possible, should be videotaped (after proper legal consultation), should be conducted by interviewers with advanced knowledge of child development, and should be observed by other professionals.

Children should be encouraged to talk about what they are enacting with the dolls so that the interpretation of the sexual doll play can be based, in part at least, on the statements of the child. Whether the interview can be admitted as evidence should depend on an evaluation of the interview by a forensic child psychologist and on whether other evidence corroborates the claims made.

Far too little is known about the effects of sexually detailed dolls to think of them as a validated instrument for either research or investigation, let alone as a test for the occurrence or nonoccurrence of sexual abuse. But there are strong indications in the research that has been done that unusual sexual or violent enactments with sexually detailed dolls are not normal responses to the dolls and, therefore, merit further inquiry.

### Interpreting the Results of Child Interviews

The methods used to interpret the results of interviews with children will depend on the purpose for which the interview was conducted, what was expected of the child in the interview, and what use will be made of the information that the child has given. However, our ability to evaluate the information given in the interview will depend on the nature of the interview record. Since no postinterview evaluation of children's statements is possible without a record, we will discuss what kind of record should be kept of interviews and why. We will then move on to methods that can be used to analyze the interview record.

*Making Interview Records.* The information resulting from an interview can best be understood in relation to the context in which it was given. The context of an interview statement includes, but is not limited to, the events leading up to the interview, the inteview setting, all previous questions and statements of the interviewer, the previous statements of the child, nonverbal messages given by the interviewer (for example, displaying affect or pacing questions), the child's understanding of all of the above, and the child's feelings about it. An interview record is a record of the interview and the relevant features of its context.

The most common interview record, which consists of the formal interview schedule and the interviewer's highly selective on-the-spot notations about what the child said, is not a valid description of questions and responses. We have seen that up to 40 percent of the questions asked in formal interviews vary significantly from the interview schedule. It is the question asked, rather than the question intended, to which the child responds. If we are to interpret the child's responses we must have an accurate record of the questions to which he responds.

*Practice Guideline 9.16: If the meaning of the child's responses in an interview is to be understood, it is essential that a record be made both of those responses and of the questions that elicited them.*

While the interviewer may not be asking the questions on the interview schedule, she will be listening for answers to them. When she makes selective notes summarizing the interview, she is likely to choose those parts of the response that sound most like those answers. Selective recording is an act of interpretation that may preclude further interpretation of the meaning of interview responses. Again, it is the answers that we want to interpret, not the interviewer's impressions of them.

The record of interview speech must be as complete and accurate as possible; high-quality videotaping is ideal, provided it is done in a way that permits those who analyze the tape to see the nonverbal communication of the interviewer and child. This is especially true for young children, who rely heavily on nonverbal channels of communication, even when props are not being used. It can be very difficult to interpret a child's statements without seeing his nonverbal communication; it will be impossible in unfamiliar, stressful situations where his language fails him. If videotaping is not possible, audiotape recording can be successful, provided the interviewer or an observer can also take notes that record key visual aspects of the interview. Note-taking can be distracting and may not seem appropriate in some child interviews. In such cases the interviewer may wish to shorten the interview and record significant visual memories immediately following the interview. Mere audiotape recording is a dramatic improvement over note-taking, and it will be accurate to the degree to which speech becomes the child's main means of communication.

Interpreting the meaning and significance of the child's statements is easier if one can work from a transcript in conjunction with a videotape or audiotape. A transcript of the interview should represent the actual features of speaking—pauses, interruptions, false starts, nonlexical expressions ("um-hm"), and unclear speech. No transcript can represent all the features of an interview, but it is important to represent the interview as speech. In interviews where the actual questions the child is answering are at issue (for example, in sexual abuse interviews, where post-event suggestion is an issue), this is especially important; not only do interviewers deviate from the interview schedule, but interviewer and respondent often negotiate the meaning of the question through their conversation (Mishler, 1986). In transcripts where there is no videotape it is also helpful to record certain movements of the interviewer and child. The interviewer's movements (such as moving closer to the child) may be interpreted as cues by the child; the child's movements (such as fidgeting) can help the analyst see shifts in the child's attention to the interview.

With the transcript should be relevant contextual information—the time, date, and place of the interview, a description of the setting in which the interview was conducted, an account of any interactions that occurred immediately before the interview, an account of how the child learned of the interview, the names of those present (either in the room or waiting outside) and their relationship to the child, the length of the interview, a description of the mood of the child, and any other information that would bear on the interpretation of the communication that occurred between the interviewer and the child (Mishler, 1986; Briggs, 1986).

*Interpreting Interview Records.* A critical problem for all interviewers of children is understanding the meaning of children's statements. A key feature of speech is that statements do not just point to phenomena; they also refer to other statements and to other aspects of their interactional context. Meaning is grounded in interactional contexts, and one must understand those contexts in order to understand meaning. We have stressed being careful about creating a complete and accurate record of the interview so that those who analyze the interview record will have the information necessary to interpret the meaning of the child's statements.

Briggs (1986), Mishler (1986), Agar and Hobbs (1982), and Paget (1983), among others, have described in detail methods for interpreting the meaning of interview statements that are consistent with the approach adopted here. However, there are no simple mechanisms for analyzing interviews with children, or, for that matter, any other type of interview. Analysis of interview texts is a process of interpretation, an art that requires considering many different kinds of information, formulating an idea of their significance, and returning to the interview text to evaluate the idea, again and again (Honey, 1987).

*Practice Guideline 9.17: The interview analyst should have a sense of the organization of the interview as a whole prior to analysis of any interview segment.*

Two important aspects of the organization of the interview are themes and sequence. Themes are topics of discussion or expression in the interview, such as friends, numbers, or fears. While the interview schedule may group questions according to their themes, children may sprinkle statements concerning a particular theme throughout the interview. Often themes can only be recognized by examining an interview record. Briggs suggests that listening to a tape of the interview while reviewing one's notes is a good way to find the major themes of the interview (Briggs, 1986).

A second aspect is sequence. A clinical interview, for instance, might include the following segments: arrival, separation of the child from his parent, a brief period of play, questions, another period of play, and return to parent. The different segments may be more or less clear and the order and number of steps may vary with the purpose of the interview. Events such as the ringing of a telephone, or the late arrival of an observer, can spontaneously segment the interview. The quality of the transition from one part to another can be important contextual information. The interview analyst should sketch both the themes and the linear order of the interview before attempting analysis of the child's statements.

Having completed a sketch of the overall themes and order of the interview, the analyst may proceed to statements. One approach to the analysis of a statement is to determine the apparent meaning of the words in the statement itself and then to compare it to the question to which it is ostensibly a response. Having a notion of the key themes of the interview and of its linear segmentation, the analyst may consider whether a given statement is best understood as a response to a question, a development of a theme, the demarcation of an interview segment, or a combination of these. It may be, for instance, that the interviewer's question and the child's statement develop different themes, in which case there are grounds for seeking the other questions to which the child is responding. The child may be continuing (by association) to respond to a previous question; he may be misinterpreting the meaning of the interviewer's question; or he may be responding to a perceived demand by the interviewer. Relating statements to interview themes and segments grounds our interpretation of their meaning in the interview as a whole, helping us avoid misinterpreting a statement completely.

The child has a coherent perspective that can, with sufficient effort, be understood by the adult. While the child may err in his interpretation of the social interaction in an interview, he does not do so randomly. The child is assumed to be responding to something in the interview or its immediate context when he makes a statement. If the analyst can discover what the child is responding to and determine the child's interpretation, what the child is doing will appear reasonable on the basis of his assumptions. Repeated divergence of interviewer and child themes suggests that the interviewer has not been successful in adjusting the interview to the communicative competence of the child.

Research interviews, for instance, seek to compare a number of children's responses to the same questions in order to make generalizations. There are a number of potential problems with such comparisons. First, there is considerable variation in the way that interviewers ask questions—did the interviewers in fact ask the children the same question? Second, assuming that the interviewers asked the same question, did they ask it in a way that was consistent with the communicative competence of this developmental age group? Third, assuming that the language and cognition requirements of the question were appropriate for this group of children, does analysis of the question-response pairs yield the finding that the children's statements were responses to the same question? One cannot simply assume that statements that follow the same or similar questions are comparable—it must be demonstrated.

Investigative interviews require perhaps the most stringent analysis of any adult interview of children. The justice system, in order to protect accused persons from punishment for crimes they did not commit, seeks to find and disallow questionable testimony. This is appropriate, because more is at stake in criminal investigations than in research—a criminal conviction can result in the incarceration of a human being.

Investigative interviews differ from research interviews in that the focus of the evaluation is the competence and independence of the child. In order for a child's statement to be accepted as evidence in court, it must be clear that the child is developmentally competent to testify or make evidential statements. His competence in language, perception, memory, and reasoning must be sufficient for him to make reliable statements about past events. In addition, the present state of the child's language, perception, memory, and reasoning ability must be consistent with the competence required to make the particular statement he is making. Finally, it must be clear that the child's statements were made voluntarily, that he was not influenced by either indoctrination or more subtle post-event suggestion. The child's adherence to these standards must be evaluated by a trained professional.

The interview record and method of interpretation described above will be most useful in evaluating the voluntariness of the child's statement and in determining whether post-event suggestion has played a significant role in the investigative interview of the child. *Suggestion,* in this context, is a forensic term for children's context sensitivity in language use. Suggestion can occur in any interview, but young children have been shown to be more vulnerable than older children. The most reliable method of interviewing suspected child victims of sexual abuse is by eliciting free reports, but young children are not likely to give spontaneous free reports without some interviewer assistance. There is some concern about the encouragement of free reports of young children. Research is desperately needed on the use of gestures and comments, on the one hand, and of props, on the other, to facilitate free report statements by younger children. As was described above in the discussion of sexually detailed dolls, little is known about the suggestive effects of presenting reconstructive or facilitative props to such children (King and Yuille, 1987). Statement analysis, a method of testimony validation that has been used with apparent success in Germany and Sweden, would rule out much testimony elicited through reconstructive techniques because it is not considered to be spontaneous (Raskin and Yuille, forthcoming). In the absence of relevant research, this method would effectively exclude the testimony of three- and four-year-olds from validity checks. Until such research has been completed, it will be necessary to have professionals with advanced training in child development evaluate interviews done with reconstructive techniques.

In addition to the standards referred to above, an evaluating professional must consider the following possibilities (Nurcombe, 1986): (1) The child is truthful but has misinterpreted an innocent incident. (2) The child is delusional (for example, he has a false but steadfast conviction of having been physically or sexually abused). (3) The child is relating a personal fantasy that he believes is real, and or he is fabricating—that is, deliberately lying. Both are most likely to occur in children who are severely disturbed and who either fear abandonment or seek relief from unhappy circumstances.

## Conclusions

What we learn from children in interviews will necessarily depend on the communicative competence of the child, the professional qualities and personal characteristics of the interviewer, the purposes for which information is sought, and the specific interview techniques, including the context of the interview. Through the adaptation of interviewing, which is an adult method of obtaining information, to the communicative competence of children, we can obtain highly reliable accounts of events and of the process by which the accounts of the events were produced. We can, through careful analysis of properly prepared interview records, understand much of the communicative process in child interviews. This will enable us to determine with substantial accuracy the meaning of statements made by children in interviews and enhance the validity of our research concerning development.

Research needs to be done on the use of props and verbal facilitators such as phatics to elicit free reports from young children. Standards for the use of such reconstructive and facilitative techniques in interviewing children need to be established. Every effort must be made to ensure that valid statements of young children can be used, while protecting accused persons from improperly obtained evidence. Interviewing will never be a mechanical test of the validity of a child's statements about sexual abuse or anything else. The basis for interviewing is speaking, and nothing about interviewing exempts it from the interactive dynamics, rules, and conventions that are spoken communication.

CHAPTER 10

# Using Tests
# and Other Instruments

Clinicians and other professionals utilize testing as one of the tools available to them for gathering information about children's adaptive and maladaptive functioning. Testing data are examined and interpreted by clinicians for several purposes—among them educational placement, prediction of school success, diagnosis of emotional disturbance, and assessment of developmental delay. Testing is also employed for the purpose of addressing legal questions concerning children, such as making recommendations in child custody cases and cases involving sexual abuse.

Formal testing is often part of a larger assessment process that is initiated when a concerned adult identifies and refers a child for an evaluation. In a comprehensive evaluation, the process may include gathering information from several methods of inquiry. For example, the identified child may be tested, interviewed, and observed in various contexts or settings; the parents and teacher may also be interviewed. Under the best of circumstances, results from all these methods of inquiry are combined and integrated to describe the child's functioning and to determine diagnosis and recommendations.

In the United States many children experience testing in one form or another, be it developmental screening in a preschool setting, educational testing in a school setting, or intellectual and personality testing in a clinical setting. Because testing is often part of a child's early experience and is often used to make crucial decisions that affect a child's life, it is important for all professionals and paraprofessionals working with children (teachers, psychologists, lawyers, child development specialists, paraprofessional program staff, and students in training) to be informed of the strengths and limitations of testing children. Professionals and paraprofessionals need to know what information and what questions can and cannot be answered by tests.

## Factors Affecting the Use of Tests

The success of testing as a method of gathering valid information and addressing specific questions about children's functioning depends on the role of the tester, the social and cultural context of testing, the technical properties of the test, and the quality of the overall clinical assessment.

*The Role of the Tester.* The role of the tester or evaluator is of paramount importance in evaluating the quality of formal assessments. Clinicians and other professionals typically operate in a culturally prescribed manner. They are familiar with different types of tests, including their purposes, norms, strengths, and limitations.

For example, consider the case of Ramona, a four-and-a-half-year-old diagnosed as mildly mentally retarded. Ramona is seen by Dr. Horowitz, a clinical psychologist, in individual psychotherapy for treatment of depression. Ramona's parents are concerned about the retardation diagnosis because, although their daughter is depressed, she has always functioned well cognitively. In reviewing the testing report Dr. Horowitz discovers that the diagnosis was based on administration of the Denver Developmental Screening Test, a test designed to screen for possible developmental delay. Dr. Horowitz's familiarity with tests leads her to have Ramona reevaluated with the Wechsler Preschool and Primary Scales of Intelligence, a test designed to diagnose intellectual delay. The parents' knowledge of their daughter is confirmed; she achieves an above-average intelligence quotient on the test. The original tester was not well informed about the uses of tests; fortunately for Ramona, the psychologist was.

Formal assessments are done by several types of professionals, including psychologists, school evaluators, developmental evaluators, and learning disability specialists. Regardless of their profession, testers have in common the role of assessing whether children are developing according to culturally accepted milestones, both in terms of the wider culture and the child's particular racial or ethnic group. In evaluating children, clinicians with a developmental perspective are aware that children's capacities change over time and that what is accepted by the wider culture also can change over time.

The theoretical model the tester endorses influences what tests are chosen to be administered, how the tests will be interpreted, and what the written or oral test report will be like. A tester may endorse one of several theories—such as psychoanalytic, behavioral, or cognitive behavioral—or take an atheoretical approach to assessment. The tester must make strong inferences based on adequate data yet must be careful not to overinterpret those data. The use of theory to guide interpretations and the availability of information from a number of sources (tests, interviews, and observations) increase the validity of the assessment.

*Practice Guideline 10.1: The evaluator's knowledge of tests, particularly their purposes and the information that can be derived from them, and the evaluator's use of theory to guide test interpretation lay the foundation for a valid assessment.*

***Social and Cultural Contexts.*** Testing, like other methods of evaluating children, is interactive and embedded in various physical, social, and cultural contexts. On one level, the child interacts with the testing materials and tasks. The meaning the child ascribes to the tasks influences the child's responses and is important to the interpretation of the data. Another level of interaction is between the tester and the child, each of whom brings his or her own cultural and ethnic values and expectations to the testing situation. On yet another level, the tester interacts with the tests by interpreting the data. The clinician must weight the child's test responses together with biological, situational, familial, and sociocultural variables to explain the child's functioning.

Cultural context refers to the particular value and belief system that the child shares with his particular reference group. The child's cultural and social context can be vastly different from that of the tester. For example, Michael, an eight-year-old, poor, black child, is referred for a psychological evaluation because of behavior problems in school. Ms. Updegrove, a student in clinical psychology training, performs the evaluation under the close supervision of Dr. Smith, an experienced psychologist. During supervision Dr. Smith comments that many of Michael's responses on the Rorschach Inkblot Test seem pathological and may indicate a psychotic process, particularly his perception of a couple of blots as "chicken backs which are about to be eaten by a family." Dr. Smith, who comes from a wealthy background, further states that "no one eats chicken backs." Ms. Updegrove gently indicates to Dr. Smith that poor families, blacks included, often eat all the parts of the chicken and that these particular responses should be considered within normal limits given the child's social and cultural background.

In addition, tests may not be normed for the particular ethnic or racial group to which the child belongs; this increases the difficulty of accurately interpreting the test data. For example, Ariella and Shira, two five-year-old girls, are to be screened for entry into kindergarten. Shira was born in New York City to an upper-middle-class, religious Jewish family. Shira's chances of passing the test are high, because tests are often normed on urban, middle-class children. However, Shira's heritage and religion may contribute significantly to understanding her performance. Ariella was born in a rural part of Mexico to a poor, working-class family. She and her family moved to the United States two years ago and live in a poor, working-class Hispanic neighborhood. Ariella's cultural context is highly influenced by her Mexican heritage. Both her heritage and her membership in a minority group can be relevant to understanding her performance.

*Practice Guideline 10.2: To understand a particular child's test performance, the clinician weights and integrates the test norms together with the child's reference group norms (such as membership in an ethnic or racial minority or a low-income family). The goal is to consider the contribution made by social and cultural variables to the child's performance.*

**Psychometric Properties of the Test.** Standardization procedures were developed to help determine the meaning of a person's test score in relation to those of similar people and to establish a system for evaluating whether tests measure accurately what they are supposed to measure (Anastasi, 1976; Martin, 1977).

Standardized tests by definition are objective in the sense that they are built on uniform procedures for gathering and interpreting data. A major assumption made is that the role of the tester is controlled or remains constant. Typically, constraints are placed on the amount and type of feedback or encouragement the tester is allowed to give the child. This uniformity is to control for error that might enter into the child's score as a result of tester variables. However, as stated earlier, it is impossible to ignore the dynamic interaction between the tester and the child in the face of growing evidence of its often negative influence (Brown and Ferrara, 1985).

As part of a larger study examining the language-using abilities of Hispanic and Anglo-American elementary school children, Mehan (1973) found that testers do not always act in a uniform manner toward children they are testing. Children and testers were videotaped and it was discovered that items were not presented in standardized form and that testers often gave both verbal and nonverbal prompts about whether or not a response was correct. In addition, items did not always have the same meaning for the tester and the child. This last finding speaks to the issue of taking context—the child's particular worldview or interpretive frame—into account when interpreting a child's behavior or performance.

A test is unfair or discriminatory if members of one group typically score lower on a measure than members of another group for reasons unrelated to the characteristics targeted by the test. For example, a height measure that finds blacks on average to be taller than Hispanics is not unfair, whereas a measure of memory used to test blacks but written in Spanish would be. Several landmark cases related to bias have been fought in the courts, often with much confusion regarding validity and unfairness; some have resulted in the banning of tests that disproportionately place minority children in special classes or programs (Reschly, 1984).

*Overall Clinical Assessment.* For the purpose of answering referral questions, a single test can rarely give conclusive answers about a child's adaptive and maladaptive functioning. Obtaining valid and conclusive results often rests upon using a battery of tests.

The validity of the results increases when the child presents similar content throughout one test and consistent content across different tests. Test results are further validated when similar results are found in other methods of inquiry, such as interviews or observations.

*Practice Guideline 10.3: Using a battery of tests and different methods of investigation increases the clinician's confidence in his or her interpretations of the child's functioning.*

### Intellectual and Educational Assessment

Intelligence, achievement, and learning disability evaluations are usually carried out by trained professionals, such as psychologists and learning disability specialists. Children typically referred for these types of evaluations are those who demonstrate poor, questionable, or superior cognitive functioning. The evaluation is often initiated by concerned parents, teachers, or clinicians. For example, through skilled observation or administration of a screening instrument teachers may determine the need for a more comprehensive cognitive evaluation.

*Intelligence Tests.* Intellectual and cognitive assessments typically serve one or more of the following purposes: to predict how well a child will function academically in school; to diagnose cognitive delay or retardation; to screen for learning problems or disabilities; to give a description or profile of the child's cognitive strengths and weaknesses; and to make recommendations regarding school placement or the need for remediation or intervention. The McCarthy Scales of Children's Abilities (MSCA), the Stanford-Binet Intelligence Test (SB), the Wechsler Preschool and Primary Scales of Intelligence (WPPSI), and the Wechsler Intelligence Scale for Children—Revised (WISC-R) are representative of tests used to assess children's intellectual ability.

The MSCA is a general intelligence test that can be used with children aged two and a half to eight and a half. The child is assessed in five specific skill areas, namely, verbal, perceptual, quantitative, memory, and motor functioning. The SB can be used with a broader age span, from age two to adulthood. One of the strengths of the SB is its usefulness in assessing older retarded children. In addition to obtaining an intelligence quotient (IQ), the tester is able to obtain a useful picture of the retarded child's skills and strengths. The SB is of limited use with younger children with language difficulties because of a high concentration of language items at the lower age levels of the test.

The WISC-R was developed as a general intelligence test for children from six to sixteen. The WPPSI was developed later as a downward extension of the WISC-R and can be used with children from four to six and a half. The Wechsler tests are divided into two broad scales, a verbal scale and a performance scale, each of which contains several subtests. For example, the verbal scale assesses such areas as vocabulary, comprehension, and similarities, while the performance scale assesses such areas as object assembly, coding, and block design. A major strength of the Wechsler tests, especially the WISC-R, is the profile that can be obtained of the child's significant intellectual strengths and deficits. A major limitation is its usability with retarded children in the lower ages for which the test is normed. For example, a retarded four-year-old can fail all the items of the WPPSI and receive an IQ score of 50. Although the score aids us in ranking the extent of retardation, it does not tell us what the child is capable of doing.

*Achievement Tests.* The Wide-Range Achievement Tests, the Stanford Achievement Tests, and the Iowa Tests of Basic Skills are representative of tests used to measure achievement. These tests were developed to be used in educational settings for the purpose of assessing student learning or mastery of curriculum. Achievement tests are now used for several other purposes, including classification, placement, and evaluation of instructional effectiveness (Fox and Zirkin, 1984). Although they are often used in this manner, achievement tests are of limited use for comparing groups of children, classrooms, or schools.

*Learning Disability Evaluation Tests.* A child with a learning disability is one who exhibits a significant discrepancy between expected and actual achievement. The discrepancy in functioning can occur in one or more of the following areas: receptive language, expressive language, reading, writing, or mathematics. These children have difficulty processing information because of deficits in attention, perception, memory, symbolization, conceptualization, or motor functioning.

The purpose of a learning disability evaluation is threefold: to diagnose the learning problem, to determine the specific area or areas where the child is experiencing difficulties (such as reading) and the specific learning systems that might underlie the difficulties (such as memory), and to make recommendations for remediation. Because the learning disability specialist is interested in locating and focusing on very specific deficits, a broad variety of tests are used. The Woodcock-Johnson Psycho-Educational Battery, the Goldman-Fristoe-Woodcock Test of Auditory Discrimination, the Developmental Test of Visual-Motor Integration, and the Peabody Picture Vocabulary Test are representative of tests used to assess specific abilities and deficits.

*Critique of Intellectual and Educational Assessment.* The strengths of intellectual and educational tests as clinical tools are many, particularly in regard to measuring prior learning and predicting academic achievement. These types of tests give a standardized evaluation of a child's cognitive functioning, which may not be readily available through observation of the child in a classroom, clinic, or home setting. For example, from observation a teacher may suspect that a child has a learning problem. However, it takes formal testing to determine the diagnosis and, more important, to discover the learning process involved and the specific area of deficit. Administering a standardized test can be especially useful when there are discrepant views about the child's cognitive functioning. Further, when the time available for an evaluation is limited, formal testing is helpful because it can provide a great deal of information about the child in a short time.

Many of the cognitive tests mentioned above provide the tester with a profile or pattern of the child's strengths and weaknesses. The WISC-R, for example, provides the tester with a verbal IQ, a performance IQ, and a full scale IQ. In addition, the child's intellectual strengths and weaknesses can be determined by examining his performance on each of the eleven subtests. The following is an excerpt from a testing report on an eight-year-old Caucasian boy referred for testing because of academic problems at school:

Clearly one of Jack's strengths is his arithmetic reasoning, which is in the high-average range compared to other children his age. His abstract concept formation (the ability to see the relationship between objects) is also a strength. One factor which seems to have lowered some of his verbal subtest scores was the low amount of speech which he produced. This does not appear to be the result of anxiety, distractibility, or motivation. Jack may have an expressive language or word finding problem. He performed roughly 25 IQ points lower on those subtests which required a high degree of language output (Information, Vocabulary, and Comprehension) than on those verbal subtests where one or two word answers were sufficient. While this may reflect a motivational problem to some degree, I would not have expected him to do as well as he did on Arithmetic and Digit Span if motivation were affecting his scores so much. Overall Jack is stronger in verbal skills than spatial ones. Although he demonstrated good visual organizational abilities, his visual scanning, non-verbal planning abilities, and visual motor speed were areas of relative weakness [Gutierrez, 1984, p. 2].

This information is invaluable in considering further assessment and remediation. Although Jack scored in the average range of intelligence, his profile indicated a possible learning problem. He was referred for a learning disability evaluation, which confirmed a learning disability, and remediation was recommended.

Standardized tests also allow the clinician to compare the child's intellectual and educational functioning to that of his peer group. In addition, testing allows the clinician to monitor a child's cognitive functioning over a period of time. For example, a child who has suffered a head injury may be tested every six months over several years to monitor progression or regression in cognitive functioning.

*Practice Guideline 10.4: Intelligence and other cognitive tests are excellent clinical tools for measuring independent problem-solving skills and prior learning and for predicting academic achievement.*

However, intellectual and educational tests are limited in several areas. One of the major criticisms of intellectual testing is the narrow manner in which intelligence is defined and assessed. Intelligence can be broadly defined as the capacity to function in life and the capacity to create new ideas. However, the capacities that are needed may vary from culture to culture and from society to society. Gardner (1987) views intelligence as the ability to solve problems. In his pluralistic view of intelligence, he asserts that individuals have different cognitive strengths and contrasting cognitive styles that they use to solve problems. Of the seven types of intelligence he lists, linguistic intelligence and logical-mathematical intelligence are the only two typically assessed by traditional intelligence tests. Intelligence tests do not typically elicit information about the other types of intelligence or other ways in which children solve problems. For example, if a child's cognitive strength or cognitive style is in social or relational intelligence, he is likely to do poorly on traditional intelligence tests. It appears that in Western societies linguistic and logical skills are more valued and more likely to be elicited from children.

In addition, Hundeide (1980) suggests that problem solving is different in different cultures or societies. How a person approaches or solves a problem is influenced by her worldview or interpretive frame. Hundeide's review suggests that people who live in simple societies solve problems by using everyday life experience as a framework. In contrast, in more complex societies an abstract, logical problem-solving method is more valued and expected. A difficulty occurs, however, when a child with one kind of interpretive frame is asked to solve a problem requiring another interpretive frame. The child may not understand what is being asked or expected of her. Hilliard (1982) states that traditional intelligence tests create this difficulty for children, especially poor children from ethnic or racial minorities; the children's poor performance is then attributed, not to a problem in the interaction between the child and the tester, but to a deficiency in the child's capacity. Culture-fair or culture-free tests have been developed to help eliminate the bias caused by the failure to take a child's social and cultural context into account (Mercer, 1975). However, many of these tests do not overcome the biases they were intended to eliminate (Hennessy, 1981).

There has been considerable legal debate about the validity of some educational and intellectual standardized assessments. For example, in 1979 in California, the use of IQ tests for educational placement of black children was banned on the grounds that the tests were biased (Cordes, 1986; Reschly, 1984). Some educators have called for cognitive tests to be either abandoned or reconstructed (Hilliard, 1982).

Another major criticism of intelligence and educational tests is related to the interpretation of the results. For example, as mentioned above, it it often assumed that the child's test score reflects the child's capacity or ability, rather than some other mediating factor. Hilliard (1980, 1982) has criticized the utility of current cognitive tests because they are designed to predict school achievement or to categorize children as gifted, average, or retarded. According to Hilliard, the tests tell us what the child does not know—that is, they reveal failure in prior learning—but give no information on why the child does not know it. One cannot be sure if a child's poor test score reflects a lack of learning ability, a lack of opportunity for learning, or a lack of motivation on the child's part.

***Dynamic Cognitive Assessments.*** Traditional intelligence assessments measure the child's independent problem-solving ability and are concerned with the child's prior learning. However, when the purpose of the cognitive assessment is to assess what a child *can* learn, a dynamic, interactive format is required. In this format, the tester interacts with the child to guide her through the learning assessment process in an attempt to determine the process by which the child learns and the strategies or interventions that will improve the child's potential. Dynamic cognitive assessment has been largely influenced by Vygotsky's theory of a zone of proximal development. The zone of proximal development is defined as "the distance between the actual developmental level as determined by independent problem solving and the level of potential development as determined through problem solving under adult guidance or in collaboration with more capable peers" (Vygotsky, 1978, p. 86). Vygotsky's theory provides support for a dynamic, interactive method of determining learning potential.

Several investigators have developed procedures for assessing learning potential. Among these are Budoff's test-coach-retest approach and Feuerstein's Learning Potential Assessment Device model. Budoff's work focuses on the learning potential of the educable mentally retarded. He developed a test-coach-retest procedure to identify a child's ability to benefit from training. Utilizing Raven's (1947) progressive matrices and blocks, children are given prompts until they solve a puzzle. Budoff identified three groups—gainers, nongainers, and high scorers prior to coaching. He found that coaching improved the performance of gainers and high scorers in special education classes (Budoff, 1968).

The goals of a Feuerstein's (1979) assessment are to measure the child's problem-solving skills and to determine whether they can be enhanced through mediated experience. To meet these goals Feuerstein designed the Learning Potential Assessment Device and the Instrumental Enrichment program. These utilize standardized tests—such as Raven's progressive matrices, the verbal and figural analogy test, and human figure drawings—in a nonstandard test-train-retest format. Feuerstein has generally found support for his approach by demonstrating that children's cognitive capacities can be modified (Feuerstein, 1979).

Feuerstein's and Budoff's dynamic assessment might also prove useful with learning-disabled children who have difficulty learning through traditional methods. A limitation of this type of approach is that it depends a great deal on the role of the tester. For example, the tester may not sample or discover the particular mediating strategy that will be helpful to a particular child.

*Practice Guideline 10.5: If the purpose of the assessment is to determine what a child can learn and which learning strategies will improve learning, a dynamic, interactive testing format is needed.*

## Developmental Screening and Assessment

The major task of infancy and childhood is to maintain development (Flapan and Neubauer, 1976). Therefore, a developmental evaluation should fulfill two goals. The first is to determine whether the child is developing according to an agreed-upon developmental agenda; this includes the notion that children develop in several domains—cognitive, physical, social, and emotional—simultaneously. The second is to determine whether a disorder is interfering with developmental progress in any domain of functioning. To meet these goals, clinicians need models of healthy and pathological development. Models and theories of development help clinicians think about how children's capacities unfold, how to assess these capacities formally, and how to determine the extent of adaptive and maladaptive functioning.

Freud, Erikson, and other psychoanalytic theorists have contributed to our understanding of socioemotional development. Piaget, Vygotsky, and other cognitive theorists have contributed to our understanding of cognitive development. These and other recent models have provided clinicians with a blueprint for assessing developmental progression and regression. Formal assessment instruments are one of the clinical tools available for assessing whether the child is maintaining development. Developmental screening tests and developmental assessment tests are two types of instruments available to clinicians evaluating infants and young children.

*Developmental Screening Tests.* Developmental screening evaluations are typically done by professionals and paraprofessionals, such as child development specialists, preschool teachers, parent-infant educators, and trained program staff. Screening is part of a larger assessment process used to identify children who are at risk for developmental delay by providing a quick and limited evaluation of the child. Children found at risk are referred for a more comprehensive developmental assessment for the purpose of diagnosis and intervention.

Developmental screening tests are designed to assess overall developmental status or to evaluate specific areas of concern, such as language or visual-motor functioning. The McCarthy Screening Test, the Minnesota Preschool Screening Instrument, the Receptive-Expressive Emergent Language Scale, and the Denver Developmental Screening Test (DDST) are representative of tests used to screen infants and children.

The DDST is one of the most widely used developmental screening instruments. The DDST is designed to be used with

children up to six years of age. The child is screened in the areas of
personal-social, fine motor, gross motor, and language development. Because it can be administered by paraprofessionals with no
specialized training in testing, the DDST is appropriate for use in
many settings, such as schools, hospitals, clinics, and community-
based developmental programs.

For example, the Ounce of Prevention Developmental
Program in Illinois uses the DDST along with the Parent-Infant
Observation Guide, a screening instrument developed to assess
socioemotional functioning in parent-child dyads (Bernstein,
Percansky, and Hans, 1987). The Ounce of Prevention Fund works
with community-based programs to help prevent family problems,
particularly with adolescent parents and young families (Musick
and Stott, forthcoming). The infants are often at risk and in need of
early identification for a number of reasons, including prematurity
and low birth weight, their parents' limited knowledge of child
care, and the many sociocultural constraints that are the result of
poverty. These screening instruments provide paraprofessional staff
with structured evaluation tools for assessing children, as well as a
means for improving their understanding of how children develop.

Developmental screening instruments are useful clinical
tools for early identification of children at risk for future problems.
Because they can be administered by paraprofessionals quickly and
inexpensively, many children can be tested who otherwise might
not be.

Screening instruments are not designed to be used to predict
school success or readiness. School success is best predicted by
standardized intelligence tests, while school readiness is best
determined by a readiness test. Educational readiness tests are used
to identify whether a child has the skills and knowledge necessary to
benefit from a specific academic program or curriculum (Meisels,
1986). The Boehm Test of Basic Concepts and the Metropolitan
Readiness Test are representative of tests designed to assess
educational readiness. Screening instruments are also not meant to
be used as diagnostic instruments; they are not intended to be used
for determining specialized placement or for labeling children.

*Developmental Assessment Tests.* Infants, toddlers, and
preschoolers are often seen in early intervention programs, child

development centers, and mental health centers for a formal developmental assessment of their cognitive, language, motor, and social capacities. The distinction between developmental screening tests and developmental assessment tests lies in the specific purpose of the testing and the type of tests employed. As mentioned earlier, the purpose of developmental screening is prevention through early identification. On the other hand, developmental assessment tests provide for a more comprehensive evaluation of the child's cognitive, socioemotional, motor, and language abilities with the intention of determining a diagnosis and making recommendations for remediation. The assessment typically serves one of several purposes, such as assessing the child's developmental status, diagnosing developmental deficits in specific capacities or domains, directing children to specialized placement or intervention, and tracking or monitoring developmental progression or regression over time.

*Practice Guideline 10.6: Developmental screening is a preventive strategy used to identify children who may have developmental delay, while developmental assessment is a treatment strategy used for diagnosis and to plan remediation.*

The Bayley Scales of Infant Development and the Gesell Developmental Schedules are representative of tests used to assess the developmental status of infants and toddlers. The Bayley is a widely used and well-known developmental assessment test that assesses cognitive, motor, and behavioral functioning in infants and toddlers up to thirty months of age. It is designed to be administered by trained professionals for the purpose of diagnosing developmental delay.

The Bayley is one of the tools used in the clinical assessment of infants in infant mental health programs, such as the Child Development Project developed by Selma Fraiberg (1980). The project was created for infants and parents who are at risk for cognitive, emotional, and familial problems. One of the main areas of concern is parent-infant attachment. Because the staff of the project are concerned with the infant's overall developmental functioning, the parent's emotional functioning, and the emotional bond between parent and infant, they do a comprehensive, process-oriented clinical assessment. They want to know why the infant is at risk, what developmental areas are affected, and what might be interfering with development (Fraiberg, 1980). The clinical assessment is done by combining home visits and clinic visits where the parent and infant are observed, interviewed, and tested. The staff of the Child Development Project work very hard at establishing a trusting relationship with the family, since they believe, like the staff of many other clinical programs, that their relationship with the family is crucial for promoting change.

In 1965 Anna Freud eloquently emphasized the need for clincians evaluating and treating children to assess their total personality and capacities. She was concerned that clinicians often assessed isolated parts of the child's functioning and used these limited assessments to make decisions and recommendations (Freud, 1965). All of the infant's or child's capacities or domains of development (cognitive, motor, language, social, and emotional) need to be evaluated; evidence exists that these different domains may not all develop in the same way and on the same schedule. In addition to evaluating the infant's individual capacities, clinicians should assess the caretaking environment and the way the infant and the caretaking system interact to determine developmental status and outcome.

Can developmental tests or any combination of tests actually evaluate children's total functioning and the important caretaking environment? We can begin to address this question by examining how well developmental tests assess the multiple lines or domains of development.

Developmental assessment tests are useful clinical tools for objectively assessing cognitive functioning. For example, the Bayley is an excellent test for assessing cognitive delay in infants and toddlers. Yet the Bayley and other developmental instruments are not predictive of later cognitive abilities; they should be considered descriptive of the child's current developmental status (Self and Horowitz, 1979). They tend to be better predictors of later abilities for infants with handicapping conditions (McCall, 1979). Intelligence and achievement tests are excellent tools for assessing preschool children's cognitive abilities and prior learning. However, if the purpose is to assess specific learning strategies or the range of cognitive capacities, other types of procedures are needed, such as observation, Piagetian probes, and dynamic, mediated assessment procedures.

Developmental tests often fail to assess emotional and social functioning comprehensively (Fraiberg, 1980). Assessing social development in very young children involves gaining information about their relationships with significant adults, peers, and strangers. Unfortunately, testing is not the best method available to us for gathering information about a child's ability to interact socially and to form relationships. Testing also does not help us assess the quality of these relationships. When developmental tests are employed, the results are of limited value. The tests often have few items measuring social development and often do not require the child to show interactive abilities; thus, it is difficult to make comprehensive statements about the child's social functioning. In addition, it is difficult to interpret data derived from more projective techniques, such as children's drawings. Currently, the best methods available to us are observing children interacting with others (parents, other adults, and peers) and interacting with the children ourselves in structured and unstructured settings.

There is no standardized test in common clinical use that evaluates emotional functioning and parent-infant attachment in children younger than four. Our best assessment techniques have typically been structured and unstructured observations and interviews with significant adults. However, in the last decade or two, researchers and clinicians like Greenspan (1979, 1981; Greenspan and Lieberman, 1980; Greenspan and Porges, 1984) and Ainsworth (Ainsworth and Wittig, 1969; Ainsworth, Blehar, Waters, and Wall, 1978) have developed procedures for assessing emotional functioning in very young children. Greenspan integrated developmental theory, existing research, and the literature on clinical case studies to formulate the clinical developmental structuralist approach to assessment and diagnosis. His diagnostic system consists of determining whether the child has met the organizational tasks of each developmental level and whether adaptive and maladaptive patterns have been established. Ainsworth's work is more specifically related to assessing the quality of infant attachment. Both assessment procedures rely heavily on combining observational techniques with developmental theory to determine the infant's level of emotional functioning.

Gaining valid and sufficient information about infants' and young children's adaptive and maladaptive capacities and the caretaking environment that influences these capacities depends largely on employing a combination of methods of assessments (tests, interviews, and observation). Each method of investigation provides the clinician with pieces of useful information. It is the clinician's role to put together all these pieces of information into a cohesive, integrated picture of the child's functioning and caretaking system.

## Personality Assessment

Assessing socioemotional or personality functioning in children older than four is like putting together the pieces of a complicated jigsaw puzzle. Each piece gives a clearer picture of the whole puzzle. Like a puzzle piece before it is fitted into place, the behavior that children display can have many meanings. It is the job of the clinician to attempt to put the pieces together and discover their combined meaning. To be effective, the clinician needs to understand both the child's external behavior and experience and her internal and subjective experience, as well as the parenting and sociocultural environment.

Personality tests are typically administered by clinical psychologists who have received specialized training in their administration and interpretation. Children are usually referred for a diagnostic interview evaluation by teachers, parents, protective service workers, or clinicians who have noticed difficulties in emotional functioning that may be due either to situational stress or to a long-standing problem. The initial diagnostic interview often leads to a recommendation for psychological testing, which includes an evaluation of personality functioning. Determining whether the symptoms are related to situational stress (such as parental divorce) or to psychopathology (such as psychosis) is part of any personality assessment.

The information obtained from a personality evaluation is typically used for determining the child's conflicts, fantasies, and feelings; for diagnosis; for making recommendations for psychological treatment; for placement in classrooms for emotionally disturbed children; and, if necessary, for referring the child for a psychiatric evaluation to assess the need for medication. The specific tests used often depend on the referral question and other questions formulated by the psychologist; typical referral questions include the following:

- Is the child's socioemotional functioning interfering with academic or cognitive functioning?
- Is the child anxious, depressed, or experiencing another type of affective disorder?
- Are the behavioral problems displayed by this child related to an underlying emotional concern?
- What seems to be causing this child to have difficulty relating to peers?
- Does the child have problems with reality testing? Is there any indication of a thought disorder or possible psychosis?
- Should the child's custody be granted to the mother or father?
- Has this sexually abused child experienced significant difficulties in emotional functioning?

Personality tests are either objective and structured or projective and unstructured. The Minnesota Multiphasic Personality Inventory and the Rotter Incomplete Sentence Blanks are examples of objective tests that present the child with unambiguous items to which he is to respond. These tests are assumed to elicit more conscious information about the child's personality (Shneidman, 1949). Projective personality tests, such as the Rorschach Inkblot Test and the Thematic Apperception Test (TAT), present the child with ambiguous stimuli. The child's internal organization is believed to determine the style and content of his response (Goldman, Stein, and Guerry, 1983). These tests are assumed to elicit unconscious and preconscious information about the child's personality, specifically conflicts, wishes, defenses, and coping mechanisms (Graham and Lilly, 1984).

Projective personality tests often help the psychologist evaluate the child's subjective experience of a problem or situation.

Often the clinician is more concerned with the psychological truth or the meaning the child has given to a particular situation than with the objective facts of the situation. For example, in sexual abuse cases, the most important therapeutic issue often is the way the child perceived and internalized the abuse and the meaning she ascribed to the situation. Projective tests provide a method of arriving at the subjective world of what the child is feeling and thinking. Chapter Twelve, which covers children in clinical settings, discusses more thoroughly the difference between subjective data and objective data and their importance in evaluating children's emotional functioning.

Three widely used projective techniques are the Rorschach, the TAT, and projective drawings. The Rorschach was originally developed to be used with adults. Ames and Exner have both normed the test for children aged two and older (Ames, Learned, Metraux, and Walker, 1974; Exner, 1978). The Rorschach is a valuable tool for providing information about underlying dynamics, such as areas of conflict, defenses, and affect (Erdberg and Exner, 1984). Often the child is not aware of the underlying conflicts and thoughts that are believed to motivate and influence feelings and behavior. For example, a child may unconsciously experience unmet dependency needs. In addition, the Rorschach can give information about the quality of the child's reality testing and problems related to thought processes; for example, the child may be psychotic or may distort reality in a less severe manner.

The TAT was developed to elicit perceptions, fantasies, and wishes from children and adults by asking them to tell stories in response to cards with human-figure scenarios. However, because the scenarios depicted on the TAT cards were not thought to be relevant to children, the Children's Apperception Test (CAT) was developed. The CAT provides the child with animal scenarios. In addition to eliciting fantasy material, these tests are useful in obtaining information about the child's perceptions and wishes regarding interpersonal relationships. They also can be used to obtain information about the child's self-esteem. The child is often only partly aware of these perceptions and wishes (preconscious) or not aware at all (unconscious).

*Practice Guideline 10.7: Eliciting information about chil-*

*dren's perceptions, fantasies, expectations, motives, and coping*
*mechanisms can aid in understanding children's behavior. How*
*children adjust or adapt to situations is often related to these more*
*subjective feelings and thoughts.*

A major strength of personality testing is that it offers the
clinician a method for collecting data on the child's internal and
subjective experience as well as the child's external behavior and
objective experience. Personality testing can thus augment material
obtained by observing children in structured and unstructured
settings, such as play, and by interviewing children and parents.

The problems involved in personality assessment are often
most apparent when clinicians are asked to answer questions that
no specific test is equipped to address. For example, caution must be
used when evaluating children involved in custody litigation and
allegations of sexual abuse. Testing, especially projective testing, is
often used in custody evaluations. Evaluators typically use a
combination of personality tests, including the Rorschach, the
CAT, and the House-Tree-Person Test. However, none of these tests
can conclusively determine whether the child is best served by
giving custody to the mother, the father, or another significant
adult. To help answer the custody question, an assessment of the
quality of the parent-child relationship is needed. This assessment
is best accomplished by observing the child with each parent and
gathering information from significant adults such as grandparents, teachers, and baby-sitters. The psychologist's report and
testimony are best used as additional information, rather than as a
final recommendation. Some professionals have recommended that
personality tests not be used to determine custody in court, largely
on the basis of the difficulty of interpreting these tests (Gardner,
1982).

Bresee, Stearns, Bess, and Packer (1986) have outlined a
therapeutic assessment model to be used when sexual abuse
allegations have been made in a custody case. They state that
whether or not the sexual abuse is confirmed, the fact that
allegations were made is enough to indicate that the child is at risk.
In their model, both parents and child are interviewed and tested
with the objective of differentiating victims of sexual abuse.

Children from three to six years old are tested using the Draw-a-Person Test, the Draw-a-Family Test, the Conger Children's Sentence Completion Test, the CAT, and the Rorschach test. In addition to these tests, children from six to twelve also are given the Children's Manifest Anxiety Scale and the Piers-Harris Children's Self-Concept Test. The tests are intended to find signs or symptoms of abuse, such as changes in personality and behavior, developmental regression, sexual preoccupations and acting out, and submissiveness. Although this diagnostic system is well thought out, it cannot determine conclusively whether a child has been sexually abused. No test exists that can answer this question conclusively. However, this testing model may help the clinician understand the way the child perceives the situation and the meaning the child ascribes to this stressful period. Testing may also help in making the necessary recommendations for treatment.

Personality tests are best used to determine underlying conflicts and feelings and to diagnose emotional disturbance. Even when they are used this way, however, much caution is needed because the data are very difficult to interpret. Clinicians have been criticized both for overinterpreting and for underinterpreting testing data in diagnosing psychopathology. Material derived from any one personality test allows the clinician to form hypotheses about the child. The confirmation of hypotheses is dependent on finding consistent content across different tests and different methods of inquiry. The clinician must be cautious when answering any referral question having to do with emotional functioning in young children. This makes it even more difficult to address child custody and sexual abuse questions.

When evaluating children using objective and projective personality tests, it is also important to be cognizant of situational regression that might be caused by a temporary stressor. For example, preschool children generally know the difference between fantasy and reality. However, when these children experience stress they are less likely to differentiate the two, a phenomenon Gould (1972) calls "fluctuating certainty" (pp. 77–84). For example, children who are hospitalized for medical procedures often show regressions in functioning. If a child presents distortions in reality, the clinician must determine whether the distortions are caused by a stressful situation or by severe psychopathology.

Another major concern is the validity of projective tests and the technical properties of personality tests. The Rorschach, for example, was standardized on normal children from middle-class backgrounds (Goldman, Stein, and Guerry, 1983). Children of different cultures or ethnic groups may present TAT stories or Rorschach responses that are divergent from what is considered emotionally healthy but within normal limits for their particular reference groups. Care must be taken not to see psychopathology where none exists.

## Conclusions

This chapter has provided the untrained consumer of test results with a framework for evaluating the strengths and weaknesses of formal assessments and for understanding what information can and cannot be provided and what questions can and cannot be answered by intellectual, developmental, and personality tests. Although tests and other instruments can be useful clinical tools, they can only provide one piece of the necessary information that forms the bigger picture. To put the picture together, additional information must be gathered from other methods, such as interviews and observation of the parents and the child. Unfortunately, there is not the kind of certainty in testing that can be found in litmus paper. Valuable information is to be found in testing, however, when sensitive clinicians take the time to know the tests they are administering, when they use theory to guide their interpretations, and when they consider the contribution made by social and cultural variables to the child's performance.

CHAPTER 11

# Children at Home, in School, and in Day Care

**M**any of the issues parents and caregivers face in coping with child-care settings are concerns about obtaining and evaluating information from children. Parents wonder: How will I know if the care arrangement is working out for my child? Can I rely on what my child tells me? How should I interpret my child's appearance at the end of the day? What meaning should I attach to the way he feels about going in the morning? How do I go beyond "It's okay, mom. Nothing happened" when I ask my child about being home alone after school? How do I get young baby-sitters to tell me what happened when I was gone? What if I suspect that the child-care center is inadequate but I have no specifics to back me up?

Caregivers ask: How much do I need to know about the family? What if the child seems unhappy but the parents say nothing's wrong? What if a child consistently does not want to go home? What if a child tells me information that contradicts what her parents have told me? If a child tells other children about intimate family relationships, do I stop her? Do I pursue the ideas if they seem to be troubling to the child? How do I draw the line between my curiosity about the family and the information that I need in order to care for the child?

*Note:* The authors acknowledge the invaluable contributions of Judith Bertacchi, Maggie Faulkenberry, Carol Pardo, Laura Schreisheim, and Bonnie Wishne. They shared their experiences as directors and consultants to child care programs, providing us with a deeper understanding of the issues; clear guidelines on how to approach caregivers, children, and families; and rich case examples.

In this chapter, we focus on two issues vital to a child's functioning as a source of information. First, what is the child-care provider's response to information that the child gives about the family? Second, what is the family's response to information that the child gives about the child-care setting? Adults must make decisions about their own behavior in response to what children tell them through words or actions. The focus of this chapter is on communications that can be understood and handled within the context of the child-care setting and the family. We do not address situations that require protective service involvement (for a discussion of protective service issues in child-care settings, see Garbarino, 1987). Many types of knowledge and many concerns inform parents' and caretakers' decisions about what to do in everyday situations:

- Knowledge about the particular child (Does the adult generally believe this child? Is this behavior typical?)
- Knowledge about children in general ("It's normal for three-year-olds to wet their pants every now and then—I don't want to make a big deal out of it when the parents pick her up" or "My daughter came home and told me that one of the boys pinched her when she was at your house. How can you let such a terrible thing happen?")
- Knowledge about each other ("This is a teacher I can't talk to because she will take it out on my child" or "This is a parent who will understand and not punish the child if I tell her.")
- Knowledge about the setting ("I've seen other day-care centers and I know that five-year-old children should not be allowed to go to the basement unsupervised for long periods of time" or "I don't know how to take care of kids. It must be okay if Mrs. Cordillo lets you do it.")
- Feelings about giving feedback ("I just keep my peace. I don't like to upset others" or "If that happened to my child, I'd go and talk to the provider. I don't let things go for very long before I speak up.")
- Their own history in similar situations ("I was hit by our baby-sitter when my parents weren't home and it didn't bother me or my brothers. We needed it or otherwise we would have wrecked

the house" or "I remember when I was in fourth grade and my mom left me alone after school. It was horrible. I was afraid that the old man who came by to ask if he could sharpen scissors would come back and get me.")

Traditional descriptions of teachers and parents as occupying clearly different roles blur when we look at child-care settings, particularly home-care and family day-care environments. Parents placing a six-week-old infant in the care of an in-home provider often expect, whether consciously or unconsciously, that the provider will love their child, not just care for him. Parents are looking for an attachment that goes beyond the typical teacher role, yet they may also hope for a more objective impartiality that will enable the provider to tell them if something is wrong.

Further, family day care offers a homelike atmosphere with naturally occurring activities set in the ebb and flow of the daily routine of family life. While there may be an expectation of greater attachment, a valuing of spontaneity and less structure, most parents still expect that appropriate activities will be available and that their child will be attended to. Thus, for example, watching TV or playing outside unsupervised all day is not acceptable.

This mix of expectations between the parenting role and the professional role in child-care settings both simplifies and complicates communication between parent and provider. The parent-provider relationship is basically symmetrical—the two parties engage in similar, but not identical, types of behavior in relation to the child. This symmetry facilitates communication, unlike an asymmetrical relationship (such as a physician-patient relationship), where one member is of higher status than the other and possesses information and skills the other lacks.

However, the role sharing of parents and providers—particularly their overlapping attachments to the child—and their mutual dependency without the intermediary of a sponsoring agency can inhibit one party from questioning the other. The provider may hesitate to bring up potentially sensitive information without the protection of social distance and professional authority, which typically buffer the communication between professionals and their clients. Likewise, parents may hesitate to give a provider feedback because of the intimate role they have asked her to play in their lives. There is a tendency for parents to view child-care providers as doing them a favor, rather than as contracting with them for services. As one hesitates to tell a guest that her help with dinner is not appreciated, one may hesitate to tell a provider that her kitchen is not clean enough. These issues seem less prevalent for providers in center-based settings; here, the traditional role differences tend to be in place and child-care providers can process their concerns and develop strategies for communicating with parents with the assistance of other adults, such as the center's director, social worker, mental health consultant, or other providers.

### Family Day-Care Providers

Alston (1984) describes nine roles of the family day-care provider: nurse, teacher, nutritionist, social worker, accountant, paramedic, architect and interior decorator, psychologist, and student of human development. The provider as nurse needs information about the overall physical condition of the child and any immediate concerns—illnesses, injuries, disruptions in sleep or feeding patterns, or any acute event (such as immunization) affecting the mood, energy level, or daily routines of the child. Information about the child's physical status and immediate concerns is usually obtained directly from parents. However, children themselves can be sources of information in this domain. Some toddlers and older preschool children may tell the provider about injuries or illness. Just as often, the provider will need to obtain the information through observation, particularly for infants, and through sensitive questioning and discussions with toddlers and preschoolers.

The provider as teacher wants to know about the child's developmental capabilities, interests, preferred activities, and friendship patterns as well as the parent's educational goals for the child. This information can be obtained by asking parents, by asking children, or by observing them as they interact with the environment. As nutritionist, the provider asks parents about the child's likes and dislikes and the family's preferences and restrictions about foods. For infants, she needs to know the frequency and amount of feedings and any individualized care routines, such as laying one infant on his tummy after feeding and seating another upright in an infant seat to reduce spitting up.

The provider's role as social worker is perhaps the most controversial. How much information does the family day-care provider need about the family to adequately care for the child? How involved should the provider be in family conflicts that affect the child—such as issues around discipline, behavior, or learning problems, behavioral upsets following marital discord or divorce, disruptions in the child's routines tied to the travel or work schedules of parents? We will return to this role when we discuss the topic of child abuse and neglect.

As accountant, the provider needs to record information about the child's attendance and the payment of fees. Unlike teachers and other human service workers, the family day-care provider is a small business owner responsible for initiating and maintaining a business, satisfying her customers—adults and children—and making a profit. To succeed, the provider must know the expectations of the parents and must be able to communicate to them and the public what her services and goals are. As paramedic, the provider needs to know how to reach the family and others in an emergency, who the insurance carrier is, who the pediatrician or family physician is, which hospital to take the child to, and so on. This information typically is obtained directly from the parents. As architect and interior decorator, the provider observes the children's functioning in her setting and makes adjustments as needed. An important concern in this domain is protecting children from being injured by environmental hazards and by their own behavior (such as mouthing objects, ingesting liquids, and exploring heights). Being able to interpret the child's need for protection is an important skill for caregivers.

As psychologist and student of human behavior, the provider is knowledgeable about child development; she knows how to set developmentally appropriate expectations for children, how to encourage positive social behavior, and how to intervene on the child's behalf in situations where the child needs redirection, information, comfort, or limits. The provider obtains the necessary information primarily by observing children's behavior.

Clearly, the family day-care provider has a wide-ranging set of responsibilities, from providing first aid to teaching children to dress themselves; from advising parents to managing tax records, dealing with state-supported food programs, and meeting licensing requirements; from negotiating with her own family about the use of space and time to redesigning her backyard for young toddlers as well as older preschoolers.

Some family day-care providers supply excellent care. But it is hardly surprising that many do not function in all the roles described above. The Aurora Home Child Care Project (Gilkerson, Nesphachel, and Trevino, 1987) has interviewed unlicensed providers caring for two to three times as many children as the law allows, with few or no toys, in ill-lit homes where several children are fed out of the same bowl with the same spoon and where others eat on the floor. Providers may be paid as little as five dollars a day to care for children whose parents do not bring food and do not pick up their children until hours after the agreed-upon departure time. In these settings, the information needs of parents and providers may appear to be low-priority issues. Getting through the day is the provider's concern and having some type of care that does not cost too much is the parents'. Establishing the importance of children as sources of information in such child-care settings is tied to the need to upgrade the quality of care.

Some providers and parents alike are unable to give direct negative feedback. In interviews with family day-care providers, Gilkerson and her colleagues (Gilkerson, Nesphachel, and Trevino, 1987) identified the "I Don't Dare" phenomenon in parent-provider communication. Providers did not dare tell parents about behavioral problems with their child, about their anger at parents who came late and forgot to bring food, or about their dissatisfaction with the low pay they were receiving. They feared either losing the income or harming the child. Parents did not dare tell providers that they disliked the way the provider yelled at the children or the fact that their child was still in his pajamas at the end of the day, that they thought the provider's kitchen was dirty, or that they worried about roaches crawling on the baby bottles. Parents feared losing the provider, who often charged a low fee, or hurting her feelings.

Giving negative feedback is one of the hardest tasks that well-prepared administrators and supervisors have to do. It is no wonder that untrained providers and parents struggle with the difficulties of being assertive when their relationships are so interdependent and ambiguous. Whether for self-protection or for want of communicative skill, where the quality of care is low both parents and providers may find it desirable to engage in a conspiracy of silence, involving children as participants in that conspiracy.

*Practice Guideline 11.1: There may be powerful incentives for adults to suppress or ignore information from children about the quality of care; even if unconsciously held, parental and caregiver disbelief can be a powerful inhibiter to children as suppliers of information.*

## Center-Based Care Providers

While most conceptualizations of infant and toddler programs cover the same content, authors differ in the emphasis that they place on particular aspects of care. Roles for caregivers also reflect these varying priorities. Caregiving roles should be organized around four types of infant and toddler learning: basic care and routines, play, guided learning, and excursion-travel (Fowler, 1980).

The preschool teacher likewise has four roles: nurturing, instructing, relating, and decision making (Spodek, 1978). As nurturers, teachers must be concerned with noninstructional elements that affect a child's ability to learn—such as whether the child is hungry, ill, or frightened. Here, the information needs of the preschool teacher are similar to those of the family day-care provider in the roles of nutritionist, nurse, and social worker. Teachers must provide love and comfort, physical nurturing, and support to families as well as educational opportunities for children.

As instructors, early childhood teachers are responsible for providing both direct instruction (giving children new information) and, more often, indirect instruction (creating a learning situation, planning an environment that invites the child to explore, asking questions that encourage a child to think or test reality). Their information needs are related to children's present developmental levels, ability to learn new information, learning styles, preferred activities, and past school or child-care experiences.

The relational aspects of teaching include the teacher's responsibility to create an atmosphere where a child can trust and where a child feels warmth and acceptance. Here, the teacher's role focuses on the development of those "emotionally validating and developmentally challenging relationships" that are the foundation for social competence and self-esteem, combining personal warmth with high expectations (Garbarino, Guttmann, and Seeley, 1986).

The decision making role overlaps to a certain extent with all other roles. Teachers are constantly making decisions as they move through their day interacting with children and other adults (staff and parents). In this component of the role, we look at not only what decisions teachers make but also the bases on which decisions are made—underlying belief system, philosophical orientation, training, and personal style.

Authoritarian adults lodge all authority in their own hands in their dealings with children: I am the adult, and therefore you will follow my definition of reality. Permissive adults, on the other hand, lodge the definition of reality with the child: You are the child, and therefore I will adjust to your version of reality. Neither of these views does justice to the process of adult-child communication.

The authoritative model recognizes the adult's responsibility to represent social reality in contrast to the child's idiosyncratic self; it simultaneously asserts the adult's obligation to respect the child's reality as a starting point for a renegotiation of the self: I am the adult and know something of the world; you are the child and have a legitimate perspective, but one that must adjust to social realities, with my help.

Of course, all this has an effect on the kind of relationships most teachers consider to be possible with children. In contrast to the very idiosyncratic and uncritical nature of the parent-child relationship, the teacher introduces the social dimension of "public truth," the objective reality that stands in contrast to the subjective reality of the love between parent and child. Getzels (1974) makes a similar distinction between particularistic and universalistic ap-

proaches to children. The former emphasizes who a child is, while
the latter emphasizes what a child does. Thus, when the teacher is
able to respond to the child as a unique individual (and on the basis
of his specific relationship with the child), he is operating in the
domain of the particularistic. When he responds to the child as an
example of a class of children (macho boys, bossy girls, bright
children, impoverished children, liars, dreamers, high-risk children), he is operating in the universalistic domain.

The contrast between the particularistic and universalistic
domains is one thing that distinguishes home from school (and
family from child care). Outside the home, the issues are always
whether the child can meet social standards for communication and
whether the teacher can be adequately responsive to the child as a
unique individual. In the home, the issues are whether the parent
can support the child in becoming communicatively socialized and
whether the child can adjust idiosyncratic communicative patterns
to increasing parental demands for socially constructed ones.

Teachers are the bridge between home and the larger social
environment for children. Unlike other professionals, the teacher
generally is not selected by the primary client—the parent—nor is
the teacher directly responsible to the primary client. Legally,
teachers are expected to serve in loco parentis, that is, to stand in the
relationship of parent and guardian to students. Teachers also have
a broader responsibility to the community and the general public.

### How Children Communicate About the Family

Two themes permeate the discussion of the way children
provide information about the family. The first theme is that
children communicate information about their experiences in at
least three ways: by answering direct questions; by providing
spontaneous reports about family experiences; and by communicating indirect messages nonverbally, particularly in infancy and early
childhood. Adults must hear what children are saying through their
behavior and through their language.

The second theme is that the philosophy of care determines
in part how a provider will pursue the leads that children offer. Katz
(1970) has described three traditional role models for early child-

hood educators. The maternal role model focuses on keeping children safe, comfortable, busy, and happy. The therapeutic model places a priority on the child's mental health and, consequently, expects the teacher to help the child understand his own inner feelings and work out his inner conflicts. The instructional model describes the teacher's role in transferring knowledge and teaching skills. Each of these role models places a priority on a different domain of information about the family. For example, if a caregiver's focus is primarily on taking care of the child's physical needs and supplying adequate stimulation so that the child's development can proceed, sensitive questioning about a child's response to a family crisis such as divorce might not occur. In a therapeutic setting, the caregiver would focus on the divorce and help the child process the experience. And in a setting focused on providing instruction, the divorce might lead to a storybook unit on alternative family forms.

For the caregiver, the underlying criteria for pursuing a child's communication about the family are two. First, does the information have important consequences for the child's development or well-being? Second, can I use the information constructively? Examples of potentially sensitive family information that children have shared with their caregivers provide a context within which to examine the caregivers' decisions about their responses.

Graham, a six-year-old boy, bounded into the after-school program and enthusiastically told his caregiver, who was surrounded by four other new arrivals, "My daddy had a vasectomy and his penis is all black and blue." The provider responded, "Oh, really." She did not pursue this piece of family information for several reasons. First, it was about private family business that is not typically in the domain of public conversation. Second, the child did not appear troubled by the information and did not pursue it in other conversations, in stories, or in play with materials. Third, the provider knew that Graham's family was close and valued giving children accurate information about the world; she thought it likely that the family had explained the vasectomy so that the child did not have misconceptions about what had happened to his father's penis. Fourth, other families in the school would be offended if their children were involved in a discussion about vasectomies and penises as part of the after-school program. Fifth, the information was not related to the accepted curriculum of the program and knowing more about it was not necessary to protect or care for the child. Finally, the provider was experienced, confident in responding to children's spontaneous comments, and able to express acceptance of the child without encouraging discussion. She neither communicated disapproval nor encouraged elaboration; a supportive yet neutral tone characterized her responses.

The provider also chose not to mention Graham's comment to the family. Had he pursued the topic and wanted to go into greater detail, the provider might have said to him privately: "I appreciate your wanting to talk about this and this is a topic that is more appropriate for you to discuss with your family."

What if this experience affected Graham's behavior? Suppose he stopped using the bathroom at school, appeared much more anxious, and began to withdraw from the group during outside play. In this situation, the provider would be advised to contact the family and discuss the possible reasons for the child's behavior. If the provider had a hunch that it was related to the father's vasectomy, she might start out more generally: "Something has come up very recently at school and I can't seem to figure out the cause. Maybe you can help me understand if there are things happening out of school or in the home that might be related." After she explained the change in the child's behavior, the family might volunteer that the change was related to the vasectomy or perhaps to something else. If the provider believed that the vasectomy was a possible contributor, she might say: "I noticed that this behavior began after Graham told me that his dad had a vasectomy." Here she might need to reassure the parents that it was fine with her that he had told her this and that she hoped not to embarrass them, but thought the vasectomy might be related to what Graham was feeling now. Depending on how therapeutic the environment is, the provider might go further with the child's individual response. In a more instructional setting, the provider might focus on the general need of children in the class for information.

Consider another example of a child's report of family behavior that was noted but not pursued. Susan, a five-year-old, presented her drawing of her family to her center-based child-care provider. Her picture was lively and had many people in it. On further examination, the provider realized that there were one man, three women, and many children in the picture. The child said: "This is my daddy. This is Mommy Sara. This is Mommy Sue, and this is Mommy Karen, and these are all my brothers and sisters." The teacher was surprised because she had no idea that the child lived in this family constellation, having seen only the father and one of the "mothers." While the information was startling to the provider, she determined that it was benign in the context of the child's adequate functioning in school, and that she had satisfactory communication with the father and the woman she assumed was the mother. The teacher chose not to pursue the topic with Susan at that time, nor did she attempt to investigate further to find out more about how this family functioned.

To provide a contrast, we can review two examples where the child's information about the home was pursued because the situation had clear implications for the child's well-being. The first is an example of an indirect communication through the child's behavior. Charles, a three-year-old in a Title XX day-care setting, was absent from school for several days without notification from home. The first day he came back, he was accompanied by a man whom the teacher did not recognize and who was not on the list of persons expected to pick up the child. Further, his clothes were dirty and he looked very tired. The teacher reported this incident to the director, who pursued the situation on the spot. She asked the man who he was and why Charles had not been to school. She learned that Charles's mother was in the hospital and that he was staying with a neighbor. Upon further questioning, the director learned that Charles's mother and father had had a fight and that the father had cut the mother's hand so badly that the mother required emergency surgery. The father disappeared after the fight and had not been seen since. The child was staying with the neighbor, who was unemployed and lived alone.

The director was concerned about the child's welfare: How adequate was the care of the child by the neighbor? How long would the mother be hospitalized and what condition would she be in on her return? How safe was the home—were there other knives or weapons around the house? Were they within the child's reach? Had the child witnessed the fight? What was the child's understanding of what had happened to his mother and to his father? Had the child been harmed? The director consulted with the staff and with the program's mental health consultant and decided to make contact with the public child welfare agency. A home visit by an agency caseworker resulted in temporary foster placement of the child.

In the second example, a teacher decided to pursue information communicated in an after-school setting. The art teacher reported to the director that two eight- and nine-year-old brothers were describing to other children very graphic information about intercourse between two males, one of whom was their uncle. They were obsessed with these descriptions to the extent that other children no longer wanted to sit by them and began to isolate them socially from the group. The parents were divorced; the brothers lived with the mother and visited the father on weekends. The director knew the family well enough that he did not fear that the boys were being molested or that they were observing this intercourse, but he did know that it was negatively affecting their school life.

After consulting with the art teacher, the director called the mother. He began: "I want to tell you about conversations that the boys have been having at school so that we can help deal with the problem they are having." Then he explained what was happening and how the other children were reacting. What eventually turned up was that the children were watching X-rated cable TV at their mother's apartment. They had not, in fact, observed their uncle but had projected the TV images onto his behavior. The parents conferred and were able to stop the secret TV watching. The director talked with the children about what was appropriate conversation for school and what was not. The art teacher helped the children reintegrate socially. Since this was not a therapeutic setting, underlying issues of sexuality and adult supervision were not explored. The matter was closed after the phone call and the conference with the director.

Child-care settings are particularly challenged when information from the child contradicts what the school or provider has been told by the parent. For example, a mother reports on intake that there is no father in the home and that the family is eligible for Aid to Families with Dependent Children (AFDC) benefits, including child care. She mentions that her brother lives with them and will help in transporting the child. When the "brother" comes to pick up the child, the child runs to him shouting, "Daddy!" What do the center's staff do now? Should they acknowledge the father's presence and include him in center activities? Should they go along with the pretense that this is the uncle? Should they report the family to Public Aid? The key to handling this situation and others involving sensitive family information in a center setting is to use an organized team process to review the events, to review staff responses to what is happening, and to develop strategies for communicating with families that take into account the context of the staff's relationship with the family and the family's relationship with their child.

Particularly when children are the source of information, it is crucial to weigh the cost to the child of sharing information with the family, as well as the gain. For example, telling a family that uses harsh physical punishment about a toileting accident may not be in the best interests of a child, even if the accident seems to accompany a generalized increase in anxiety that one would like to discuss with the family. Similarly, children may come to school and report that their parents had a fight that morning or the night before. For children for whom this is particularly troubling—such as those from homes where privacy is highly valued and children are punished for telling family business—caregivers may offer support around these issues without informing the parents.

Team process and consultation about issues in communicating with families are rarely available in family day-care settings and virtually nonexistent in in-home care. While family day-care networks and provider support groups are beginning to grow in number, the provider is more than likely to resolve on her own the complexities of what family information she should pursue and what is out of her ballpark.

Because the provider often lacks the resources to provide help or knowledge of referral options, she may hesitate to get involved even when she sees that the child's welfare is affected. If there is no existing team in which she can participate, then one role for the professional agency (a day-care network) is to establish such a consultation and support team.

*Practice Guideline 11.2: Two criteria should guide professionals in determining whether or not to pursue information from a child about the family: Does the information have important consequences for the child's development or well-being? Do I have a constructive use for the information?*

*Practice Guideline 11.3: Each child-care setting should have an organized team process in place that can serve as a forum for review, consultation, and dissemination of information about the handling of sensitive family situations. This team process should include defined policies and procedures for handling sensitive situations as well as discussion of relevant cases.*

*Practice Guideline 11.4: Family day-care networks should provide consultation and support to providers and parents for their communication with one another. Special assistance should be provided in giving and receiving direct feedback, particularly if the feedback is perceived to be negative.*

### How Children Communicate About Child Care

Communication between children and parents about child care takes place in the context of the characteristic dynamics of the family and the individual. Some families avoid sensitive topics as a way of avoiding hurt or conflict. For example, a family may conspire to avoid mentioning a child who died in infancy. Individuals may do the same to defend themselves—for example, by forbidding her children to discuss their father, a woman may protect herself against her rage or pain at her ex-husband. Thus, domains of silence (Halpern and Larner, 1987; Musick and Stott, forthcoming) can be broadly cultural or narrowly experiential in origin. The former are generally easier to anticipate.

Among the many common everyday situations in which adults seek information from children, nonparental child care is rapidly gaining in importance. How does a parent know whether this care is working well for the child? Direct observation of the child while in care and direct feedback from the caregiver provide some information. However, a primary source of information is the child's own testimony. How does the child provide testimony about the experience of nonparental child care? The child does so in at least three ways: by answering direct questions posed by the parent, by providing spontaneous reports, and by communicating indirect messages nonverbally.

Direct questions to children often yield little useful information if they are posed in a way that permits uninformative answers. "How was school today?" "OK." "What did you do in school today?" "Nothing" or "I can't remember." Nonetheless, direct questions can serve a useful purpose by providing occasions for communication when the child is interested and ready. Even a simple one-word answer can be useful if the tone with which it is delivered invites further exploration, or if the parent can elicit elaboration. For example, a child who says that school was "Okay . . . I guess" may be inviting gentle probing by a parent. This is one way for a child to test a parent's interest without appearing to be a complainer. Children do seem to test parents, to find out if they really want to hear what the child has to say. In an extreme case, this could include whether or not the parent is prepared to hear about abusive experiences outside the home.

Direct questioning about nonparental care can be frustrating, but it is important. A child needs repeated assurance: "I am interested; I care; I will listen." Parents may become skillful in posing questions in ways that elicit discursive responses. For example, instead of asking, "How was school today?" a parent might ask, "What did you make in art today? I'd like to see." or "How about showing me how you draw in school? Here's some paper and crayons." Of course, this approach presupposes the parent taking the time to arrange and follow through. Librarians refer to this process as "question negotiation" because it involves an attempt to reach clarity and specificity in response to an initially vague or ill-formed request that does not elicit the appropriate references.

Perhaps of greater value are spontaneous reports. Children

who seem uncommunicative under direct questioning may open up spontaneously at other times. This is one problem with the view that small amounts of "quality time" can substitute for larger quantities of time together, whether at home or in the child-care setting. For children to make spontaneous reports about their experience, they need blocks of time with their parents. Many of the most important reports from children come in the course of routine, low-key activities—doing the dishes, taking a walk, riding in the car, preparing for bed, having breakfast, weeding the garden.

The crucial quality of informal occasions that generate spontaneous accounts from children is that they establish an unself-conscious pattern of interaction in which information can flow smoothly. Particularly with young children, these times together may evoke memories and stimulate associations. Young children may make casual comments that provide important, even dramatic, information for the parent. For example, some cases of out-of-home sexual abuse are discovered through seemingly innocuous comments. While folding laundry with her mother, a preschooler reported, "I wish my underpants were as nice as Mr. Tom's." This led eventually to an account of molestation by the day-care center's janitor. These spontaneous reports are often positive, of course. While watching him make a sandwich, a little boy told his father that he had learned how to make his own sandwich at school, and proceeded to show him his new skill. The same child had earlier reported, "Nothing," when asked what he had done at school.

*Practice Guideline 11.5: Child-initiated accounts of experiences in nonparental care can be particularly helpful in understanding the child's point of view. These spontaneous reports often occur during informal times between parent and child. Child-care providers and parents should encourage ample amounts of low-key, routine contacts.*

Children also communicate indirect messages about the nonparental care; young children tell their story through play and social behavior. This is at the heart of recent criticism of the psychosocial impact of day care on infants in the first year of life (Belsky, 1986). Belsky believes evidence from a variety of sources indicates that day care in the first year of life leads to insecurely attached relationships, as measured by the Strange Situation paradigm (in which children and their parents are observed when separated and reunited in a strange situation as a measure of the quality and tone of the parent-infant attachment). Others have disputed Belksy's interpretation, arguing that the infants are simply indicating a nonpathological adaptation to the repeated separations and reunions characteristic of living with infant day care. The key, of course, is to know how to interpret the infant's behavior and its significance for the future.

A terrified child may be sending an important message, one that needs a serious parental response. A child who shows deteriorating functioning (perhaps regressing to less mature speech) may be reporting indirectly about a negative child-care situation. As society has finally come to face up to the reality of sexual molestation, for example, parents have become attuned to the possible significance of a negative response to attending day care. Many parents of children who attended the McMartin Preschool in California reported that their children had shown such negative responses, but that at the time they had not attached any significance to these messages.

Krugman and Krugman (1985) reported on a whole class of third graders that was being psychologically abused by a teacher. For some time parents were unaware of the problem, although they recognized negative symptoms in their own children, such as fear of school, nightmares, bed-wetting, and anxiety. Only when a few parents happened to discuss the problems they were having at home with their children did the parents begin to interpret the children's messages correctly. The same thing has happened often in child-care abuse cases. Here, as elsewhere, adults should be open to many alternative hypotheses in receiving information from children.

*Practice Guideline 11.6: Children communicate messages about nonparental care through their play and social behavior. Child-care providers and parents must be attuned to children's indirect communication as well as their direct responses.*

One of the most important child-care issues facing today's parents is the question of when children can care for themselves. Often called latchkey children, children in self-care pose a serious challenge to the information-seeking and information-processing skills of parents. At what age can a child succeed in self-care? How does a child feel about self-care? How can a parent tell if it is working?

All these questions need to be answered, both to protect the child and to protect the parent. While research on the dynamics and consequences of self-care is far from definitive, many observers believe that some children have very negative experiences, while others are unaffected or may even respond positively (Robinson, Rowland, and Coleman, 1987). The keys seem to be the quality of adult supervision (does the child feel like she is being monitored by the parent even if the parent is not physically present?), the perceived character of the home environment (is it safe or dangerous?), and the maturity of the child (younger children are generally more at risk of fear and loneliness; older children are more confident and competent but more likely to "get into trouble"). How does a parent use the child as a source of information in addressing these issues?

Direct questions are of some value. A parent can ask, "Is it okay with you to come home alone after school?" Of course, a yes answer may not be acceptable at face value. Children may underestimate the task, may be unable to predict their reaction, may wish to appear grown-up, and, perhaps most important, they may desire to help the parent solve the child-care problem. The same issues present themselves whenever a parent is trying to evaluate an ongoing self-care arrangement.

Direct questioning may be more useful in assessing a child's knowledge and skills. Indeed, there is now a large and growing set of "survival skills" and child safety programs. These programs (which include do-it-yourself books for parents) often rely on a child's feedback to judge their success. Children are asked questions to determine whether or not they have the knowledge needed to be safe at home. Some use the child's behavior in hypothetical situations or stage tests to find out if the child has the requisite skills and knowledge.

One way to make use of the programs is as an opportunity for parent-child dialogue. The structured discussion of safety may help the child send messages that otherwise might remain unsent, and these guided interactions may produce behavior that is readily interpretable to a parent. Gray's (1986) evaluation of a group safety skills program is interesting in this regard. A questionnaire completed by children as part of a series of survival skills programs revealed that even when they mastered the skills, the children still preferred to have a parent home and had negative feelings about self-care. The training program increased skills and confidence but left the children with unchanged negative feelings.

However, the program also provided occasions for parents and children to discuss feelings in the context of an agenda of concrete issues. Some parents chose not to go forward with self-care arrangements after completing the program. Thus, one program outcome was to increase the effectiveness of what the children could tell their parents. The parents were able to receive information that previously was unavailable to them for a variety of reasons.

In another study, this particular model (the "I'm in Charge" curriculum) was compared with an approach that emphasized rehearsing behavioral skills related to safety. The evaluation showed that the skills approach produced superior performance by fifth graders at the end of the training, but that the more discussion-oriented "I'm in Charge" approach produced better results during a four-week follow-up. The investigators attributed this effect to the family discussions prompted by the "I'm in Charge" approach.

### Conclusions

This chapter has explored the special difficulties parents and children face when communicating about important matters of day-to-day care. Parents and providers each have relationships with children. These relationships overlap to some degree, but they also differ. Ideally, these two sets of relationships for a child will complement each other. When this happens children have new avenues of communication, and parents have alternative ways to obtain and clarify information from children. Providers similarly can make use of their different relationships with children and parents to gain information useful in the task of providing good care. Of course, in some situations (most notably child abuse and neglect) the fact that providers and parents have different "channels" with children can be crucial for the well-being of the child. Diversity and pluralism are important.

A discussion-oriented approach presents a good model. One way to improve the communication between children and their parents about everyday life is to provide a diverse set of situations (some formal, some informal) in which discussion of facts and feelings can flourish. And that, of course, is the point of our efforts. For children to serve effectively as sources of information for adults, children and adults must engage in a dialogue that is emotionally validating and developmentally appropriate in the home, in the child-care setting, and anywhere else that adults and children are engaged in the process of living and learning together.

CHAPTER 12

# Children in Clinical Settings

Most troubled children are unable to understand or to voice their complaints directly. Usually it is up to professionals who evaluate and treat psychological problems to elicit information from and about the child. These professionals bring different perspectives and purposes, each of which necessarily dictates the nature and interpretation of the information obtained. This process partially accounts for the confusion and common misunderstandings about the meaning and validity of information from and about children in clinical settings.

In Chapter One we raised the issue of professionals working at cross-purposes in connection with allegations of sexual abuse and psychological maltreatment of young children, such as those emerging from the McMartin Preschool case. Similar issues were raised in a recent professional meeting convened to examine bizarre sexual abuse in preschool centers across the United States. Representatives from the legal system, the police and FBI, the mental health system, researchers, and parents of the abused children were in attendance.

Many of the children in these cases had told chilling stories about being forced to pose for pornographic movies, being raped and sodomized, seeing pets (and in some cases human babies) sacrificed, and being frightened into keeping quiet. Therapists who were treating these children and the children's parents told of witnessing the children repeating the same bizarre themes over and over in their play—and displaying many symptoms of psychological problems. The mental health professionals, parents, and prosecutors believed the children's stories. However, many of the police officers and protective service workers who investigated these

247

cases, as well as some defense attorneys, genuinely felt that since there was no physical evidence of the bizarre activities, they had not occurred. They felt that even in those cases in which sexual abuse was medically corroborated, the children's stories about the more bizarre activities were not valid—that they were the products of either suggestion or fantasy.

While it is unlikely that truth can ever be fully known or justice completely served, we can strive to understand how professional roles influence the ways in which information is sought and interpreted by adults. In this case, those persons trying to serve the criminal justice system were seeking objective, reliable information. Their approach to information gathering was investigative and questioning. Parents and therapists, on the other hand, were more interested in creating a context for healing than for fact-finding. Whether or not the more grotesque activities actually took place was less important to parents and therapists than the fact that the children (possibly deluded) believed what they said. The therapeutic or healing process requires that adults understand and empathize with the child's subjective experiences regardless of the objective truth. The child can then be helped to move on so that a traumatic experience does not become the focus of his life and identity.

This tension between objective information seeking and the therapeutic process is not characteristic only of such extreme cases. It occurs frequently and across a variety of situations. For example, evaluators of children of divorce may dismiss a young child's feeling that he caused his parents' divorce by too quickly assuring the child that it is not so. If the evaluator's goal is to assess each parent's ability to parent, she has less need to understand the child's subjective experience in order to help him. On the other hand, if the evaluator is also interested in assessing the effect of a divorce on the child's development, she needs to attend to both objective and subjective information. And at some point, the therapeutic process may necessitate the validation of the child's feelings in order to help the child work them through.

We use the term *clinician* in this chapter to refer to those professionals who have received specific clinical training in the diagnosis and treatment of psychological problems, such as social workers, psychologists, counselors, and psychiatrists. There are a variety of possible roles within the broad category of clinician. Child clinicians have been called on as advocates to lobby for resources and to increase the accountability and responsiveness of social institutions affecting children. They also serve as expert witnesses who testify on behalf of or about children in court. They function as investigators conducting fact-finding interviews in child abuse cases and as researchers seeking to understand children under stress. They serve as clinical evaluators who assess psychopathology or the effects of stress and as therapists who create the context for healing. Further, each role may be carried out quite differently, depending on factors outside a particular family or child—such as the training and theoretical orientation of those who seek to help. The focus of this chapter will be on the roles of evaluator and therapist.

*Practice Guideline 12.1: Professional roles and theoretical orientations influence the nature and interpretation of information sought and obtained from children in clinical settings.*

## Clinical Evaluation of Children

Children are typically evaluated by clinicians for one of three major reasons. One reason is that the child is considered to be a witness to someone else's crime, or is herself suspected of being the victim of abuse or neglect. The purpose of the evaluation may ultimately be to discover the facts about what actually happened, and perhaps to use the child's testimony as evidence to prosecute the perpetrator. Fulfilling this purpose requires adherence to the standards set by the criminal justice system, which may be antithetical to clinical evaluation (MacFarlane and others, 1986; Summit, 1986). That is, if the goal is to discover and help victims, the techniques required to elicit information, such as asking potentially leading questions, may not be conducive to prosecuting the perpetrators.

A second major reason for a clinical evaluation is that the child is displaying developmental problems or symptomatic behavior. When the child presents a problem, the evaluator's primary goal is to assess the presence and level of psychopathology.

The evaluator attempts to understand the possible causes and meanings of the child's developmental problem or symptomatic behavior. In conducting a diagnostic evaluation the clinician seeks to determine the history of the problem, to identify symptoms, to look for clues to biological or environmental causes, to be alert to attendant risks (such as suicide), and to identify coping mechanisms and strengths. This information then points to appropriate treatment measures.

A third major reason for an evaluation is that the child has experienced a stressful event that may place him at risk for psychological problems. While the child may not be presenting an immediate problem, the stressful event may provoke a short-term disturbance that requires the child to change or adapt or that may lead to a psychological disorder.

Understanding the effects of stress on the developmental process is a central concern in clinical evaluation and the design of interventions for children. Rutter (1983) suggests five main ways in which early stressful experiences may be linked with disorder some years later. First, a distressing experience (such as the violent death of a parent) may precipitate a disorder in childhood that persists into adult life. Second, early events may lead to bodily changes (for example, in the neuroendocrine system) that in turn influence later functioning. Third, early events may lead to altered patterns of behavior that take the form of an overt disorder only some years later (for example, a series of substitute caregivers during the first two years of life may create attentional problems that later result in a learning disability or behavioral problem). Fourth, early events (such as parental death or divorce) may lead to changed family conditions (such as diminished or over-anxious parenting) that in turn predispose the child to disorder. Fifth, early events (such as maladaptive parenting) may alter sensitivities to stress or modify coping styles; these may then predispose the child to disorder in the presence of later stressful events.

*Practice Guideline 12.2: Stressors that place a child at risk for major psychopathology appear to involve either some form of loss or disappointment or disturbed interpersonal relationships.*

The most common reason for evaluating children who have

experienced stressful life events is to determine the need for intervention. The clinician's goal is not primarily the assessment of psychopathology but rather the assessment of the child's overall response, or the degree to which he remains developmentally on track. Diagnostic categories, especially those used with adults, are seldom directly helpful and may in fact obscure important aspects of the child's attempts to cope (Kelly and Wallerstein, 1977). Posttraumatic stress disorder, for example, may not be an appropriate diagnosis for children's anxiety reactions to stress (Garmezy, 1986).

*Practice Guideline 12.3: Whatever the stressor, it is important to sort out those responses that are in the service of eventual coping from those that lead to psychological problems.*

In order to understand the child's response to a stressor, the clinician uses several methods. First, the coping process is considered in terms of the multiple transactions among child, parental, and environmental characteristics (Sameroff and Chandler, 1975). An evaluation of environmental factors, such as resources and available support systems, is made. Resources may include adequate housing, medical care, a relatively safe neighborhood, and so on. Support can be instrumental (someone to baby-sit) and emotional (someone to talk to). Parental capacity to respond adequately to and care for the child is also evaluated. Parents play a particularly important role in how their children cope because of their direct responses and strategies in a stressful situation. For example, if a child has experienced sexual abuse at the hands of a stranger and her mother responds by saying, "How could you do this to me?" or "How could this happen to us?" the child will have to overcome more guilt than she might otherwise. Parents are also important because of their indirect role as mediators of the environment. A parent can exacerbate a stressful event by becoming depressed or excessively anxious; on the other hand, a parent can serve as a buffer between the child and the stressor or act as a model who demonstrates that trauma is surmountable.

Second, a developmental assessment is made to determine if the child has achieved age-appropriate milestones or if his development has been arrested. This requires the evaluator to have knowledge of developmental norms. In some domains, standardized tests (which state the norms) are appropriate. In other areas, particularly social and personality development, the clinician is more likely to use techniques such as observation, interviewing, and play, which require theoretical knowledge and experience in order to judge whether or not the child is behaving in developmentally appropriate ways. The evaluator may also turn to other sources (parents, teachers, and peers) for information about the child.

Third, an assessment is made that focuses on how the child has understood the stressful event, what the accompanying emotional reaction is, and what coping strategies the child is employing. This requires the clinician to have some understanding of both conscious and unconscious coping mechanisms in the child. Children (as well as adults) often deal with traumatic or painful events by defending against conscious awareness of reality or feelings or by distorting their understanding or feelings. For example, it is not uncommon for children to defend against their fear in the initial stages of an evaluation with either aggressive actions (a young child may keep bumping into the clinician) or false bravado (an older child may use obscenities).

Thus, evaluation of a child's response to a stressful experience entails multiple sources of information and an understanding of what kind of information is needed. The following sections examine various sources and types of information used in making evaluation and treatment decisions both for children who have a presenting problem and for those who are at risk.

### Sources of Information

In general, using multiple sources of information about a child can increase the accuracy and completeness of the evaluation. Additional sources that provide different perspectives can be integrated with the clinician's view in order to provide a more coherent and objective picture of the child and his family. Greater emphasis can be placed on those patterns that are consistently reported and observed across differing circumstances and contexts. If, for example, a child behaves the same way at home, at camp, and at school, the behavior is more likely to be something the child brings to all relationships rather than the result of the demands of a particular context. Each additional source, however, has its advantages and disadvantages. It is therefore important to understand the perspective and merits of a source before it is used.

*Teachers and Peers.* In many ways, teachers and peers offer the most objective and developmentally appropriate measures of childhood adjustment. Schools are the first major social institution children face outside the family setting and are fundamental to both social and intellectual development. Teachers are in a unique position to assess a child's coping strategies as well as competence, both as an individual and in comparison with local and national norms. Teacher evaluations (conducted in such a way that the teacher is unaware of the child's risk status) have been found to be valid descriptions of present development as well as effective predictors of maladjustment (Weintraub, Neale, and Liebert, 1975; Pekarik and others, 1976).

Peer evaluations may offer a somewhat different picture from that of teacher ratings. In studies that have asked both teachers and peers to rate all the children in a class, for example, peers were better than teachers at identifying children at risk for psychological problems (for example, Rolf and Hasazi, 1977; Fisher, Harder, Kokes, and Schwartzman, 1982). It may be that teachers do not perceive the more subtle aspects of behavior and adjustment that peers experience in everyday encounters, or that children open up with each other and are more guarded with teachers. It may also be that certain things are less salient for teachers than for peers—they place different values on different behaviors. Teachers, peers, and siblings who are aware of a child's circumstances are also often able to offer important information about the child's functioning as well as to provide support to the child.

*Parents.* Parents can be extremely valuable sources of information about their own children. For example, Rutter and his colleagues (Rutter, Tizard, and Whitmore, 1970) found that an interview with a parent that focused on the details of the child's current behavior was in closer agreement with a final overall clinical rating of psychiatric disturbance than were a structured psychiatric interview with the child himself or questionnaires completed by his teacher or parent. There are also circumstances in which parents provide less valid and reliable data, such as maternal psychiatric illness (Stott, Cohler, and Musick, 1985).

Even if parents do not provide wholly accurate and objective data about their child to outside observers, their subjective experiences or perceptions of their child are a vital part of a thorough assessment. Because parental perceptions and feelings can strongly influence parental behavior, they are usually crucial to the long-term adjustment of children. The parent contributes to the child's social and emotional (as well as cognitive) development by attributing meaning to the infant's behavior, thereby slowly bringing the infant's behavior to match the parent's expectations (Fraiberg, Adelson, and Shapiro, 1975; Stern, 1985; Cramer, 1986). By interpreting the child's behavior according to their perceptions, feelings, values, intentions, and goals for the child (whether conscious or unconscious), parents either reinforce or discourage the infant's behaviors; in this way meaning is mutually created.

In order to uncover this subjective layer, clinicians listen to the ways in which parents describe their child's characteristics and problems. (Such narrative accounts formed the basis for the major work on childhood temperament by Thomas, Chess, and Birch, 1968.) Clinicians often seek this information when they take the case history of a child from the parents. They ask for a history of the parents' own lives. As the parents speak of past or current relationships, the clinician may detect connections between the child and the parent's other relationships. As she listens to parents discussing their pasts, pleasures, anxieties, and failings, the clinician may also detect that the parent has projected or transferred his own unconscious anxieties or meanings onto the child. The child then, unfortunately, lives up to these parental expectations in a self-fulfilling prophecy.

Cramer (1986) has outlined three variations of the parent's representation of the child that are frequently found in clinical practice. First, the child may represent an important person in the parent's past. If, for example, a child reminds a mother of her own hated older sister, the mother's resentment may cause her to withhold comfort or pleasures from the child because she's "already too demanding and spoiled." Thus, buried relationships return as "ghosts in the nursery" (Fraiberg, Adelson, and Shapiro, 1975).

Second, the child may be supposed to take the place of a dead relative (usually a grandparent). The child is given the name of the deceased and expected to fill the void by becoming a replica of the dead relative. Third, the child may represent a repressed or split-off part of the parent's own self. The parent projects aspects of his own unconscious issues onto the child. For example, a father who has unresolved grief over the loss of his own father may view his nonathletic and relatively calm son as depressed, when in actuality it is he who is depressed.

### Types of Information

We seek to draw a distinction between what some have called children's public and private selves (Wolff, 1978), or the "objective" child and the "clinical" child (Stern, 1985). In order to evaluate and make treatment decisions, clinicians msut be concerned with both aspects of children. Clinicians often face the difficult task of having to be aware of the outward manifestations of children's behavior while also moving into the subjective world of children's thinking and feeling.

*Objective Information.* Objective information about a child is that which is observable or can be assessed in a reliable manner. It can include her outward behaviors (such as friendliness or aggression), capacities (such as memory or school achievement), symptoms (such as hyperactivity or depression), and verbal accounts of an event that she has experienced. Objective data can be collected from a child through direct observation, through formal assessment (including psychological testing), or through interviews with the child (which may be validated by external sources). Objective data about a child can also be collected from other sources, such as teachers and parents.

Objective information gathered from and about a child is very useful in trying to discover what actually happened in a particular event that the child witnessed or personally experienced. This information (which is sought by parents and teachers all of the time) is required by investigators who are seeking evidence as well as by clinicians who need to understand the child's reality in order to evaluate and possibly treat the child.

Objective information also enables the clinician to understand the child's developmental achievements (such as walking,
speaking in sentences, reading a second-grade book) and identify
symptoms (such as separation anxiety or bed-wetting). These data
can be checked against our theories of how development proceeds in
order to evaluate the effects of a stressful experience on the child, or
against scientific studies that have established links between a
specific stressful experience and subsequent behavior. The identification and measurement of behaviors that are characteristic of a
particular stressor are helpful in focusing treatment on those aspects
of the child's functioning that have been affected by a particular
stressful experience. For example, it has been found that preschool
children of divorce often display regressed behaviors. These
findings might suggest a treatment strategy that focuses on helping
the parents understand both their child's behavior and the need to
provide greater consistency of care.

*Practice Guideline 12.4: Objective information is useful
when trying to discover the child's behaviors and symptoms, his
developmental achievements, and what happened in a particular
situation he witnessed or experienced.*

**Subjective Information.** In order to be personally helpful to
the child, clinicians also need to get to the child's subjective
experience. This mode of understanding focuses on personal
understanding of the child—of his motives, his affect, and the
meaning of his experiences, beliefs, attitudes, and expectations.
Seeking to make sense of their experiences, children and adults
construct a subjective chain of reasoning with which they link their
life events. For example, a woman may tell herself that her husband
left her for his secretary because he was incapable of running his
business alone and needed the secretary's help, when, in fact, he left
his wife because he no longer loved her. Or a man may tell himself
that he has not heard from his editor because his manuscript was
terrible, when his editor may simply have gotten behind in her
work. This subjective chain of reasoning may be conscious, as in
these examples, or outside a person's awareness.

Since subjective information may bear little resemblance to
reality, it is not sought by clinicians who are trying to establish facts

(such as evidence required in litigated custody or abuse cases) or those who need reliable or quantifiable data. It is also not always easily obtained in a diagnostic evaluation because children are more likely to share their thoughts and feelings in the context of a trusting relationship, which generally takes time to establish. Therefore, subjective information is sometimes obtained by a sensitive and knowledgeable evaluator, but it is more often the province of therapists.

The ways in which the clinician comes to know the child's subjective experience also depend on the child's developmental level. During the first two years of life, the infant experiences her world in a perceptual, action-oriented, nonverbal fashion. Because infants cannot tell us about their subjective world, we can only infer how they experience the sights and sounds around them or the care they receive. Psychoanalytically oriented clinicians have traditionally based their inferences on reconstructed clinical material supplied by older patients. However, when one uses adults' self-narrations as sources of inference about infant social experience, there is always a risk of attributing adultlike thoughts and feelings to a small child, or "adultomorphizing" (Stern, 1985). Attempts have also been made to use observations of infants' emotions and behaviors as the basis for hypotheses about infants' subjective experience. For example, in describing the approach of the clinician-researcher (as opposed to the experimental psychologist), Emde (1983) gives the following example of the way in which Rene Spitz arrived at some of his inferences of the subjective experiences of institutionalized infants in the 1940s: "Spitz followed a number of infants longitudinally and noticed that after separation from their mothers, they became weepy, had sad facial expressions, and were immobile; their faces often had dazed looks; and they sometimes engaged in autoerotic activities. Spitz felt saddened and was reminded of the adult state of depression. Even though infants could not tell him how they felt, he felt they were depressed, and he related their plight to the loss of a loved one. Spitz felt something inside himself that was communicated by these infants, and he made use of that feeling to facilitate a widened perception. After this, he was able to see a clinical syndrome that included a pattern of behavior, emotional communication, and events occurring over time" (p. 85).

More recently, investigators such as Bowlby (1980), Emde (1980), and Stern (1985) have used research on infants' capacities to develop hypotheses about infants' subjective experiences. Thus, for example, an eight-month-old infant is considered to have built up memories of many specific ways of being cared for by the same person. A change of caretaker would therefore elicit uncertainty and, it may be inferred, would be experienced as an abandonment.

The advent of language and symbolic thinking between eighteen and twenty-four months brings about the ability to share meanings with other people. It also permits the child to link his life events by constructing a narrative of his own life. The ability to symbolize and use language, however, also allows the child to distort and transcend reality. A person can, for example, knowingly or unknowingly feel one thing and say another, or call something by another name. Additionally, young children's sense of causality is not always logical. Thus, children now can create narratives with mistaken causal attributions, such as "I caused my parents' divorce" or "I brought on my own abuse because I was bad."

Symbolic play is a time-honored method used by clinicians to help young children communicate about their subjective feelings, beliefs, and expectations. The clinician draws inferences from the way a child relates to and uses the toys and materials in the playroom. Unacknowledged or difficult-to-verbalize conflicts and feelings may be expressed through dolls, other toys, drawing, or actions. Bertacchi and Coplon (1988) provide the following example of the way a young child was able to symbolize her subjective experience through her actions even though she could not express her feelings in language:

Lisa, aged two and a half, was cared for by unfamiliar caretakers while her mother was in the hospital having a baby. Lisa was able to state in words that her mother was having a baby and her father was helping her mother, giving the impression that she understood the reason for the absence. Her father returned late the first night at which point Lisa, who had been manageable with the unfamiliar caretaker, began to tantrum. The next day Lisa was taken to the hospital to visit her mother and to visit her new baby sister. The visit went well, including the good-bye to mother. But as Lisa and her father prepared to leave the hospital, Lisa refused to put her gloves on and eventually engaged in what her father described as the worst tantrum of her life. . . . During the next several days of her mother's absence Lisa ritualistically put on her coat, boots and gloves while sitting in the house. She carefully presented this to her caretaker, particularly emphasizing that she had put on her gloves. Never during her mother's four-day absence did Lisa state in words that she missed her mother or was confused about the reason for her absence [p. 2].

*Practice Guideline 12.5: Just because a young child can use language to express an idea does not necessarily mean that it accurately reflects her subjective experience.*

The clinician also draws upon the feelings evoked within herself in interactions with a particular child and notes how these have changed over time. The feelings elicited by a child (such as anger, affection, or disgust) can be useful clues for the clinician, leading her to a deeper understanding of how the child feels about himself and indicating the kinds of reactions the child is accustomed to eliciting from others. For example, a four-year-old girl who is constantly making the clinician angry by acting out and testing limits may herself be an angry and frightened child who often elicits angry feelings from her caretakers.

*Practice Guideline 12.6: It is important for a clinician to have enough self-awareness to be able to distinguish between those times when a feeling elicited by a child reflects the child's subjective feelings and those times when it reflects the clinician's own issues.*

By age seven, children develop metacognition (an awareness of their own thinking and of what they know and do not know) and the ability to think more logically. With the development of these capacities, children are open to rational explanations. Thus, for example, school-age children are more likely to attribute the cause of their parents' divorce to their parents than to themselves (Wallerstein and Kelly, 1980). Therefore, the first step in trying to uncover the subjective experience of a child older than six (in most cases) is often to elicit a direct account of his subjective experience, a "phenomenal investigation." As Allport (1942, p. 37) put it, "If we want to know how people feel: what they experience and what they remember, what their emotions and motives are like, and the reasons for acting as they do—why not ask them?" The problem with children is that they have particular difficulty with reporting on a purely verbal basis and frequently do not report all they know. They may be deliberately withholding information, since their more mature cognitive capacities enable them to be more aware of allegiances to others and of possible consequences. Or they may not be able to verbalize because their feelings and motives are beyond their conscious awareness.

Like younger children, school-age children (as well as adults) may unconsciously create magical narratives to account for stressful events. An illustration of this comes from the movie *My Life as a Dog*, which portrays the subjective experience of a twelve-year-old boy whose mother dies of tuberculosis. During much of the movie the boy seems to be in a haze of confusion and unreality—not facing facts and postponing feelings. First he denies that she is dying; after her death, he seems to be numb to his sadness and pain. Toward the end of the movie he blurts out an indication of his distorted perception to his beloved uncle when he says, "I didn't kill her!" and "Why didn't she want me?" He thus reveals his feelings of guilt, anger, and rejection.

Because subjective information is so difficult to obtain, psychodynamic clinicians turn to free association, play, and stories, as well as conversation with older children, as basic clinical tools for uncovering defenses, identifying repressed traumatic material, and understanding the child's sense of self and view of the world. As discussed in earlier chapters, when subjective material is interpreted there is a danger of misreading the message in the child's play or stories. Since much of the material is symbolic and metaphorical, a clinician's interpretation may not match the child's experience. In addition, it is sometimes difficult to ascertain whether enactments in play or stories reflect fantasies or real-life experiences (such as abuse). There is also the danger of interpreting unconscious meaning in an indiscriminate manner. Offering premature interpretations, for example, may undermine the child's attempts to cope with a stressful experience. Despite the dangers, the value of correctly interpreting subjective material is that it offers the child some hope of being understood and perhaps even helped. This is no small matter, for it may be that, as Basch says, "though we tend not to be aware of it, the need to communicate on some level with other human beings—that is, to make ourselves understood or understandable, and in doing so feel cared for, safe, stimulated, and appreciated—remains the prime motivator for all that we do or don't do" (Basch, 1980, p. 174).

### Therapies for Children

The theoretical model behind the treatment style determines the sources and types of information sought about and from children. While there are a number of theoretical frameworks for the treatment of children, the three dominant models are behavior theory, family systems theory, and psychoanalytic theory (Koocher and Pedulla, 1977). These illustrate differing emphases on sources of information beyond the child and the use of objective and subjective information.

The behavioral model holds that maladaptive behavior results from inappropriate environmental responses to the child. The application of this model therefore requires a referred problem to be behaviorally identified and defined. Objective information is then carefully collected and analyzed in order to determine an intervention paradigm. While the child is the focus of inquiry, subjective information is neither sought nor interpreted. Techniques such as systematic desensitization, positive and negative consequences following a child's behavior, and modeling adaptive behavior are utilized in the treatment process.

Since a key feature of learning theory is the specificity of the intervention to the problem, approaches that apply the theory have been applied to a wide array of problems (Schaefer, Millman, Sichel, and Zwilling, 1986). Offering a powerful methodology that yields observable results, this approach works especially well when particular behaviors are targeted (such as behavior management in a special education classroom or desensitization of a phobia) or when the child's problem has a physiological component (such as toilet training a retarded child).

When the aim of therapy is to address the underlying psychic cause of a problem rather than to initially change the overt behavior, psychodynamic approaches are used. In addition to family systems therapy and psychoanalysis, examples of such frameworks include Gestalt and client-centered or nondirective play therapy. These approaches seek both objective and subjective information from and sometimes about children. Implicit in these therapies is the view of a fundamental need to communicate on some level with another person. In making themselves understood, children can feel cared for and validated and eventually reverse some of their self-defeating processes.

The philosophy of family therapy advocates that the entire family as a unit or system should be the primary focus of treatment. According to this point of view, the family system operates according to a specific but often unconscious belief structure or mythology that provides the rules for functioning. All members of the system are involved in the creation, maintenance, and modification of all family patterns, both adaptive and maladaptive.

Since the child's problem is also a symptom of current family dysfunction and psychopathology is redefined as a relationship problem (Haley, 1970), diagnosis becomes an interactional assessment of the entire family. In addition to objective information, subjective information is often sought in order to understand the special meaning a presenting problem or symptom has to family members. For example, a mother's concern about her child's acting out may serve, in part, as a displacement of her anger toward her husband. Treatment involves changing maladaptive family relationships that contribute to or maintain symptoms. Depending on the particular conceptualization of family therapy, approaches to systemic change vary in the emphasis they give to family dynamics, structural patterns, and communication processes (Walsh, 1983).

Psychodynamic concepts are applied in some forms of family therapy as well as in situations in which the child is treated individually. Psychoanalytically oriented therapies rely principally on the child-therapist relationship. This therapeutic alliance, developed on the basis of trust, allows the child to depend on the therapist and share his subjective thoughts and feelings. Since this is a relationship model, the personal characteristics of the therapist are considered to be important. The essential traits of the therapist have been described as a capacity to identify with the patient without loss of personal identity, a capacity to contain the conflicts of the patient and wait for a resolution instead of anxiously looking around for a cure, and an absence of the tendency to retaliate under provocation (Winnicott, 1971). As the therapist comes to know the child's feelings through an empathic understanding in a continuing commitment over time, she can begin to be helpful.

In interpreting subjective material, psychoanalytically oriented therapists often work deductively from the general principles of their theory to the details of the particular case. Thus, for example, Freud's psychosexual phases, Erikson's psychosocial phases, or Mahler's phases of separation-individuation are used to pinpoint potential periods of fixation. If the developmental conflict of a particular stage is not resolved, the anxiety and characteristics of the conflict may dominate the child's personality and result in later psychopathology.

The danger in this method is that the formulation of the child's personality derived from theory may not correspond to either the subjective or objective ordering of the child's life. For example, a child's subjective experience of a stressful event will not necessarily include oedipal fantasies just because the child was four years old at the time of the event. If an interpretation does not correspond to the child's subjective experience, it is likely to be a misinterpretation and the child, consciously or unconsciously, will feel misunderstood.

A lack of correspondence with the child's objective reality, however, may mean that the therapist is responding empathically to what the child is subjectively experiencing. When a therapist somehow conveys that she knows that a child is feeling responsible for something the child had no control over, for example, she is communicating understanding. As Wolff (1978) points out, the validity of psychoanalytic theories about emotional development rests on their clinical helpfulness rather than on their performance as causal explanations for behavior. Wolff further states, "So long as we are clear that psychodynamic explanations of an individual's behavior and experiences can be psychologically even if not scientifically true and that for psychological interventions but not for scientific purposes their validity is unchallenged, we shall avoid both logical confusion and therapeutic nihilism" (p. 94).

Those who observe psychodynamic therapies must understand this distinction between reality and psychological truth. The children's fantasies (or the narratives they have constructed) need to be understood in order to explain the behavioral manifestations by which such fantasies are expressed and affect the child. Thus, as suggested above, in order to be empathic, a therapist may accept (albeit temporarily) the child's feeling that he is to blame for his abuse or his parents' divorce. At the same time, the therapist keeps the objective facts of the divorce or abuse in mind in order to eventually guide the child to a better understanding of reality.

*Practice Guideline 12.7: A rigidly held theoretical perspective or factionalism can create unwarranted negative judgments of the effectiveness of therapy. Each theoretical orientation pays specific attention to factors the others overlook or spend little time on and therefore has a contribution to make.*

There is considerable confusion in both professional writing and clinical practice as to whether or not the person who evaluates the child should also be the person who treats the child (and possibly the family). This depends on the purpose of the evaluation. If the purpose is to make a recommendation in a custody dispute or to discover whether sexual abuse has occurred, the evaluator may need to remain impartial and objective (Gardner, 1982). As noted earlier, a therapeutic alliance between child and therapist often reduces the therapist's objectivity. A therapist who agrees to participate in a custody evaluation also runs the risk of alientating one parent or the other, thereby decreasing his ability to act as an advocate for the child's well-being. The separation of the roles of evaluator and therapist may reduce the effects of personal bias, and the combination of two perspectives may be more valuable (Dodds, 1987).

On the other hand, there are some advantages to having the same person conduct both the initial evaluation and the subsequent treatment. In this way, ongoing therapy can be used both to treat the problem and to produce further evidence or reduce uncertainty about what actually happened to the child. Thus, authors such as Bresee, Stearns, Bess, and Packer (1986) advocate an assessment model for sexual abuse cases that places the evaluation in the context of a program of treatment for the child. Another advantage is continuity for the child and parents. Further, as suggested earlier, subjective information is more likely to be obtained in the context of an ongoing relationship.

## Conclusions

This chapter has addressed issues of adult orientation and competence. The primary orientation issue rests with the role of the clinician, which necessarily dictates the purposes of evaluations and interventions for children. Since there are often tensions between the requirements of the roles of advocate, investigator, researcher, evaluator, and therapist, it is important to keep in mind the perspectives of each.

The form an evaluation of a child takes also depends on the perceived determinants of the child's problem and on the effect of the problem on the child's development. Adult competence influences the choice of techniques and the nature of information elicited from children in clinical settings. This chapter has focused on the various sources and types of information used in making evaluation and treatment decisions. In particular, a distinction has been made between objective and subjective information. The lack of such a clear distinction has often led to confusion and, in some instances, anger and blame. For example, therapists have long understood that children do not freely voice their complaints. Therefore, evaluation and treatment often depend on inferences drawn from a child's play or stories. However, this information cannot be used as evidence to prove that a child did or did not experience a particular stressful event. On the other hand, the task of an evaluator or researcher seeking factual or replicable information requires reduced intrusiveness and interpretation. There are a place and time for both objective reality and psychological truth. Thus, there is a clinical need for both scientific and more interpretive methods.

CHAPTER 13

# Children in Medical Settings

An abundant literature exists on the patient-practitioner relationship (see, for example, Parsons, 1951, 1975; Bloom, 1963; Freidson, 1961, 1970, 1975; Wolinsky, 1980), especially on issues of patient compliance, patient satisfaction, and practitioner control (Pendleton, 1983; Stone, 1979; Waitzkin, 1983). The growing literature on communication reflects the increased concern over this aspect of the medical encounter (Pendleton and Hasler, 1983; Mishler, 1984; Cassell, 1985a, 1985b; West, 1984; Bernstein and Bernstein, 1985; Fisher and Todd, 1983; Gumperz, 1982; Cicourel, 1982). However, adults more often than children are the focus of inquiry. While investigators have examined children's concepts of health and illness, the psychological effect of illness on children and their families, and topics such as the impact of pediatric hospitalization (Vernon, Foley, Sipowicz, and Schulman, 1965; Thompson, 1985; Thompson and Stanford, 1981; Petrillo and Sanger, 1980), much less attention has been paid to the place of the child in the patient-practitioner relationship and the special problems encountered when children are the source of information for health practitioners.

Adults have many roles as health practitioners in their interactions with children as patients. Depending on whether the practitioner is a physician, nurse, technician, or other health provider, the methods of communication and the kinds of information being exchanged may vary. The primary goal of the physician, for example, is to cure disease and to provide medical support when a cure is not attainable. In the management of a patient's illness, the physician evaluates the problem, decides on a diagnosis, and determines a course of treatment. Physicians need information from both the child and the family to determine the medical problem.

The relationship with the child develops in the context of physical examinations, medical interviews, and procedures.

Similarly, nurses interact with children during physical exams, informal and formal discussions, and activities such as changing dressings, inserting IV needles, and giving medications and injections. Traditionally, the nursing role includes both a technical or clinical component and an affective, nurturing component. The combined dimensions of this role result in what many nurses describe as the holistic treatment of patients. Nurses play an important role in monitoring the medical care of patients and they are in a unique position in relation to children as patients. Nurses can become effective communication mediators or "gatekeepers" between children and their families and other health care professionals.

Important services are available to the child patient through medical technicians, social workers, occupational therapists, child life therapists, dietitians, and aides. Medical personnel have different needs in relation to the child as a patient, and each requires different kinds of information from the child. The information obtained by these professionals is used in a variety of ways throughout the treatment of an illness; inevitably, there are limitations on the usefulness of the data gathered by the individual practitioners.

Although their responsibilities differ in relation to children's needs, health providers act as a team in caring for the child. In fact, it is rare for a child to see only one type of health practitioner in the course of being treated for an illness or injury. Regardless of the professional status of the health practitioner, both the structure and content of medical discourse and the child's and adult's mutual understanding of each other influence the way in which information is exchanged and managed in pediatric encounters.

## Medical Terminology and Interview Style in Pediatric Interactions

Problems surrounding the use of medical vocabulary in patient-practitioner interactions have been documented in numerous studies (McKinlay, 1975; West, 1984). Indeed, in his examination of the doctor-patient relationship, Shuy (1983) suggests that medical jargon is one of the primary deterrents to successful communication. While its precision may be useful between experts, technical language is not helpful when it is not understood. In a classic study, Korsch and Negrete (1972) found that in more than half of 800 interviews between mothers and pediatricians, the physicians used medical terminology that confused or mystified the mothers—not to mention the children.

The use of medical terminology with children can be especially problematical. A boy of four, for example, was told by his physician that he needed to have a CAT scan. During the interaction the boy nodded his head, indicating that he understood the doctor's explanation of what was involved. Later, however, he expressed his fears to his mother. He believed the CAT scan was a giant cat with green eyes that "could see right through you," and that he was going to be "laid on a table and slid into the cat's mouth like he's gonna eat you and the table too" (Patricia Marshall, pers. comm., 1987). CAT scans are a relatively unfamiliar phenomenon for most children and most adults. Making sense of a description of a CAT scan without seeing the equipment or experiencing the process requires abstract and imaginative thinking from people of all ages, not just children.

*Practice Guideline 13.1: It is sometimes difficult for children to separate adult reality from their own, often more "magical" reality; consequently, information may be distorted and logically explained from the child's point of view.*

Another source of interference in pediatric interactions is the structure of medical discourse. The one-sided, asymmetrical style of medical interviews may provide a focused method for collecting factual information, but other important details can be overlooked. The physician, for example, is interested in data that will inform the diagnosis and prognosis, but the patient's feelings about pain, hospitalization, medical treatments, and the interview experience itself are often neglected, sometimes to the detriment of the treatment.

The public nature of bedside rounds conducted by physicians in teaching hospitals demonstrates the way in which the social structure of the medical interaction sometimes contributes to the depersonalization of the patient. A fifteen-year-old girl, having undergone surgery to remove a tumor on her upper thigh, was surrounded by ten physicians, including several residents and medical students. Most of them were male. Throughout the examination, the attending physician directed questions to the patient and then to the junior staff. The girl's answers were short and she would not look directly at any of the faces around her. When asked how she was feeling, the girl replied, "Fine." The physician continued his inquiry without a moment's hesitation. When the group left the room, the girl began to cry as she pulled the sheet up close to her shoulders and turned away from the door.

Adolescents are extremely concerned about sexual identity and body image. Being exposed in front of strangers, especially male strangers, could account for the girl's emotional upset. Furthermore, the forced interaction of the directed interview did little to alleviate her sense of vulnerability and helplessness. Later that day, the girl told the pastoral counselor, "It didn't matter what I said. He just wanted to put on a good show for the students and I was part of his lesson for the day" (Patricia Marshall, pers. comm., 1987).

Silverman's (1987) analysis of communication in a cleft-palate clinic provides a good example of how adults shape the responses of children. The following is a transcript of a discussion between a surgeon and a twelve-year-old boy about physical appearance and the possibility of future surgery:

*Surgeon:*   Mm. Let's have a look. (examines mouth)

*Surgeon:*   Now then. This has got rather an ugly scar line hasn't it? It's rather a lot of stitch marks. Isn't terribly handsome, is it? What do you think about your looks?

*Barry:*   I don't know.

*Surgeon:*   You. (laughs) Doesn't worry you a lot. You don't lie awake at night worrying about it or anything?

*Barry:*   (hesitates) No.

*Surgeon:*   No. No. It could be improved . . . er . . . because I think that scar line isn't brilliant but it's, you're the customer, if you're happy with things the way they are then that's . . .

*Barry:*   (hesitates) Well I hope to have it done [p. 167].

Silverman points out the interactional confusion that results when the clinical reality of the surgeon examining scar tissue is superimposed on the everyday reality of discussing one's satisfaction with one's appearance. The physician's explicit comments about the scar and the excessive number of stitch marks reveal his own assessment of Barry's looks. But it is difficult in this situation for Barry, as it would be for most people, to separate the clinical dimension of the question "What do you think about your looks?" from the everyday interpretation. In fact, Barry's noncommittal response reveals an adherence to the rules governing normal conversation about appearances rather than his inner feelings about his looks. At the age of twelve, Barry understands that, while others may comment on one's appearance, modesty is more appropriate than excessive self-consciousness. Hence, Barry says he does not worry at night over his scar. The physician treats Barry's response as an expression of his true feeings when actually Barry wants to have surgery to lessen the scar, as he indicates in his final remark.

In this case, apart from the verbal side-stepping, both the patient and the physician were in agreement about the decision to proceed with reconstructive surgery. What would happen, however, in the same situation if a child did not want to have the facial reconstruction? Given the physician's clear expression of dissatisfaction with the technical inadequacies of the scar, it is unlikely that any patient would be comfortable communicating his disagreement.

*Practice Guideline 13.2: The physician's ability to influence a desired outcome is further augmented by the traditional authority and autonomy associated with the profession of medicine; in most encounters, patients take their cues from the physician's verbal and nonverbal directives and questions.*

Communication is affected by children's understanding and expectations of what adults want from them. In physicians' interactions with children this has important implications, especially in situations where another adult, usually the mother or another family member, is present. In this case, children must anticipate and respond to the expectations of at least two adults.

*Practice Guideline 13.3: Regardless of whether the parent or other significant adult is actually present during a medical encounter, children carry with them mental templates of the behavioral norms they are expected to accommodate.*

What does this mean in child-physician interaction? For example, a child who wants to please her doctor might supply the "correct" answers to questions and hesitate to report symptoms that are not reviewed in the medical interview. However, investigators have found that in pediatric encounters, physicians usually share information and discuss treatment plans with parents more often than with the child who is the patient (Beuf, 1979; Pantell and others, 1982). Yet in 26 percent of the pediatric visits investigated, Korsch and Negrete (1972) found that the mother's primary concerns were never mentioned because the physician did not encourage her to talk about her concerns or provide the opportunity to do so. In a more recent study of medical discourse, Frankel (forthcoming) found that 99 percent of over 3,500 utterances produced in medical dialogue with patients were initiated by the physician; of these, the majority were questions.

Thus, children are confronted with a communication hierarchy that involves, at one level, child-parent interaction and, at another level, parent-practitioner interaction. As Korbin and Zahorik (1985, p. 338) point out, "The sick role for children is modified by parental responsibility. Parents must recognize a child's complaints as legitimate before alternative or biomedical professionals are consulted. . . . Children must convince their parents that they are 'really' sick rather than wanting to avoid a test at school." In turn, parents must convince the physician that their child's symptoms are authentic and require medical attention.

How do children let adults know that they are feeling ill? Korbin and Zahorik (1985) reported that in initial interviews with urban American schoolchildren about illness and health, the majority of the children (94.1 percent) said that someone else, usually their mother, knew they were ill without being told. The chief indicator was a change in mood or activity level. In contrast to the initial interviews, in weekly follow-up interviews fewer children (53 percent) reported that someone knew they were not feeling well without being told. In their weekly assessments of responses to symptoms, Korbin and Zahorik found that the children indicated that they would seek adult assistance, but that more often they used strategies over which they had some independent control. Resting, "putting my head down for a few minutes," and eating or drinking (or not eating or drinking) were viewed as particularly restorative.

Children's understanding of symptoms tends to be grounded in the degree to which children experience symptoms as interfering with everyday activities. Symptom recognition may be specific ("My tummy hurts," "I have a headache and a cough"), or symptoms can represent a more general malaise ("I just don't feel good"). In either case, a deviation from normal behavior and affect provides the strongest clue that something is wrong. It is important to note that adults use similar processes of symptom recognition.

*Practice Guideline 13.4: Children are more likely to label or define a symptom, whether it is a localized pain or general emotional ill-being, when the symptom disrupts routine affairs.*

## Adult Expectations of Children

A further complication in pediatric interactions arises from health professionals' expectations concerning appropriate demeanor in children as patients. Regardless of the professional status of the adults who interact with injured or ill children, a recognition of the child's cognitive ability can facilitate effective and comprehensible communication (Perrin and Gerrity, 1981; Bibace and Walsh, 1979, 1981; Turiel, 1969). As Perrin and Perrin (1983) have demonstrated, however, health practitioners are not always accurate in their estimation of the cognitive capacities of children. In their study, physicians, nurses, and students in child development were asked to estimate the ages of children on the basis of their responses to questions about health and illness. Ages were identified correctly in less than 40 percent of the cases. Professionals tended to underestimate the age of children twelve to fifteen years old and overestimate the age of children four to seven years old.

These findings have important implications for pediatric interactions, especially those that involve explanations of the illness and medical procedures. An older child might be infantilized in the process of treatment and a younger child might be unable to comprehend the situation. However, as Robinson (1987) points out in her discussion of preschoolers' conceptualizations of health and illness, an accurate perception of a child's cognitive development is not always sufficient to ensure effective communication. According to Robinson (1987, p. 95), "When working with preschoolers, what is done and how this influences the children's sensory experiences may be even more critical to their understanding than what is said. Health care professionals working with young children must pay attention to the congruency of verbal and experiential messages that these children receive."

Silverman's account of an interaction with a fourteen-year-old diabetic adolescent in England reflects the health professional's belief that teens should be responsible for testing their own urine samples:

*Health Visitor:* Rajiv, you're doing the testing?

*Rajiv's Mother:* Sometimes.

*Health Visitor:* Rajiv, it's your urine. (To mother) He's a young man now. Come on Rajiv, do your own wees. It's a bit undignified. It's not your Mum's job [1987, p. 213].

Although the health visitor is promoting independent self-care for adolescents, she is also giving a somewhat guilt-inducing message to Rajiv, making it clear to him that she disapproves of his continual reliance on his mother.

*Practice Guideline 13.5: Adult expectations of age-appropriate behavior can have a significant impact on the way in which medical treatments are managed; for example, young children are often told, "Act like a big girl" or "Don't be a cry-baby" when undergoing an invasive medical procedure.*

Adults also have expectations about children's understanding of disease and symptoms. In some cases, adults underestimate children's awareness of their physical condition and related symptoms and therapy. However, Bluebond-Langer's (1978) investigation of terminally ill leukemic children, Beuf's (1979)

account of pediatric hospitalization, and other research on perceptions of health and illness (such as Korbin and Zahorik, 1985;
Robinson, 1987; Brewster, 1982; Bibace and Walsh, 1981) suggest
that children have well-developed notions and often a clear
understanding of the signs of sickness, the nuances of symptoms,
illness trajectories, drug therapies, and treatment strategies.

Robinson (1987) reported that preschoolers knew that
illnesses varied in severity and duration and that, for example, not
all coughs were indicative of the same sickness. In Bluebond-
Langer's (1978) study, the children with leukemia "were well aware
of the extremely toxic side effects of many of the drugs. . . . They
knew . . . that prednisone created mood swings and weight gain:
[one child reported,] 'Prednisone makes me eat like a pig and act
like a brat'" (pp. 158–159). A child's ability to understand problems
related to her health care should neither be assumed nor discounted.
Compliance with medical care and cooperation with health
personnel are more likely to occur when children are given
explanations of their illness that are appropriate for their age and
when they are included in discussions about treatment strategies.

### Information Management in Pediatric Encounters

Beliefs that adults have about a child's awareness of disease
processes and the consequences of treatment influence the way in
which information is revealed to and withheld from children.
Adults who think that a child is too young to understand the effect
of drug therapy will be less likely to make an attempt to communicate the effect. Adults who believe that it is better to protect children
from the pain of knowledge will avoid discussing a problem,
provide vague answers to specific questions, or, in some cases,
simpy lie ("Oh, don't worry. Everything is going to be fine. You'll
be back at school in no time").

*Practice Guideline 13.6: Sometimes the expressed desire to
protect children is an indication of the adult's own discomfort with
the issues of loss, pain, illness, or death.*

Pediatric terminal illness and death are two areas in which
the impact of information management is significant. Beuf (1979)

provides a poignant account of what can happen when hospital staff try to camouflage communication:

> A colleague told me that one hospital had attempted to resolve fears of death by never speaking of it to the young patients and by developing a code word for it: as the hospital had only six floors, they referred to death as "the seventh floor." A child who asked the whereabouts of a deceased companion would be told, "Mary is on the seventh floor." Unfortunately, this hospital was not totally self-sufficient, and from time to time a child would have to be taken over to the adjoining adult hospital (a larger and taller building) for testing. My colleague recalled vividly an occasion when she had to take a child over for a test that was to be performed on the seventh floor of the adult hospital. When the child saw her push the button labelled "7," she became hysterical. At some level, she had broken code and thought she was going to die [p. 106].

Adults are not alone in their attempts to control the channels and content of information in pediatric settings. Building on the work of Glaser and Straus (1965), Bluebond-Langer (1978) sensitively describes the interactional phenomenon of mutual pretense. In her study, she cites examples of child-practitioner collusion in mutual pretense where both parties knew the child was dying of cancer but acted as if they did not. In these cases, the child and adult were active participants in concealing and disguising information. According to Bluebond-Langer, children and adults understand and adhere to the conversational and behavioral rules that help maintain mutual pretense about illness and death; for example, they avoid topics such as the child's appearance or future plans, or discuss them only as long as no one becomes tearful.

By practicing mutual pretense, leukemic children help protect and sustain the child-parent or child-practitioner relationship in the face of serious threats to personal and social integrity (Bluebond-Langer, 1978). When the child acts in the expected way, the parents and health care team are allowed to assume the reciprocal role and act accordingly. Moreover, mutual pretense demonstrates that children not only understand their social obligations but are competent in managing social relations.

An alternative to mutual pretense is open awareness, in which children and adults openly ackowledge the inevitability or imminence of death. While parents and staff who practiced open awareness in their interactions with terminally ill children reported feeling good about their honesty, Bluebond-Langer notes that it did not protect them from experiencing the same conflicts and dilemmas faced by those practicing mutual pretense. Difficulties with issues of separation, guilt, anger, and delegation of responsibility were concerns for both groups. Similarly, children who practiced open awareness were very much like children who practiced mutual pretense in most behaviors. For example, all of the children avoided using the names of those who had died and they all used symbols of death and disease in art activities and creative play. The processes of open awareness and mutual pretense have implications for pediatric encounters of all kinds. Perhaps most important is the implicit suggestion that individual communication styles function to support, sustain, and manage social relations.

*Practice Guideline 13.7: Forcing children and adolescents (and adults, for that matter) to disclose feelings, beliefs, or fears when self-disclosure is not a normal interactive mode will contribute to discomfort, misunderstanding, and alienation for everyone involved; likewise, to thwart, inhibit, or ignore a sincere desire to acknowledge or express concerns about symptoms or medical treatments can also result in alienation.*

Thus, the challenge for parents and health practitioners is to maintain a communication and information management style that maximizes interactional comfort for the child and themselves. Meeting this challenge is not always easy. However, achieving an effective and comfortable interaction style with children who are ill or hospitalized can be personally and professionally rewarding. The child life specialist, for example, plays an important role in caring for the emotional and developmental needs of hospitalized children (Thompson and Stanford, 1981; Thompson, 1985; Ricks and Faubert, 1981). While the goal of minimizing the negative impact of illness and hospitalization is achieved through the provision of a variety of services, it is perhaps best articulated in the relationship that develops between the child life specialist and the patient and family. In the words of one child life worker, "The relationship is our strongest tool" (Mary Jean Adkins, pers. comm., 1987). This relationship normally develops in directed or nondirected therapeutic play (DelPo and Frick, 1988) with infants and young children and age-appropriate activities (Francis, Myers-Gordon, and Pyper, 1988) for adolescents.

The positive impact of child life specialists in pediatric settings is significant; in certain cases, the relationship that develops between the child life specialist and a patient creates an opportunity for important clinical information to come to the surface. In one case, a child life specialist trained in music therapy was able to determine the cause of a young boy's strong fear of getting shots (Mary Jean Adkins, pers. comm., 1987). The seven-year-old boy, hospitalized for encopresis, was extremely afraid of shots and his behavior mystified and concerned the staff. Using her recorder, the child life specialist enlisted the boy's participation in writing a song about being in the hospital. One verse of his song was quite revealing:

> I hate shots.
> They hurt me because probably
> blood comes out my arm, you probably get killed.
> My mama tells us to get out of the room
> when she gets her shots.
> My stepbrother's mama be gettin' shots too.
> The end.

The child life specialist was able to determine that the boy's fear of needles was directly related to his mother's drug habit. The boy's mother and his "stepbrother's" mother were heroin addicts who would inject themselves in his presence. In this example, the young patient revealed his fears using the expressive medium of music and song. This revelation might never have occurred outside the context of the relationship that was established with the child life specialist.

## Development and Communication in Pediatric Care

The interactive quality of communication between children and health practitioners of all professions influences the meaning attached to what is said, what is heard, and what is observed. In addition, pediatric encounters vary depending on the child's developmental characteristics and the sociocultural backgrounds of both child and health provider. In this section, actual cases are used to demonstrate developmental concerns in pediatric care.

*Case One: A Preschool Child.* As a result of brain damage at birth, Peter's motor coordination on his right side was limited. At the age of two, he had an operation to lengthen his Achilles tendon and improve his ability to walk. Six weeks after the operation, Peter was fitted for a brace; as part of the fitting, a cast was made of his foot. During the process of removing the casting with a small saw, Peter screamed in terror and repeatedly cried out, "No, Mama! No! No! Mama!"

Every six months Peter went through the same process of casting so that the brace would fit comfortably inside his shoe. On subsequent visits, Peter's mother reported that he remained calm until they entered the physician's office and he was placed on the examining table. At this point, she said, "he would cry out and clutch at me. . . . I would be on one side of the table and doctor would try to examine him. . . . He would tighten up and that's exactly what we didn't want him to do because it made it impossible to check his foot properly."

At the age of four Peter shouted repeatedly, "He's gonna saw my leg off!" when the doctor attempted to remove the cast. When Peter turned five, his mother said, "everything seemed to fall into place. . . . If he was going to see the pediatrician he knew that he would get a shot and have to take all his clothes off. . . . He'd take shots real good. . . . If he was going to the neurologist, Peter knew that he'd just talk to him and shine the flashlight in his eyes. . . . If he was going to the other doctor, Peter would ask, 'Is he going to use the hammer?' on his knee."

Developmental experts recognize that the impact of illness or hospitalization depends upon the age of the child (Thompson and Stanford, 1981; Thompson, 1985; Petrillo and Sanger, 1980; Dixon and Stein, 1987). Peter's case clearly demonstrates the way in which developmental changes are reflected in response to medical treatment. At the age of two, Peter was unable to express his emotional distress in words. He could not name what it was that frightened him. At the age of four, his verbal skills allowed him to communicate his fear effectively. However, his cognitive development had not yet reached the level where he could understand the procedure being performed.

Peter's fantasy and misconception about the removal of the cast are classic indications of his preoperational developmental stage. The fear of mutilation or castration is common for children at this age. Peter understood that his foot was in a cast, but he was unable to differentiate the act of having his cast sawn off from the act of having his leg cut off. From his perspective, the physician was using the saw on his leg and this meant he was in danger of losing it.

As noted in Chapter Three, preschool children are capable of causal reasoning in certain familiar contexts. However, in unfamiliar settings, physical and psychological causality are often confused. David, a boy of five, was hospitalized for an infected leg that was not responding to treatment. During his hospitalization, David had blood drawn at least once a day for testing. Each time someone tried to take blood from David he became increasingly hysterical. Through therapeutic play it was discovered that David believed his heart was a beaker, a vessel, and that each time blood was taken his beaker was being depleted. David thought that eventually he would die because the vessel would be empty. Like Peter, David was unable to grasp effectively the causal relationship between an action (blood being drawn or a cast being sawn off) and its consequences.

In addition to their cognitive difficulties in understanding the nature or purpose of medical equipment, preschool children may interpret intrusive procedures—such as blood tests, injections, the insertion of IV needles, or spinal taps—as hostile acts or punishments. In Brewster's (1982) investigation of chronically ill children between the ages of five and twelve, children younger than seven viewed illness as the result of their own actions. Moreover, the younger children also viewed medical treatments—regardless of how benign they might appear to an adult—as forms of punishment for misbehavior. Both Peter and David experienced intrusive procedures that easily could be construed, from their perspective, as punishments. Young children need reassurance that getting sick is not their fault and that medical treatments are not punishments for being bad. It should be noted, however, that recent investigations (Robinson, 1987; Perrin, 1984; Perrin and Gerrity, 1981) have shown that young children do not necessarily use self-blame in their explanations of illness.

Maturation, experience with medical procedures, and the caring attention of health providers and parents increase a young child's tolerance of medical treatment. Peter's mother explained, for example, that as he grew older, Peter was able to manage the doctor visits more successfully. In preparation for a consultation, both she and her husband would play with him, imitating some of the procedures they knew would occur. They would take turns using a "hammer" like the one the doctor used to check reflexes and they would use a flashlight to check their eyes. This kind of play is especially effective in preparing children of this age for medical procedures. In fact, as Thompson and Stanford (1981, p. 33) point out, "preparation for preschoolers is a necessity. It is important that they receive simple, reassuring explanations of forthcoming procedures, with emphasis placed on what they will see, feel, hear, smell, or taste during the event. Since abstract thought is beyond their current cognitive ability at this level, the preschoolers' information should be as concrete as possible."

Studies of children's conceptualizations of health and illness, illness causality, medical procedures, and medical personnel demonstrate that their explanations become increasingly complex with developmental age (Young, McMurray, Rothery, and Emery, 1987; Perrin and Gerrity, 1981; Bibace and Walsh, 1979; Spicher, 1982; Robinson, 1987). School-age children are much less vulnerable than preschoolers to psychological problems associated with illness or hospitalization. At this stage of development, magical fantasies are less likely to distort a child's understanding of medical treatment and procedures. Indeed, as Putnam (1987, p. 307) points out, "for the first time the child has the mental capacity to appreciate that a surgical procedure will cause discomfort, yet produce a desired result."

***Case Two: A School-Age Child.*** Robin, a girl of ten, was hospitalized for a bone marrow transplant. Prior to the day of the transplant, Robin and her mother met several times with a child life specialist for therapeutic play sessions. During these sessions, Robin acted out the bone marrow transfusion with a life-size doll. She played the part of the doctor and instructed the child life therapist and her mother to be the "nurses." Robin repeatedly gave her "patient" messages that the transplant might hurt but that it was being done to help her get better. Robin was also well versed in what her "patient" might expect to feel after the transplant and, consequently, provided detailed explanations about post-transplant recovery. Not all ten-year-olds are as verbally fluent as Robin, but her understanding that a potentially painful treatment can have a positive effect reflects her developmental maturation.

In addition to cognitive development, the school-age child is also developing emotional and social resources that increase the tolerance for medical encounters and treatments. Children of this age, for example, are able to manage separation from parents much more effectively than preschool children. This is due in part to the child's growing ability to understand the reasons for separation and the concept of time. Separation from parents is no longer perceived as a condition that could last indefinitely. At this age, the child is also actively developing social relationships with friends outside the home. Thus, in the hospital setting, most school-age children are able to identify with and relate to other patients their age. The development of relationships with children and health providers in the hospital helps offset the impact of separation anxiety.

Combined with a rapid increase in cognitive, social, and physical capacities in the school-age child is a sense of achievement, mastery, and control in activities, bodily functions, and emotions. Among children who are sick or hospitalized, the fear of losing control is commonly expressed as a concern about death or resistance to anesthesia. Theresa, a nine-year-old girl hospitalized for abdominal surgery, was less concerned about the possibility of a surgical scar than about being "put to sleep" during the operation. This issue was especially problematical for Theresa because several months earlier, the family dog had been "put to sleep" after an extended illness. As Theresa's anxiety increased, so did her need to ask questions about the procedure: "How do they do it?" "What's the difference between being put to sleep and being dead?" "Will I remember the operation?" "Will I know how to wake up when the operation is done?"

The hospital staff were able to alleviate some of Theresa's fears by answering her questions simply and directly. A much more difficult situation arises when a child is uncomfortable expressing fears or asking adults questions. As mentioned in Chapter Four, children are more likely to be talkative when they are playing with peers, siblings, or adults, especially in nonthreatening situations that involve routine activities. Hospitalization and surgery are the antithesis of a routine event. The child is faced with physical trauma and confronted with many new and unfamiliar faces. Parents, health care providers, and other adults need to be extremely sensitive to affect and body cues that indicate discomfort or anxiety. In some cases, it is helpful to anticipate a child's concern and raise issues indirectly—by suggesting, for example, that "sometimes kids have questions about anesthesia." This creates an opportunity for the child to identify with other children who have been in similar circumstances and suggests that she is not alone in experiencing fears. It also provides the child with an opportunity to legitimately ask questions about a procedure.

### Sociocultural Issues and Communication in Pediatric Care

The substantial and growing literature on sociocultural issues in the experience and treatment of illness demonstrates the importance of ethnicity and health beliefs in understanding interactions within the context of medical care. Cultural background has been shown to influence responses to pain (Zborowski, 1958, 1969), attitudes toward and explanations of physical symptoms (Zola, 1966; Kleinman, 1980; Good and Good, 1981; Helman, 1985; Blumhagen, 1982); and the process of identifying and seeking medical care (Chrisman, 1977; Friedson, 1975).

*Case One: Cultural Conflict and Diagnostic Testing.* A recent immigrant from Haiti arrived at the emergency room with Marie, her four-year-old daughter. Marie, unconscious, was immediately admitted to the hospital. The staff were concerned that Marie might be in a diabetic coma. The usual testing was begun.

Routine procedures called for blood samples at regular intervals. During the first day of hospitalization, Marie's mother watched quietly while hospital staff conducted their examinations. She asked very few questions and when she did speak, the staff were unable to understand her broken English. During the second day, Marie remained in a coma and routine examinations continued to be performed. Marie's mother became increasingly agitated, especially when blood samples were drawn. The situation reached a crisis when she physically struggled with a technician in order to prevent him from drawing a blood sample from Marie. Additional staff were called to the room. An interpreter was contacted and arrived several hours later.

Marie's mother told the interpreter that she was afraid that the blood being drawn would be used to practice voodoo sorcery against her child. She was reluctant to admit this because she was a foreigner in a new community. At that time she was staying with distant relatives and was not well integrated into either the Haitian or English-speaking community. Marie's mother also revealed that in Haiti she had had a daughter who was "poisoned" and then taken to a clinic where she died.

In Marie's case, serious problems developed because her mother and the health care team had significantly different views about the nature and purpose of drawing blood. This problem was exacerbated by a language barrier that prevented both parties from communicating their concerns. From the health providers' point of view, everything possible was being done to care for Marie. Testing blood samples is routine in evaluating and monitoring a patient's condition and determining a diagnosis. In the scientific and modern environment of the hospital, voodoo sorcery falls into the realm of the exotic and magical; it has no place in "rational" medicine. On the other hand, voodoo sorcery was not only a part of Marie's mother's belief system, it was also a devastating reality in the realm of her own experience. Her violent outburst with the technician drawing blood demonstrates the degree to which she felt Marie's life was threatened because of the possibility of ritualistic contamination or use of her blood. Having already lost one daughter to sorcery, she was determined to protect Marie. While her behavior might have been construed as irrational, belligerent, and defiant by the staff, Marie's mother was taking protective action on the basis of her knowledge of the danger in blood being taken from her child.

Korbin and Johnson (1982) report on a similar case in their discussion of the resolution of cultural conflicts in pediatric hospitals. A four-year-old girl, the daughter of a woman from Belize, was brought to the emergency room of a large, metropolitan hospital. She was lethargic and had a high fever and back pain. The differential diagnosis was meningitis or sepsis. She was treated with antibiotics and intravenous fluids and her symptoms resolved after a thirteen-day course of treatment. Throughout her hospitalization, the child's mother was so resistant to diagnostic treatment procedures that the hospital obtained legal constraints against her. Her resistance was anchored in the belief that the staff were actively harming her child with repeated and unnecessary blood tests. Medical records indicated that the staff believed her behavior was "erratic. . . irrational . . . and secondary to ignorance versus mental illness versus child abuse" (Korbin and Johnson, 1982, p. 260).

Throughout the Caribbean, blood loss generates concern. In the first example, blood being drawn was suggestive of black magic. This might have been a factor in the second case; however, it is also clear that the woman from Belize was concerned about her child being physically depleted by the procedure. "She felt the amount of blood taken from her daughter was particularly dangerous since the child was small and there is a limited amount of blood in the body. She further believed that remedial action was critical and planned to administer an 'herbal medicine' to her daughter 'to build her blood back up' immediately upon discharge from the hospital" (Korbin and Johnson, 1982, p. 261). In this case, conflicting beliefs about the etiology of the child's illness also created major difficulties for the hospital staff and the mother. The girl's mother believed her sickness was the result of an injury sustained from falling down concrete steps.

These examples call attention to the potential for conflict when patients and health providers have different explanatory models of illness. Explanatory models are the culturally patterned beliefs and expectations that people have about health and illness. According to Kleinman and his associates (Kleinman, Eisenberg, and Good, 1978, p. 254), "Patient-doctor interactions are transactions between explanatory models often involving major discrepancies in cognitive content as well as therapeutic values, expectations, and goals." In pediatric interactions, parents or other adults act as brokers between children and health practitioners in determining when and what type of therapeutic action should be taken. In order to provide effective care to a sick child, the practitioner must be sensitive to the entire family's belief system in relation to the particular problem. Being sick and getting well involves a process of negotiated exchanges between the child and the practitioner, the practitioner and the family, and the child and the family.

Language barriers present unique problems in pediatric settings, especially when the child is bilingual but the family is not. A young girl dying of bone cancer, for example, had relapsed and had been hospitalized. The girl spoke English and Spanish fluently. Her family, which spoke only Spanish, was extremely attentive and stayed close to her throughout her hospitalization. When the doctors, nurses, and other staff visited, the girl usually translated what was said. When the girl died, the family was very upset because it had not fully understood the critical course the daughter's illness had taken. Although the staff believed that the family understood the seriousness of the daughter's condition, the girl had been reassuring the family that this hospitalization would be like other times and she would get better and go home.

Whether they are reflected in dialect or in attitudes and beliefs about illness, socioeconomic and ethnic differences have the potential to thwart effective pediatric care. In an early study of social psychological determinants in the patient-professional relationship, Simmons (1958) concluded that trust, cooperation, and respect between the patient and provider were inversely related to social distance. Health professionals were more likely to establish rapport and effective communication with patients whose values and life-styles were similar to their own. Similarly, in a more recent study, Triandis (1975) noted that as distance between cultures increases, the effectiveness of communication decreases.

The impact of social and cultural distance on the patient-practitioner relationship has serious implications for pediatric encounters, especially in the area of compliance with recommended therapy. Parents and other adult caretakers of children are the primary figures in determining the level of pediatric compliance or follow-through with therapeutic activities. Lock (1984), for example, cited the case of a first-generation Greek mother of a twenty-month-old obese child. During visits with her pediatrician she was encouraged to change the baby's diet to reduce its weight. The mother refused these recommendations because she believed that a fat baby was a model of good health and a sign of family prosperity. Consequently, she did not return to the clinic.

*Case Two: Culture and Compliance with Therapy.* Kim, a ten-year-old child of Chinese descent, was diagnosed with an ulcer and hospitalized in order to stabilize her condition. During her hospital stay, Kim was placed on a bland diet consisting of foods such as cold milk, tomato soup, macaroni and cheese, and Jello with fruit. Kim's family was wary of the hospital food and insisted on bringing meals to Kim that were prepared at home. The meals included a variety of items, many of which were prepared with the traditional stir-fry method using oil.

The hospital staff were upset because the meals represented a total disregard for the prescribed bland diet. Staff were also concerned about the number of family members visiting Kim. They complained that the family entourage interfered with Kim's rest and with their ability to provide efficient care. On the other hand, Kim's family believed that the preparation of home-cooked meals and the presence of family would facilitate Kim's recuperation.

As in the cases described above, differences in the sociocultural backgrounds of the staff and the patient's family created communication difficulties that resulted in dissatisfaction and resentment on both sides. In this case, the problems arose over visitation privileges and diet, not diagnostic testing. The issue of etiology remains, however, because of the cultural significance of certain dietary restrictions indicated by Kim's condition.

Very often, children in Kim's position are caught in the middle of a power struggle between two powerful adult authorities for control over therapeutic regimens. On one hand, Kim is dependent on her family's support. When she goes home, they will certainly feed her according to their own beliefs about an appropriate diet for someone who is ill. On the other hand, while Kim is hospitalized, she is dependent on the doctors, the nurses, and the dietitian, who have clear ideas about what she needs to eat in order to become well again. In this situation, Kim must please two masters.

As Chapter Five points out, cultural beliefs and values are not always explicit; more often they are unconscious definitions of what is right and, therefore, represent guides for normal behavior. What is normal at home is not necessarily normal in the hospital. The continuous presence of Kim's family members was upsetting to the staff. From the staff's perspective, many visitors in the room might disturb the patient, who needed to sleep. Perhaps more important is their perception that too many people in the room disrupted their ability to carry out routine activities. In a similar case, a nurse complained repeatedly to the family of a five-year-old boy from a small town in eastern Kentucky, hospitalized with a broken leg, that she "simply couldn't get a thing done with all of them sittin' around his bed takin' up all the space and the chairs . . . and anyway . . . I told them he wasn't supposed to have so many visitors at once." The mother of the boy spoke for the family when she told the nurse, "You don't understand, we're not visitors, we're family!"

The expectation that family members should be present and available when one of them is hospitalized is shared by many cultures and is not limited to the care of a child. Anderson, Toledo, and Hazam (1982), in their study of Mexican-American resistance to pediatric heart care, reported an instance where "an 18-year-old was undergoing surgery. His wife, mother, father, two sisters, aunt, uncle, great aunt, grandmother, and two female cousins all came to wish him well and be present during the operation" (p. 334). As they point out, this familial attention provides support to the parents as well as the patient.

When pediatric medical encounters involve conflicting beliefs about illness and appropriate therapeutic activities, successful care of the child is more likely to be achieved if the practitioner keeps in mind two goals: communication and compromise. If the child or the family speaks another language, every attempt should be made to enlist an interpreter. Adults should anticipate that a child who is sick and cannot communicate in his own language, especially if he is alone, is likely to experience a greater level of anxiety and fear than a child who can use his own language. Furthermore, when possible, traditional cultural beliefs about remedies, patient care, and disease etiology should be accommodated. Working with the family's traditional beliefs enhances the possibility of a recovery unencumbered by family-staff conflicts. Accommodation of cultural values also facilitates patient compliance.

## Conclusions

Communication between children and adults in the context of medical care is important in shaping the experience and understanding of childhood illness, injury, or hospitalization. Adjustment to an illness, whether it is acute or chronic, and coping with the physical debilitation and emotional stress are articulated and transformed in adult-child interactions. These interactions may occur within the bounds of a significant relationship, such as that between a parent and child. They may also occur within idiosyncratic or time-limited relationships of the sort that develop between nurses and hospitalized children.

In either case, pediatric encounters are influenced by the child's developmental characteristics and the sociocultural backgrounds of the child, the family, and the health provider. Medical terminology, the social construction of medical interactions, adult expectations of children in pediatric settings, and information management between children and adult caretakers all affect issues of health and illness.

Although illness and hospitalization are often stressful events for the child, family, and practitioners, an understanding of the critical factors affecting pediatric care can facilitate effective communication and promote a child's recovery. Sensitivity to a child's developmental concerns is especially important. For example, developmental experts agree that in a hospital situation, in order to counteract the negative effect of separation anxiety, parental participation in the treatment and medical care of both older and younger infants should be maximized (Thompson and Stanford, 1981; Brill and others, 1987). In addition, children in the sensorimotor stage of development, roughly between birth and age two, depend on repetitive explorations of bodily movements and manipulation of objects for their developmental growth. Stimulation activities for children in this stage are thus extremely important, especially in the hospital setting, where opportunities for activity are restricted.

Parental involvement in medical activities and maintenance of familiar routines throughout illness are as important for toddlers as they are for infants (Petrillo and Sanger, 1980; Thompson and Stanford, 1981; Brill and others, 1987). Because of their limited capacity for verbal expression, play is an important method of communication for toddlers. Therefore, health practitioners and adults need to be observant of the messages communicated through play. Play is also an important means of expression for children of preschool age; opportunities for expressive play should be provided for preschoolers who are ill or hospitalized. Directed or unstructured play therapy is particularly beneficial for achieving a sense of control and predictability. Play can be used effectively in preparing a preschooler for medical procedures or treatments.

Clinicians working with school-age children should take advantage of their increased capacity for logical thinking. Yet they must not forget that under stress, children may revert to patterns of understanding and behavior more typical for the child of preschool age. Once again, parental involvement, medical preparation, the provision of opportunities to play, and the maintenance of normal activities when possible help to counteract the detrimental impact of illness or hospitalization.

In addition to developmental issues, sociocultural factors also play an important role in pediatric encounters, especially in cases where health providers and the child and family have different beliefs and values in relation to the occurrence and treatment of illness. In these situations, every attempt should be made to accommodate the patient's understanding of appropriate treatment. Culturally sensitive medical care increases and promotes the patient's recovery and the provider's satisfaction.

Situational context, like developmental and sociocultural characteristics, also influences pediatric interactions. The time, location, and structure of interactions between children and adults in medical settings can profoundly affect the outcome of medical interviews, examinations, and even therapeutic treatments. The quality and extent of information received from children in pediatric settings depend, in part, on contextual and verbal cues given by adults.

A child who is ill or injured does not become well in isolation. Recovery and treatment take place within the context of negotiated interactions with family members, significant caretakers, and health practitioners. Adult sensitivity to a child's behavior and affect facilitates understanding of the medical problem and increases the potential for effective and emotionally supportive communication.

CHAPTER 14

# Children as Witnesses

Evaluating and dealing with the legal system present a special challenge for child advocates, those who are concerned with the well-being of children. This is particularly true in the United States, where legal precedent and the Constitution have established a complex web of ground rules governing the dos and don'ts of behavior by all parties in legal encounters. The interaction of these ground rules with the developmental psychology of children highlights three principal issues: the appropriateness of adversarial proceedings for issues involving children, the importance of incorporating a child's perspective in the design of legal settings and processes, and the importance of adults' understanding of the nature of their roles in relation to children involved in legal proceedings.

Our goal is to maximize the degree to which the legal system acts in the interest of children, to make sure that children can be both safe and competent in legal proceedings. Thus, we put the well-being of children and the developmental appropriateness of legal policies and procedures first. Conventional concerns with adult civil liberties and due process are secondary in our discussions; children come first.

## An Ecological Perspective

We must recognize that the habitat of the child in the legal system includes family, friends, neighborhood, church, and school, as well as less immediate forces that constitute the social geography and climate (such as laws, institutions, and values) and the physical environment of the legal system. The interplay of social forces and physical settings with the individual child defines the range of issues in the forefront of an ecological perspective on children in the legal system. The most important characteristic of an ecological perspective is that it both reinforces our inclination to look inside the individual child and simultaneously encourages us to look beyond the individual child to the environment for questions and explanations about individual behavior and development in relation to the legal process. It leads us to recognize that the performance of a child as a witness is the joint product of the child's capacities and the adult's definitions of the legal context (Melton, 1985).

No discussion of children in legal settings can avoid the issue of the competence of the child to bear witness. Certainly, a major change in the relation of children to the legal system over recent decades has been an increasing presumption of competence. Melton (1981) sets out the features of this essential competence:

> The child [must have the] ability to differentiate truth from falsehood, to comprehend the duty to tell the truth, and to understand the consequences of not fulfilling this duty. . . . The child [must] have cognitive skills adequate to comprehend the event he or she witnessed and to communicate memories of the event in response to questions at trial. . . . Thus, competency to testify implies some measure of competency at the time of the event witnessed as well as at the time of the trial. The child must be able to organize the experience cognitively and to differentiate it from his or her other thoughts and fantasies. . . . [The child] must be able to maintain these skills under psychological stress and under pressure, real or perceived, from adult authority figures to shape his or her responses in a particular way. Particular kinds of testimony may require further specific skills. Testimony by children on sexual abuse may require verification of the child's comprehension of the meaning of sexual terms and behavior [Melton, 1981, pp. 74–75].

Competence is important, of course, but the crucial issue is the capacity of the legal system to respond appropriately to the needs of children with different capacities and competencies (Donald Bross, pers. comm., 1988). Here as elsewhere, it is the match of child to setting (and vice versa) that is our principal concern.

*Practice Guideline 14.1: Children should be presumed competent unless proven otherwise; however, adults must be knowledgeable about and sensitive to the conditions under which children perform competently.*

Thus, the focus here is the social and physical environment presented by legal institutions. Throughout, we must acknowledge that the legal system has different goals from the clinical setting or the scientific study. The law aims at justice; the clinic at psychological benefit; science at truth (Melton and others, 1987). This simple statement stands behind some of the conflicts among professionals in these three knowledge systems.

### The Roles of Adults

Particularly where children are concerned, the roles of investigator, clinical evaluator, and therapist can become inappropriately tangled, even compromised, when individuals serve more than one master—like the clinician who serves the court. Some say this happens frequently (E. Bruce Nicholson, pers. comm., 1988). Sometimes this role conflict arises out of sympathy with the child—for example, when an investigator avoids seeking legally important evidence because gathering it might compromise a child's development. Many observers believe the more common error is to subordinate the needs of the child to the collection of legally useful evidence—for example, when a clinician refrains from therapeutic questioning because it might compromise the admissibility of a child's testimony. Therefore, underlying this chapter is the recognition of five distinct roles for adults vis-à-vis children in the legal system:

1. The *impartial evaluator* possesses expertise about the strengths and limitations of the child as a source of information and uses that expertise to assess facts and their significance.
2. The *advocate* is allied with the child, begins from the belief that

the child is a valid reporter, and seeks an interpretation of events and a resolution of the legal processes that maximize the child's prospects for growth and development.

3. The *guardian* assumes responsibility for the child's overall well-being and protection as the child interacts with others in the legal system; the guardian is presumed to be the child's parent unless the parent is disqualified for that role (in which case someone else is appointed to fulfill this function).

4. The *therapist* seeks to preserve and restore the mental health of the child and is guided by the child's condition and subjective interpretation of reality.

5. The *decision maker* (judge) is responsible for maximizing justice in the legal process, for assuming control of the interactive process on the basis of laws setting minimum standards for due process and substantive concerns.

Once we might have thought that these roles were clearly defined and understood; we recognize now that conflicts and ambiguities are common, as difficult sexual abuse and custody cases have demonstrated. For example, many now believe that the conventional adversarial relationships characterizing the legal process are antithetical to the mental health needs of children in custody disputes, and that fundamental ethical issues are raised by professional participation in adversarial roles (for example, when a professional represents one side in a custody dispute).

The forensic clinician needs access to all parties in the dispute in order to serve the interests of the child. This requires the clinician to work for the court rather than one of the parties to the dispute (Melton and others, 1987; Weithorn, 1987). A psychiatrist well versed in custody disputes put it this way when discussing protracted parental conflicts (admittedly a minority of all custody proceedings): "My main criticism of attorneys involved in custody conflicts is that via their commitment to the adversary system—as a first step in resolving custody conflicts—they are bringing about psychopathology when it doesn't exist and exacerbating and prolonging it when it does" (Gardner, 1982, p. 21).

## A Systems Approach to the Legal System

Our goal here is to use an ecological systems approach to development in ways that will clarify the complexity we face in seeking to understand children as participants in the legal system (whether as witnesses or the objects of a dispute). A systems approach helps us discover the connections between what might at first seem to be unrelated events. It also can help us see that what often seems an obvious solution may actually make the problem worse. Jay Forrester (1969), a systems analyst, concluded that because systems are linked, and therefore influence each other through feedback, many of the real solutions to social problems are not readily apparent. They may even be exactly the opposite of what seems sensible on the face of things (that is, they are counterintuitive).

According to Hardin (1966), the first law of ecology is that we can never do just one thing. Intersystem feedback ensures that any single action may reverberate and produce unintended consequences. This will become apparent as we proceed, particularly as we examine efforts to protect the child in the courtroom. For example, some observers have hypothesized that some efforts (such as televising testimony) may, paradoxically, produce more rather than less stress for children because they create a totally unfamiliar situation (being on camera). Others (such as Raskin and Steller, forthcoming) have argued that in sexual abuse cases, efforts to make the child more comfortable or to load the interview in favor of a child's allegation may actually produce evidence of inferior quality that eventually may rebound against the child's best interest.

When asked whether $x$ causes $y$, the ecologically prudent answer is always that it depends. We cannot reliably predict the future of a system without knowing something about the other systems with which it is linked and in which it is embedded. We see this when we ask, Does courtroom participation as a witness harm a child's development? We answer, It depends on the child's age and level of development, the presence of psychopathology (which can impair accurate reporting by distorting memory or cognition), the emotional state of the child, the quality of adult support and demands in the courtroom, the timing of interrogations, and the quality of the judge's motivations and training, as well as the child's understanding of the proceedings. In short, it depends.

This, while frustrating, is the truth of the matter. For example, preliminary reports from a study of child witnesses in one state suggest that children experienced the act of witnessing as empowering (Runyan and others, 1988), while other reports suggest that similar experiences produced a sense of being victimized (MacFarlane and others, 1986).

Many observers have concluded that gross mistreatment of child witnesses is tactically unwise (regardless of the personal or professional scruples of the attorneys). It may create sympathy for the child and cause the attacker to be characterized as a bully (with negative repercussions for the client's case). This is not to say that horror stories are unknown. Even within the same trial, the experience of children as witnesses can be very different, and the experience of some children much better than others. For example, Gary Moylen, a lawyer and child advocate, presents this scenario for a group molestation case: "If a prosecutor has 18 to 20 child victims, he may have 5 or 6 who will make strong witnesses. The prosecutor might allow the defense attorney to verbally abuse 3 to 4 of the less competent witnesses to get sympathy from the jury. He then puts on his 5 or 6 strong witnesses to make the facts of his case. Tactically, it's a great move—he gets the sympathy he needs plus his facts—but at the expense of 3 or 4 children" (Little, 1987, pp. 1-2).

As we said in Chapter One, we see the individual's experiences as subsystems within systems within larger systems, "as a set of nested structures, each inside the next, like a set of Russian dolls" (Bronfenbrenner, 1979, p. 22). In asking and answering questions about development, we can and should always be ready to look at the next level of systems to find the questions and the answers (Garbarino and Associates, 1982). If we see parents and practitioners in conflict over the involvement of children in the legal system, we need to look beyond, to the community that establishes laws and policies regulating a child's participation and leads parents to fear for their child's emotional safety in the court. This is precisely the kind of dynamic that generates advocacy efforts such as "Believe the Children," an advocacy and support group for child victims and their parents (P.O. Box 1358, Manhattan Beach, CA 90266; 213/379-3514).

Further, we should look to the culture that defines the courtroom experience for all concerned: what is normal, what is permissible, what is prescribed, what is proscribed. We must look, too, within the individual (as a set of psychological systems that are affected by conscious and changing roles, unconscious needs, and motives) to know why and how they adjust to the events of being a witness. In addition, we must look at how the several systems involved (family, social services, social network, and legal) adjust to new conditions.

These social forces are the keys to our analysis of children as witnesses. Since they exist as linked social systems, intervention can take place at each system level; further, intervention and effects in one system may well spill over to others. For example, a change in policy that permits videotaped child testimony may lead to defense-originated "discovery" motions that open up all videotaped records to hostile scrutiny. This may aid the cross-examining defense attorney in attacking the interview process and the child as a witness. Does this facilitate justice? The American model works from the presumption of innocence; thus, anything that increases access to evidence is theoretically desirable. Nonetheless, in this case, the child's task might be easier without the videotape, because the defense would only have the in-court testimony to use (Gary Melton, pers. comm., 1987).

*Practice Guideline 14.2: Some procedural innovations designed to improve the child's experience inadvertently may increase its stressfulness.*

We approach these issues from an ecological perspective. This perspective focuses on the interplay of social systems in shaping human behavior (Bronfenbrenner, 1979). The immediate relationships and situations of the child's life are called *microsystems*. Family, school, peer group, and church are all microsystems. The connections among these microsystems are called *mesosystems*. These are the systematic relationships between immediate settings, for example, the school-home mesosystem. Settings that influence the child's life but in which the child does not play a direct role are called *exosystems.* These include the microsystems of the child's parents in which the child does not participate but which affect the child through their influence on the parent, for example, the parent's place of work. Exosystems also include governmental bodies that make decisions affecting the child, for example, local government or a court in which the child does not testify but which makes custody decisions. Finally, there are the *macrosystems,* the broad cultural, economic, and political systems that provide the blueprints for day-to-day life. Macrosystems include institutions such as government, as well as cultural patterns such as the Bill of Rights. Macrosystems provide the context in which other social systems operate.

**Legal Microsystems.** Microsystems evolve and develop much as individuals themselves do, from forces generated both within and without. The quality of microsystems depends on their ability to sustain and enhance development, to provide a context that is emotionally validating and developmentally challenging. This in turn depends on their capacity to operate in what Vygotsky (1986) called the zone of proximal development—the range between what the child can accomplish alone (the level of actual development) and what the child can do when helped (the level of potential development).

This is crucial in assessing the competence of children in the legal system. A child who appears competent when interviewed by a supportive and skillful therapist or a specially trained and intuitively sensitive prosecutor may appear incompetent when cross-examined by a hostile and intimidating defense attorney bent on undermining the child. The same child might not say anything at all to a bored, brusque judge.

*Practice Guideline 14.3: A child's account may develop when the child is inteviewed by an investigator or therapist.*

This might, paradoxically, weaken the child's credibility in court; naive (or cunning) observers might interpret the developmental changes as discrepancies and inconsistencies and as evidence of "tampering." Some practitioners in the field have reported precisely this experience (MacFarlane and others, 1986).

Others have sought to develop objective techniques for

assessing the credibility of the accounts offered by children (Raskin and Steller, forthcoming). These approaches seek to increase adult competence by incorporating an understanding of the expectable errors of children at various stages of development into the procedures for assessing the validity of narrative accounts. The most exciting innovation on this score is statement validity analysis. Pioneered in Germany, this technique provides specific guidelines for evaluating the credibility of accounts presented by children. It has been used in thousands of investigations in Germany and Sweden and is now becoming available for North Americans in a refined form through the efforts of David Raskin, John Yuille, Max Steller, and others.

The validity of the technique depends on the success of the interviewer in eliciting an open-ended and unprompted narrative account in four phases (Farr and Yuille, 1988). In the initial phase, conversation and routine questions are used to establish rapport. In the free recall phase, the child gives a free narrative of events. In the specific question phase, the interviewer asks specific, open-ended clarification questions. In the suggestibility phase, the interviewer uses leading questions to check the child's suggestibility.

The actual statement analysis relies on an assessment of the internal structure of the child's statement and its congruence with accepted norms about the likely and unlikely mistakes and ambiguities of such child-delivered narratives (Farr and Yuille, 1988; Raskin and Steller, forthcoming). It provides a formalized scheme for implementing the criteria developed (often impressionistically) by experts in the field in recent years (Farr and Yuille, 1988). The technique appears to possess a high level of accuracy when used correctly on appropriate narrative data, yielding 90 percent correct conclusions (Steller, Raskin, and Yuille, forthcoming).

Like the polygraph (which may be inappropriate for use with children; Raskin and Steller, forthcoming), this technique may be useful in the investigatory and even the adjudicatory phases of legal proceedings involving children over the age of six. Introduction of statement analysis into the legal system would set in motion a set of changes, the course and side effects of which are a focal point of an ecological analysis. A courtroom may be very different after a judge attends a special training session on children in court.

Naturally, children themselves change and develop, as do others in the setting. By operating in the child's zone of proximal development, a prosecutor or clinician can train the child to perform better in the courtroom as a witness (however, he can also distort the natural flow of the child's narrative unitl it becomes unsuitable for evaluation via statement analysis).

The courtroom itself can do this, as when judges create a setting designed to maximize a child's performance. This can be done by reorganizing furniture and layout to make them more child-sized, by permitting only brief periods of testimony, and by using puppets to talk with children (Schudson, 1989). The Cambridge, Massachusetts, district attorney's office has prepared a kit for making the court more child-oriented. This acknowledges the importance of a phenomenological approach to the child in the legal process. Such an approach recognizes that each participant operates on the basis of a particular conception of what is real, an emergent social map that is a phenomenological record and projection of experience.

*Practice Guideline 14.4: Repeated involvement in the witnessing process may have both positive and negative effects on the child's social map of the courtroom. It may desensitize the child to the stressful aspects of testifying, or it may reinforce its aversive characteristics.*

Some observers have noted that the legal process can validate the child's sense of self-worth by demonstrating that the child's experience of victimization is being taken seriously, and that justice is being served on the child's behalf. Achieving that validation is a goal for all who are responsible for administering the legal system.

*Legal Mesosystems.* We measure the richness of mesosystems by the number and quality of their connections. For example, in the mesosystem of the courtroom, we ask, do staff visit the child at home prior to trial? Do the child's parents know the court staff? What role do the parents play in shaping the process of testifying? For example, sitting on a parent's lap may reassure a young child while testifying because it transfers the security of home to the courtroom. Is the child the only one to participate in both home and court? If the linkage is only this, the mesosystem is weak and that weakness may place the child at risk.

Research suggests that the strength of the mesosystem linking the setting in which intervention is implemented to the settings in which a person spends most significant time is crucial to the long-term effectiveness of the intervention and the maintenance of effects (Whittaker, Garbarino, and Associates, 1983). This may apply to the child's experience of the legal system as well.

*Practice Guideline 14.5: Children who have experience at home or in school with formal social settings that rehearse the legal process may transfer this experience to that of being a witness in a courtroom.*

Children who are accustomed to being closely questioned about school after they arrive home may be better prepared for the interrogative process of being a legal witness than are children who are not routinely interviewed. Children who participate in student courts in school may be prepared likewise for becoming real witnesses. Indeed, Melton and others (1987) have gone so far as to suggest that informing children about the legal process is one of the most important ways to reduce any negative effects of being a witness. Noting that by about age seven or eight children have much the same concept of fairness as adults, they argue that making a full disclosure in order to maximize a child's understanding is most likely to create a sense of fairness and thereby a buffer against feelings of victimization (assuming, of course, that the legal system is in fact being fair to the child—a dubious assumption in some cases). Building a sense of fairness implies making only promises that can be kept, for example. The naive adult may wish to reassure the child or elicit cooperation by promising, "Everything is going to be all right if you just tell what you know." This promise may be false, however—even patently false—and may lead only to suspicion and opposition from the child in future encounters with professionals—whether allied with the legal system or not.

*Practice Guideline 14.6: Honesty in the context of a warm, supportive, and empathic child advocacy is the best policy for improving the child's role in the legal process.*

*Legal Exosystems.* One form of intervention aims at transforming exosystems (in which children do not participate) into microsystems (in which they do) by initiating greater participation in important institutions by isolated, disenfranchised, and powerless clients. For example, a child might be taken to visit the courtroom prior to testifying; all children might be routinely exposed to courtrooms as part of citizenship education in order to prepare them for the possibility of serving as a witness. Does the court see the parent as a collaborator or as an enemy? What about the therapist's role in the court? Are both involved in the legal process? These are some of the important exosystem issues.

Another important exosystem issue is found in policy-making. When legislators alter the rules of evidence to make them more compatible with the needs of children, they enhance the courtroom as a setting for child witnesses. When they insist on adult-oriented rules of evidence that violate the special needs of children, they may create artificial conditions of social risk for children as witnesses. The Canadian senate recently conducted a debate on such policies and chose to support child-oriented rules of evidence.

The issue of the child-centeredness of powerful decision makers has an individual aspect as well, for example, in whether or not parents have the "pull" to get a child assigned to a child-oriented prosecutor or judge. Here, the experience of powerful, well-connected people can have far-reaching social significance. The fact that President John F. Kennedy's sister was mentally retarded stimulated national policy. A similar effect might be observed if a president's child were a witness in a court case.

Unfortunately, the fact that most legislators are themselves lawyers can work against reforms that diminish the degree to which the legal system is lawyer-driven and lawyer-oriented. The current system is often short on justice and long on procedures that generate possibilities for expensive litigation. Children rarely are the ones who profit from this system.

*Legal Macrosystems.* Macrosystems are the blueprints for the ecology of human development. These blueprints reflect a people's shared assumptions about how things should be done, as well as the institutions and demographic configurations that represent those assumptions. In discussing children as witnesses we are always operating within the context of broad legal constraints (in the United States, for example, the constitutional protections of due process under the Fourteenth Amendment and confrontation under the Sixth). In other societies the same constraints may not apply; discussions might proceed on the matter of maximizing the performance of children as witnesses without the constraint of contending with a mandate that defendants must be able to confront witnesses against them. For all the legal discussion of confrontation as a vital process for producing justice, the validity of this and other such requisites remains a matter largely untested by empirical research. When children are witnesses, for example, there is a good case to be made that confrontations may actually decrease truth and thus result in a miscarriage of justice.

### The Adversarial System and the Problem of Confrontation

We begin with suspicion of the adversarial system where children are concerned. We do so even with the recognition that this may not do justice to existing supports for children within the legal system. Even the adversarial system can sometimes operate in ways that provide protection for children (Donald Bross, pers. comm., 1988).

*Practice Guideline 14.7: By identifying legal resources that can insulate the child from harmful experiences in the legal setting, lawyers, clinicians, and advocates can sometimes accomplish a great deal on behalf of a child. Nonetheless, we should retain a basic skepticism about the compatibility of the adversarial system and the psychological needs of children.*

This is particularly true of custody disputes. "In a child custody dispute no one wins. This is one point that psychiatrists and attorneys can agree upon" (Weiner, Simons, and Cavanaugh, 1985, p. 59). Of course, we must recognize that in many ways the current situation represents a clear historical advance (Weiner, 1985). Child custody laws once operated on the principle that children were the property of parents (fathers being the principal beneficiaries of these laws). They now have moved to a standard of serving the child's best interest. This is real progress. What is more, the last fifteen or twenty years have seen many changes in practice, changes that include greater use of mediation (sometimes mandated by law or judicial decree), court-affiliated counseling services, child assessment services specializing in custody disputes, and the routine use of attorneys for children in custody cases. The list is long and growing.

However, greater sensitivity to the potentially deleterious effects of mishandled custody litigation has coincided with an increase in the number of children entering the legal system because of divorce-related custody disputes. This has produced a heightened sense of alarm about the process; concern that the system is authoritarian and biased has been replaced with concern that greater equality between competing spouses has led to an unfortunate increase in the adversarial nature of the proceedings. As Weiner put it, "As the entire area of family law evolves, the only certainty that exists for the foreseeable future is that the divorce rate will remain high, profoundly affecting the involved children, and issues such as custody, visitation and child support will continue to be litigated" (Weiner, 1985, pp. 842–843). All the ameliorating mechanisms are at work in a context in which more and more children are involved in legal proceedings concerning custody arrangements, and reports of horror stories continue with alarming frequency.

An overriding concern about the legal system is that it exhibit procedural justice—that it be fair (and be perceived as fair). This concern lies behind much of the debate over what can and cannot be done, as well as what should and must be done. Survey research and experimental studies suggest that most people will accept as just the legal conclusions that flow from a system and process perceived to be fair (Melton and others, 1987). The challenge lies in developing an approach to children in the legal system that is fair to them—that respects their developmental needs—and fair to adults—that respects their rights.

Just as our system recognizes that the accused adult needs special protection when confronted by the police power of the state in a criminal proceeding, so we should recognize that children need special protection when confronting the power of adults, whether those adults be perpetrators of abuse, attorneys, competing parents, or judges (Donald Bross, pers. comm., 1988). The more vulnerable a person is before the power of the legal system, the greater should be the safeguards for that person in a confrontation with the legal system.

*Practice Guideline 14.8: Those who operate within the legal system must be—or at least must be advised by—informed and sensitive child development experts who can interpret the system for children and interpret children to the system.*

Such experts must be more than passive interpreters, however. They must assume a child advocacy role. Perhaps the institutional role that most clearly models this is that of the hospital-based child life specialist, discussed in Chapter Twelve. These professionals are steeped in child development knowledge and take as their mission the job of making the experience of hospitalization (and medical care more generally) less developmentally threatening to children.

In a recent study, the U.S. Department of Justice conducted in-depth interviews with court-related personnel in four cities on the topic of children as witnesses in criminal proceedings (Whitcomb, Shapiro, and Stellwagen, 1985). They asked, "What exactly is it about the criminal justice system that may be difficult or troublesome?" (p. 17). The fear most frequently reported among children was facing the defendant. As the investigators point out, "This fear was mentioned by virtually all respondents, including police, social workers, advocates, therapists, doctors, and judges" (p. 18). Other investigators, such as Goodman, have verified this finding. Fortunately (from a child advocate's point of view), most cases involving children are handled outside criminal courts, and the experience of confrontation thus is rare (E. Bruce Nicholson, pers. comm., 1988).

Our concern here is twofold: first, that children are frightened, and second, that their performance is impaired (and thus justice is not well served). Many anecdotal reports testify to this. For example, a child would only testify when the bailiff stood next to her, hand on gun, ready to protect her. The social conventions of the criminal court (for example, that the defendant will not attack) may need very concrete verification to reassure a child. However, what is not clear from the existing research and clinical observation is whether children are any more likely than adults to feel intimidated by the courtroom. At least one observer doubts that they are (Gary Melton, pers. comm., 1987).

## Interaction of Systems

*Microsystem Effects.* A microsystem is defined by the roles, relationships, activities, furnishings, and equipment that distinguish it. What about the legal system as a set of microsystems for children? Much of the current debate about the involvement of children in legal proceedings (particularly the prosecution of sexual abuse cases and the litigation of custody disputes) focuses on two sets of questions:

- What features of the legal process as a set of microsystems affect children as sources of information for adults?
- What features of the court as a microsystem make up the constitutionally mandated format for legal proceedings? What features are optional? What alternatives are possible?

The microsystem of the courtroom is under the control of many forces. One such force is the statutory classification of the proceedings. For example, the burden of proof differs markedly as one moves from civil to criminal proceedings. In civil dependency and neglect proceedings in some states, it is possible to shift the burden of proof to parents, who must show why presumptive evidence of the child's endangerment is not what it appears to be (Donald Bross, pers. comm., 1988). This provides greater latitude for the child to be a source of information in shaping the outcome of the case than do criminal proceedings, where the more stringent rule applies that a defendant is innocent until proven guilty beyond a reasonable doubt. We believe that many cases involving children (such as sexual abuse cases) are best served in civil proceedings (or, indeed, in extralegal settings entirely).

Beyond such matters of statutory rule there is the Supreme Court's interpretation of the U.S. Constitution. For example, in a sexual abuse case in Kentucky, a trial judge excluded the defendant (but not his attorney) from an in-chambers hearing to determine the competence of two alleged victims to testify (Demchak, 1987). The children then testified about the sexual abuse in court during the trial—with some repetition of questions asked during the hearing. The defendant was convicted. On appeal to the state supreme court the conviction was reversed, but the Supreme Court reinstated it (*Kentucky* v. *Stincer*, 482 U.S. 730). The appeal was argued on the Sixth Amendment right of the accused to confront witnesses (Demchak, 1987).

The majority of the justices indicated that direct confrontation is required by the Constitution whenever it will assist in cross-examination, but decided that events in this particular case did not violate this principle. This case illustrates that the process of sorting out what is permissible (as opposed to desirable from the point of view of the child witness) is still uncertain. The six-to-three Supreme Court ruling still leaves three members opposed to anything that dilutes the constitutional mandate to have witnesses testify in the presence of the accused at all stages of the court procedings. In 1988, the Supreme Court held, six to two, that placing a screen between the accused and child victims during their testimony violated the accused's right of confrontation (*Coy* v. *Iowa*, 108 S.Ct. 2798).

This view was upheld in a decision by the Texas court of criminal appeals that voided a statute allowing admission into evidence of a videotaped interview of a child in a sexual abuse case (Constantikes, 1987). This ruling was based on the same appeal to the Sixth Amendment (*Long* v. *State of Texas*, 694 S.W.2d 185). The intention of the statute in question was to spare children the stressful encounter with a perpetrator in the courtroom (although as written, it allowed the introduction of videotaped statements only when the child was available to testify at the trial). That the legal system is in flux on the matter of children as witnesses is clear from the many cases that are reaching appeals courts for decisions on evidentiary and other issues (see, for example, the American Bar Association's *Juvenile and Child Welfare Law Reporter*).

**Mesosystem and Exosystem Effects.** How are other social systems beyond the legal system relevant? Here the principal issue is the degree to which a positive congruence exists between the court and other settings with which the child is familiar—home, school, and church, for example. Does the child confront people and roles in the court that he knows from home, school, or church? For example, does the child participate in the court with adults known to him in other settings? Some courts allow or even encourage the presence of familiar adults to support the child. This evidences a strong mesosystem.

Is the child familiar with the peculiar social roles of the courtroom? Is there in the child's experience an analogue to a judge in black robes? To a defense attorney? To cross-examination? In some homes, loud arguments lead to physical assault. Will the courtroom's argument stimulate fear of impending assault? The key here is the degree to which connections and parallels between the court and the other microsystems in a child's life affect the child, whether positively or negatively.

In the matter of exosystem effects, legislators and judicial superiors do much to set the standard of care for children in the legal process. Systematic variation is evident in this standard of care. The juvenile courts in most jurisdictions treat the testimony of children differently from family or criminal courts (E. Bruce Nicholson, pers. comm., 1988). In contrast to criminal and family proceedings, the juvenile court involves children as parties. In juvenile court children have their own attorneys and the judge has a broader range of dispositional powers. The standards of evidence and testimony are different, and the proceedings are more likely to be conversational and to resemble the everyday experience of children in nonlegal settings.

In recent years, statutory reform in states across the country has changed policies and procedures regarding children in the juvenile courts (usually for the better). In some jurisdictions, informed, progressive judicial leadership has raised the standard of care. In others, lax or uninformed leadership has left the standard low. Thus, for example, Judge Pamela Iles, South Orange County Municipal Court, New Jersey, does not permit questions to children that are too long (that contain more words than the child's age plus one). She deliberately and actively protects children who testify in her court. Others do not. Iles states unequivocally that the judge is responsible for the conduct of her court and must be answerable and held accountable for how children fare. Other leaders (such as Schudson, 1989) endorse this hard line.

Thus, effective and sensitive legal action in matters affecting children hinges on a shared set of definitions and assumptions. That shared conception, in turn, depends on the active involvement of judges in programs that educate and raise consciousness about child development. When done well, such programs can alter what is taken for granted in the direction of meeting the needs of children.

Another important exosystem effect concerns how the responsibility for dealing with children is assigned. A community's power structure may reserve adjudication of situations involving children to the court; in most U.S. jurisdictions this means a separate and special juvenile or family court.

This is not the only possible model, however. The community may allocate the function to administrative review, as U.S. communities do in the earlier and less intrusive stages of assessing and dealing with child maltreatment cases, or to lay citizen panels, as some U.S. communities do with foster care case review. Whether or not this is permissible, plausible, or likely presumably becomes a macrosystem issue, however, since it impinges on the matter of institutional expressions of culture.

We can see this clearly in the observation that such alternatives to judge- and lawyer-oriented courts are found most readily in cultures and contexts beyond the United States mainstream—for example, in Puritan New England of the seventeenth and eighteenth centuries, where religious tribunals dominated; in Native American communities, where tribal courts dominated (and still do in some areas); and in Scotland, where a state-authorized system of children's hearings operates. These alternatives do not necessarily provide better service to the needs of children, of course. Structural forms that permit more collaborative and informal proceedings may even work against children if the ideology guiding those settings is adult- rather than child-oriented. For example, this may be true of some of the Native American tribal courts.

The Scottish system is worth noting briefly here. Scottish law provides for five-member panels to hear cases in which "the child is beyond the control of parents; is exposed to moral danger; is being caused unnecessary suffering or serious impairment to health or development through lack of parental care; is failing to attend school; is indulging in solvent abuse; or has committed an offense" (Scottish Information Office, 1987, p. 1).

The children's hearing deals with cases involving children and youth under the age of sixteen. An official reporter is responsible for directing cases to the hearing on the basis of information communicated by professional and lay sources. Thus, when someone identifies children in difficulty, telling the reporter is the appropriate course of action.

Who serves on the hearing panels? All members are appointed by the government after screening and receive training. They are meant to be representative of the community and to "have experience of and interest in children and the ability to communicate with them and their families" (Scottish Information Office, 1987, p. 3). An important limitation is that the child and parents must accept all the grounds for referral. If they do not, a court referral is made for the adjudication of facts; the case is referred back to the hearing for deposition.

Most of the hearings deal with delinquency, but 5 percent involve lack of parental care. For our purposes, the key to the children's hearing is that it operates as an informal discussion in which the child is a participant, except where the hearing panel decides that parts of such discussions could cause distress. This focus on informal, common-language discussion among citizens contrasts with the conventional courtroom scene. The system is set up to guard against abuses by permitting appeal to the sheriff; a high appeal to a court is available on points of law or "irregularity" only. Included in the system is a child advocate (a "safeguarder"), who also may appeal the hearing's decision. The children's hearing may provide some ideas for improving on the conventional courtroom as a mechanism for serving the best interests of a child.

*Practice Guideline 14.9: Our goal is a legal system that makes human sense to children; reducing adult-oriented procedures and roles is one way to accomplish that goal.*

**Macrosystem Effects.** Here, our concern is with the impact of the culture's blueprints on children in the courts. Do the culture and its dominant institutions enhance or diminish the child's functioning as a source of information for adults? A macrosystem effect that has received extensive discussion is the role of the U.S. Constitution in limiting the range of options available to those trying to reduce the traumatic and presumably truth-distorting effects of confronting child witnesses with alleged adult perpetrators.

This issue is most pertinent to the criminal courts, where the dominant concern is avoiding false convictions of innocent parties who are accused of crimes. The constitutional insistence on a defendant's right to confront witnesses has been cited as the basis for refusing to allow videotaped statements and other techniques designed to protect the testimony of children from implicitly coercive confrontations with adult perpetrators. That this macrosystem effect can impair justice by reducing the effectiveness of children as witnesses is possible, although not yet empirically verified (Melton and others, 1987). However, most cases involving children are conducted in juvenile and family courts, where less stringent rules of evidence operate.

Another macrosystem issue is the culture's stereotypes of children and youth. Young children are generally seen in terms of sympathetic stereotypes by well-meaning adults. The concern of these adults is that children are incompetent as witnesses, rather than that they are malicious. However, where adolescents are concerned, the issue is more likely to be one of suspicion. Adolescents are generally viewed in a negative light by adults in our society (Garbarino and Associates, 1985). Marie Winn (1983, p. 14) observes that the dominant image with respect to teenagers is "the myth of the teenage werewolf." In Winn's view, most adults ascribe monstrous images to adolescents, even when they defined the same individuals positively as children.

This is relevant to our consideration of children as witnesses because it suggests that adult jurors will bring to adolescents a culturally sanctioned mistrust. We saw this in Chapter Six when we reviewed Everson and Boat's (1986) study of child protective services workers. Everson and Boat reported that workers were much more likely to be suspicious of reports of sexual abuse from adolescents than from children.

Of course, these stereotypical views of adolescents are rein-
forced by a certain measure of reality. For example, Jones and
McGraw (1987) found that teenagers who had had prior experience
of victimization were more likely than children to make false
accusations of sexual abuse. Similarly, Ralph Welsh (pers. comm.,
1988) reports that many adolescent victims of abuse make poor
witnesses because one adaptation to being abused is a pattern of
aggressive acting out, belligerence, and social incompetence. This
resonates with the negative stereotypes of adolescents to conspire
against the teenager as a witness. Here, macrosystem forces act in
concert with microsystem (and individual developmental) influences to produce a potentially serious problem.

### Children's Competence as Witnesses

The courts do not have a history of responsiveness to the
special needs of children as sources of information. British
common-law tradition established a presumption of competency
only for adolescents (those over fourteen). This tradition assumed
that the competency of all children below the age of fourteen was
intrinsically suspect. A special inquiry was required to determine
whether a particular child might be competent. In the United
States, statutory guidelines were rare and case law prevailed. Where
they existed, guidelines generally set ten as the age of competence:
younger children were presumed incompetent, older children and
youth were presumed competent. But these presumptions could be
challenged on a case-by-case basis.

The trend has been in the direction of a generalized case-by-
case determination for children (Melton, 1981). Recently, the
tendency has been to do away with competency requirements
outright and presume competency (E. Bruce Nicholson, pers.
comm., 1988). In some cases children as young as four have been
approved. Taking this trend to its logical conclusion, Terr (1985)
has presented an analysis of the processes for employing infants as
witnesses. Being a witness in this sense includes providing
photographs and other documentation of the child's condition, as
well as data relevant to paternity if that is at issue: "In issues of
paternity, the baby is his own best witness. He must be allowed to

donate his direct evidence, his blood, in order to get on with the business of 'psychological attachment' " (Terr, 1985, p. 316).

Terr suggests direct "testimony" by infants in some cases, for example, where the issue before a judge is who is the psychological parent of an eight-month-old. Differences in the baby's responsiveness to the parents should be introduced directly to the judge as evidence (perhaps in chambers). Such direct testimony by infants may also be relevant in cases where foster and biological parents dispute and in marital breakups, where the issue is which parent *really* took care of the baby.

Terr recognizes that infants may misrepresent the reality of their relationships in such settings, perhaps as a result of being manipulated by adults (for example, a parent may pinch the baby while handing it over to create the impression that the baby was upset by the change from one person to another). But she believes court personnel can control these problems, particularly if they utilize the services of infant specialists as consultants (for example, by having a member of the court handle the transferring of children and by using multiple tests).

Others add that personnel must ensure that plenty of time is used in making such evaluations, that consistency across different settings is assessed, that participants are sensitive to the child's need for emotional comfort, and that multiple observers are used to increase the reliability and validity of judgments (Donald Bross, pers. comm., 1988). Terr's suggestion that infants serve as witnesses does not sit well with some observers (one attorney's response was simply, "This is garbage"). Of course, there are those who have much the same response to some forms of adult testimony (such as psychiatric testimony concerning the insanity plea as a homicide defense).

In recent years the American Bar Association's National Legal Resource Center for Child Advocacy and Protection has advocated rules that presume competency to allow children in general to testify. These rules require that the "trier of fact" (the judge or jury) evaluate the child's testimony as it would any testimony. We have yet to achieve that objective. The key is to be found in communicating a better general understanding of children as sources of information for adults, not in any single procedural reform (no matter how important it is for solving a specific problem).

Once we create momentum in the macrosystems and exosystems for child-centered legal proceedings, specific reform initiatives will come more easily and will contribute to the creation of positive feedback loops in the experience of children as witnesses. In 1895, the Supreme Court affirmed a decision to permit a five-year-old's testimony, stating, "While no one would think of calling as a witness an infant only two or three years old, there is no precise age which determines the question of competency" (Melton, 1981, p. 74). Terr and others (such as Jones and Krugman, 1986) have now challenged even the first part of the Supreme Court's statement. What is more, there is enough evidence available to allow us to assume that the normal, expectable capacities of children are a sufficient foundation if adults make good use of them. This is Melton's conclusion as well: "Liberal use of children's testimony is well founded, to the extent that the primary consideration is the child's competence to testify. Memory appears to be no more of a problem than in adult eyewitnesses when recollection is stimulated with direct questions. Children are no more prone to lying than adults" (Melton, 1981, pp. 81–82).

## Conclusions

Once again, it is the adults' competence and orientation that make the difference. They determine how the legal system will affect the well-being and competence of children. Most important in all this are three things: First, the adult-oriented adversarial system must be subordinated to policies and procedures that encourage dialogue and cooperation. The adversarial system is designed to produce a relentless process of competition between parties. While this may have some advantages, in certain contexts it tends to lead to a "winner-loser" mentality for all concerned. It is not the kind of climate in which the needs of children are met well. This is evident in families, schools, games, and anywhere else that children encounter adults and each other. The costs of the adversarial model are seen most clearly when children are the objects of parental custody disputes. Where children are the spoils that go to the victor, the result is likely to be damaged goods. The same is true within families when parents compete for the affection and loyalty of children. It is also true in the legal proceedings surrounding child maltreatment cases. The child's first need is for protection and support. In courtrooms as well as in families this need is most likely to be met when the situation is cooperative rather than adversarial in nature.

Second, courtrooms must be child-sized in layout and child-oriented in process. This means that judges and court administrators must scrutinize every feature of the court from the perspective of the child. This will require consultation with child development specialists. It includes the furniture, the language used, the scheduling of events, access to reassuring presences, and everything else now known to reassure children and thus to boost their competence.

Finally, adults must maintain the distinctions among the roles of advocate, therapist, evaluator, investigator, and judge. Creating a cooperative ethos in the legal system does not deny the possibility of multiple roles. If anything, it highlights the fact that different adults have different agendas. It is the melding of these agendas into a cooperative whole guided by the goal of preserving the child that exemplifies the desirable process. Once we accomplish these three goals we can feel confident that children in the legal setting will be safe and competent.

# Epilogue

We began with a desire to improve the ethical and technical quality of child-adult communications, to improve the effectiveness of children as sources of information for adults. Our goal has been to pursue the issues of orientation and competence by inspecting research, collecting clinical lore, and drawing on our firsthand experiences with children.

Translating this desire to serve children well into a practical perspective with which to approach the issues of orientation and competence introduced in Chapter One has proven very difficult. We must fit every research finding and clinical conclusion into a framework that is developmentally sound and respects the integrity of the child. We find many suggestions for the practitioner, but we recognize (sometimes reluctantly) that few assertions can stand naked without the cloaking caveat "It depends."

It depends on issues of identity and relationship, of meaning and sequence. It depends on who the child is as an individual as well as in the broad sense of cultural identity. It depends on who the adult is in both personal orientation and professional role. It depends on who the child and adult are to each other—on where they have been and where they are going as a dyad.

It depends on the value we attach to children. Recall Dostoyevski's Grand Inquisitor. He asks the story's central character if he would be willing to torture one child if doing so meant the salvation of the world. While the choices presented to us are not so dramatic, we can see that many professionals are asked to make the same sort of decision when investigating cases of victimization (sexual abuse, criminal assault, even some divorce proceedings), particularly when the legal system is involved. Whose needs come first? How do we balance a child's need for reassurance and validation with a court's need for testimony or a defendant's constitutional right to cross-examination? We have come down on the side of the child. We put the child's need first. This is our orientation.

In the matter of competence, we have found support for our view that it is not so much the child's lack of competence that creates problems but rather the adult's lack of competence in all too many situations. The psychologist Lev Vygotsky (1986) provides the inspiration for a perspective that emphasizes the role of the adult in mediating the child's level of functioning. The task is to prepare adults to recognize and operate in the child's zone of proximal development—the range between what the child can and will do alone and what he or she can do with the assistance of a competent teacher. We must set a standard for adults to produce the greatest possible competence on the child's part by providing contextual support. That is, the onus is on the adult to understand, support, have positive expectations, and, when appropriate, guide and assist the child. The thrust of our discussions of competence has therefore been to improve adult capacity. This is how we deal with the issue of competence.

We believe that when adults adopt an empathic orientation to children and demonstrate the highest possible level of competence, the process of adult-child communication can succeed well beyond conventional expectations, expectations that are based on a devaluing of children and less than optimal adult performance. Children can tell us more than we thought possible, if we adults are ready and able to play our part.

# References

Achenbach, T. M. "The Child Behavior Profile: I. Boys Aged 6-11."
*Journal of Consulting and Clinical Psychology,* 1978, *46,* 478-
488.

Achenbach, T. M., and Edelbrock, C. S. "The Child Behavior
Profile: II. Boys Aged 12-16 and Girls Aged 6-11 and 12-16."
*Journal of Consulting and Clinical Psychology,* 1979, *47,* 223-
233.

Agar, M., and Hobbs, J.R. "Interpreting Discourse: Coherence and
the Analysis of Ethnographic Interviews." *Discourse Processes,*
1982, *5,* 1-32.

Ainsworth, M., Blehar, M., Waters, E., and Wall, S. *Patterns of
Attachment: A Psychological Study of the Strange Situation.*
Hillsdale, N.J.: Erlbaum, 1978.

Ainsworth, M., and Wittig, B. "Attachment and Exploratory
Behavior of One-Year-Olds in a Strange Situation." In B. Foss
(ed.), *Determinants of Infant Behavior.* Vol. 4. London: Meth-
uen, 1969.

Allport, G. W. "The Use of Personal Documents in Psychological
Science." Social Science Research Council, Bulletin 49, 1942.

Alston, F. K. *Caring for Other People's Children: A Complete
Guide to Family Day Care.* Baltimore, Md.: University Park
Press, 1984.

American Academy of Child and Adolescent Psychiatry. *Journal of
the American Academy of Child and Adolescent Psychiatry,* 1987,
*26* (5), 611-669.

American Bar Association. *Juvenile and Child Welfare Law Reporter.* Washington, D.C.: ABA National Legal Resource Center
for Child Advocacy and Protection.

Ames, L. B., Learned, J., Metraux, R. W., and Walker, R. N. *Child Rorschach Responses: Developmental Trends from Two to Ten Years.* (Rev. ed.) New York: Brunner/Mazel, 1974.

Anastasi, A. *Psychological Testing.* (4th ed.) New York: Macmillan, 1976.

Anderson, B. G., Toledo, J. R., and Hazam, N. "An Approach to the Resolution of Mexican-American Resistance to Pediatric Heart Care." In N. Chrisman and T. Maretzki (eds.), *Clinically Applied Anthropology.* Dordrecht, the Netherlands: D. Reidel, 1982.

Anthony, E. J. "The Influence of Maternal Psychosis on Children — Folie à Deux." In E. J. Anthony and T. Benedek (eds.), *Parenthood.* Boston: Little, Brown, 1970.

Asch, S. E. "The Doctrine of Suggestion, Prestige, and Imitation in Social Psychology." *Psychological Development,* 1951, *35,* 250–276.

Ashmead, D. H., and Perlmutter, M. "Infant Memory in Everyday Life." In M. Perlmutter (ed.), *Children's Memory.* New Directions for Child Development, no. 10. San Francisco: Jossey-Bass, 1980.

Attias, R., and Goodwin, J. "Knowledge and Management Strategies in Incest Cases: A Survey of Physicians, Psychologists, and Family Counselors." Paper presented at the Fifth International Conference on Child Abuse and Neglect, Montreal, Canada, Sept. 1984.

Axline, V. M. *Play Therapy.* Boston: Houghton Mifflin, 1939.

Basch, M. F. *Doing Psychotherapy.* New York: Basic Books, 1980.

Bateson, G. "A Theory of Play and Fantasy." In J. S. Bruner, A. Jolly, and K. Sylva (eds.), *Play.* New York: Basic Books, 1976.

Bell, R. Q. "A Reinterpretation of the Direction of Effects in Studies of Socialization." *Psychological Review,* 1968, *75,* 81–95.

Belsky, J. "Infant Day Care: A Cause for Concern?" *Zero to three.* National Center for Clinical Infant Programs, Washington, D.C., Sept. 1986.

Bernstein, B. "Social Class and Linguistic Development: A Theory of Social Learning." In A. A. Halsey, J. Floyd, and C. A. Anderson (eds.), *Education, Economy and Society.* New York: Free Press, 1961.

Bernstein, L., and Bernstein, R. *Interviewing: A Guide for Health*

*Professionals.* East Norwalk, Conn.: Appleton-Century-Crofts, 1985.

Bernstein, V., Percansky, C., and Hans, S. "Screening for Social-Emotional Impairment in Infants Born to Teenage Mothers." Paper presented at the biennial conference of the Society for Research in Child Development, Balimore, Md., Apr. 1987.

Bertacchi, J., and Coplon, L. "The Effects of Divorce on Parenting: Developmental, Preventive, and Clinical Considerations for Families with Very Young Children." Unpublished manuscript, Virginia Frank Child Development Center of the Jewish Family Service, Chicago, 1988.

Bettelheim, B. *The Uses of Enchantment: The Meaning and Importance of Fairy Tales.* New York: Knopf, 1976.

Beuf, A. H. *Biting Off the Bracelet.* Philadelphia: University of Pennsylvania Press, 1979.

Bibace, R., and Walsh, M. E. "Developmental Stages in Children's Conceptions of Illness." In G. C. Stone, F. Cohen, N. E. Adler, and Associates, *Health Psychology—A Handbook: Theories, Applications, and Challenges of a Psychological Approach to the Health Care System.* San Francisco: Jossey-Bass, 1979.

Bibace, R., and Walsh, M. E. "Children's Conceptions of Illness." In R. Bibace and M. Walsh (eds.), *Children's Conceptions of Health, Illness, and Bodily Functions.* New Directions for Child Development, no. 14. San Francisco: Jossey-Bass, 1981.

Blanck, P. "The Appearance of Justice: Judges' Verbal and Nonverbal Behavior in Criminal Jury Trials." *Stanford Law Review,* 1985, *38,* 89-164.

Bloom, S. W. *The Doctor and His Patient: A Sociological Interpretation.* New York: Free Press, 1963.

Bluebond-Langer, M. *The Private World of Dying Patients.* Princeton, N.J.: Princeton University Press, 1978.

Blumhagen, D. "The Meaning of Hypertension." In N. Chrisman and T. Maretzki (eds.), *Clinically Applied Anthropology.* Dordrecht, the Netherlands: D. Reidel, 1982.

Boat, B. W., and Everson, M. D. "Using Anatomical Dolls: Guidelines for Interviewing Young Children in Sexual Abuse Investigations." Unpublished manuscript, School of Medicine, University of North Carolina, Chapel Hill, 1986.

Boat, B. W., and Everson, M. D. "The Anatomical Doll Project: An Overview." Unpublished manuscript, Department of Psychiatry, University of North Carolina, Chapel Hill, 1988.

Boggs, S. T. "The Meaning of Questions and Narratives to Hawaiian Children." In C. B. Cazden, V. P. John, and D. Hymes (eds.), *Functions of Language in the Classroom*. New York: Teachers College Press, 1972.

Borke, H. "Piaget's Mountains Revisited: Changes in the Egocentric Landscape." *Developmental Psychology*, 1975, *11*, 102–108.

Bowlby, J. *Attachment and Loss*. Vol. 3: *Loss: Sadness and Depression*. New York: Basic Books, 1980.

Bradburn, N. M., Sudman, S., and Associates. *Improving Interview Method and Questionnaire Design: Response Effects to Threatening Questions in Survey Research*. San Francisco: Jossey-Bass, 1979.

Breger, L. *From Instinct to Identity*. Englewood Cliffs, N.J.: Prentice-Hall, 1974.

Brenner, M. "Patterns of Social Structure in the Research Interview." In M. Brenner (ed.), *Social Method and Social Life*. Orlando, Fla.: Academic Press, 1981.

Brenner, M. "Response Effects of 'Role-Restricted' Characteristics of the Interviewer." In W. Dijkstra and J. van der Zouwen (eds.), *Response Behavior in the Survey Interview*. Orlando, Fla.: Academic Press, 1982.

Bresee, P., Stearns, G. B., Bess, B. H., and Packer, L. S. "Allegations of Child Sexual Abuse in Child Custody Disputes: A Therapeutic Assessment Model." *American Journal of Orthopsychiatry*, 1986, *56* (4), 560–569.

Brewster, A. B. "Chronically Ill Hospitalized Children's Concepts of Their Illness." *Pediatrics*, 1982, *69*, 355–362.

Briggs, C. L. *Learning How to Ask: A Sociolinguistic Appraisal of the Role of the Interview in Social Science Research*. Cambridge, England: Cambridge University Press, 1986.

Brill, N., and others. "Caring for Chronically Ill Children: An Innovative Approach to Care." *Children's Health Care*, 1987, *16*, 105–113.

Bronfenbrenner, U. *The Ecology of Human Development*. Cambridge, Mass.: Harvard University Press, 1979.

Bross, D., and Michaels, L. *Foundations of Child Advocacy*. Longmont, Calif.: Bookmakers Guild, 1986.

Brown, A. L. "The Development of Memory: Knowing, Knowing About Knowing, and Knowing How to Know." In H. W. Reese (ed.), *Advances in Child Development and Behavior*. Vol. 10. Orlando, Fla.: Academic Press, 1975.

Brown, A. L. "Knowing When, Where and How to Remember: A Problem of Metacognition." In R. Glaser (ed.), *Advances in Instructional Psychology*. Vol. 1. Hillsdale, N.J.: Erlbaum, 1978.

Brown, A. L., Bransford, J. D., Ferrara, R. A., and Campione, J. C. "Learning, Remembering and Understanding." In J. H. Flavell and E. M. Markman (eds.), *Handbook of Child Psychology*. Vol. 3: *Cognitive Development*. New York: Wiley, 1983.

Brown, A. L., and Ferrara, R. A. "Diagnosing Zones of Proximal Development." In J. V. Wertsch (ed.), *Culture, Communication and Cognition: Vygotskian Perspectives*. Cambridge, England: Cambridge University Press, 1985.

Brown, A. L., and others. "Intrusion of Thematic Ideas in Children's Comprehension and Retention of Stories." *Child Development*, 1977, *48*, 1454-1466.

Budoff, M. "A Learning Potential Assessment Procedure: Rationale and Supporting Data." In B. W. Richards (ed.), *Proceedings of the 1st Congress of the International Association for the Scientific Study of Mental Deficiency*. Reigate, England: M. Jackson, 1968.

Burton, R. "Honesty and Dishonesty." In T. Lickona (ed.), *Moral Development and Behavior: Theory, Research, and Social Issues*. New York: Holt, Rinehart & Winston, 1976.

Cannell, C. F., Lawson, S. A., and Hausser, D. L. *A Technique for Evaluating Interviewer Performance*. Ann Arbor: Survey Research Center of the Institute for Social Research, University of Michigan, 1975.

Cassell, E. *Talking with Patients*. Vol. 1: *The Theory of Doctor-Patient Communication*. Cambridge, Mass.: MIT Press, 1985a.

Cassell, E. *Talking with Patients*. Vol. 2: *Clinical Technique*. Cambridge, Mass.: MIT Press, 1985b.

Cazden, C. B. "Play with Language and Meta-Linguistic Awareness: One Dimension of Language Experience." In J. S. Bruner, A. Jolly, and K. Sylva (eds.), *Play*. New York: Basic Books, 1976.

Cazden, C. B. "Spontaneous and Scientific Concepts: Young Children's Learning of Punctuation." Paper presented at the Conference on English Education at the National Council of Teachers of English, Washington, D.C., Nov. 1982.

Cazden, C. B. "Peekaboo as an Instructional Model: Discourse Development at School and at Home." In B. Bain (ed.), *The Sociogenesis of Language and Human Contact: A Multi-Disciplinary Book of Readings*. New York: Plenum, 1983.

Ceci, S. J., Ross, D. F., and Toglia, M. P. "Age Differences in Suggestibility: Narrowing the Uncertainties." In S. J. Ceci, M. P. Toglia, and D. F. Ross (eds.), *Children's Eyewitness Memory*. New York: Springer-Verlag, 1987.

Chagoya, L., and Schkolne, M. A. "Children Who Lie: A Review of the Literature." *Canadian Journal of Psychiatry*, 1986, *31*, 665–669.

Chi, M. T. H. "Knowledge Structures and Memory Development." In R. S. Siegler (ed.), *Children's Thinking: What Develops?* Hillsdale, N.J.: Erlbaum, 1978.

Chilcott, J. "Where Are You Coming From and Where Are You Going?" *American Educational Research Journal*, 1987, *24* (2), 199–218.

Chrisman, N. J. "The Health Seeking Process: An Approach to the Natural History of Illness." *Culture, Medicine and Psychiatry*, 1977, *1*, 351–377.

Chukovsky, K. *From Two to Five*. Berkeley: University of California Press, 1971.

Cicourel, A. "Pragmatic Issues in the Construction of Recent History from Interview Narratives." In H. Parret and others (eds.), *Possibilities and Limitations of Pragmatics*. Studies in Language Companions Series, vol. 7. Amsterdam: John Benjamins, 1981.

Cicourel, A. "Interviews, Surveys, and the Problem of Ecological Validity." *American Sociologist*, 1982, *17*, 11–20.

Cicourel, A. "Elicitation as a Problem of Discourse." In *Sociolinguistics: An International Handbook of the Science of Language and Society*. Berlin: Walter de Gruyter, 1986.

Claman, L. "The Squiggle-Drawing Game in Child Psychotherapy." *American Journal of Psychotherapy*, 1980, *34* (3), 414–425.

Cohen, D. H., and Stern, V. *Observing and Recording the Behavior of Young Children*. New York: Columbia University Teachers College, 1958.

Cole, C. B., and Loftus, E. F. "The Memory of Children." In S. J. Ceci, M. P. Toglia, and D. F. Ross (eds.), *Children's Eyewitness Memory*. New York: Springer-Verlag, 1987.

Cole, M. "The Zone of Proximal Development." In J. V. Wertsch (ed.), *Culture, Communication and Cognition: Vygotskian Perspectives*. Cambridge, England: Cambridge University Press, 1985.

Cole, M., and Bruner, J. "Cultural Differences and Inferences About Psychological Processes." *American Psychologist*, 1972, *26*, 867–876.

Cole, M., Dore, J., Hall, W. S., and Dowley, G. "Situational Variability in the Speech of Preschool Children." In M. Ebihara and R. Gianutsos (eds.), *Papers in Anthropology and Linguistics*. New York: New York Academy of Sciences, 1978.

Cole, M., and Scribner, S. *Culture and Thought*. New York, Wiley, 1974.

Constantikes, P. "Videotaped Statement of Sex Abuse Victim Inadmissible, Says Texas High Court." *Youth Law News*, 1987, *8* (3), 6–7.

Coopersmith, S. *The Antecedents of Self-Esteem*. New York: W. H. Freeman, 1967.

Cordes, C. "Assessment in San Francisco." *APA Monitor*, Apr. 1986, p. 16.

Cotton, N. S. "The Development of Self-Esteem and Self-Esteem Regulation." In J. E. Mack and S. L. Ablon (eds.), *The Development and Sustaining of Self-Esteem in Childhood*. New York: International Universities Press, 1983.

Cramer, B. "Assessment of Parent-Infant Relationships." In T. B. Brazelton and M. Yogman (eds.), *Affective Development in Infancy*. Norwood, N.J.: Ablex, 1986.

Daehler, M. W., and Greco, C. "Memory in Very Young Children." In M. Pressley and C. J. Brainerd (eds.), *Cognitive Learning and Memory in Children*. New York: Springer-Verlag, 1985.

Davies, G., Stevenson, Y., and Flin, R. "The Reliability of Children's Testimony." *International Legal Practices*, forthcoming.

"Debate Forum." *Journal of the American Academy of Child and Adolescent Psychiatry*, 1988, *27* (3), 387–388.

DelPo, E. G., and Frick, S. B. "Directed and Nondirected Play as Therapeutic Modalities." *Children's Health Care*, 1988, *16*, 261–267.

Demchak, T. "Child Sex Abuse Defendant May Be Excluded from Competency Hearing." *Youth Law News*, 1987, *8* (3), 4–5.

DeMonbreun, B. G., and Mahoney, M. J. "The Effect of Data Return Patterns on Confidence in an Hypothesis." In M. J. Mahoney (ed.), *Scientist as Subject: The Psychological Imperative*. Cambridge, Mass.: Ballinger, 1976.

Demos, V. "A Perspective from Infancy Research on Affect and Self-Esteem." In J. E. Mack and S. L. Albon (eds.), *The Development and Sustaining of Self-Esteem in Childhood*. New York: International Universities Press, 1983.

Dent, H. "The Effects of Interviewing Strategies on the Results of Interviews with Child Witnesses." In A. Trankell (ed.), *Reconstructing the Past*. Deventer, the Netherlands: Kluwer, 1982.

Dent, H., and Stephenson, G. M. "An Experimental Study of the Effectiveness of Different Techniques of Questioning Child Witnesses." *British Journal of Social and Clinical Psychology*, 1979, *18*, 41–51.

DePaulo, B., and Pfeifer, R. "On-the-Job Experience and Skill at Detecting Deception." *Journal of Applied Social Psychology*, 1986, *16* (3), 249–267.

DePaulo, B., Zuckerman, M., and Rosenthal, R. "Humans as Lie Detectors." *Journal of Communications*, Spring 1980, *30*, 129–139.

de Villiers, P. A., and de Villiers, J. G. *Early Language*. Cambridge, Mass.: Harvard University Press, 1979.

Dexter, L. A. *Elite and Specialized Interviewing*. Evanston, Ill.: Northwestern University Press, 1970.

deYoung, M. "A Conceptual Model for Judging the Truthfulness of a Young Child's Allegation of Sexual Abuse." *American Journal of Orthopsychiatry*, 1986, *56* (4), 550–559.

Dijkstra, W., van der Veen, L., and van der Zouwen, J. "A Field Experiment on Interviewer-Respondent Interaction." In M. Brenner, J. Brown, and D. Canter (eds.), *The Research Interview: Uses and Approaches*. Orlando, Fla.: Academic Press, 1985.

Dillon, J. T. "The Multidisciplinary Study of Questioning." *Journal of Educational Psychology*, 1982, *74* (2), 147-165.

Dixon, S. D., and Stein, M. T. *Encounters with Children: Pediatric Behavior and Development*. Chicago: Year Book Medical Publishers, 1987.

Dodds, J. B. *A Child Psychotherapy Primer*. New York: Human Sciences Press, 1987.

Donaldson, M. *Children's Minds*. New York: Norton, 1979.

Eberhart, M. A. "Therapeutic Storytelling with Preschoolers." *Journal of the American Academy of Child Psychiatry*, 1979, *18*, 119-127.

Edelbrock, C., and Costello, A. "Structured Psychiatric Interviews for Children and Adolescents." In G. Goldstein and M. Hersen (eds.), *Handbook of Psychological Assessment*. Elmsford, N.Y.: Pergamon Press, 1984.

Edelbrock, C., and others. "Age Differences in the Reliability of the Psychiatric Interview for the Child." *Child Development*, 1985, *56*, 265-275.

Ekman, P. *Why Kids Lie*. New York: Scribner's, 1989.

Elkind, D. "Strategic Interactions in Early Adolescence." In J. Adelson (ed.), *Handbook of Adolescent Psychology*. New York: Wiley, 1980.

Emde, R. N. "Toward a Psychoanalytic Theory of Affect." In S. I. Greenspan and G. H. Pollock (eds.), *The Course of Life: Psychoanalytic Contributions Towards Understanding Personality Development*. Vol. 1: *Infancy and Childhood*. Washington, D.C.: National Institute of Mental Health, 1980.

Emde, R. N. (ed.). *René A. Spitz: Dialogues from Infancy*. New York: International Universities Press, 1983.

Emde, R. N., Gaensbauer, T. J., and Harmon, R. J. *Emotional Expression in Infancy: A Biobehavioral Study*. Psychological Issues: A Monograph Series, Vol. 10, no. 37. New York: International Universities Press, 1976.

Erdberg, P., and Exner, J. E., Jr. "Rorschach Assessment." In G. Goldstein and M. Hersen (eds.), *Handbook of Psychological Assessment.* Elmsford, N.Y.: Pergamon Press, 1984.

Erickson, F., and Schultz, J. *The Counselor as Gatekeeper: Social Interaction in Interviews.* Orlando, Fla.: Academic Press, 1982.

Erikson, E. *Childhood and Society.* New York: Norton, 1950.

Erikson, E. *Identity and the Life Cycle.* New York: International Universities Press, 1959.

Evans-Pritchard, E. E. *Social Anthropology and Other Essays.* New York: Free Press, 1962.

Everson, M., and Boat, B. "Lying About Sexual Abuse: In the Eye of the Beholder?" Paper presented at the Fourth National Conference on Sexual Victimization of Children, New Orleans, May 1986.

Exner, J. E., Jr. *The Rorschach: A Comprehensive System.* Vol. 2: *Current Research and Advanced Interpretation.* New York: Wiley-Interscience, 1978.

Fagan, J. F. "Memory in the Infant." *Journal of Experimental Child Psychology,* 1970, *9,* 217–226.

Fagan, J. F. "Infants' Delayed Recognition Memory and Forgetting." *Journal of Experimental Child Psychology,* 1973, *16,* 424–450.

Fantz, R. L., Fagan, J. F., and Miranda, S. B. "Early Visual Selectivity." In L. B. Cohen and P. Salapatek (eds.), *Infant Perception: From Sensation to Cognition.* Vol. 1. Orlando, Fla.: Academic Press, 1975.

Farr, V., and Yuille, J. "Assessing Credibility." *Preventing Sexual Abuse,* 1988, *1* (1), 8–13.

Fenichel, O. "The Economics of Pseudologia Phantastica." In O. Fenichel, *Collected Papers.* New York: Norton, 1954.

Fenson, L., Kagan, J., Kearsley, R. B., and Zelazo, P. R. "The Developmental Progression of Manipulative Play in the First Two Years." *Child Development,* 1976, *47,* 232–236.

Feuerstein, R. *The Dynamic Assessment of Retarded Performers: The Learning Potential Assessment Device, Theory, Instruments, and Techniques.* Baltimore, Md.: University Park Press, 1979.

Finkelhor, D. *Child Sexual Abuse.* New York: Free Press, 1984.

Fisher, L., Harder, D., Kokes, R. F., and Schwartzman, P. *School Functioning of Children at Risk for Behavioral Pathology.* Monographs of the Society for Research in Child Development, no. 197. Chicago: University of Chicago Press, 1982.

Fisher, S., and Todd, A. D. (eds.). *The Social Organization of Doctor-Patient Communication.* Washington, D.C.: Center for Applied Linguistics, 1983.

Fitzpatrick, J., and Travieso, L. "The Puerto Rican Family: Its Role in Cultural Transition." In M. Fantini and R. Cardenas (eds.), *Parenting in a Multicultural Society.* New York: Longman, 1980.

"Five Freed in Sex-Abuse Case; Parents Urge State Action." *Chicago Tribune,* Jan. 18, 1986, p. 1.

Flapan, D., and Neubauer, P. B. *The Assessment of Early Child Development.* New York: Jason Aronson, 1976.

Flavell, J. H. "Metacognition and Cognitive Monitoring." *American Psychologist,* 1979, *34,* 906-911.

Flavell, J. H. *Cognitive Development.* (2nd ed.) Englewood Cliffs, N.J.: Prentice-Hall, 1985.

Flavell, J. H. "The Development of Children's Knowledge About the Appearance-Reality Distinction." *American Psychologist,* 1986, *41* (4), 418-425.

Flavell, J. H., Friedrichs, A. G., and Hoyt, J. D. "Developmental Changes in Memorization Processes." *Cognitive Psychology,* 1970, *1,* 324-340.

Flavell, J. H., Green, F. L., and Flavell, E. R. *Development of Knowledge About the Appearance-Reality Distinction.* Monographs of the Society for Research in Child Development, no. 212. Chicago: University of Chicago Press, 1986.

Flavell, J. H., and Wellman, H. M. "Metamemory." In R. V. Kail and J. W. Hagen (eds.), *Perspectives on the Development of Memory and Cognition.* Hillsdale, N.J.: Erlbaum, 1977.

Florio-Ruane, S. "Sociolinguistics for Educational Researchers." *American Educational Research Journal,* 1987, *24* (2), 185-197.

Ford, C., King, B., and Hollender, M. "Lies and Liars: Psychiatric Aspects of Prevarication." *American Journal of Psychiatry,* 1988, *145,* 554-562.

Forrester, J. *Urban Dynamics.* Cambridge, Mass.: MIT Press, 1969.

Fowler, W. *Infant and Child Care: A Guide to Education in Group Settings.* Newton, Mass.: Allyn & Bacon, 1980.

Fox, L. H., and Zirkin, B. "Achievement Tests." In G. Goldstein and M. Hersen (eds.), *Handbook of Psychological Assessment.* Elmsford, N.Y.: Pergamon Press, 1984.

Fraiberg, S. *The Magic Years.* New York: Scribner's, 1959.

Fraiberg, S. (ed.). *Clinical Studies in Infant Mental Health.* New York: Basic Books, 1980.

Fraiberg, S., Adelson, E., and Shapiro, V. "Ghosts in the Nursery: A Psychoanalytic Approach to the Problem of Impaired Infant-Mother Relationships." *Journal of the American Academy of Child Psychiatry,* 1975, *14,* 387–422.

Francis, S., Myers-Gordon, K., and Pyper, C. "Design of an Adolescent Activity Room." *Children's Health Care,* 1988, *16* (4), 268–273.

Frankel, R. M. "Talking in Interviews: A Dispreference for Patient-Initiated Questions in Physician-Patient Encounters." In G. Psathas (ed.), *Interaction Competence.* New York: Irvington, forthcoming.

Freidson, E. *Doctoring Together: A Study of Professional Social Control.* New York: Elsevier, 1975.

Freidson, E. *Patients' Views of Medical Practice: A Study of Subscribers to a Prepaid Medical Plan in the Bronx.* New York: Russell Sage Foundation, 1961.

Freidson, E. *Profession of Medicine: A Study of the Sociology of Applied Knowledge.* New York: Harper & Row, 1970.

Freud, A. *The Ego and the Mechanisms of Defense.* London: Hogarth Press, 1937.

Freud, A. *The Psycho-Analytic Treatment of Children.* London: Imago, 1950.

Freud, A. *Normality and Pathology in Childhood: Assessments of Development.* New York: International Universities Press, 1965.

Friedman, V., and Morgan, M. *Interviewing Sexual Abuse Victims Using Anatomical Dolls.* Eugene, Ore.: Shamrock Press, 1985.

Garbarino, J. "How to Detect and Prevent Child Abuse." *Child Care Center,* 1987, *2* (5), 18–19.

Garbarino, J., and Ebata, A. "The Significance of Ethnic and

Cultural Differences in Child Maltreatment." *Journal of Marriage and the Family,* Nov. 1983, pp. 773–783.

Garbarino, J., and Gilliam, G. *Understanding Abusive Families.* Lexington, Mass.: Lexington Books, 1980.

Garbarino, J., Guttmann, E., and Seeley, J. *The Psychologically Battered Child: Strategies for Identification, Assessment, and Intervention.* San Francisco: Jossey-Bass, 1986.

Garbarino, J., and Associates. *Children and Families in the Social Environment.* New York: Aldine, 1982.

Garbarino, J., and Associates. *Adolescent Development: An Ecological Perspective.* Westerville, Ohio: Merrill, 1985.

Gardner, H. "Beyond the IQ: Education and Human Development." *Harvard Educational Review,* 1987, *57,* 187–193.

Gardner, R. *Therapeutic Communication with Children: The Mutual Storytelling Technique.* New York: Science House, 1971.

Gardner, R. *Family Evaluation in Child Custody Litigation.* Caskill, N.J.: Creative Therapeutics, 1982.

Garfinkel, H. *Studies in Ethnomethodology.* Englewood Cliffs, N.J.: Prentice-Hall, 1967.

Garmezy, N. "Children Under Severe Stress: Critique and Commentary." *Journal of the American Academy of Child Psychiatry,* 1986, *25* (3), 384–392.

Garvey, C. *Play.* Cambridge, Mass.: Harvard University Press, 1977.

Gelman, R., and Baillargeon, R. "A Review of Piagetian Concepts." In J. H. Flavell and E. M. Markman (eds.), *Handbook of Child Psychology.* Vol. 3: *Cognitive Development.* New York: Wiley, 1983.

George, C., and Main, M. A. "Social Interactions of Young Abused Children: Approach, Avoidance, and Aggression." *Child Development,* 1979, *50,* 306–318.

Getzels, J. W. "Socialization and Education: A Vote on Discontinuities." *Teacher's College Record,* 1974, *76,* 218–225.

Gibson, E. J., and Spelke, E. S. "The Development of Perception." In J. H. Flavell and L. Ross (eds.), *Social Cognitive Development: Frontiers and Possible Futures.* New York: Cambridge University Press, 1983.

Gilkerson, L., Nesphachel, S., and Trevino, R. "Issues in Family

Day Care." Unpublished manuscript, Erikson Institute for Advanced Study in Child Development, 1987.

Glaser, B., and Straus, A. *Awareness of Dying: A Study of Social Interaction.* Hawthorne, N.Y.: Aldine, 1965.

Goffman, E. *Strategic Interaction.* Philadelphia: University of Pennsylvania Press, 1969.

Goldberg, A. "On Telling the Truth." In S. C. Feinstein and P. L. Giovacchini (eds.), *Adolescent Psychiatry: Developmental and Clinical Studies.* Vol. 2. New York: Basic Books, 1973.

Goldman, J., Stein, C., and Guerry, S. *Psychological Methods of Child Assessment.* New York: Brunner/Mazel, 1983.

Goleman, D. *Vital Lies, Simple Truths: The Psychology of Self-Deception.* New York: Simon & Schuster, 1986.

Goleman, D. "Who Are You Kidding?" *Psychology Today,* Mar. 1987, pp. 24–30.

Goleman, D. "Analyzed: Mental Disorders or Normal Growth?" *New York Times,* May 17, 1988, p. 19.

Good, B. J., and Good, M. D. "The Meaning of Symptoms: A Cultural Hermeneutic Model for Clinical Practice." In L. Eisenberg and A. Kleinman (eds.), *The Relevance of Social Science for Medicine.* Dordrecht, the Netherlands: D. Reidel, 1981.

Goodenough, F. L. *Anger in Young Children.* Minneapolis: University of Minnesota Press, 1932.

Goodman, G. "The Child Witness: Conclusions and Future Directions." *Journal of Social Issues,* 1984a, *40,* 157–175.

Goodman, G. "Children's Testimony in Historical Perspective." *Journal of Social Issues,* 1984b, *40* (2), 9–31.

Goodman, G., and Aman, C. "Children's Use of Anatomically Correct Dolls to Report an Event." Paper presented at the biennial meeting of the Society for Research in Child Development, Baltimore, Md., Apr. 1987.

Goodman, G., Aman, C., and Hirschman, J. "Child Sexual and Physical Abuse: Children's Testimony." In S. J. Ceci, M. P. Toglia, and D. F. Ross (eds.), *Children's Eyewitness Memory.* New York: Springer-Verlag, 1987.

Goodman, G., Golding, J., and Haith, M. "Jurors' Reactions to Child Witnesses." *Journal of Social Issues,* 1984, *40,* 139–156.

Goodman, G., Hirschman, J., and Rudy, L. "Children's Testimony: Research and Policy Implications." Paper presented at the biennial meeting of the Society for Research in Child Development, Baltimore, Md., Apr. 1987.

Goodman, G., and Reed, R. S. "Age Differences in Eyewitness Testimony." *Law and Human Behavior,* 1986, *10,* 317–332.

Goody, E. N. (ed.). *Questions and Politeness: Strategies in Social Interaction.* New York: Cambridge University Press, 1978a.

Goody, E. N. (ed.). "Towards a Theory of Questions." In E. N. Goody (ed.), *Questions and Politeness: Strategies in Social Interaction.* New York: Cambridge University Press, 1978b.

Gould, R. *Child Studies Through Fantasy: Cognitive-Affective Patterns in Development.* New York: Quadrangle Books, 1972.

Graham, J. R., and Lilly, R. S. *Psychological Testing.* Englewood Cliffs, N.J.: Prentice-Hall, 1984.

Gray, E. *An Evaluation of Latchkey Programs.* Chicago: Committee for Prevention of Child Abuse, 1986.

Gray, E., and Cosgrove, D. "Ethnocentric Perception of Childrearing Practices in Protective Services." *Child Abuse and Neglect,* 1985, *9,* 389–396.

Greenspan, S. I. "Intelligence and Adaptation: An Integration of Psychoanalytic and Piagetian Developmental Psychology." *Psychological Issues,* 1979, *47/48* (entire issue #12).

Greenspan, S. I. *Psychopathology and Adaptation in Infancy and Early Childhood: Principles of Clincial Diagnoses and Preventive Intervention.* New York: International Universities Press, 1981.

Greenspan, S. I., and Lieberman, A. F. "Infants, Mothers, and Their Interaction: A Quantitative Clinical Approach to Developmental Assessment." In S. I. Greenspan and G. H. Pollock (eds.), *The Course of Life: Psychoanalytic Contributions Toward Understanding Personality Development.* Vol. 1: *Infancy and Early Childhood.* Washington, D.C.: U.S. Government Printing Office, 1980.

Greenspan, S. I., and Porges, S. W. "Psychopathology in Infancy and Early Childhood: Clinical Perspectives on the Organization of Sensory and Affective-Thematic Experience." *Child Development,* 1984, *55,* 49–70.

Groth, N. "The Psychology of the Sexual Offender: Rape, Incest, and Child Molestation." Workshop presented by Psychological Associates of the Albemarle, Charlotte, N.C., Mar. 1980.

Gumperz, J. *Discourse Strategies*. New York: Cambridge University Press, 1982.

Gutierrez, J. Unpublished psychological testing report, pp. 1–5, Chicago, 1984.

Gutierrez, J. "A Model for Studying Children as Sources of Information." Paper presented at the annual conference of the National Association for the Education of Young Children, Chicago, Nov. 1987.

Haake, R. J., Somerville, S. C., and Wellman, H. M. "Logical Ability of Young Children in Searching a Large-Scale Environment." *Child Development*, 1980, *51*, 1299–1302.

Hale, J. *Black Children*. Provo, Utah: Brigham Young University Press, 1982.

Haley, J. "Approaches to Family Therapy." *International Journal of Psychiatry*, 1970, *9*, 233–242.

Hall, J. *Nonverbal Sex Differences*. Baltimore, Md.: Johns Hopkins University Press, 1985.

Halpern, R., and Larner, M. "Lay Family Support During Pregnancy and Infancy: The Child Survival/Fair Start Initiative." *Infant Mental Health Journal*, 1987, *8* (2), 130–155.

Hardin, G. *Biology: Its Principles and Implications*. New York: W. H. Freeman, 1966.

Harter, S. "Developmental Perspectives on the Self-System." In E. M. Hetherington (ed.), *Carmichael's Manual of Child Psychology*. Vol. 4: *Social and Personality Development*. New York: Wiley, 1983.

Harter, S., and Connell, J. P. "A Comparison of Alternative Models of the Relationship Between Academic Achievements and Children's Perceptions of Competence, Control, and Motivational Orientation." In J. Nicholls (ed.), *The Development of Achievement-Related Cognitions and Behaviors*. Greenwich, Conn.: J.A.I. Press, 1982.

Haynes-Seman, C., and Hart, J. S. "Doll Play of Failure to Thrive Toddlers: Clues to Infant Experience." *Zero to Three*, Apr. 1987, pp. 10–13.

Helman, C. "Psyche, Soma and Society: The Social Construction of

Psychosomatic Disorders." *Culture, Medicine, and Psychiatry,* 1985, *9,* 1-26.

Hennessy, J. J. "Clinical and Diagnostic Assessment of Children's Abilities: Traditional and Innovative Models." In P. Merrifield (ed.), *Measuring Human Abilities.* New Directions for Testing and Measurement, no. 12. San Francisco: Jossey-Bass, 1981.

Henry, J. *Pathways to Madness.* New York: Vintage Books, 1973.

Herzberger, S. D. "Identifying Cases of Child Abuse: A Social Psychological Phenomenon." *Victimology,* 1985, *10,* 87-96.

Herzberger, S. D., and Tennen, H. "The Effect of Self-Relevance on Judgments of Moderate and Severe Disciplinary Encounters." *Journal of Marriage and the Family,* 1985, *47,* 311-318.

Herzog, J. M. "So Sad You'd Think the World Was About to End: Perceptions of and Adaptions to Suffering in Three Preschool Siblings." *Zero to Three,* Feb. 1986, *6,* 6-10.

Hilliard, A. G. "Educational Assessment: Presumed Intelligent Until Proven Otherwise." *Journal of School Health,* 1980, *50,* 256-258.

Hilliard, A. G. "The Learning Potential Assessment Device and Instrument Enrichment as a Paradigm Shift." Paper presented at the annual meeting of the American Educational Research Association, New York, Mar. 1982.

Hines, P., and Boyd-Franklin, N. "Black Families." In M. McGoldrick, J. Pearce, and J. Giordano (eds.), *Ethnicity and Family Therapy.* New York: Guilford Press, 1982.

Hodges, K., McKnew, D., Burbach, D., and Roebuck, L. "Diagnostics Concordance Between the Child Assessment Schedule (CAS) and the Schedule for Emotional Disorders and Schizophrenia for School-Age Children (K-SADS) in an Outpatient Sample Using Lay Interviewers." *Journal of the American Academy of Child and Adolescent Psychiatry,* 1987, *26* (5), 654-661.

Hoffman, A. D., Becker, R. D., and Gabriel, H. P. *The Hospitalized Adolescent.* New York: Free Press, 1976.

Holmes, D. L., Reich, J. N., and Pasternak, J. F. *The Development of Infants Born at Risk.* Hillsdale, N.J.: Erlbaum, 1984.

Honey, M. A. "The Interview as Text: Hermeneutics Considered as a Model for Analyzing the Clinically Informed Research Interview." *Human Development,* 1987, *30* (1), 69-82.

Howe, A. Herzberger, S., and Tennen, H. "The Influence of Personal History of Abuse and Gender on Clinicians' Judgments of Child Abuse." *Journal of Family Violence,* 1988, *3* (2), 105–119.

Hughes, M. "Egocentrism in Preschool Children." Unpublished doctoral dissertation, Edinburgh University, 1975.

Hundeide, K. "The Origins of the Child's Replies in Experimental Situations." *Quarterly Newsletter of the Laboratory of Comparative Human Cognition,* 1980, *2,* 15–18.

Hymes, D. "Models of the Interaction of Language and Social Life." In J. J. Gumperz and D. Hymes (eds.), *Directions in Sociolinguistics.* New York: Holt, Rinehart & Winston, 1967.

Hymes, D. "Competence and Performance in Linguistic Theory." In R. Huxley and E. Ingram (eds.), *Language Acquisition: Models and Methods.* Orlando, Fla.: Academic Press, 1971a.

Hymes, D. "Sociolinguistics and the Ethnography of Speaking." In E. Ardener (ed.), *Social Anthropology and Linguistics.* London: Tavistock, 1971b.

Inhelder, D. "The Sensory-Motor Origins of Knowledge." In D. Walcher and D. C. Peters (eds.), *Early Childhood: The Development of Self-Regulatory Mechanisms.* Orlando, Fla.: Academic Press, 1971.

Isaacs, S. *Intellectual Growth in Young Children.* New York: Schocken Books, 1972. (Originally published 1930.)

Izard, C. E. *Human Emotions.* New York: Plenum, 1977.

Jalali, B. "Iranian Families." In M. McGoldrick, J. Pearce, and J. Giordano (eds.), *Ethnicity in Family Therapy.* New York: Guilford Press, 1982.

James, J., Womack, W. M., and Strauss, F. "Physician Reporting of Sexual Abuse of Children." *Journal of the American Medical Association,* 1978, *240,* 1145–1146.

Johnson, M. K., and Foley, M. A. "Differentiating Fact from Fantasy: The Reliability of Children's Memory." *Journal of Social Issues,* 1984, *40* (2), 33–50.

Jones, D., and Krugman, R. "Can a Three-Year-Old Child Bear Witness to Her Sexual Assault and Attempted Murder?" *Child Abuse and Neglect,* 1986, *10,* 253–258.

Jones, D., and McGraw, J. M. "Reliable and Fictitious Accounts of

Sexual Abuse in Children." *Journal of Interpersonal Violence,* 1987, *2,* 27–45.

Jones, D., and McQuiston, M. *Interviewing the Sexually Abused Child.* Denver, Colo.: C. Henry Kempe National Center for the Prevention and Treatment of Child Abuse and Neglect, 1985.

Kagan, J. *The Second Year: The Emergence of Self-Awareness.* Cambridge, Mass.: Harvard University Press, 1981.

Kail, R. *The Development of Memory in Children.* (2nd ed.) New York: W. H. Freeman, 1984.

Kail, R. V., and Levine, L. E. "Encoding Processes and Sex-Role Preferences." *Journal of Experimental Child Psychology,* 1976, *21,* 256–263.

Katz, L. G. "Teaching in Preschools: Roles and Goals." *Children,* 1970, *17,* 43–48.

Katz, P. "Development of Children's Racial Awareness and Intergroup Attitudes." In L. Katz (ed.), *Current Topics in Early Childhood Education.* Vol. 4. Norwood, N.J.: Ablex, 1982.

Kaufman, J., and Zigler, E. "Do Abused Children Become Abusive Parents?" *American Journal of Orthopsychiatry,* 1987, *57* (2), 186–192.

Kaye, K. *The Mental and Social Life of Babies: How Parents Create Persons.* Chicago: University of Chicago Press, 1982.

Keenan, E. O., Schiefflin, B., and Platt, M. "Questions of Immediate Concern." In E. N. Goody (ed.), *Questions and Politeness: Strategies in Social Interaction.* New York: Cambridge University Press, 1978.

Kelly, J. B., and Wallerstein, J. S. "Brief Interventions with Children in Divorcing Families." *American Journal of Orthopsychiatry,* 1977, *47* (1), 23–39.

King, M. A., and Yuille, J. C. "Suggestibility and the Child Witness." In S. J. Ceci, M. P. Toglia, and D. F. Ross (eds.), *Children's Eyewitness Memory.* New York: Springer-Verlag, 1987.

Kister, M. C., and Patterson, C. J. "Children's Conceptions of the Causes of Illness: Understanding of Contagion and Use of Immanent Justice." *Child Development,* 1980, *51,* 839–846.

Klein, M. *The Psycho-Analysis of Children.* London: Hogarth Press, 1949.

Kleinman, A. *Patients and Healers in the Context of Culture.* Berkeley: University of California Press, 1980.

Kleinman, A., Eisenberg, L., and Good, B. "Culture, Illness and Care." *Annals of Internal Medicine,* 1978, *88,* 251–258.

Kohut, H. "Reflections on Advances in Self-Psychology." In A. Goldberg (ed.), *Advances in Self-Psychology.* New York: International Universities Press, 1980.

Koocher, G. P., and Pedulla, B. M. "Current Practices in Child Psychotherapy." *Professional Psychology,* Aug. 1977, pp. 275–287.

Korbin, J. *Child Abuse and Neglect: Cross-Cultural Perspectives.* Berkeley: University of California Press, 1981.

Korbin, J., and Johnson, M. "Steps Toward Resolving Cultural Conflict in a Pediatric Hospital." *Clinical Pediatrics,* 1982, *21* (5), 259–263.

Korbin, J., and Zahorik, P. "Childhood, Health, and Illness: Beliefs and Behaviors of Urban American School Children." *Medical Anthropology Quarterly,* Fall 1985, pp. 337–353.

Korsch, B. M., and Negrete, V. F. "Doctor-Patient Communication." *Scientific-American,* 1972, *227,* 66–74.

Krugman, R. and Krugman, M. "Emotional Abuse in the Classroom." *American Journal of Diseases in Children,* 1984, *138,* 284–286.

Kuhn, D. "Cognitive Development." In M. H. Bornstein and M. E. Lamb (eds.), *Developmental Psychology.* Hillsdale, N.J.: Erlbaum, 1984.

Labov, W. "The Logic of Nonstandard English." In F. Williams (ed.), *Language and Poverty.* Chicago: Markham Press, 1970.

Labov, W. "Some Principles of Linguistic Methodology." *Language in Society,* 1972a, *1* (1), 97–120.

Labov, W. "The Logic of Nonstandard English." In R. Abrahams and R. Troike (eds.), *Language and Cultural Diversity in American Education.* Englewood Cliffs, N.J.: Prentice-Hall, 1972b.

Lazarus, R. S., and Launier, R. "Stress-Related Transactions Between Person and Environment." In L. A. Pervin and M. Lewis (eds.), *Perspectives in Interactional Psychology.* New York: Plenum Press, 1978.

Lewis, M., Stanger, C., and Sullivan, M. "Deception in Three-Year Olds." *Developmental Psychology.* 1989, *25* (3), 439-443.

Lewis, O. "The Culture of Poverty." *Scientific American,* 1966, *215,* 19-25.

Lind, N. "The Development of Causal Reasoning: Guidelines for Adults Evaluating Children's Causal Judgements." Unpublished manuscript, Erikson Institute for Advanced Study in Child Development, 1987.

Lindfors, J. W. *Children's Language and Learning.* (2nd ed.) Englewood Cliffs, N.J.: Prentice-Hall, 1987.

Little, B. "An Advocate for Children." *Believe the Children Newsletter,* 1987, *5,* 1-2.

Lock, M. "The Relationship Between Culture and Health or Illness." In J. Christie-Seely (ed.), *Working with the Family in Primary Care.* New York: Praeger, 1984.

Loftus, E. F., and Davies, G.M.T. "Distortions in the Memory of Children." *Journal of Social Issues,* 1984, *40* (2), 51-67.

Luborsky, L., Blinder, B., and Schimek, J. "Looking, Recalling, and GSR as a Function of Defense." *Journal of Abnormal Psychology,* 1965, *70,* 270-280.

Lumsden, C., and Wilson, E. *Genes, Mind, and Culture.* Cambridge, Mass.: Harvard University Press, 1981.

McAdoo, H. "Family Therapy in the Black Community." *Journal of the American Orthopsychiatric Association,* 1977, *47* (1), 75-79.

McAdoo, H. *Black Families.* Newbury Park, Calif.: Sage, 1981.

McCall, R. B. "The Development of Intellectual Functioning in Infancy and the Prediction of Later IQ." In J. D. Osofsky (ed.), *Handbook of Infant Development.* New York: Wiley, 1979.

Maccoby, E., and Jacklin, C. *The Psychology of Sex Differences.* Stanford, Calif.: Stanford University Press, 1974.

MacFarlane, A. *The Psychology of Childbirth.* Cambridge, Mass.: Harvard University Press, 1977.

MacFarlane, K., and others. *Sexual Abuse of Young Children: Evaluation and Treatment.* New York: Guilford Press, 1986.

McGoldrick, M. "Ethnicity and Family Therapy: An Overview." In M. McGoldrick, J. Pearce, and J. Giordano (eds.), *Ethnicity and Family Therapy.* New York: Guilford Press, 1982.

Mack, J. E. "Self-Esteem and Its Development: An Overview." In J. E. Mack and S. L. Albon (eds.), *The Development and Sustaining of Self-Esteem in Childhood*. New York: International Universities Press, 1983.

McKinlay, J. B. "Who Is Really Ignorant?—Physician or Patient." *Journal of Health and Social Behavior*, 1975, *16*, 3-11.

McLane, J. B. "Interaction, Context and the Zone of Proximal Development." In M. Hickmann (ed.), *Social and Functional Approaches to Language and Thought*. Orlando, Fla.: Academic Press, 1987.

McNamee, G. D. "The Social Origins of Narrative Skills." *The Quarterly Newsletter of the Laboratory of Comparative Human Cognition*, 1979, *1* (4), 63-68.

Mahler, M. S., Pine, F., and Bergman, A. *The Psychological Birth of the Child: Symbiosis and Individuation*. New York: Basic Books, 1975.

Mahoney, M. "Self-Deception in Science." Paper presented at the annual meeting of the American Association for the Advancement of Science, Philadephia, May 1986.

Mandler, J. M. "Representation." In J. H. Flavell and L. Ross (eds.), *Social Cognitive Development: Frontiers and Possible Futures*. New York: Cambridge University Press, 1983.

Markman, E. M. "Realizing That You Don't Understand: A Preliminary Investigation." *Child Development*, 1977, *48*, 986-992.

Martin, C. L., and Halverson, C. F. "The Effects of Sex-Typing on Young Children's Memory." *Child Development*, 1983, *53*, 563-574.

Martin, D. W. *Doing Psychology Experiments*. Pacific Grove, Calif.: Brooks/Cole, 1977.

Masson, J. M. *The Assault on Truth: Freud's Suppression of the Seduction Theory*. New York: Farrar, Straus & Giroux, 1984.

Mehan, H. "Assessing Children's Language Using Abilities: Methodological and Cross Cultural Implications." In M. Armer and A. D. Gumshaw (eds.), *Comparative Social Research: Methodological Problems and Strategies*. New York: Wiley, 1973.

Mehan, H. *Learning Lessons*. Cambridge, England: Cambridge University Press, 1979.

Meisels, S. J. "Testing Four- and Five-Year-Olds: Response to Salzer and to Shepard and Smith." *Educational Review,* 1986, *44* (3), 90-92.

Melton, G. "Children's Competency to Testify." *Law and Human Behavior,* 1981, *5,* 73-85.

Melton, G. "Training Child Clinicians as Child Advocates." In J. M. Tuma (ed.), *Proceedings of the Conference on Training Clinical Child Psychologists.* Baton Rouge, La.: Section on Clinical Child Psychology, 1985.

Melton, G. "Litigation in the Interest of Children: Does Anybody Win?" *Law and Human Behavior,* 1986, *10,* 337-353.

Melton, G., and Thompson, R. "Getting Out of a Rut: Detours to Less Traveled Paths in Child Witness Research." In S. J. Ceci, M. P. Toglia, and D. F. Ross (eds.), *Children's Eyewitness Memory.* New York: Springer-Verlag, 1987.

Melton, G., and others. *Psychological Evaluations for the Courts: A Handbook for Mental Health Professionals and Lawyers.* New York: Guilford Press, 1987.

Mercer, J. R. "Psychological Assessment and the Rights of Children." In N. Hobbs (ed.), *Issues in the Classification of Children: A Sourcebook on Categories, Labels, and Their Consequences.* San Francisco: Jossey-Bass, 1975.

Millar, S. *The Psychology of Play.* Baltimore, Md.: Penguin Books, 1969.

Miller, A. *For Your Own Good: Hidden Cruelty in Children and the Roots of Violence.* New York: Farrar, Straus & Giroux, 1983.

Miller, A. *Thou Shalt Not Be Aware: Psychoanalysis and Society's Betrayal of the Child.* New York: Farrar, Straus & Giroux, 1984.

Miller, T. W., Veltkamp, L. J., and Janson, D. "Projective Measures in the Clinical Evaluation of Sexually Abused Children." *Child Psychiatry and Human Development,* 1987, *18* (1), 47-57.

Miller, W. B. "Lower Class Culture as a Generating Milieu of Gang Delinquency." *Journal of Social Issues,* 1958, *14,* 5-19.

Mishler, E. G. "Studies in Dialogue and Discourse III: Utterance Structure and Utterance Function in Interrogative Sequences." *Journal of Psycholinguistic Research,* 1978, *7,* 279-305.

Mishler, E. G. *The Discourse of Medicine: Dialectics of Medical Interviews.* Norwood, N.J.: Ablex, 1984.

Mishler, E. G. *The Research Interview: Context and Narrative.* Cambridge, Mass.: Harvard University Press, 1986.

Mitroff, I. I. *The Subjective Side of Science.* New York: Elsevier, 1974.

Motley, M. "What I Meant to Say." *Psychology Today,* Feb. 1987, pp. 24–28.

Moustakis, C. E. *Children in Play Therapy.* New York: McGraw-Hill, 1953.

Murphy, L. B. *The Widening World of Childhood.* New York: Basic Books, 1962.

Murphy, L. B., and Moriarty, A. E. *Vulnerability, Coping and Growth.* New Haven, Conn.: Yale University Press, 1976.

Musick, J., and Stott, F. "Paraprofessionals, Parenting and Child Development: Understanding the Problems and Seeking Solutions." In S. Meisels and J. Shonkoff (eds.), *Handbook of Early Intervention.* New York: Cambridge University Press, forthcoming.

National Committee for Prevention of Child Abuse. "Public Attitudes and Actions Regarding Child Abuse and Its Prevention: The Results of a Louis Harris Public Opinion Poll." Unpublished manuscript, Chicago, 1987.

Nelson, K. *Event Knowledge: Structure and Function in Development.* Hillsdale, N.J.: Erlbaum, 1978.

Nelson, K., and Ross, G. "The Generalities and Specifics of Long-Term Memory in Infants and Young Children." In M. Perlmutter (ed.), *Children's Memory.* New Directions for Child Development, no. 10. San Francisco: Jossey-Bass, 1980.

Nurcombe, B. "The Child as Witness: Competency and Credibility." *Journal of American Academic Child Psychiatry,* 1986, *25* (4), 473–480.

Ogbu, J. *Minority Education and Caste.* Orlando, Fla.: Academic Press, 1978.

Paget, M. A. "On the Work of Talk: Studies in Misunderstandings." In S. Fisher and A. Todd (eds.), *The Social Organization of Doctor-Patient Communication.* Washington, D.C.: Center for Applied Linguistics, 1983.

Paley, V. G. *Wally's Stories.* Cambridge, Mass.: Harvard University Press, 1981.

Paley, V. G. *Mollie Is Three*. Chicago: University of Chicago Press, 1986.

Pantell, R., and others. "Physician Communication with Children and Parents." *Pediatrics,* 1982, *70,* 396-401.

Parker, W. C. "Interviewing Children: Problems and Promise." *Journal of Negro Education,* 1984, *53,* 18-28.

Parsons, T. *The Social System.* New York: Free Press, 1951.

Parsons, T. "The Sick Role and the Role of the Physician Reconsidered." *Milbank Memorial Fund Quarterly,* 1975, *53,* 257-277.

Parten, M. B. "Social Participation Among Preschool Children." *Journal of Abnormal and Social Psychology,* 1942, *27,* 243-269.

Patterson, G. R., Reid, J. B., Jones, R. R., and Conger, R. E. *A Social Learning Approach.* Vol. 1: *Families with Aggressive Children.* Eugene, Ore.: Castalia, 1975.

Patterson, O. "Context and Choice in Ethnic Allegiance." In N. Glazer and D. Moynihan (eds.), *Ethnicity.* Cambridge, Mass.: Harvard University Press, 1975.

Pekarik, E., and others. "The Pupil Evaluation Inventory." *Journal of Abnormal Child Psychology,* 1976, *4,* 79-83.

Peller, L. E. *On Development and Education of Young Children.* New York: Philosophical Library, 1978.

Pendleton, D. "Doctor-Patient Communication: A Review." In D. Pendleton and J. Hasler (eds.), *Doctor-Patient Communication.* Orlando, Fla.: Academic Press, 1983.

Pendleton, D., and Hasler, J. (eds.). *Doctor-Patient Communication.* Orlando, Fla.: Academic Press, 1983.

Perrin, E. C. "Children's Development of Concepts About Illness." In W. K. Frankenburg and S. M. Thorton (eds.), *Child Health Care Communications.* New York: Praeger, 1984.

Perrin, E. C., and Gerrity, P. S. "There's a Demon in Your Belly: Children's Understanding of Illness." *Pediatrics,* 1981, *67,* 841-847.

Perrin, E. C., and Perrin, J. M. "Clinicians' Assessments of Children's Understanding of Illness." *American Journal of Diseases of Children,* 1983, *137,* 874-878.

Peters, D. "Influence of Stress and Arousal on the Child Witness."

Paper presented at the annual meeting of the American Psychological Association, Atlanta, Ga., Aug. 1988.

Petrillo, M., and Sanger, S. *The Emotional Care of Hospitalized Children.* Philadelphia: Lippincott, 1980.

Piaget, J. *The Origins of Intelligence in Children.* New York: International Universities Press, 1952.

Piaget, J. *The Construction of Reality in the Child.* New York: Basic Books, 1954. (Originally published 1937.)

Piaget, J. *Play, Dreams and Imitation in Childhood.* New York: Norton, 1962.

Piaget, J. *The Child's Conception of Physical Causality.* Totowa, N.J.: Littlefield, Adams, 1972. (Originally published 1930.)

Piaget, J. *The Child and Reality.* New York: Penguin Books, 1976.

Piaget, J. *The Child's Conception of the World.* Totowa, N.J.: Littlefield, Adams, 1979. (Originally published 1929.)

Piaget, J., and Inhelder, B. *The Child's Conception of Space.* Boston: Routledge & Kegan Paul, 1956.

Price, D.W.W. "The Development of Children's Comprehension of Recurring Episodes." Unpublished doctoral dissertation, University of Denver, Colo., 1983.

Putnam, N. "Seven to Ten Years: Growth and Competency." In S. D. Dixon and M. T. Stein (eds.), *Encounters with Children: Pediatric Behavior and Development.* Chicago: Year Book Medical Publishers, 1987.

Pynoos, R. S., and Eth, S. "The Child as Witness to Homicide." *Journal of Social Issues,* 1984, *40* (2), 87–108.

Raskin, D. C., and Steller, M. "Assessing Credibility of Allegations of Child Sexual Abuse: Polygraph Examinations and Statement Analysis." In H. Wegener, F. Loesel, and J. Haisch (eds.), *Criminal Behavior and the Justice System.* New York: Springer-Verlag, forthcoming.

Raskin, D. C., and Yuille, J. C. "Problems in Evaluating Interviews of Children in Sexual Abuse Cases." In S. J. Ceci, D. F. Ross, and M. P. Toglia (eds.), *Children Take the Stand: Adult Perceptions of Children's Testimony.* New York: Springer-Verlag, forthcoming.

Raven, J. C. *Progressive Matrices, Sets I and II.* Dumfries, Scotland: The Chrichton Royal, 1947.

Reschly, D. J. "Aptitude Tests." In G. Goldstein and M. Hersen (eds.), *Handbook of Psychological Assessment*. Elmsford, N.Y.: Pergamon Press, 1984.

Ricks, R., and Faubert, T. "Canadian Child Life/Non-Medical Programs in Hospitals." *Children's Health Care*, 1981, *10*, 16–19.

Robinson, B., Rowland, B., and Coleman, M. *Latchkey Kids: Unlocking Doors for Children and Their Families*. Lexington, Mass.: Lexington Books, 1986.

Robinson, C. A. "Preschool Children's Conceptualizations of Health and Illness." *Children's Health Care*, 1987, *16* (2), 89–96.

Rogler, L., Malgady, R., Costantino, G., and Blumenthal, R. "What Do Culturally Sensitive Mental Health Services Mean?" *American Psychologist*, June 1987, *42*, 565–570.

Rogoff, B., Gauvain, M., and Ellis, S. "Development Viewed in Its Cultural Context." In M. H. Bornstein and M. E. Lamb (eds.), *Developmental Psychology*. Hillsdale, N.J.: Erlbaum, 1984.

Rogoff, B., and Wertsch, J. V. (eds.). *Children's Learning in the "Zone of Proximal Development."* New Directions for Child Development, no. 23. San Francisco: Jossey-Bass, 1984.

Rolf, J. E., and Hasazi, J. "Identification of Preschool Children at Risk and Some Guidelines for Primary Prevention." In J. Joffee and G. Albee (eds.), *The Issues: The Primary Prevention of Psychopathology*. Vol. 1. Hanover, N.H.: University Press of New England, 1977.

Rommetveit, R. "Language Acquisition as Increasing Linguistic Structuring of Experience and Symbolic Behavior Control." In J. Wertsch (ed.), *Culture, Communication and Cognition: Vygotskian Perspectives*. Cambridge, England: Cambridge University Press, 1985.

Rosenberg, M. *Conceiving the Self*. New York: Basic Books, 1979.

Rosenblatt, D. "Developmental Trends in Infant Play." In B. Tizard and D. Harvey (eds.), *Biology of Play*. Philadelphia: Lippincott, 1977.

Rosenthal, R. S. "Biasing Effects of Experimenters." *Etc.*, 1978, *34*, 253–264.

Rosenthal, R. S. *Pygmalion in the Classroom*. New York: Holt, Rinehart & Winston, 1968.

Rowland, A. "Do Dentists Know When It Hurts?" *Psychology Today*, Aug. 1987, p. 12.

Runyan, D., and others. "Impact of Legal Intervention on Sexually Abused Children." *Journal of Pediatrics*, 1988, *113* (4), 647–653.

Rutter, M. "Stress, Coping, and Development: Some Issues and Some Questions." In N. Garmezy and M. Rutter (eds.), *Stress, Coping, and Development in Children*. New York: McGraw-Hill, 1983.

Rutter, M., Tizard, J., and Whitmore, K. (eds.). *Education, Health and Behavior*. New York: Longman, 1970.

Sacks, H., Schegloff, E., and Jefferson, G. "A Simplest Systematics for the Organization of Turn-Taking for Conversation." *Language*, 1974, *50*, 696–735.

Sameroff, A., and Chandler, M. "Reproductive Risk and the Continuum of Caretaking Casualty." In F. D. Horowitz (ed.), *Review of Child Development Research*. Vol. 4. Chicago: University of Chicago Press, 1975.

Sarnoff, C. *Latency*. New York: Aronson, 1976.

Saywitz, K. "Children's Testimony: Age-Related Patterns of Memory Errors." In S. J. Ceci, M. P. Toglia, and D. F. Ross (eds.), *Children's Eyewitness Memory*. New York: Springer-Verlag, 1987.

Schaefer, C. E. *Therapeutic Use of Child's Play*. New York: Aronson, 1976.

Schaefer, C. E., Millman, H. L., Sichel, S. M., and Zwilling, J. R. *Advances in Therapies for Children*. San Francisco: Jossey-Bass, 1986.

Schellenbach, C. J., and Susman, E. J. "Parental Stress Responses to Normal Childhood Illness." Paper presented at the annual meeting of the American Psychological Association, Los Angeles, Aug. 1981.

Schneider, J. W. "Suggestibility in Children: What Role Does Memory Play?" Unpublished paper, Erikson Institute for Advanced Study in Child Development, 1987.

Schudson, C. *On Trial: Sexually Abused Children in America's Courts*. Boston: Beacon Press, 1989.

Scottish Information Office. "Children's Hearings." Factsheet Dd. 8036485. Scottish Information Office, Edinburgh, Apr. 1987.

Self, P. A., and Horowitz, F. D. "The Behavioral Assessment of the Neonate: An Overview." In J. D. Osofsky (ed.), *Handbook of Infant Development.* New York: Wiley, 1979.

Shade, B. "Afro-American Cognitive Style: A Variable in School Success?" *Review of Educational Research,* 1982, *52* (2), 219–244.

Shantz, C. U. "The Development of Social Cognition." In E. M. Hetherington (ed.), *Review of Child Development Research.* Vol. 5. Chicago: University of Chicago Press, 1975.

Shatz, M., and Gelman, R. *The Development of Communication Skills: Modifications in the Speech of Young Children as a Function of Listener.* Monographs of the Society for Research in Child Development, no. 152. Chicago: University of Chicago Press, 1973.

Shneidman, E. S. "Some Comparisons Among the Four Picture Test, Thematic Apperception Test and Make a Picture Story Test." *Journal of Projective Techniques,* 1949, *13,* 150–154.

Shuy, R. "Three Types of Interference to an Effective Exchange of Information in the Medical Interview." In S. Fisher and A. Todd (eds.), *The Social Organization of Doctor-Patient Communication.* Washington, D.C.: Center for Applied Linguistics, 1983.

Siegler, R. S. "The Origins of Scientific Reasoning." In R. S. Siegler (ed.), *Children's Thinking: What Develops?* Hillsdale, N.J.: Erlbaum, 1978.

Silver, L., Barton, W., and Dublin, C. "Child Abuse Laws: Are They Enough?" *Journal of the American Medical Association,* 1967, *199,* 65–68.

Silverman, D. *Communication and Medical Practice: Social Relations in the Clinic.* Newbury Park, Calif.: Sage, 1987.

Simmons, O. "Implications of Social Class for Public Health." In E. G. Jaco (ed.), *Patients, Physicians, and Illness.* New York: Free Press, 1958.

Sinclair, H. "The Transition from Sensory-Motor Behavior to Symbolic Activity." *Interchange,* 1970, *1,* 119–125.

Singer, J. L. *The Child's World of Make-Believe.* Orlando, Fla.: Academic Press, 1973.

Sivan, A. B., Schor, D. P., Koeppl, G. K., and Noble, L. D. "Interaction of Normal Children with Anatomical Dolls." *Child Abuse and Neglect,* 1988, *12,* 295–304.

Skolnick, A. "The Limits of Childhood: Conceptions of Child Development and Social Context." *Law and Contemporary Problems,* 1975, *39* (3), 38–77.

Smith, J. H. "The First Lie." *Psychiatry,* 1968, *31,* 61–68.

Spicher, C. M. "Children's Perceptions of Their Covered Operative Sites." *Maternal-Child Nursing Journal,* 1982, *11,* 181–192.

Spodek, B. *Teaching in the Early Years.* (2nd ed.) Englewood Cliffs, N.J.: Prentice-Hall, 1978.

Starr, R. H. (ed.). *Child Abuse Prediction: Policy Implications.* Cambridge, Mass.: Ballinger, 1982.

Steller, M., Raskin, D., and Yuille, J. "Sexually Abused Children: Interview and Assessment Procedures." In H. Wegener, F. Loesel, and J. Haisch (eds.), *Criminal Behavior and the Justice System.* New York: Springer-Verlag, forthcoming.

Stern, D. N. *The First Relationship: Infant and Mother.* Cambridge, Mass.: Harvard University Press, 1977.

Stern, D. N. *The Interpersonal World of the Infant.* New York: Basic Books, 1985.

Steward, M. S. "Review of the Literature: Selected References and Issues." Paper presented at the Symposium on Interviewing Children sponsored by the Children's Bureau of the National Center on Child Abuse and Neglect, Washington, D.C., Sept. 1987.

Stone, G. C. "Patient Compliance and the Role of the Expert." *Journal of Social Issues,* 1979, *35,* 34–59.

Stone, L. J., and Church, J. *Childhood and Adolescence.* New York: Random House, 1979.

Stott, F. M., Cohler, B. J., and Musick, J. S. "Competence and Vulnerability in School-Aged Children of Psychiatrically Ill and Well Mothers." Unpublished manuscript, William T. Grant Foundation, 1985.

Summit, R. "Foreword." In K. MacFarlane and others (eds.), *Sexual Abuse of Young Children: Evaluation and Treatment.* New York: Guilford Press, 1986.

Super, C., and Harkness, S. "The Development of Affect in Infancy and Early Childhood." In D. A. Wagner and H. Stevenson (eds.), *Cultural Perspectives on Child Development.* New York: W. H. Freeman, 1982.

Tammivaara, J., and Enright, D. S. "On Eliciting Information: Dialogues with Child Informants." *Anthropology and Education Quarterly*, 1986, *17*, (2), 218–238.

Terr, L. "Life Attitudes, Dreams, and Psychic Trauma in a Group of 'Normal' Children." *Journal of the American Academy of Child Psychiatry*, 1983, *22* (3), 221–230.

Terr, L. "The Baby as Witness." In D. Schetky and E. Benedek (eds.), *Emerging Issues in Child Psychiatry and the Law*. New York: Brunner/Mazel, 1985.

Thomas, A., Chess, S., and Birch, H. G. *Temperament and Behavior Disorders in Children*. New York: New York University Press, 1968.

Thompson, R. H. *Psychosocial Research on Pediatric Hospitalization and Health Care*. Springfield, Ill.: Thomas, 1985.

Thompson, R. H., and Stanford, G. *Child Life in Hospitals*. Springfield, Ill.: Thomas, 1981.

Todd, C. M., and Perlmutter, M. "Reality Recalled by Preschool Children." In M. Perlmutter (ed.), *Children's Memory*. New Directions for Child Development, no. 10. San Francisco: Jossey-Bass, 1980.

Tores-Matrullo, C. "Acculturation, Sex-Role Values and Mental Health Among Mainland Puerto Ricans." In A. Padilla (ed.), *Acculturation*. AAAS Selected Symposium no. 39. Boulder, Colo.: Western Press, 1980.

Triandis, H. C. "Culture Training, Cognitive Complexity and Interpersonal Attitudes." In R. W. Brislin, S. Bochner, and W. J. Lonner (eds.), *Cross-Cultural Perspectives on Learning*. New York: Wiley/Halstead, 1975.

Tulkin, S. "An Analysis of the Concept of Cultural Deprivation." *Developmental Psychology*, 1972, *6*, 326–339.

Turiel, E. D. "Developmental Processes in the Child's Moral Thinking." In P. Mussen, J. Langer, and M. Covington (eds.), *New Directions in Developmental Psychology*. New York: Holt, Rinehart & Winston, 1969.

Van Ornum, W., and Mordock, J. B. *Crisis Counseling with Children and Adolescents: A Guide for Nonprofessional Counselors*. New York: Continuum, 1983.

Vernon, D. T. A., Foley, J. M., Sipowicz, R. R., and Schulman, J. L.

*The Psychological Responses of Children to Hospitalization and Illness.* Springfield, Ill.: Thomas, 1965.

Vygotsky, L. S. *Mind in Society.* Cambridge, Mass.: Harvard University Press, 1978.

Vygotsky, L. S. *Thought and Language.* Cambridge, Mass.: MIT Press, 1986.

Waitzkin, H. *The Second Sickness: Contradictions of Capitalist Health Care.* New York: Free Press, 1983.

Wallerstein, J. S., and Kelly, J. B. *Surviving the Breakup: How Parents and Children Cope with Divorce.* New York: Basic Books, 1980.

Walsh, F. "Family Therapy: A Systematic Orientation to Treatment." In A. Rosenblatt and D. Waldfogel (eds.), *Handbook of Clinical Social Work.* San Francisco: Jossey-Bass, 1983.

Weiner, B. "An Overview of Child Custody Laws." *Hospital and Community Psychiatry,* 1985, *36* (8), 838–843.

Weiner, B., Simons, V., and Cavanaugh, J. "The Child Custody Dispute." In D. Schetky and E. Benedek (eds.), *Emerging Issues in Child Psychiatry and the Law.* New York: Brunner/Mazel, 1985.

Weintraub, S., Neale, J. M., and Liebert, D. E. "Teacher Ratings of Children Vulnerable to Psychopathology." *American Journal of Orthopsychiatry,* 1975, *43,* 838–845.

Weithorn, L. *Psychology and Child Custody Determinations: Knowledge, Roles and Expertise.* Lincoln: University of Nebraska Press, 1987.

Wertlieb, D., Weigel, C., and Feldstein, M. "Measuring Children's Coping." *American Journal of Orthopsychiatry,* 1987, *57* (4), 548–560.

Wertsch, J. V. "Adult-Child Interaction and the Roots of Metacognition." *Quarterly Newsletter of the Institute for Comparative Human Development,* 1978, *2* (1), 15–18.

Wertsch, J. V. (ed.). *Culture, Communication and Cognition: Vygotskian Perspectives.* Cambridge, England: Cambridge University Press, 1985a.

Wertsch, J. V. *Vygotsky and the Social Formation of Mind.* Cambridge, Mass.: Harvard University Press, 1985b.

Wertsch, J. V., McNamee, G. D., McLane, J. B., and Budwig, N. A.

"The Adult-Child Dyad as a Problem Solving System." *Child Development,* 1980, *51,* 1215-1221.

West, C. *Routine Complications: Troubles with Talk Between Doctors and Patients.* Bloomington: Indiana University Press, 1984.

Whitcomb, D., Shapiro, E., and Stellwagen, L. "When the Victim Is a Child—Issues for Judges and Prosecutors." ABT Associates, Inc., U.S. Department of Justice. Washington, D.C.: U.S. Government Printing Office, 1985.

White, R. W. *Ego and Reality in Psychoanalytic Theory.* New York: International Universities Press, 1963.

White, S. H., and Pillemer, D. B. "Childhood Amnesia and the Development of a Socially Accessible Memory System." In J. F. Kihlstrom and F. J. Evans (eds.), *Functional Disorders of Memory.* Hillsdale, N.J.: Erlbaum, 1979.

White, S., Strom, G., and Santilli, G. "A Clinical Protocol for Interviewing Young Children with the Sexually Anatomically Correct Dolls." Unpublished manuscript, Case Western Reserve School of Medicine, 1986.

Whittaker, J., Garbarino, J., and Associates. *Social Support Networks.* Hawthorne, N.Y.: Aldine, 1983.

Wilson, J. H. "The 'New' Science Teachers Are Asking More and Better Questions." *Journal of Research in Science Teaching,* 1969, *6,* 49-53.

Wilson, R. N. *The Sociology of Health: An Introduction.* New York: Random House, 1970.

Wilson, W. J. *The Truly Disadvantaged.* Chicago: University of Chicago Press, 1987.

Winn, M. *Children Without Childhood.* New York: Pantheon, 1983.

Winnicott, D. W. *The Maturational Processes and the Facilitating Environment.* London: Hogarth Press, 1965.

Winnicott, D. W. *Therapeutic Consultations in Child Psychiatry.* New York: Basic Books, 1971.

Wise, F., and Miller, N. "The Mental Health of the American Indian Child." In G. Powell (ed.), *The Psychosocial Development of Minority Group Children.* New York: Brunner/Mazel, 1983.

Wolff, S. "The Case History in Child Care." In *Good Enough Parenting*. Central Council for Educators and Training in Social Work, London: Derbyshire House, 1978.

Wolinsky, F. D. *The Sociology of Health: Principles, Professions and Issues*. Boston: Little, Brown, 1980.

Wood, D. J., MacMahon, L., and Cranstoun, Y. *Working with Under Fives*. Ypsilanti, Mich.: High/Scope, 1980.

Wood, H., and Wood, D. "Questioning the Pre-School Child." *Educational Review*, 1983, *35* (2), 149-162.

Winawer-Steiner, H., and Wetzel, N. "German Families." In M. McGoldrick, J. Pearce, and J. Giordano (eds.), *Ethnicity and Family Therapy*. New York: Guilford Press, 1982.

Yamamoto, K. "Brief Reports: Children's Ratings of the Stressfulness of Experiences." *Developmental Psychology*, 1979, *15* (5), 581-582.

Yarrow, M. R., and Zahn Waxler, C. "Observing Interaction: A Confrontation with Methodology." In R. B. Cairns (ed.), *The Analysis of Social Interaction*. Hillsdale, N.J.: Erlbaum, 1979.

Yates, A., and Terr, L. "Anatomically Correct Dolls: Should They Be Used as the Basis for Expert Testimony?" *Journal of the American Academy of Child and Adolescent Psychiatry*, 1988, *27* (3), 387-388.

Young, J. G., O'Brien, J. D., Gutterman, E. M., and Cohen, P. "Research on the Clinical Interview." *Journal of the American Academy of Child and Adolescent Psychiatry*, 1987, *26* (5), 613-620.

Young, M. H., McMurray, M. B., Rothery, S. A., and Emery, L. A. "Use of the Health and Illness Questionnaire with Chronically Ill and Handicapped Children." *Children's Health Care*, 1987, *16* (2), 97-104.

Yussen, S. R. "Determinants of Visual Attention and Recall in Observational Learning by Preschoolers and Second Graders." *Developmental Psychology*, 1974, *10*, 93-100.

Zajonc, R. "On the Primacy of Affect." *American Psychologist*, 1984, *39*, 117-123.

Zaragoza, M. S. "Memory, Suggestibility, and Eyewitness Testimony in Children and Adults." In S. J. Ceci, M. P. Toglia, and D. F.

Ross (eds.), *Children's Eyewitness Memory*. New York: Springer-Verlag, 1987.

Zborowski, M. "Cultural Components in Responses to Pain." *Journal of Social Issues*, 1958, *8*, 16–30.

Zborowski, M. *People in Pain*. San Francisco: Jossey-Bass, 1969.

Zola, I. K. "Problems of Communication, Diagnosis, and Patient Care: The Interplay of Patient, Physician and Clinic Organization." *Journal of Medical Education*, 1963, *38*, 829–838.

Zola, I. K. "Culture and Symptoms: An Analysis of Patients Presenting Complaints." *American Sociological Review*, 1966, *31*, 615–630.

Zuckerman, M., DePaulo, B., and Rosenthal, R. "Verbal and Nonverbal Communication of Deception." In L. Berkowitz (ed.), *Advances in Experimental Social Psychology*. Vol. 14. Orlando, Fla.: Academic Press, 1981.

# Name Index

## A

Achenbach, T. M., 147–148
Adelson, E., 254
Adkins, M. J., 277
Agar, M., 198
Ainsworth, M., 24, 144, 219
Allport, G. W., 260
Alston, F. K., 229
Aman, C., 55, 57, 175, 176, 185, 186, 194
Ames, L. B., 222
Anastasi, A., 207
Anderson, B. G., 287
Anthony, E. J., 37
Ariella, 206
Asch, S. E., 108
Ashmead, D. H., 44
Attias, R., 114
Axline, V. M., 161

## B

Baillargeon, R., 41
Barry, 269–270
Barton, W., 114
Basch, M. F., 261
Bateson, G., 158
Bell, R. Q., 139
Belsky, J., 242–243
Bergman, A., 160
Bernstein, B., 99
Bernstein, L., 266
Bernstein, R., 266
Bernstein, V., 216
Bertacchi, J., 226n, 258–259

Bess, B. H., 154, 223, 265
Bettelheim, B., 162
Beuf, A. H., 271, 273, 274–275
Bibace, R., 272, 274, 280
Birch, H. G., 19, 254
Blanck, P., 115
Blehar, M., 24, 144, 219
Blinder, B., 132
Bloom, S. W., 266
Bluebond-Langer, M., 273, 274, 275–276
Blumenthal, R., 98, 105
Blumhagen, D., 282
Boat, B. W., 116–119, 187, 190, 192, 193–194, 311
Boggs, S. T., 181
Borke, H., 41, 49
Bowlby, J., 258
Boyd-Franklin, N., 100
Bradburn, N. M., 172
Bransford, J. D., 50
Breger, L., 27
Brenner, M., 171, 172
Bresee, P., 154, 223, 265
Brewster, A. B., 274, 279
Briggs, C. L., 173, 198
Brill, N., 288, 289
Bronfenbrenner, U., 8, 296, 297
Bross, D., 127, 293, 303, 305, 306, 313
Brown, A. L., 42, 50, 51, 55, 59, 64, 65, 207
Bruner, J. S., 95, 103, 104
Budoff, M., 214
Budwig, N. A., 41
Burbach, D., 186
Burton, R., 117

# Subject Index

## A

Abuse: of adolescents, 116, 118; and adult biases and expectations, 108–135; adult's previous experience of, 111; community judgment on, 92–93, 103, 110; and disorganized behavior, 144; expectations about, 109–110; false allegations and retractions of, 114, 116–117, 128; and fantasies, 128–129; of infants and toddlers, 116, 117; intergenerational transmission of, 113; policy and practice on, 127–134; in preschool period, 116, 117; and reporting practices, 114–115; in school-age period, 116, 117; and sexually detailed dolls, 192–195; and testing, 222, 223–224

Acceptance, and self-esteem, 21, 27

Achievement, tests of, 209

Adjacency pair, in interviews, 180

Adolescents: abuse allegations by, 128, 129; abuse of, 116, 118; autonomy and lying for, 123; in legal setting, 311–312; in medical settings, 268–269, 273, 287

Adults: and assumption about children's behaviors, 148–151; biases and expectations of, 108–135; competence of, 16–17; inquiry by, format of, 14–15; as interviewers, 183–195; legal setting role of, 293–294; and lying, 121–127; lying to children by, 124–

125; medical setting expectations of, 272–274; orientation of, 16; play and storytelling role of, 163–167

Adversarial system, and confrontation, 303–306

Age, and cultural identity, 96

Aid to Families with Dependent Children (AFDC), 239

American Academy of Child and Adolescent Psychiatry, 186, 194

American Bar Association, 307, 313

Asian children: caregiving for, 103, 104; and compliance with therapy, 286–287; and racism, 99–100

Aurora Home Child Care Project, 231

## B

Bayley Scales of Infant Development, 25, 26, 45, 217, 218

Behavior: aspects of observing, 136–153; assumptions about, 148–151; context of, 151–152; observable, 139–146; social, 142–144

Believe the Children, 296–297

Belizean child, and diagnostic testing, 284

Bias, confirmatory, 120–121, 130, 134

Biases and expectations: adult, about communication, 108–135; background on, 108–110; conclusions on, 134–135; and decision making, 114–121; and lying, 121–127;